CLASSIC *f*M

THE BIG BOOK OF CLASSICAL MUSIC

CLASSIC *f*M

THE BIG BOOK OF CLASSICAL MUSIC

1,000 YEARS OF MUSIC IN 366 DAYS

**DARREN HENLEY, SAM JACKSON
AND TIM LIHOREAU**

Illustrations by Lynn Hatzius

First published 2014 by
Elliott and Thompson Limited
27 John Street, London WC1N 2BX
www.eandtbooks.com

ISBN: 978-1-90965-326-9

Illustrations © Lynn Hatzius
Design: www.gradedesign.com and Jon Wainwright, Alchemedia Design
Jacket design: Chris Skinner and Jon Wainwright

9 8 7 6 5 4 3 2 1

A catalogue record for this book is available from the British Library.

Printed in China by 1010 Printing International Ltd

Contents

Introduction

Quite simply, this is the biggest book we have ever written at Classic FM, with more words on more pages than any of the other books we have published over the years. So, when we sat down to discuss what to call it, we found that we kept on referring to it as our 'big book'. In the end, the name stuck.

Together we have made tens of thousands of hours of radio programmes for Classic FM. Often, these include music that is pegged to a particular moment in time, or a particular story or incident from the history of classical music. But, we have never before gathered everything together in one place.

Over the next four hundred or so pages you will find a daily compendium of some of the biggest happenings in classical music, including: the births and deaths of the major composers and performers; details of premieres of many of the major works in the classical music repertoire; and some of the headline events that took place on the particular day in question.

You will also find a series of short feature articles which delve into different aspects of the genre, whether it be the lives of the great composers; a definition of a particular piece of musical terminology; or a profile of a significant orchestra or musician. We have also sprinkled through the book quotations from the great and the good (and the sometimes not so good) of the classical music world.

Each page also includes a recommended recording from the Classic FM Hall of Fame, our annual poll of the UK's most popular classical works, as voted by our listeners. Especially for this book, we have created an aggregated chart based on all of the entries to the annual Classic FM Hall of Fame Top 300 countdowns every year from when we first began canvassing for votes back in 1996. This has enabled us to produce a brand new Top 366 based on 18 years of votes, which is listed at the bottom of each daily page. We've listed the number 1 choice on 1st January, running through to number 366 on 31st December.

This book is big, but it's not so big that we pretend to have included absolutely everything that ever occurred in classical music. If we had set out to do that job, the resulting weighty tome would have needed to have been bundled with free delivery in its own articulated lorry. Instead, we have picked out some of the most interesting people and stories from classical music, tying our choices in to the music that you are most likely to hear on Classic FM. We make no claims as to the definitive nature of what has been included, so if you think that there is something or someone that has been overlooked, then please do get in touch by going online at www.classicfm.com/bigbook and filling in the contact form. We will update the daily pages in future editions of this book and would love to hear your thoughts.

In the meantime, do make sure you keep listening to Tim Lihoreau's *More Music Breakfast* each weekday morning between 6 a.m. and 9 a.m., as he dips into *The Big Book of Classical Music* on a daily basis, playing some of the music that brings to life the personalities and events featured here.

Janua

01

JANUARY

> 'In order to compose, all you have to do is remember a tune that nobody else thought of.'
>
> **ROBERT SCHUMANN, COMPOSER**

🕐 BIRTHS & DEATHS

1760 Bohemian organist and composer Jan Dussek is born in Čáslav.

1782 German composer Johann Christian Bach dies in London.

🎭 FIRST PERFORMED

1846 Robert Schumann's *Piano Concerto* is premiered in Leipzig with his wife Clara as the soloist.

1879 Johannes Brahms' *Violin Concerto* is premiered with the composer conducting and soloist Joseph Joachim.

☀ TODAY'S THE DAY

1764 The young Wolfgang Amadeus Mozart gives a concert for King Louis XV of France, at the age of just seven years old.

1827 Gioachino Rossini signs a deal to write operas for the King of France, Charles X. Rossini is rather grandly known as the 'senior composer to the king and inspector general of singing in France'.

1891 Antonín Dvořák is appointed professor of music at the Prague Conservatoire.

1908 Gustav Mahler conducts in the USA for the first time: a performance of Wagner's opera *Tristan and Isolde* at the New York Metropolitan Opera.

1957 Herbert von Karajan becomes director of the Vienna State Opera.

COMPOSER PROFILE:

Robert Schumann

Although a brilliant musician, Schumann led a troubled life. His plans to become a concert pianist suffered a setback when, at the age of 22, he began to develop problems with his right hand, probably as a symptom of mercury poisoning (he was being treated with the chemical to combat syphilis). At the same time, Schumann was pursuing the hand of the aforementioned Clara, totally against the wishes of her father. Determined not to be beaten, Schumann went to court to fight her father's objections to the marriage, but in the end the couple had to wait until she was old enough to marry without her parental consent. When he reached 33, Schumann started teaching at the conservatoire Felix Mendelssohn had founded in Leipzig, though he found time to journey with his wife on a concert tour of Russia (in one instance being asked by a concertgoer, 'Are you a musician too?'). Soon after this, Schumann suffered his first bout of severe depression. These attacks were to become more serious as time went by until, when he was 44, he tried to drown himself by jumping off a bridge into the River Rhine. On being rescued by some passing boatmen, he asked to be taken to an asylum. He remained there for two years until his death.

🎵 HALL OF FAME HIT

Sergei Rachmaninov: *Piano Concerto No. 2*

Recommended Recording

Stephen Hough (piano); Dallas Symphony Orchestra conducted by Andrew Litton; Hyperion CDA 67501/2

> 'I love Wagner's music better than any other music. It is so loud that one can talk the whole time without people hearing what one says. That is a great advantage.'
>
> OSCAR WILDE, *THE PICTURE OF DORIAN GRAY* (1891)

02
JANUARY

BIRTHS & DEATHS

1726 Italian composer Domenico Zipoli dies in Santa Catalina, Argentina.

1837 Russian composer Mily Balakirev is born in Nizhny Novgorod.

1905 English composer Michael Tippett is born in London.

FIRST PERFORMED

1843 Richard Wagner's opera *The Flying Dutchman* is premiered in Dresden.

TODAY'S THE DAY

1678 Hamburg's first opera house, the Gänsemarkt theatre, opens.

1825 Munich Opera House re-opens after being burned down when the scenery caught fire.

1835 Composer Robert Schumann didn't just write music; he also enjoyed a career writing about it. The first edition of the magazine *Neue Zeitschrift für Musik* appears today with Schumann as editor.

1926 Ukrainian-born pianist Vladimir Horowitz makes his concert debut in Berlin, aged 22, setting him on the road to international superstardom.

1955 Canadian pianist Glenn Gould makes his debut performance in the USA at the Phillips Gallery in Washington.

Humming along

The highly idiosyncratic, but nonetheless brilliant, Glenn Gould performed at the Town Hall in New York a week after his debut US recital in Washington. The very next morning he was offered a contract by the label Columbia Masterworks, for whom he recorded for the rest of his life. Gould was one of classical music's great eccentric geniuses. He often hummed throughout his recordings, which is either rather charming or intensely irritating, depending on your point of view. Watching him perform must have been a bizarre experience, as he insisted on sitting on a chair that was just fourteen inches high, which meant that his eyes were at the same level as the keyboard. This chair was made for him by his father and he continued to use it even when it was worn through. He always kept a glass of distilled water on the floor near by, while the piano itself always had to be placed on a rug. He absolutely hated personal contact and refused to shake hands with anyone, including the conductors on stage at his performances. Gould even went as far as creating pseudonyms, which allowed him to publish scathing reviews of his own works. Among the best known of these were the German musicologist 'Karl-Heinz Klopwisser', the English conductor 'Nigel Twitt-Thornwaite' and a New York cabbie turned music reviewer, 'Theodore Slutz'.

HALL OF FAME HIT

Wolfgang Amadeus Mozart: *Clarinet Concerto*

Recommended Recording

Alessandro Carbonare (clarinet); Orchestra Mozart conducted by Claudio Abbado; Deutsche Grammophon 477 9331

03

'I don't mind what language an opera is sung in so long as it is a language I don't understand.'

EDWARD APPLETON, PHYSICIST

BIRTHS & DEATHS

1909 Danish piano-playing musical comedian Victor Borge is born in Copenhagen.

1926 English composer George Martin is born in London.

1944 English conductor David Atherton is born in London.

FIRST PERFORMED

1738 George Frideric Handel's opera *Faramondo* has the first of eight performances at London's King's Theatre.

1799 Antonio Salieri's opera *Falstaff* (based on Shakespeare's play *The Merry Wives of Windsor*) is premiered in Vienna.

1843 Gaetano Donizetti's opera *Don Pasquale* is premiered in Paris.

TODAY'S THE DAY

1867 The first 'ballad concert' featuring a big-name artist performing popular contemporary songs takes place starring Charlotte Stainton-Dolby, one of the most successful ballad singers of the day.

1964 New Victoria Hall (now the Civic Hall) opens in Halifax, West Yorkshire.

1985 American soprano Leontyne Price takes her final operatic curtain call as Aida at the New York Metropolitan Opera. She had spent almost a quarter of a century with the company.

COMPOSER PROFILE:

Antonio Salieri

An Italian composer and conductor from Legnano, near Milan, Salieri originally studied singing in Venice. When he was 16, he moved, with the help of the Bohemian composer Florian Leopold Gassmann, to Vienna. He worked there, chiefly producing operas, until he was 28, at which point he returned to Italy. In his mid-thirties, he moved to take over from Gluck at the Paris Opéra, before returning to Vienna, where he became court conductor from 1788 until the year before his death. Despite being considered Mozart's rival and arch enemy – the two were certainly competing for commissions in the opera marketplace – Salieri almost certainly did not have him poisoned, despite the popular myth that holds that he did.

Classic Beatles

Composer George Martin is better known as the Beatles' record producer. The Fab Four's links to classical music extend way beyond Paul McCartney's reinvention as a classical composer. Beethoven's *Symphony No. 9* and Wagner's *Lohengrin* both feature in the Beatles' movie *Help*.

HALL OF FAME HIT

Max Bruch: *Violin Concerto No. 1*

Recommended Recording

Nigel Kennedy (violin); English Chamber Orchestra conducted by Jeffrey Tate; EMI Classics CDC 7496632

'The pedestal upon which his fame was erected.'

ONE OF THE FIRST OBITUARIES OF WOLFGANG AMADEUS MOZART – REFERRING TO HIS OPERA *THE ABDUCTION FROM THE SERAGLIO* – IS PUBLISHED TODAY IN 1792

BIRTHS & DEATHS

1710 Italian composer Giovanni Battista Pergolesi is born in Iesi, near Ancona.

1874 Czech composer Josef Suk is born in Křečovice.

1951 English conductor and composer Ronald Corp is born in Wells, Somerset.

1969 Russian pianist Boris Berezovsky is born in Moscow.

FIRST PERFORMED

1881 Johannes Brahms' *Academic Festival Overture* is premiered in Breslau.

1941 Sergei Rachmaninov's *Symphonic Dances* is premiered by the Philadelphia Orchestra, conducted by Eugene Ormandy.

TODAY'S THE DAY

1751 George Frideric Handel completes his last orchestral work, his *Organ Concerto in B flat* (*Opus 7 No. 3*) He begins to go blind just a few weeks later, which severely curtails his ability to compose.

1840 Hungary presents a ceremonial sword of honour to one of its most favoured sons, the composer Franz Liszt, as the nation battles for independence from Austria.

Academic success

Brahms wrote the *Academic Festival Overture* to celebrate being given an honorary degree. At its first performance, the largely student audience was delighted to hear the tune to the favourite student song, '*Gaudeamus Igitur*', included in the music. It's said that they cheered and threw their hats in the air. It was quite a move up in the world for Brahms, who had earned a living playing the piano in taverns around his native Hamburg in the early part of his career. He continued to tour as a pianist and was regarded as a master of every type of music, except for opera, to which he never turned his hand.

Brahms might have been musical in the daytime, but at night his snoring was a far from sweet sound. One conductor, forced to share a room with him, described how 'the most unearthly noises issued from his nasal and vocal organs'. Brahms would never have won the award for 'best-turned-out composer' in daylight hours either. He seems to have had particular problems in the trouser department. He hated buying new clothes and often wore baggy trousers, which were covered in patches and nearly always too short. Once, his trousers nearly fell down altogether in the middle of a performance. On another occasion, he took a tie from around his neck and looped it around his waist in place of a belt.

 HALL OF FAME HIT

Ralph Vaughan Williams: *The Lark Ascending*

Recommended Recording

Julia Fischer (violin); Orchestre Philharmonique de Monte Carlo conducted by Yakov Kreizburg; Decca 478 2864

05

JANUARY

'Composers shouldn't think too much – it interferes with their plagiarism.'

HOWARD DIETZ, SONGWRITER

🎵 BIRTHS & DEATHS

1660 Austrian composer Joseph Fux is born near St Marein, Styria.

1762 Austrian soprano Constanze Mozart (née Weber), wife of Wolfgang Amadeus, is born in Zell.

1931 Austrian pianist Alfred Brendel is born in Wiesenberg, Moravia.

1942 Italian pianist Maurizio Pollini is born in Milan.

🎵 FIRST PERFORMED

1745 George Frideric Handel's oratorio *Hercules* is premiered at London's King's Theatre.

1868 Max Bruch's *Violin Concerto No. 1* is given its first performance, in Bremen, with Joseph Joachim as the soloist. There had been earlier versions, but this is the one that we know and love today.

1884 Gilbert and Sullivan's operetta *Princess Ida* makes its debut at London's Savoy Theatre.

1932 Maurice Ravel's *Piano Concerto for the Left Hand* is premiered by the Vienna Symphony Orchestra, after being commissioned by the soloist for the evening, Paul Wittgenstein, who had lost his right arm during the First World War.

☀️ TODAY'S THE DAY

1708 The Salone Margherita theatre in Milan burns to the ground.

1713 Composer Arcangelo Corelli writes his will, leaving his collection of violins to his favourite pupil, Matteo Fornari.

1763 The Mozart family returns home to Salzburg after a first tour to Vienna. Wolfgang and his sister Maria Anna have gone down a storm with Viennese high society.

1912 Composer Engelbert Humperdinck suffers a stroke, resulting in the permanent paralysis of his left hand. It doesn't prevent him from continuing to compose for a further decade though.

COMPOSER PROFILE:

Arthur Sullivan

It was in 1869, some 15 years before the premiere of *Princess Ida*, that the 33-year-old W. S. Gilbert, previously a lawyer but now a writer and dramatist, was introduced to a 27-year-old budding composer, Arthur Sullivan – a man who already had his *Irish Symphony* and *Overture in C* under his belt. Nothing much came of the meeting at first; *Thespis*, the first piece they wrote together, was a relative failure. Then the young impresario Richard D'Oyly Carte commissioned the partnership to produce a supporting piece for his production of Offenbach's *La Périchole*. The result, *Trial by Jury*, was a riotous success. It was the first of the so-called 'Savoy Operas', named after the theatre built by D'Oyly Carte in which Gilbert and Sullivan flourished (and the first to be lit completely by electric light). By 1890, the relationship had ruptured. The two men got together again to produce two more operettas; neither was a success.

🎵 HALL OF FAME HIT

Ludwig van Beethoven: *Piano Concerto No. 5* ('Emperor')

Recommended Recording

Alfred Brendel (piano); Vienna Philharmonic Orchestra conducted by Simon Rattle; Philips 468 6662

'A loss to the musical world.'

WOLFGANG AMADEUS MOZART REFLECTS ON THE DEATH OF FELLOW COMPOSER JOHANN CHRISTIAN BACH IN A LETTER TO HIS FATHER, LEOPOLD MOZART

06

JANUARY

🗓 BIRTHS & DEATHS

1695 Italian composer and oboist Giuseppe Sammartini is born in Milan.

1838 German composer Max Bruch is born in Cologne.

1868 Italian composer Vittorio Monti is born in Naples.

1872 Russian composer Alexander Scriabin is born in Moscow.

☀ TODAY'S THE DAY

1782 Composer Johann Christian Bach is buried in St Pancras churchyard in London, leaving behind major money worries for his widow.

1923 A British National Opera Company performance of Engelbert Humperdinck's *Hansel and Gretel* at Covent Garden is the first broadcast of a complete opera in Europe. And just to be absolutely clear – the Humperdinck to whom we refer in this book is the German composer born in 1854 – and definitely not the crooner who enjoyed an unexpected resurgence in interest when he came second last as the UK's entrant in the Eurovision Song Contest in 2012. Born Arnold George Dorsey in 1936, he took the opera composer's name during the 1960s.

Bach again . . . and again . . .

The Bach dynasty's influence on classical music through the years should not be underestimated. Johann Sebastian had twenty children, of whom four became composers: Wilhelm Friedemann Bach (1710–1784); Carl Philipp Emanuel Bach (1714–1788); Johann Christoph Friedrich Bach (1732–1795); and Johann Christian Bach (1735–1782). Music historians have come up with handy nicknames to tell which of J.S.'s composer sons are which. Johann Christian Bach goes under the alias of the 'London' Bach. C. P. E. Bach is known as the 'Berlin' or 'Hamburg' Bach, and J. C. F Bach as the 'Bückeburg Bach', while W. F. Bach is given the moniker of the 'Halle' Bach.

🎵 HALL OF FAME HIT

Edward Elgar: *Cello Concerto*

Recommended Recording

Jacqueline du Pré (cello); London Symphony Orchestra conducted by John Barbirolli; EMI Classics 567 3412

'Give me a laundry list and I will set it to music.'

GIOACHINO ROSSINI, COMPOSER

JANUARY

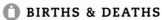

🕐 BIRTHS & DEATHS

1899 French composer Francis Poulenc is born in Paris.

1912 The appropriately named German conductor Günter Wand is born in Elberfield.

1941 English violinist and conductor Iona Brown is born in Salisbury.

🎵 FIRST PERFORMED

1842 Gioachino Rossini did actually compose the version of his *Stabat Mater* that receives its first performance at the Théâtre-Italien. The first version, debuted a decade earlier, was not composed entirely by him.

1898 Nikolai Rimsky-Korsakov's opera *Sadko* is premiered in Moscow.

☀ TODAY'S THE DAY

1738 Antonio Vivaldi is the conductor for a performance celebrating the centenary of the Schouwburg theatre in Amsterdam.

1762 Modena may be associated with opera performances by Luciano Pavarotti in the minds of modern classical-music lovers, but the Italian composer and cellist Luigi Boccherini is recorded as playing in the Italian city more than two centuries before the big opera star.

1924 George Gershwin began working on the piano score of his classical and jazz fusion *Rhapsody in Blue*. It was premiered just a few weeks later.

COMPOSER PROFILE:

George Gershwin

Born in New York, George Gershwin was the son of Russian Jewish migrants. He was brought up on classical music, but his own personal tastes ran far wider. After leaving school, at the age of 15, he worked as a song-plugger on what was then known as 'Tin Pan Alley'. Gershwin was soon plugging his own songs, with 'Swanee' his first big hit in 1920. In fact, he made so much money from this one song over the years that it allowed him to spend his time writing just about anything else he liked. By the time he composed *Rhapsody in Blue*, he was a multimillionaire, living in a swanky house on New York's Upper West Side. As well as his other big classical hits, such as *An American in Paris* and his *Concerto in F*, he also wrote his massively popular opera, *Porgy and Bess*, featuring the song 'Summertime'. Gershwin died at the tragically young age of 38 from a brain tumour. He continued to take lessons on writing for orchestra well into his thirties and it seems certain that, had he lived, he could well have gone on to become an even greater success as a classical composer. His music remains hugely popular on both sides of the Atlantic today, not least because the knack of being able to pen an infectiously catchy tune, which he honed on Tin Pan Alley, never left him.

🎵 HALL OF FAME HIT

Ludwig van Beethoven: *Symphony No. 6 ('Pastoral')*

Recommended Recording

Anima Eterna conducted by Jos van Immerseel; Zig Zag 3700 55173 2227

'I stayed on deck during the entire crossing, so as to gaze my fill of that great monster, the ocean.'

A LETTER WRITTEN BY THE COMPOSER JOSEPH HAYDN TODAY IN 1791 ABOUT A JOURNEY ACROSS THE ENGLISH CHANNEL FROM CALAIS TO DOVER

08

JANUARY

BIRTHS & DEATHS

1713 Italian composer and violinist Arcangelo Corelli dies in Rome.

1830 German conductor and composer Hans von Bülow is born in Dresden.

1831 Moravian composer and violinist Franz Krommer dies in Vienna.

1948 Austrian (later British) tenor Richard Tauber dies in London.

1998 English composer Michael Tippett dies in London.

2003 English composer and conductor Ron Goodwin dies in London.

FIRST PERFORMED

1705 George Frideric Handel's opera *Almira* is premiered in Hamburg.

1735 Handel's *Ariodante* is premiered at London's Covent Garden.

1963 Dmitri Shostakovich's opera *Lady Macbeth of the Mtsensk District* received its original premiere in 1934, but its revised debut as *Katerina Izmaylova* happens today in Moscow some 29 years later.

TODAY'S THE DAY

1750 Handel finishes writing the music for the play *Alceste*. For reasons that have been lost in the mists of time, the words to the play don't survive but Handel's music is still with us.

1755 Composer Johann Christoph Friedrich Bach marries singer Lucia Elisabeth Münchhausen. Both of them work at the court of Bückeburg, which gave rise to his nickname, the 'Bückeburg Bach'.

1861 Pope Pius IX rules that Princess Carolyne von Sayn-Wittgenstein's marriage is annulled, allowing her to wed the composer Franz Liszt. But later, at the eleventh hour, the authorities in Rome change their minds and the wedding is not allowed to go ahead on the grounds that the Princess had perjured herself at the original hearing. They were never married.

Operatic tragedy

Hans von Bülow married Cosima, the daughter of his piano teacher, the composer Franz Liszt. But she carried on a passionate affair with the composer Richard Wagner behind von Bülow's back, eventually leaving her husband and setting up home with Wagner in Bayreuth. The distraught von Bülow gave up his job as court conductor in Munich, a role in which he had been responsible for championing much of Wagner's work, including giving the premiere performances of the operas *Tristan and Isolde* (in 1865) and *Die Meistersinger von Nürnberg* (in 1868).

 HALL OF FAME HIT
Edward Elgar: *Enigma Variations*

Recommended Recording
Hallé Orchestra conducted by Mark Elder; Hallé CDHLL 7501

09

JANUARY

'One ought to wash one's hands after dealing with one of his scores.'

FELIX MENDELSSOHN, COMPOSER, ON HECTOR BERLIOZ

 BIRTHS & DEATHS

1939 Austrian composer Johann Strauss III dies in Berlin.
1962 English oboist and conductor Nicholas Daniel is born.

 FIRST PERFORMED

1879 Hector Berlioz's *Symphonie Fantastique* gets its first outing in front of British audiences in Manchester, conducted by Charles Hallé.

 TODAY'S THE DAY

1816 Ludwig van Beethoven is awarded custody of his nephew Karl by an Austrian court as part of a long tug-of-love battle with his sister-in-law Johanna, following the death of Ludwig's brother Caspar Carl.
1888 Gabriel Fauré completes the *Introit and Kyrie* and the *Sanctus* for his *Requiem*. A version of it is first performed at an architect's funeral in Paris just a week after completion.

INSTRUMENT FOCUS:

Oboe

A member of the woodwind family, the oboe is the instrument to which all others in the orchestra tune. This is because it can easily be heard above the rest and also because it holds its note well. It gets its name from the French words *haut* (high) and *bois* (wood). To play, the oboist blows through a double reed, uncovering or covering the holes on the instrument's body. The metal attachments (which look a little like jewellery) allow the player to open and close the holes with ease. The interior chamber is conical, rather than cylindrical like those of flutes and clarinets, and this gives it its unique sound.

The instrument has been a popular choice for concerto composers: Vivaldi, Albinoni and Mozart wrote particularly fine examples. In more modern times, Ravel wrote a central part for the oboe in his celebrated *Boléro*, while fellow French composer Jean Françaix gives it a starring role in the *Malabar Jasmine* movement of *The Flower Clock*. Richard Strauss's *Oboe Concerto* was one of his last masterpieces.

 HALL OF FAME HIT

Ludwig van Beethoven: *Symphony No. 9 ('Choral')*

Recommended Recording

Various soloists; Staatskapelle Berlin and the Chorus of German State Opera conducted by Daniel Barenboim; Warner Classics 2564 618902

> 'When I am . . . completely myself, entirely alone . . . or during the night when I cannot sleep . . . my ideas flow best and most abundantly.'
>
> **WOLFGANG AMADEUS MOZART, COMPOSER**

BIRTHS & DEATHS

1941 English composer, violinist and conductor Frank Bridge dies in Eastbourne.

1948 Latvian (latterly Israeli) cellist Mizcha Maisky is born in Riga.

1985 Welsh harpist Claire Jones is born in Pembrokeshire.

FIRST PERFORMED

1713 The premiere of Handel's opera *Teseo* in London is not a happy one. Two nights into the run, the theatre manager makes off with all the box-office takings. The angry singers and the composer are left empty-handed. Despite further technical difficulties with the performance, they vow that the show must go on, but it will be more than 200 years before the opera is revived.

GENRE FOCUS:

Opera

The word opera is the plural of the Latin word *opus* (work). It originates from the phrase *opera in musica*, which means 'musical works', but over the years it has been shortened. Put at its simplest, opera is the combination of singing, drama and musical accompaniment, a genre whereby the music and the plot are as one. This is what differentiates operas from musicals, which generally speaking are dramas with breaks for musical numbers. In an opera, the drama and the music are not separated in the same way.

Opera in the form that we know it began to take shape in the dying years of the 16th century. It was the idea of a group of arts-loving intellectuals known as the Florentine Camerata. They wanted to resurrect Greek drama, with music, and the first offering came from a composer and singer called Jacopo Peri. Most musical historians consider his work *Dafne*, written around 1597 and now lost, to be the first real opera. Peri went on to write the second ever opera, *Euridice*, which is not lost, but simply no longer performed. It is an opera by Monteverdi that is the oldest still to hold the stage. By coincidence, it is on the same subject as Peri's second opera: the story of Orpheus and Eurydice. Monteverdi simply called his *La favola d'Orfeo*. It was the real starting point for a brand new genre of music that continues to thrive in the 21st century.

HALL OF FAME HIT
Johann Pachelbel: *Canon in D*

Recommended Recording
Harmonie Universelle; Eloquentia EL 0606

11

JANUARY

'The conductor has the advantage of not seeing the audience.'

ANDRÉ KOSTELANETZ, CONDUCTOR

 BIRTHS & DEATHS

1801 Italian composer Domenico Cimarosa dies in Venice.

1902 French composer and organist Maurice Duruflé is born in Louviers.

1998 German conductor Klaus Tennstedt dies in Kiel.

 FIRST PERFORMED

1940 Although Sergei Prokofiev had finished composing it in 1936, the ballet *Romeo and Juliet* wasn't actually performed in Leningrad until four years later. He did think about giving it a happy ending, but decided in the end to leave the story just as Shakespeare intended. And it was just as well – the ballet was a smash hit.

☀ **TODAY'S THE DAY**

1801 There is a whiff of scandal surrounding the death of Domenico Cimarosa. Some say that Maria Caroline, Queen of Naples and Sicily, had ordered him to be bumped off with a dose of poison. The level of public suspicion rises so high that the government goes into damage-limitation mode, publishing a medical report stating that the composer had died from natural causes.

1845 Richard Wagner completes the overture to his opera *Tannhäuser*. It takes him another two months to complete the whole work.

Playing for Scotland

Alexander Gibson was the first principal conductor and artistic director of the Royal Scottish National Orchestra. He held the role for a quarter of a century from 1959 through until 1984. To date, this is longer than any other conductor at the RSNO, which began its life as the orchestra of the Glasgow Choral Union. It became the Scottish Orchestra in 1891 and the Scottish National Orchestra in 1950. In 1990, royal status was conferred on the orchestra and it became the Royal Scottish National Orchestra. In 2003 it became Classic FM's Orchestra in Scotland. The composer Gustav Holst was once the orchestra's second trombone. At the time, the band was conducted by another famous composer, Richard Strauss. Other famous names linked to the RSNO include the father of David McCallum (Illya Kuryakin in *The Man from U.N.C.L.E.*), who was the orchestra's leader in the 1930s. The father of Lonnie Donegan, the king of skiffle, was a violinist in the orchestra at around the same time. Today, the RSNO is based in a newly built home next door to the Royal Concert Hall in Glasgow. It tours regularly around Scotland, taking in Edinburgh, Perth, Aberdeen, Dundee and Inverness. Its footprint is far wider though, with regular visits overseas, under the baton of Music Director Peter Oundjian.

 HALL OF FAME HIT
Samuel Barber: *Adagio for Strings*

Recommended Recording
Detroit Symphony Orchestra conducted by Neeme Järvi; Chandos CHAN 9169

'Clementi plays well, as far as execution with the right hand goes . . . apart from that, he has not a kreuzer's worth of taste or feeling. In short he is a mere mechanicus.'

WOLFGANG AMADEUS MOZART IN A LETTER TO HIS FATHER TODAY IN 1782 ABOUT COMPOSER AND PIANIST MUZIO CLEMENTI

12

JANUARY

🎵 BIRTHS & DEATHS

1876 Italian composer Ermanno Wolf-Ferrari is born in Venice, although he was plain old Ermanno Wolf at birth, adding in his mother's family name, Ferrari, almost 20 years later.

☀️ TODAY'S THE DAY

1885 Although there are plenty of examples in this book of one composer's spiteful behaviour or catty comments about either the music or the personality of a fellow composer, believe it or not, some of them did actually get on. Engelbert Humperdinck and Richard Strauss became pals for the rest of their lives after meeting today at a rehearsal of Strauss's *Symphony No. 2*.

1910 The first broadcast from New York's Metropolitan Opera House. The chosen opera? Act II of *Tosca*. The following day a double bill of Pietro Mascagni's *Cavalleria Rusticana* and Ruggero Leoncavallo's *Pagliacci* (known in the trade as 'Cav and Pag') was

transmitted. There has been a long tradition of broadcasting from the Met ever since. NBC began Christmas Day broadcasts in 1931 with Engelbert Humperdinck's *Hansel and Gretel* – the same opera that was the first complete European broadcast some eight years earlier.

1928 Ukrainian (later American) pianist Vladimir Horowitz performs for the first time in the USA, playing Tchaikovsky's *Piano Concerto No. 1* with the New York Philharmonic Orchestra conducted by Thomas Beecham. There was a bit of a to-do between the conductor and the soloist, with the latter feeling that the former wasn't letting him play the piece fast enough. By the final movement, Horowitz had become so exasperated that he ignored Beecham's time-keeping and played the piece at his own pace, forcing the orchestra to keep time with him rather than with their conductor.

1931 Russian composer Sergei Rachmaninov, by now resident in the USA, writes a letter to *The New York Times* which is highly critical of the political situation in his homeland. As a result, the Soviet regime bans his music not only from being performed, but also even from being studied in Russia. The ban isn't lifted for another two years.

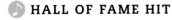

🎵 HALL OF FAME HIT
Edvard Grieg: *Piano Concerto*

Recommended Recording
Stephen Hough; Bergen Philharmonic Orchestra conducted by Andrew Litton; Hyperion CDA 67824

13

JANUARY

'The kind of opera that starts at six o'clock and after it has been going three hours you look at your watch and it says 6:20.'

DAVID RANDOLPH, CONDUCTOR, ON WAGNER'S PARSIFAL

BIRTHS & DEATHS

1904 English composer Richard Addinsell is born in London.

1961 English pianist, organist and conductor Wayne Marshall is born in Oldham.

1973 Peruvian tenor Juan Diego Flórez is born in Lima.

FIRST PERFORMED

1775 Wolfgang Amadeus Mozart's opera *La finta giardiniera* (which translates as 'The pretend garden-girl') is premiered in Munich.

1890 Pyotr Ilyich Tchaikovsky's ballet *The Sleeping Beauty* is premiered in St Petersburg.

1945 Sergei Prokofiev's *Symphony No. 5* receives its first performance, in the Great Hall of the Moscow Conservatoire. The composer himself conducts the USSR State Symphony Orchestra.

TODAY'S THE DAY

1555 Italian composer Giovanni Pierluigi da Palestrina is given a job in the Sistine Chapel, which is the Pope's dedicated musical chapel. It was an unusual decision, given that Palestrina was married, but he had successfully curried favour with Pope Julius III (the former Bishop of Palestrina) by personally dedicating his first book of Masses to the Pontiff.

1817 German composer and conductor Carl Maria von Weber arrives in the city of Dresden and begins the process of setting up a new opera company dedicated to singing in German, to go alongside the one that performs only Italian operas.

1854 American inventor Anthony Foss files a patent for the accordion.

1860 Austrian composer Anton Bruckner was a great advertisement for 'Continuous Professional Development'. Despite working full-time, he continued to study via correspondence course. And there was every sign that he was a hard grafter. In a letter dated today, his teacher praises his effort and warns him not to overdo it.

1880 Russian composer Modest Mussorgsky is sacked from his government job after a long battle with alcoholism. Friends, including his civil service boss, try to keep him on the straight and narrow by offering him money, so long as he delivers his musical commissions on time. Mussorgsky proves to be unable to resist the drink and is sadly not up to the task, dying just over a year later.

1882 German composer Richard Wagner completes his opera *Parsifal*, almost 25 years after he had first conceived the idea.

1931 Hungarian composer Béla Bartók agrees to join the rather grandly named Permanent Committee for Literature and the Arts of the League of Nations' Commission for Intellectual Co-operation. One can only wonder at the size of their business cards.

1976 American conductor Sarah Caldwell is the first woman to wield the baton at New York's Metropolitan Opera, conducting *La traviata*.

HALL OF FAME HIT

Ralph Vaughan Williams: *Fantasia on a theme by Thomas Tallis*

Recommended Recording

Britten Sinfonia conducted by Nicholas Cleobury; Sony Classical 8869 7707282

'I certainly do believe in Finnish music, regardless of the smirks of the self-appointed authorities.'

JEAN SIBELIUS, COMPOSER

🕐 BIRTHS & DEATHS

1800 Austrian musicologist Ludwig von Köchel is born in Stein.

1914 Rudolph Wurlitzer, who gave his name to the company famous for manufacturing harps and organs, dies in Cincinnati.

1943 Latvian conductor Mariss Jansons is born in Riga.

1950 English conductor, flautist and harpsichordist Nicholas McGegan is born in Sawbridgeworth, Hertfordshire.

1965 English violinist and conductor Andrew Manze is born in Beckenham.

1995 Scottish conductor Alexander Gibson dies in London.

Musical cataloguers

There's only one way to have your name attached to a masterpiece and that's to write one. Isn't it? Well, it is unless you happen to be one of the people who catalogue composers' works. Among them are:

Otto Erich Deutsch – Schubert (D. numbers)
Anthony van Hoboken – Haydn (Hob. numbers)
Ralph Kirkpatrick – Scarlatti (K. numbers)
Ludwig von Köchel – Mozart (K. numbers)
Peter Ryom – Vivaldi (RV. Numbers)

🎵 FIRST PERFORMED

1710 George Frideric Handel's music is first performed, in London. Orchestral music he composed for his opera *Rodrigo* is performed as incidental music to Ben Jonson's play *The Alchemist*.

1889 One of the great Irish composing exports of his time, Charles Villiers Stanford is asked to conduct a concert in Berlin only consisting of music that he himself has written. The soloist for the premiere of his *Suite for Violin and Orchestra* is Joseph Joachim.

1934 George Gershwin's 'I Got Rhythm' Variations is premiered in Boston, with the composer at the keyboard.

1953 Ralph Vaughan Williams' *Sinfonia Antartica* has its first performance, in Manchester, with John Barbirolli conducting the Hallé Orchestra.

☀ TODAY'S THE DAY

1690 The clarinet is reported to have been invented in Nuremberg, Germany, by the German woodwind instrument maker Johann Denner.

1792 London's Italian Opera Company faces a struggle to find a new home after its temporary residence at the Pantheon comes to an end because of a fire. The company had moved there in the first place only because its normal home, the King's Theatre, had burned to the ground in 1789. They end up moving to the Little Theatre in the Haymarket, which, as its name suggests, isn't really big enough for their needs. They return home to the King's Theatre by the end of the year.

1867 The Norwegian Academy of Music opens today, a project spearheaded by the nation's composer hero, Edvard Grieg.

1947 Covent Garden Opera House re-opens for its first complete performance after being renovated, with Bizet's *Carmen*.

🎵 HALL OF FAME HIT

Camille Saint-Saëns: *Symphony No. 3 ('Organ')*

Recommended Recording
Olivier Latry (organ); Philadelphia Orchestra conducted by Christoph Eschenbach; Ondine ODE 10945

15

JANUARY

'I write as the sow piddles.'

WOLFGANG AMADEUS MOZART, COMPOSER

BIRTHS & DEATHS

1893 Welsh composer and lyricist Ivor Novello is born in Cardiff.

2005 Spanish soprano Victoria de los Ángeles dies in Barcelona.

FIRST PERFORMED

1934 Arnold Bax's *Symphony No. 5* is premiered by the London Philharmonic Orchestra. It is dedicated to the Finnish composer Jean Sibelius.

TODAY'S THE DAY

1737 Newcastle-based composer Charles Avison marries Catherine Reynolds. They end up having nine children, but infant mortality rates are desperately high, with only three making it past their eighteenth birthday.

1785 Wolfgang Amadeus Mozart performs six new quartets for 'my dear friend Haydn and other good friends' in Vienna.

1787 Mozart writes that *The Marriage of Figaro* has caused quite a stir among operagoers in Prague, with a new work, *Don Giovanni*, being commissioned as a direct result of its success.

1896 Alexander Scriabin makes his European debut as a pianist at the Salle Erard in Paris.

Newcastle's finest

The Avison Ensemble takes its name from the English composer, conductor and organist, who has been described by the *Grove Dictionary of Music and Musicians* as 'the most important English concerto composer of the 18th century'. The members of the ensemble have set about recording his complete works on the Naxos and Divine Art labels. They also perform music from the Baroque and early Classical periods and spend a lot of their time working with thousands of children across the North-East of England. Without their efforts, the music of Charles Avison would be largely unknown today. They follow a long line of quartets named after composers, including the Borodin Quartet, the Alban Berg Quartet, the Tippett Quartet, the Pavel Haas Quartet and the Kodály Quartet.

A singer's glossary

Bel canto: literally beautiful singing, often used to refer to the type of role written by such composers as Bellini, where beauty is rated higher than dramatic punch.

Counter-tenor: the alto register as sung by a man.

Descant: from a mixture of different derivations, today descant means the improvised-sounding higher tune added to the last verse of a hymn or carol.

Perfect pitch: the ability to sing any named note, without recourse to instrumental help. Leonard Bernstein, André Previn, Yo-Yo Ma and Mozart all have/had it.

Recital: a concert by a soloist or a small number of artists (as opposed to, say, a symphony orchestra concert).

Shanty: a song originally sung at sea during hard physical work.

HALL OF FAME HIT

Gustav Holst: *The Planets*

Recommended Recording

Royal Scottish National Orchestra and Chorus conducted by David Lloyd-Jones; Naxos 855 5776

'A good conductor ought to be a good chauffeur. The qualities that make the one also make the other. They are concentration, an incessant control of attention, and presence of mind – the conductor only has to add a little sense of music.'

SERGEI RACHMANINOV, COMPOSER

16
JANUARY

BIRTHS & DEATHS

1891 French composer Léo Delibes dies in Paris.

1934 American mezzo-soprano Marilyn Horne is born in Bradford, Pennsylvania.

1943 English composer Gavin Bryars is born in Goole, Yorkshire.

1957 Italian conductor Arturo Toscanini dies in New York.

FIRST PERFORMED

1739 George Frideric Handel's oratorio *Saul* is premiered at the King's Theatre in London's Haymarket.

1869 Mily Balakirev conducts the premiere of Borodin's *Symphony No. 1*.

1888 Fauré's *Requiem* is first performed at the funeral of an architect in Paris.

TODAY'S THE DAY

1775 Italian composer Giovanni Battista Sammartini, a big name in the early days of the Classical era, is buried in the church of St Alessandro. His death certificate describes him as being 'a most excellent master and celebrated by a most brilliant renown'.

1920 The group of French composers known as 'Les Six' gets its name from a newspaper article published today. They are: Georges Auric, Louis Durey, Arthur Honegger, Darius Milhaud,

Francis Poulenc and Germaine Tailleferre.

1938 Although Robert and Clara Schumann are most often thought of as classical music's foremost composer/pianist husband-and-wife double acts, don't forget Hungary's Béla Bartók and his wife Ditta. Their first public concert features his *Sonata for Two Pianos and Percussion*.

Musical express

Composer Antonín Dvořák was well known for his passionate interest in trains, but he wasn't the only musical scribe with a passion for steam. Russian Mily Balakirev worked in an administrative job with the Warsaw railway company. But this wasn't something he did to make ends meet while he was struggling to get started in the world of music. He made the move late on in his life, when he had already proved himself to be a very successful composer and musician.

Homeless hymns

Gavin Bryars came to prominence for Classic FM listeners in the early 1990s, following the release of an arrangement of the hymn *Jesus' Blood Never Failed Me Yet*. It is based on a recorded loop of a homeless man singing the hymn, with orchestrations on top. The track was a great success, but Bryars never managed to identify the mystery singer.

HALL OF FAME HIT
Georges Bizet: *The Pearl Fishers*

Recommended Recording
Robert Merrill; Jussi Björling; RCA Victor Symphony Orchestra conducted by Renato Cellini; Alto ALC 1007

17

JANUARY

'Music helps not the toothache.'

GEORGE HERBERT, POET

🔒 BIRTHS & DEATHS

1706 American composer and politician Benjamin Franklin is born in Boston.

1712 English organist and composer John Stanley is born in London.

1734 French composer François-Joseph Gossec is born in Vergnies.

1750 Italian composer Tomaso Albinoni dies in Venice (possibly 1751).

1952 Japanese composer Ryuichi Sakamoto is born in Nakano, Tokyo.

2000 English trumpeter Philip Jones dies in London.

🎵 FIRST PERFORMED

1773 Teenage composer Wolfgang Amadeus Mozart's *Exsultate, Jubilate* is premiered in Milan. When you hear this beautiful soprano motet, does it make your eyes water? It could be because it was written originally not for soprano at all, but for the castrato Venanzio Rauzzini, who was a favourite of Mozart.

1885 Jules Massenet's opera *Manon* receives its British premiere by the Carl Rosa Opera Company in Liverpool.

☀️ TODAY'S THE DAY

1745 George Frideric Handel offers subscribers to his concert series three-quarters of their money back because he believes that he can't please them. His actions provoke a ripple of support and he's back to business as usual just a few weeks later.

1919 The celebrated international concert pianist Ignacy Jan Paderewski becomes prime minister of Poland. During his time in charge, he was one of the international statesmen who negotiated the Treaty of Versailles. Once he had sorted out things on the diplomacy front, he resigned as prime minister and went back to tinkling the ivories on a full-time basis.

COMPOSER PROFILE:

Tomaso Albinoni

A leading opera composer of his day, Albinoni was a fortunate man. Unlike many other musicians, his inheritance from his father's business, which manufactured playing cards and stationery, meant that he did not depend on patronage to make a living. At one time, though, he did have problems with an imposter touring Germany and passing off Albinoni's music as his own. Albinoni's most famous work is one that was not really composed by him.

Remo Giazotto, a 20th-century Italian musicologist, admitted he 'completed' the celebrated *Adagio in G minor* from the fragment of an otherwise lost trio sonata, though some say it is totally Giazotto's work. If you're looking for something that is definitely 100 per cent from Albinoni's pen, then try his *Oboe Concerto in D minor*.

🎵 HALL OF FAME HIT

George Frideric Handel: *Messiah*

Recommended Recording

Various soloists; Choir of King's College, Cambridge and the Academy of Ancient Music conducted by Stephen Cleobury; EMI Classics 268 1562

'Harpists spend 90 per cent of their lives tuning their harps and the other 10 per cent playing out of tune.'

IGOR STRAVINSKY, COMPOSER

BIRTHS & DEATHS

1835 Russian composer César Cui is born in Vilnius.

1841 French composer Emmanuel Chabrier is born in Ambert, Puy-de-Dôme.

FIRST PERFORMED

1908 Frederick Delius's *Brigg Fair* is premiered in Liverpool under the baton of Granville Bantock.

1930 Dmitri Shostakovich's opera *The Nose* is premiered at the Maliiy Theatre in Leningrad. The Soviet authorities carefully scrutinised all new works, and composers were required to pass a compulsory exam in Marxist ideology as part of their university studies. *The Nose* was condemned by the communist regime for its 'bourgeois decadence' and Shostakovich had to withdraw it.

TODAY'S THE DAY

1729 The financial affairs of the Royal Academy of Music are wound up at a meeting in London. The original Royal Academy of Music in London wasn't the fine teaching establishment that we know today, which trains some of the world's greatest musicians. Instead, it was a concert-promoting body that specialised in operas sung in Italian. George Frideric Handel was one of the many composers who were closely involved in its work.

1936 An article highly critical of composer Dmitri Shostakovich is published in the official Soviet newspaper *Pravda*. Under the headline 'Chaos Instead of Music', Shostakovich's reputation is shredded. The review is printed after Stalin attends a showing of Shostakovich's opera *Lady Macbeth of the Mtsensk District* and was probably inspired by the

Soviet leader's own personal views on the opera.

1958 Leonard Bernstein begins presenting his television series *What does music mean?* with the New York Philharmonic Orchestra on the American network CBS. In total, the series ran for 53 programmes, with the final one being broadcast in 1972.

1962 President John F. Kennedy holds a dinner at the White House in honour of the Russian composer Igor Stravinsky, who had emigrated to California at the start of the Second World War. The very same night back in Russia, Stravinsky's ballet *Petrushka* is being revived to great success at the Kremlin Palace of Congresses. Two years after the dinner – and following Kennedy's assassination – Stravinsky composes a vocal piece entitled *Elegy for J.F.K.*, setting to music words by the poet W. H. Auden.

HALL OF FAME HIT

Antonín Dvořák: *Symphony No. 9* ('From the New World')

Recommended Recording

Czech Philharmonic Orchestra conducted by Charles Mackerras; Supraphon SU 40412

'Incomparable.'

REVIEW OF A 1770 CONCERT BY WOLFGANG AMADEUS MOZART IN TODAY'S EDITION OF THE GAZZETTA DI MANTOVA

BIRTHS & DEATHS

1833 French opera composer Ferdinand Hérold dies in Paris.
1896 Bohemian musical instrument inventor Václav Červený dies in Königgrätz.
1955 Conductor Simon Rattle is born in Liverpool.

FIRST PERFORMED

1787 Mozart's 'Prague' Symphony (No. 38) is premiered, unsurprisingly, in Prague.

1873 Saint-Saëns' *Cello Concerto No. 1* is premiered in Paris.
1884 Massenet's opera *Manon* is premiered in Paris.

TODAY'S THE DAY

1609 Italian composer Claudio Monteverdi persuades his boss Duke Vincenzo to increase his pay, give him a housing allowance and promise him a pension. Cue a celebration in the Monteverdi household? Not really. The composer had terrible trouble prising the pension cash out of the Duke's pocket for much of the rest of his life.
1949 Industrial unrest at the Chicago Symphony Orchestra, after the musicians are asked to work with the conductor Wilhelm Furtwängler. They lay down their instruments in protest, accusing him of being a Nazi collaborator.

CONDUCTOR PROFILE:

Simon Rattle

Simon Rattle was very talented very young, rising through the Merseyside Youth Orchestra and then the National Youth Orchestra. He played the piano, violin and percussion, but it was conducting that always attracted him. He studied it at London's Royal Academy of Music from the age of 16 and three years later won the John Player International Conducting Competition. The prize was a two-year assistant conductorship with the Bournemouth Symphony Orchestra. After successes with the Nash Ensemble, the Philharmonia Orchestra (at the record-breaking age of 21) and the Royal Liverpool Philharmonic Orchestra, Rattle became music director of the City of Birmingham Symphony Orchestra in 1980. He was to remain with the orchestra for 18 years. Under him, the CBSO won an international reputation. It soon became clear that Rattle was a conductor of genius as he worked wonder after wonder with his band. His spectacular 'Towards the Millennium' series of concerts – and, indeed, the CBSO's move into the new Symphony Hall in 1991 – were highlights of his period with the orchestra. In 2002, Rattle succeeded Claudio Abbado as chief conductor of the Berlin Philharmonic, possibly the greatest orchestra in the world. After an initially stormy honeymoon, he took the orchestra to even greater heights of accomplishment, with the result that his contract has been extended to 2018, when he has announced that he will leave the orchestra.

HALL OF FAME HIT

Wolfgang Amadeus Mozart:
Requiem

Recommended Recording

Various soloists; Academy of Ancient Music conducted by Christopher Hogwood; Decca 411 7122

> 'For changing people's manners and altering their customs there is nothing better than music.'
>
> SHU CHING, 600 BC

BIRTHS & DEATHS

1855 French composer Ernest Chausson is born in Paris.

1951 Hungarian conductor Iván Fischer is born in Budapest.

2014 Italian conductor Claudio Abbado dies in Bologna.

FIRST PERFORMED

1961 Poulenc's *Gloria* is premiered in Boston by the Boston Symphony Orchestra and Chorus.

TODAY'S THE DAY

1626 Possibly the day that English composer John Dowland died. It's certainly the last day he was paid by the English royal court, although he wasn't registered as being buried for another month.

1797 Composer Joseph Haydn is given free tickets for life to all concerts promoted by the Tonkünstler-Societät in Vienna.

1802 Italian composer Luigi Boccherini is awarded a pension of 3000 francs a year by Joseph Bonaparte, brother of Napoleon.

1949 Catholic wedding ceremony for English composer William Walton and his Argentine bride Susana Gil Passo, following a civil ceremony in December 1948. William and Susana spent the rest of their married lives on Ischia, a volcanic island of in the Tyrrhenian Sea.

ERA FOCUS:

Early music: part I

Early music is a group term combining the medieval and Renaissance periods, which together cover just about all music-making up to 1600. The medieval period of early music ends around 1400, with the Renaissance period covering the next two centuries. Although there was undoubtedly music-making before 500 AD, this is the rough date from which many musical histories start. Between 500 and 1400, the principal surviving music is plainchant. It had already been handed down for centuries by the year 500. A bishop called Ambrose gave his name to an early variety (known as Ambrosian chant). Many of the formal rules around plainchant were organised by Pope Gregory the Great, who lent his name to

Gregorian chant – a sub-grouping of plainchant that has proved extremely popular in the late 20th and early 21st centuries. Pope Gregory was responsible for formalising chant through his Schola Cantorum, which was not just a papal choir but a whole system of handing down choir music from generation to generation. He also produced publications such as *The Antiphonar*, a compendium of chants. As ancient and far removed as this period might seem to us now, it was a time of amazing and exciting developments. Worthy of mention is Guido d'Arezzo, a Benedictine monk who died around 1050, but not before inventing what we now know as the musical stave – the five lines on which all music is written.

 HALL OF FAME HIT

Antonio Vivaldi: *Four Seasons*

Recommended Recording

Fabio Bondi (violin); Europa Galante; Naïve NC 40018

21

'Every composer knows the anguish and despair occasioned by forgetting ideas which one has no time to write down.'

HECTOR BERLIOZ, COMPOSER

JANUARY

BIRTHS & DEATHS

1941 Spanish tenor Plácido Domingo is born in Madrid.
1948 Italian composer Ermanno Wolf-Ferrari dies in Venice.

FIRST PERFORMED

1904 Leoš Janáček's opera *Jenůfa* is premiered in Brno.
1930 Dmitri Shostakovich's *Symphony No. 3* is premiered by the Leningrad Philharmonic Orchestra and Academy Capella Choir.

TODAY'S THE DAY

1575 The rights to print music and music paper in England are granted to the composers Thomas Tallis and William Byrd by Queen Elizabeth I.
1736 Music historians reckon that today's the day the first proper classical music concert took place in New York. The star of the show was the harpsichordist C. T. Pachelbel, whose more famous father was responsible for composing the *Canon in D*.

1751 George Frideric Handel begins composing his oratorio *Jephtha*, although by now he is struggling with his eyesight, so it takes him around seven months to complete.
1786 Luigi Boccherini is appointed the house composer to Crown Prince Wilhelm of Prussia.
1901 Giuseppe Verdi suffers a stroke in Milan from which he never recovers, dying six days later.

ERA FOCUS:

Early music: part II

Hildegard of Bingen, who lived until 1179, was a significant composer, scholar, abbess and mystic. Her close links with the ruling class around Europe enabled her to take her own unique compositions onto an international stage. Hildegard is considered part of what is now termed the *ars antiqua* (old art), a term generally applied to those working up to around the early 1300s. This period of early music also included the delightful round, 'Sumer is icumen in', often attributed to the Norfolk-born John of Fornsete. Worthy of mention, too, is Franco of Cologne, a German composer of the mid-1200s,

who standardised the measure of notes by codifying the lengths and appearance of minims, breves, crotchets and so on. After 1300, the *ars antiqua* was replaced by the *ars nova*, when plainchant gave way to polyphony. This is where a composer writes separate tunes for people with different voices (sopranos, tenors, basses and so on), which all combine together harmoniously. Among the principal composers of the *ars nova* was the Frenchman Guillaume de Machaut, who is credited with being a driving force in the development of musical polyphony.

HALL OF FAME HIT

Gregorio Allegri: *Miserere*

Recommended Recording

The Sixteen conducted by Harry Christophers; Coro COR16118

'Let me present to you the future Paganini!'

COMPOSER FRANZ LISZT ABOUT THE VIOLINIST AUGUST WILHELMJ

22
JANUARY

🎵 BIRTHS & DEATHS

1908 German violinist August Wilhelmj dies in London.
1916 French composer Henri Dutilleux is born in Angers.
1953 Korean conductor and pianist Myung-Whun Chung is born in Seoul.
1978 Maltese tenor Joseph Calleja is born in Attard.

🎭 FIRST PERFORMED

1887 Gilbert and Sullivan's operetta *Ruddigore* opens at the Savoy Theatre in London.

☀️ TODAY'S THE DAY

1720 Nine-year-old Wilhelm Friedemann begins work on the piano exercises put together for him by his father, Johann Sebastian Bach, in a book entitled *Clavier-Büchlein vor W. F. Bach*.
1922 Leoš Janáček starts to compose his opera *The Cunning Little Vixen*.

ERA FOCUS:

Early music: part III

The Renaissance period of early music ran from 1400 to 1600 and saw a rapid rebirth of styles and ideas about how music should be composed. It followed on from the medieval period and was the immediate precursor to the Baroque period. The most celebrated composers of the time include:

Joaquin des Prez (1450s–1521): a prolific Franco-Flemish composer. His Mass, *La Sol Fa Re Mi* is said to be based on the phrase *Laise faire moy* ('Leave it to me').

John Taverner (1490–1545): the most important English composer of the time, writing Masses (such as his significant *Western Wind Mass*) in Oxford. Not to be confused with the contemporary composer John Tavener (spelled with only one 'r').

Giovanni Pierluigi da Palestrina (1525–1594): Chief exponent of the Roman School of the Renaissance, a largely geographical group of choral writers, which extended into the Baroque period and later included Gregorio Allegri.

🎵 HALL OF FAME HIT

Sergei Rachmaninov: *Symphony No. 2*

Recommended Recording

Royal Liverpool Philharmonic Orchestra conducted by Vasily Petrenko; EMI 915 4732

23

JANUARY

> 'By the grace of God and with his help I will one day be a Liszt in technique and a Mozart in composition.'
>
> DIARY ENTRY FROM TODAY IN 1843 BY CZECH COMPOSER BEDŘICH SMETANA

 BIRTHS & DEATHS

1752 English composer and pianist Muzio Clementi is born in Rome in 1752.

1837 Irish composer and pianist John Field dies in Moscow.

1908 American composer Edward MacDowell dies in New York.

1962 English film composer David Arnold is born in Luton.

1976 American bass-baritone Paul Robeson dies in Philadelphia.

1981 American composer Samuel Barber dies in New York.

 FIRST PERFORMED

1895 Edward MacDowell's *Indian Suite* is premiered in New York by the Boston Symphony Orchestra.

Touring duo

The composers Muzio Clementi and John Field are linked together by more than the former being born on 23 January and the latter dying on the very same day of the year. Clementi was actually Field's teacher and in 1802 they embarked on a European tour together, which took in Paris, Vienna and St Petersburg. John Field, adopting the French word meaning 'of the night', was the first composer to use the term 'nocturne'. He wrote a series of short studies for solo piano, which had a gently romantic late-night feeling about them. They are rather dreamy pieces, with floating chords being played by the pianist's left hand, while the right plays an expressive, sometimes melancholy melody. The idea was quickly taken up by Chopin, who wrote a total of 21 nocturnes.

Trick question

You know those silly questions: 'Who wrote Beethoven's Fifth?' or 'Which country's official song is the French National Anthem?' Well, just be careful if someone asks you 'Who wrote the overture to Offenbach's *Orpheus in the Underworld?*' because it was actually added later by Carl Binder.

 HALL OF FAME HIT

Joaquín Rodrigo: *Concierto de Aranjuez*

Recommended Recording

John Williams (guitar); English Chamber Orchestra conducted by Daniel Barenboim; Sony Classical 8869 769 0542

'The heart of a melody can never be put down on paper.'

PABLO CASALS, CELLIST

BIRTHS & DEATHS

1953 Ukrainian viola player Yuri Bashmet is born in Rostov-na-Donu.

FIRST PERFORMED

1906 Sergei Rachmaninov's two one-act operas *The Miserly Knight* and *Francesca da Rimini* are premiered at the Bolshoi theatre in Moscow.

TODAY'S THE DAY

1813 The Royal Philharmonic Society is founded in London by a group of wealthy music lovers, its aim being 'to promote the performance, in the most perfect manner possible, of the best and most approved instrumental music'.

1846 Johann Strauss Senior is given the honorary position of k.k. Hofballmusik-Direktor (Imperial-Royal Director of Music for the Balls at Court) by Austria's Emperor Ferdinand I. The role stayed as a Strauss-family affair for more than half a century up until 1901, when it was given up by Eduard Strauss.

Royal Philharmonic Society

Among the many famous works composed as a result of a commission from the Royal Philharmonic Society, Beethoven's *Symphony No. 9* must rank as the greatest. During the two centuries of its existence, the society has also commissioned music from Mendelssohn, Dvořák, Vaughan Williams and Elgar. Today, the Royal Philharmonic Society continues to support contemporary composers, as well as working to provide young musicians with a concert platform and generally promoting a greater appreciation of classical music.

Disc count

It's claimed that compact discs hold 74 minutes of music to ensure that the whole of Beethoven's *Symphony No. 9* can be fitted on one disc without any interruptions.

Popular appeal

David Arnold was not only the composer of five James Bond soundtracks, he was also the music director for the closing ceremony of the London 2012 Olympic and Paralympic Games.

HALL OF FAME HIT

Pietro Mascagni: *Cavalleria Rusticana*

Recommended Recording

Various soloists; London Opera Chorus and the National Philharmonic Orchestra conducted by Gianandrea Gavazzeni; Decca 444 3912

25

JANUARY

'When I composed that, I was conscious of being inspired by God Almighty. Do you think I consider your puny little fiddle when He speaks to me?'

COMPOSER LUDWIG VAN BEETHOVEN, TO A VIOLINIST WHO BELIEVED THAT A PASSAGE WAS IMPOSSIBLE TO PLAY

BIRTHS & DEATHS

1886 German conductor Wilhelm Furtwängler is born in Berlin.

1913 Polish composer Witold Lutosławski is born in Warsaw.

1960 Italian harpsichordist, organist and conductor Rinaldo Alessandrini is born in Rome.

2012 Finnish conductor Paavo Berglund dies in Helsinki.

TODAY'S THE DAY

1672 The original Theatre Royal, Drury Lane, in London (then known as the Bridges Street Theatre) burns to the ground.

1759 Many people think of Robbie Burns, whose birthday is today, as being Scotland's greatest poet of all time. However, not everyone realises that he was also a songwriter, with more than 350 songs to his name.

1784 Wolfgang Amadeus Mozart conducts a performance of *The Abduction from the Seraglio* in Vienna.

1856 Composer Anton Bruckner has a second audition for the post of cathedral organist in Linz. He gets the job, although he very nearly hadn't applied for the role at all, throwing his hat into the ring only after encouragement from a local organ tuner.

1862 Richard Wagner finishes writing the words to *Die Meistersinger von Nürnberg*. The music won't be complete for another five years.

You can't be good at everything

Albert Einstein was the man who formulated the theories of relativity, who revolutionised our grasp of matters of space and time, and even tweaked the Brownian theory of motion. He was also a keen amateur violinist. Once, below the window of his Mercer Street apartment in Princeton, his violin teacher was heard to say, 'Oh for goodness' sake, Albert, can't you count?'

Note perfect

After he had heard a performance of Mozart's *The Abduction from the Seraglio* in 1782, Emperor Joseph II turned to the composer and said, 'Too fine for our ears, my dear Mozart, and far too many notes.' From the composer came the retort: 'Exactly as many notes as are necessary, Your Majesty.'

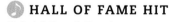

HALL OF FAME HIT
Gabriel Fauré: *Requiem*

Recommended Recording
Accentus and members of the Orchestre National de France conducted by Laurence Equilbey; Naïve V5137

'...wrestling with God.'

COMPOSER JEAN SIBELIUS, DIARY ENTRY TODAY IN 1916, ON THE SUBJECT OF COMPOSING BIG WORKS

26
JANUARY

BIRTHS & DEATHS

1795 German composer Johann Christoph Friedrich Bach dies in Bückeburg. He was the son of Johann Sebastian.

1908 French violinist Stéphane Grappelli is born in Paris.

1945 English cellist Jacqueline du Pré is born in Oxford.

1951 English conductor Roy Goodman is born in Guildford.

1981 Venezuelan conductor Gustavo Dudamel is born in Barquisimeto.

FIRST PERFORMED

1790 Wolfgang Amadeus Mozart's opera *Così fan tutte* is premiered in Vienna.

1882 Alexander Borodin's *String Quartet No. 2* is premiered in St Petersburg.

1911 Richard Strauss's opera *Der Rosenkavalier* is premiered in Dresden.

TODAY'S THE DAY

1712 Italian composer Giacomo Puccini is baptised in Lucca. His birthdate is lost in the mists of time. But be warned! This isn't the great opera composer of the same name: this Puccini specialised in church music.

ARTIST PROFILE:

Jacqueline du Pré

Giving her first public performance at the age of seven, Jacqueline du Pré made her debut at London's prestigious Wigmore Hall when she was just 16. As a performer, she was amazing to watch – player and instrument seemed to meld together as one. She studied with the great cellists Mstislav Rostropovich and Paul Tortelier. Her recordings and performances of Elgar's *Cello Concerto* are regarded as being among the best ever and she became particularly closely linked with the work. She recorded it with her husband, Daniel Barenboim, conducting the Philadelphia Orchestra and with John Barbirolli, conducting the London Symphony Orchestra.

Sadly, du Pré became ill with multiple sclerosis, gradually losing the feeling in her fingers and the ability to play. She died at the tragically young age of 42. The controversial film *Hilary and Jackie* is based on a book about her life, which was written by her brother and sister. The two cellos with which she became most associated – both made by Stradivarius – are now played by Yo-Yo Ma and Nina Kotova.

HALL OF FAME HIT
Jean Sibelius: *Finlandia*

Recommended Recording
Oslo Philharmonic Orchestra conducted by Mariss Jansons; EMI 679 1802

27

'Where the speech of man stops short, then the art of music begins.'

RICHARD WAGNER, COMPOSER

JANUARY

🎵 BIRTHS & DEATHS

1756 Austrian composer Wolfgang Amadeus Mozart is born in Salzburg.

1823 French composer Edouard Lalo is born in Lille.

1901 Italian composer Giuseppe Verdi dies in Milan.

1915 English clarinettist Jack Brymer is born in South Shields.

1937 English composer and pianist John Ogdon is born in Mansfield Woodhouse.

1962 English clarinettist Michael Collins is born in Isleworth.

1970 Swiss flautist Emmanuel Pahud is born in Geneva.

1972 Welsh tenor Wynne Evans is born in Carmarthen.

🎵 FIRST PERFORMED

1733 George Frideric Handel's opera *Orlando* opens at the King's Theatre in London's Haymarket.

1859 Johannes Brahms' *Piano Concerto No. 1* is premiered in Leipzig. It doesn't go down well with the critics.

☀ TODAY'S THE DAY

1587 The 19-year-old Claudio Monteverdi dedicates his first book of five-voice madrigals to a nobleman from Verona, Count Marco Veritá.

COMPOSER PROFILE:

Wolfgang Amadeus Mozart

Mozart lived for just 35 years. He was a native of Salzburg but spent a good deal of his early life travelling. As soon as his ambitious father Leopold realised just how phenomenal and prodigious Mozart's musical talent actually was, the young boy was propelled around Europe for years at a time.

After the age of 19, Mozart toured in his own right, with just his mother for company. He moved to Vienna, effectively as a freelance composer, taking work where he could find it. Here he married Constanze Weber. It was a very happy marriage, despite the fact that Mozart had previously pursued Constanze's sister for some years. In Vienna, he continued to compose a huge amount of music, including symphonies, piano concertos and operas, possibly the purest yet riskiest musical currency of all at the time. *The Marriage of Figaro* and *Così fan tutte* were both premiered in Vienna to great popular acclaim.

Mozart was also popular in Prague, where he premiered his opera *Don Giovanni* as well as masterpieces such as *Symphony No. 41 ('Jupiter')* and *Eine Kleine Nachtmusik*. In the final year of his life, Mozart wrote *The Magic Flute*, the *Ave Verum Corpus*, the *Clarinet Concerto* and part of a *Requiem*. He died not quite penniless but certainly with cash problems and was buried in an unmarked pauper's grave.

🎵 HALL OF FAME HIT
Felix Mendelssohn: *Violin Concerto*

Recommended Recording
Anne-Sophie Mutter (violin); Leipzig Gewandhaus Orchestra conducted by Kurt Masur; Deutsche Grammophon 477 8575

> 'You have Van Gogh's ear for music.'
> **BILLY WILDER, FILM DIRECTOR AND WRITER**

 BIRTHS & DEATHS

1791 French composer Ferdinand Hérold is born in Paris.

1887 American pianist Arthur Rubinstein is born in Poland.

1944 English composer John Tavener is born in London.

 TODAY'S THE DAY

1848 Having failed to make the grade as a concert pianist, Bedřich Smetana asks the government for permission to open a music institute in Prague.

1855 Anton Bruckner qualifies as a schoolteacher, but he ends up working as an organist instead.

1904 The tenor Enrico Caruso signs his first recording contract with Victor Records.

10 Dons in opera

Don Alfonso	Donizetti: *Lucrezia Borgia*
Don Alvaro	Verdi: *La forza del destino*
Don Basilio	Rossini: *The Barber of Seville*
Don Carlos	Rameau: *Les Indes galantes*
Don Curzio	Mozart: *The Marriage of Figaro*
Don Fernando	Beethoven: *Fidelio*
Don Giovanni	Mozart: *Don Giovanni*
Don José	Bizet: *Carmen*
Don José Martinez	Delius: *Koanga*
Don Quixote	Purcell: *Don Quixote*

Sign of the times

You know those house signs you occasionally see that are an amalgamation of the names of the couple living inside? Well, genius that he was, Rachmaninov was not above doing it, too. His house on the edge of Lake Lucerne was called 'Senar', which was short for SErgei and NAtalya Rachmaninov.

Out of this world

Composer Dmitri Shostakovich might have enjoyed a troubled relationship with his country's leaders, but that didn't stop him being able to claim one notable premiere after the first cosmonaut, Yuri Gagarin, sang Shostakovich's song '*My Homeland Hears*', over the radio link from his spacecraft back to earth.

 HALL OF FAME HIT

Wolfgang Amadeus Mozart: *Piano Concerto No. 21*

Recommended Recording

Maria João Pires (piano); Chamber Orchestra of Europe conducted by Claudio Abbado; Deutsche Grammophon 479 1435

29

JANUARY

BIRTHS & DEATHS

1862 English composer Frederick Delius born in Bradford.

1962 Austrian (later American) violinist and composer Fritz Kreisler dies in New York.

FIRST PERFORMED

1728 *The Beggar's Opera* is premiered at Lincoln's Inn Fields in London. This play, written by John Gay, with music by Johann Christoph Pepusch, is a satire on Italian opera. *The Beggar's Opera* becomes a massive success and revivals continue into the 21st century. It is at the vanguard of a new genre, known as 'ballad opera'.

1781 Mozart's opera *Idomeneo* is premiered in Munich.

TODAY'S THE DAY

1996 Venice's opera house Teatro La Fenice ('The Phoenix') is ravaged by fire for the second time in its history. It was previously destroyed by fire in December 1836. It re-opened after being rebuilt for a second time in December 2003.

COMPOSER PROFILE:

Frederick Delius

Delius's father wanted him to work in the family wool business, but instead Frederick went to Florida to run an orange plantation, where he spent more time studying music than cultivating fruit. He moved to Paris, where his friends included the composers Ravel and Fauré and the painters Gauguin and Munch.

Delius specialised in 'idylls' (short pastoral works for orchestra), as well as choral works and operas. Thanks in the main to the advocacy of the conductor Thomas Beecham, who became the composer's lifelong champion and friend, it is the 'idylls' that have endured the best – wonderful meanderings of orchestral colour, rich in fleeting melodies. They are also exquisitely crafted.

As a young man, Delius contracted syphilis. By the time he was in his sixties, he was crippled and practically blind. He needed an amanuensis, Eric Fenby, to help him to transfer the tunes from his head onto manuscript paper. Delius's intermezzo *The Walk to the Paradise Garden* sounds particularly idyllic, especially coming, as it does, from the opera *A Village Romeo and Juliet*. Sounds idyllic, that is, until you realise that the Paradise Garden is a pub. They're off for a pint!

HALL OF FAME HIT

Ludwig van Beethoven: *Symphony No. 7*

Recommended Recording

Anima Eterna conducted by Jos van Immerseel; Zig Zag 370055 1732234

'There are two golden rules for an orchestra: start together and finish together. The public don't give a damn what goes on in between.'

THOMAS BEECHAM, CONDUCTOR

 BIRTHS & DEATHS

1960 Canadian baritone Gerald Finley is born in Montreal.

1963 French composer Francis Poulenc dies in Paris.

1990 Chinese pianist Ji Liu is born in Shanghai.

2011 English film composer John Barry dies in New York.

TODAY'S THE DAY

1858 Respected pianist and conductor Charles Hallé gives the first of a new series of concerts in Manchester. Out of this series, the Hallé Orchestra is born. Contemporaneous records show that it was raining in Manchester on the night in question. The Hallé is the UK's second-oldest continuously operating professional symphony orchestra, beaten to the title of being the oldest only by near neighbours, the Royal Liverpool Philharmonic, which can trace its origin as a professional band back to 1853. The Hallé's home venue is the wonderful Bridgewater Hall in the centre of Manchester and the orchestra has a long association with the cities of Sheffield and Bradford. The orchestra is currently enjoying an artistic resurgence under Music Director Mark Elder. He follows in a long line of prestigious principal conductors, including Hans Richter, Thomas Beecham, Hamilton Harty and John Barbirolli. The orchestra's list of world-premiere performances includes Elgar's *Symphony No. 1*, Vaughan Williams' *Sinfonia Antartica* and Finzi's *Cello Concerto*.

COMPOSER PROFILE:

Francis Poulenc

Francis Jean Marcel Poulenc was as French as his names suggest. His musical education did not follow the normal path; although he did study with various composers, there are whole areas in which he never received any formal instruction. His witty, Continental style drew him to ally himself with Satie and the rest of 'Les Six' (a group of six composers all writing in France around the same time). Poulenc rediscovered his Roman Catholicism in the 1930s, resulting in some truly great choral works, such as his *Gloria*. Not surprisingly for a man who once confessed he wished he was Maurice Chevalier, another area in which he made his name was 'chanson', the French lieder tradition. He created a huge volume of songs, many for his concert partner, Pierre Bernac.

 HALL OF FAME HIT

Gustav Mahler: *Symphony No. 5*

Recommended Recording

San Francisco Symphony Orchestra conducted by Michael Tilson Thomas; Avie 8219 3600122

31
JANUARY

'I compose every morning and when one piece is done, I begin another.'

FRANZ SCHUBERT, COMPOSER

BIRTHS & DEATHS

1797 Austrian composer Franz Schubert is born in Vienna.

1831 Rudolph Wurlitzer is born in Schöneck, Saxony.

1921 American tenor Mario Lanza is born in Philadelphia.

1937 American composer Philip Glass is born in Baltimore.

1960 English composer George Benjamin is born in London.

1965 Israeli (later Canadian) cellist Ofra Harnoy is born in Hadera.

FIRST PERFORMED

1891 Arthur Sullivan's *Ivanhoe* is premiered at the opening of the Royal English Opera House in London's Cambridge Circus, built by the impresario Richard D'Oyly Carte.

TODAY'S THE DAY

1994 Barcelona's opera house, the Gran Teatro del Liceo, is destroyed by fire.

COMPOSER PROFILE:

Franz Schubert

Schubert's father was a schoolteacher in Vienna, and he taught the youngster the basic rudiments of music. After being spotted by the eminent composer Salieri when he was only seven, Schubert was enrolled into the Stadtkonvikt (the imperial boarding school) as a boy soprano. He also played violin in the school orchestra, while Salieri himself taught him musical theory and the principles of composition.

The family was always short of money, so, when Schubert left the Stadtkonvikt, he was forced to combine his musical activities with teaching in his father's school. This didn't stop him composing. By 1814, he had already produced some piano pieces, songs, some string quartets, his first symphony and a three-act opera. The following year he wrote '*Gretchen am Spinnrade*' ('*Gretchen at the Spinning Wheel*'), '*Der Erlkönig*' ('*The Earl King*') and many other great songs, plus two more symphonies, three Masses and four stage works.

Aged 20, he gave up teaching in order to compose full-time. At first, things went well for him. He produced more overtures, symphonies, theatre music and chamber music, and his works began to be performed in public. Then, in 1822, he almost certainly contracted the syphilis that eventually killed him. Nevertheless, he soldiered on composing, including *Winterreise* (*The Winter Journey*), his last and most amazing song-cycle.

HALL OF FAME HIT

Sergei Rachmaninov: *Rhapsody on a theme of Paganini*

Recommended Recording

Yuja Wang (piano); Mahler Chamber Orchestra conducted by Claudio Abbado; Deutsche Grammophon 477 9308

Febru

01

FEBRUARY

'Everything sung by individual voices and supposed to resemble an aria was empty, frozen and wretched . . . but the choruses are good and even excellent.'

LETTER WRITTEN TODAY IN 1764 BY WOLFGANG AMADEUS MOZART'S FATHER LEOPOLD ABOUT THE ROYAL CHAPEL AT VERSAILLES

🎵 BIRTHS & DEATHS

1872 English contralto Clara Butt is born in Southwick, Sussex.
1875 English composer William Sterndale Bennett dies in London.
1952 Hungarian pianist Jenö Jandó is born in Pécs.

🎭 FIRST PERFORMED

1893 Giacomo Puccini's opera *Manon Lescaut* is premiered in Turin.
1896 Giacomo Puccini's opera *La bohème* is premiered in Turin, with Arturo Toscanini conducting.

☀ TODAY'S THE DAY

1579 The man widely credited with composing the first real opera, Jacopo Peri, takes up a job as an organist in Florence.
1795 In London, King George III is present at an evening of music by Joseph Haydn put on by the composer's biggest royal fan, the Prince of Wales, who is later to become King George IV.
1864 Composer Modest Mussorgsky takes up a job as assistant head of the barracks division of Russia's Central Engineering Authority.

1878 Composer Pyotr Ilyich Tchaikovsky finishes eight months of work on the score of his opera *Eugene Onegin*.
1904 Italian tenor Enrico Caruso makes his first recording for Victor Records, his first step to immense fame and fortune.
1947 Composer Dmitri Shostakovich begins teaching at the Leningrad Conservatoire.
1949 RCA Victor Records releases the first 7-inch record. It plays at 45 revolutions per minute, signalling the end for the old 78 rpm single releases.

Mozart's letters

One of the most amazing non-musical legacies of any composer, Mozart's surviving letters span a 22-year period from his teens to just before his death. What they reveal counterbalances the traditional portrait of an angelic genius. The Mozart of the letters is coarse, rude and childish. His obsession with his own, and others', nether regions is undeniable and, while reading them might make some uncomfortable, they show a very 'humanising' side to a great mind. Comments such as the one written while he was composing *The Magic Flute*, 'Today, out of absolute tedium, I wrote an aria for the opera', serve to shed light on Mozart the man, possibly helping us to appreciate him all the more.

A box of notes

Every year, thousands of people visit Salzburg and literally eat Mozart. Don't worry, cannibalism isn't rife in Austria – Mozart is a brand of chocolate over there. It particularly appeals to visiting tourists.

🎵 HALL OF FAME HIT

Ludwig van Beethoven: *Symphony No. 5*

Recommended Recording

Berlin Philharmonic Orchestra conducted by Herbert von Karajan; Australian Eloquence 429 0392

> 'Genius is an overused word. The world has known only about a half dozen geniuses. I got only fairly near.'
>
> **FRITZ KREISLER, COMPOSER AND VIOLINIST**

BIRTHS & DEATHS

1875 Austrian (later American) violinist and composer Fritz Kreisler is born in Vienna.

1901 Russian (later American) violinist Jascha Heifetz is born in Vilnius.

1944 English conductor Andrew Davis is born in Hertfordshire.

FIRST PERFORMED

1795 Joseph Haydn's *Symphony No. 102* has its premier. Some musicologists believe this was the performance where a chandelier fell from the ceiling, narrowly missing the audience. History has attributed this event to the premiere of his *Symphony No. 96*, hence its nickname '*The Miracle*'.

1893 Charles Hallé conducts the first British performance of Tchaikovsky's *Symphony No. 5* in Manchester.

TODAY'S THE DAY

1911 The Swedish tenor Jussi Björling always considered today as his birthday, although he was in fact born three days later on 5 February. Nonetheless, 2 February is the day that he always celebrated, as this was the date that was mistakenly shown on his baptism records.

ARTIST PROFILE:

Fritz Kreisler

An amazing child prodigy, the violinist Fritz Kreisler entered the Vienna Conservatoire at the age of seven. He won the first prize at the Paris Conservatoire when he was still only 12 years old and was on tour by the time he was 14. He then turned his back on a career in music, opting instead to study medicine at university and then to become an officer in the Austrian army. He took up the violin again at the age of 24 and resumed his international performing career. In 1910, he gave the first performance of Elgar's *Violin Concerto* – the work is dedicated to him. He had to lay down his violin again to fight in the Austrian army in 1914, but was discharged after being wounded at the front. He was one of the first darlings of the gramophone age and his archive recordings can still be heard today. He claimed that many of the violin pieces that he composed to show off his own virtuosic playing were written by composers from the 1700s, when in fact they were all his own work.

 HALL OF FAME HIT

Johann Sebastian Bach: *Concerto in D minor for 2 Violins*

Recommended Recording

Nigel Kennedy; Daniel Stabrawa; Berlin Philharmonic Orchestra; EMI 629 0572

03

FEBRUARY

'Joking apart, Prince Albert asked me to go to him on Saturday at two o'clock so that I might try his organ before I leave England.'

FELIX MENDELSSOHN, COMPOSER

🕐 BIRTHS & DEATHS

1525 Italian composer Giovanni Pierluigi da Palestrina is likely to have been born today.

1809 German composer Felix Mendelssohn is born in Hamburg.

1947 Soprano and Royal Opera director Elaine Padmore is born in Yorkshire.

1960 Scottish pianist Malcolm Martineau is born in Edinburgh.

🎭 FIRST PERFORMED

1844 Hector Berlioz's *Roman Carnival Overture* is first performed in Paris with the composer conducting.

🌅 TODAY'S THE DAY

1821 Felix Mendelssohn's first major public work, *Die Soldatenliebschaft*, was performed with an orchestra in his home, as part of the celebrations for the young composer's 12th birthday.

COMPOSER PROFILE:

Felix Mendelssohn

Mendelssohn was born into a wealthy Hamburg family and showed plenty of early musical talent. In 1825, the composer Cherubini spotted his true potential, but said, 'He puts too much material into his coat' – a warning not to cram too many musical ideas into each piece. At the age of 16, Mendelssohn wrote his *Octet*, which is still considered to be one of the greatest classical music works ever composed by a teenager. He followed the success of the *Octet* with his *Overture to 'A Midsummer Night's Dream'*, although it took him a further 17 years to complete the rest of the incidental music.

Mendelssohn was a big fan of Bach, and when he was 20, he organised performances of Bach's *St Matthew Passion* to mark its centenary. This was unusual because Bach was unfashionable at the time; it was the first time the *St Matthew Passion* had been performed since Bach's death in 1750. He also revived the music of Franz Schubert, giving the premiere of his last symphony when it was rediscovered more than a decade after the older composer's death. He then got the travelling bug, journeying around Europe and spending a lot of time in Britain, with Scotland being a particular favourite destination. While he was there, he developed the ideas behind his *Hebrides Overture* and *'Scottish' Symphony*. He was lionised by music societies and festivals across the country – his oratorio *Elijah* received its premiere during the Birmingham Festival.

🎵 HALL OF FAME HIT
Pyotr Ilyich Tchaikovsky: 1812 Overture

Recommended Recording
Mariinsky Orchestra conducted by Valery Gergiev; MAR 0503

> 'Military justice is to justice what military music is to music.'
>
> **GROUCHO MARX, ACTOR AND WRITER**

04
FEBRUARY

 BIRTHS & DEATHS

1873 Romanian composer Theodor Fuchs is born in Sassin.

1894 Belgian inventor of the saxophone, Adolphe Sax, dies in Paris.

TEN FAVOURITE CHAMBER WORKS

1 Mendelssohn: *Octet*
2 Schubert: *Piano Quintet in A* (*'Trout'*)
3 Mozart: *Clarinet Quintet*
4 Schubert: *String Quintet in C*
5 Borodin: *String Quartet No. 2*
6 Schubert: *String Quartet in D minor* (*'Death and the Maiden'*)
7 Tchaikovsky: *String Quartet No. 1*
8 Beethoven: *Grosse Fugue*
9 Mozart: *Trio in E flat for clarinet, viola and piano* (*'Kegelstatt' Trio*)
10 Saint-Saëns: *Carnival of the Animals* (written originally for two pianos, string quintet, flute, clarinet, glockenspiel and xylophone)

INSTRUMENT FOCUS:

Saxophone

Born and raised in Belgium, Adolphe Sax was in his late twenties and living in Paris when he invented his saxophone in the 1840s. Like the clarinet, it is a wind instrument with a single-reed mouthpiece. However, unlike the clarinet, it has a fairly simple fingering system. It has a conical bore (wider at the bottom than it is at the top) and is very popular in military bands, not to mention jazz groups.

The Russian composer Glazunov loved the sound the saxophone produced and wrote his *Concerto for alto saxophone and strings* in 1934 after repeated requests from Sigurd Rascher, a legendary Swedish saxophonist. The combination of medieval plainchant and improvised jazz brought together by the saxophonist Jan Garbarek and the Hilliard Ensemble, a noted Early-music group, for the album *Officium* in 1993 is an enduring Classic FM favourite, with *Parce Mihi Domine* always particularly popular. Other composer fans of the instrument include Debussy, Vaughan Williams, Berlioz and Bizet. Among the current crop of performers, Britain's John Harle is near the top of the tree. As well as being a world-class saxophonist, he also composes, writing the haunting theme tune to the long-running pathology television drama *Silent Witness*.

HALL OF FAME HIT
Nikolai Rimsky-Korsakov: *Scheherazade*

Recommended Recording
London Symphony Orchestra conducted by Charles Mackerras; Telarc 80208

05

FEBRUARY

'One can't judge Wagner's opera *Lohengrin* after a first hearing, and I certainly don't intend hearing it a second time.'

GIOACHINO ROSSINI, COMPOSER

🕐 BIRTHS & DEATHS

1810 Norwegian violinist Ole Bull is born in Bergen.
1911 Swedish tenor Jussi Björling is born in Stora Tuna.
1962 French composer Jacques Ibert dies in Paris.

🔔 FIRST PERFORMED

1887 Giuseppe Verdi's opera *Otello* is premiered in Milan.

☀ TODAY'S THE DAY

1861 Eduard Strauss makes his debut as the conductor of the Strauss Orchestra, following his father Johann Strauss Senior and his even more famous brother Johann Strauss Junior into the family business.
1871 Richard Wagner completes the score for his opera *Siegfried*, the third opera in his *Ring Cycle*.

Female voices

The highest of the female registers is called a soprano. Famous sopranos include: Joan Sutherland, Renée Fleming, Emma Kirkby, Lesley Garrett, Lucia Popp and Dawn Upshaw. Mezzo-sopranos (meaning literally 'half' sopranos) sing between the soprano and alto ranges. Famous mezzo-sopranos include: Janet Baker, Christa Ludwig and Magdalena Kožená. The word 'alto' means 'high', which is a little confusing considering they are the lower of the two main female registers (this is because, originally, all parts were sung by men and 'alto' itself was short for 'contratenor altus', shortened to contralto and then alto). Famous altos include: Clara Butt, Kathleen Ferrier and Marian Anderson. Boys singing in the soprano range are known as trebles; in the 17th and 18th centuries a male soprano would have been a castrato.

Welsh National Opera

Founded thanks to the efforts of a group of miners, doctors, teachers, shop assistants and steel workers in 1943, WNO performed its first ever operas, a double bill of *Cavelleria Rusticana* and *Pagliacci*, three years later. It is now recognised as one of the most innovative opera companies in the world. An early reputation for performing rare Verdi operas preceded touring seasons in Swansea, Bristol, Birmingham and beyond, alongside the Welsh Philharmonia, which was renamed the Orchestra of Welsh National Opera in 1979.

🎵 HALL OF FAME HIT

Sergei Rachmaninov: *Piano Concerto No. 3*

Recommended Recording

Martha Argerich (piano); Berlin Radio Symphony Orchestra conducted by Riccardo Chailly; Philips 464 7322

'Music is the electrical soil in which the spirit lives, thinks and invents.'

LUDWIG VAN BEETHOVEN, COMPOSER

🏛 BIRTHS & DEATHS

1818 English composer and pianist Henry Litolff is born in London.

🐎 FIRST PERFORMED

1813 Gioachino Rossini's opera *Tancredi* is premiered in Venice.

☀ TODAY'S THE DAY

1629 The first Master of the King's Musick, Nicholas Lanier, is arrested for disorderly behaviour in the street along with other members of his family. Given his position in court society, eyebrows are raised.

1922 Thomas Beecham's British National Opera Company makes its debut performance, with Verdi's *Aida* in Bradford.

Masters of the King's/ Queen's Music

1625	Nicholas Lanier
1666	Louis Grabu
1674	Nicholas Staggins
1700	John Eccles
1735	Maurice Green
1755	William Boyce
1779	John Stanley
1786	William Parsons
1817	William Shield
1834	Christian Kramer
1848	George Frideric Anderson
1870	William George Cusins
1893	Walter Parratt
1924	Edward Elgar
1934	Walford Davies
1942	Arnold Bax
1953	Arthur Bliss
1975	Malcolm Williamson
2004	Peter Maxwell Davies

Male voices

The origin of the term 'tenor' is slightly bizarre. It means 'holding' – nothing to do with the register of the singer's voice, but all to do with its role in medieval times when the tenors sang a 'holding' tune, around which others sang counterpoints. Nowadays, tenors are very much the leading men of the opera world, almost always the heroes. Famous tenors include: Luciano Pavarotti, José Cura and Ian Bostridge. The word 'baritone' comes from the Greek barytonos, meaning deep-sounding, though, in actuality, baritones do not sing as low as all that. Fauré's *Requiem* contains a beautiful part for solo baritone. Famous baritones include: Dietrich Fischer-Dieskau, Geraint Evans, Sherrill Milnes and Thomas Allen. Basses are the lowest of the male voices and very often find themselves cast as the villains or, perhaps because of their grand nature, the kings in opera. Famous basses include: Boris Christoff, Gottlob Frick, Ruggero Raimondi, Samuel Ramey and Paata Burchuladze.

HALL OF FAME HIT

Ludwig van Beethoven: *Piano Sonata No. 14 ('Moonlight')*

Recommended Recording

Steven Osborne (piano); Hyperion CDA 67662

07

FEBRUARY

'Truly there would be reason to go mad if it were not for music.'

PYOTR ILYICH TCHAIKOVSKY, COMPOSER

BIRTHS & DEATHS

1779 English composer William Boyce dies in London.

1871 Henry Steinway dies in New York after building up the world-famous piano-making company that bears his name.

1994 Polish composer Witold Lutosławski dies in Warsaw.

FIRST PERFORMED

1792 Domenico Cimarosa's opera *The Secret Marriage* is given its first performance.

1873 Tchaikovsky's *Symphony No. 2* is premiered in Moscow.

1894 Puccini's opera *Manon Lescaut* is premiered in Milan in a version revised from the previous year's debut. The composer completely changed the ending to Act I.

TODAY'S THE DAY

1809 Joseph Haydn signs his last will, three months before his death.

1914 Claude Debussy, Edward Elgar, Engelbert Humperdinck and Camille Saint-Saëns are all granted honorary membership of the Academy of Santa Cecilia in Rome.

COMPOSER PROFILE:

William Boyce

Steeped in the traditions of English choral music, William Boyce was a boy chorister at St Paul's Cathedral. He worked as an organist in London, before becoming Composer to the Chapel Royal in 1736 and Master of the King's Musick in 1755. He was among the leading English composers of his generation, writing the music for both the funeral of George II and the coronation of George III. Boyce had to retire from his musical posts in his sixties because of his increasing deafness.

Sing for your supper

Legend suggests that the Austro-Hungarian Emperor Leopold II loved the premiere of Cimarosa's *The Secret Marriage* so much that he invited the whole cast and orchestra to dinner, before demanding that they stage the whole performance from beginning to end once again.

HALL OF FAME HIT
Tchaikovsky: *Piano Concerto No. 1*

Recommended Recording
Van Cliburn (piano); RCA Victor Symphony Orchestra conducted by Kyrill Kondrashin; Regis RRC 1391

> 'John is the most important collaborator I've ever had in my career . . . His music immediately bypasses the brain and goes straight to your heart. That's the way he's always been . . . an amazing talent.'
>
> **FILM DIRECTOR STEVEN SPIELBERG ABOUT COMPOSER JOHN WILLIAMS**

08
FEBRUARY

BIRTHS & DEATHS

1741 French (originally Belgian) composer André Grétry is born in Liège.

1932 American film composer John Williams is born in New York.

FIRST PERFORMED

1874 The revised version of Modest Mussorgky's opera *Boris Godunov* is premiered in St Petersburg. The original was not performed until 1928.

1904 The original version of Jean Sibelius's *Violin Concerto* is given its first performance in Helsinki.

1908 Sergei Rachmaninov's *Symphony No. 2* is premiered in St Petersburg, with the composer conducting.

TODAY'S THE DAY

1800 The composer Franz Süssmayr writes a letter to a publisher laying his claim to having been one of the musicians whom Mozart's wife asked to complete his *Requiem* in 1792, following the great man's death.

COMPOSER PROFILE:

John Williams

John Williams has written the music for more than a hundred different movies. And there is no doubt that the rest of the film industry appreciates his talents: he has 45 Oscar nominations (the highest number for any living person), carrying off the statuette five times. He has been nominated for 22 Golden Globes, winning four times. Of his 59 Grammy Award nominations, he was victorious on 15 occasions. Born in New York in 1932, he moved with his family to Los Angeles in 1948. He had loved music from his boyhood and, after finishing his first set of studies, he joined the American Air Force. Next, Williams moved back to New York for more studying, this time at the world-famous Juilliard School. In the evenings, he made money working as a pianist in many of the jazz clubs in the city's Manhattan area. Finally, Williams made the move back to Los Angeles, where he started to work in the film and television industry. Throughout the 1960s, he wrote the theme tunes of many successful American television programmes. Then, in 1973, Williams met the film director Steven Spielberg, with whom he has subsequently enjoyed the greatest creative partnership of his long career. Their first film was called *Sugarland Express*. Since then, their list of credits includes blockbuster after blockbuster – *Jaws*, *E.T.*, *Superman*, *Schindler's List* and *Saving Private Ryan* to name but a few. Williams also collaborated very successfully with the *Star Wars* director, George Lucas, working on the first six films in the series. Although he could choose to write his music using a computer programme, Williams prefers the old-fashioned way. He uses a piano to work out the tune, and a pencil and paper to write down what he has composed. It's hard work, too – he might have only eight weeks to write around two hours of music for a full orchestra for a film.

HALL OF FAME HIT
Dmitri Shostakovich: *Piano Concerto No. 2*

Recommended Recording
Dmitri Shostakovich Junior (piano); I Musici de Montreal conducted by Maxim Shostakovich; Chandos CHAN 8443

'In opera, anything that is too stupid to be spoken is sung.'

VOLTAIRE, PHILOSOPHER

 BIRTHS & DEATHS

1885 Austrian composer Alban Berg is born in Vienna.
1966 English soprano Amanda Roocroft is born in Lancashire.

FIRST PERFORMED

1893 Giuseppe Verdi's opera *Falstaff* is premiered in Milan.
1909 The final three of the 12 movements of Isaac Albéniz's piano suite *Iberia* are given their first performance in Paris. The work had been premiered in blocks of three movements since 1905.

TODAY'S THE DAY

1712 Georg Philipp Telemann is appointed director of music and Kapellmeister at the Barfüsserkirche in Frankfurt.
1810 Composer Carl Maria von Weber is arrested, together with his father, and charged with crimes including embezzlement.
1818 The Halifax Choral Society holds its first concert, a performance of Haydn's *Creation*.

COMPOSER PROFILE:

Isaac Albéniz

Albéniz was born in the Spanish town of Gerona. As a child, he travelled around Europe with his father, a musician who gave recitals wherever it paid him to do so. Later, Albéniz himself was something of a globetrotter, visiting musical centres as far removed as Madrid, Puerto Rico, Cuba, Leipzig, Budapest and Paris. An effortless improviser on the piano, he is best known today for his music for that instrument. Two famous names to whom he is linked are Francis Money-Coutts of the Coutts banking family, who funded Albéniz for many years, and Cecilia Sarkozy, the former wife of the former French President, Nicolas Sarkozy. She is Albéniz's great-granddaughter.

MUSICAL TERM:

Transcription

A transcription is an interpretative paraphrasing by one composer of another composer's original work, or part of it, usually, but not always, from an orchestra to a piano. It developed out of the penchant for producing 'opera fantasies', usually piano-based works that take two or more of the themes from a certain opera, and develop them further, and together, in a new piece by a different composer. Liszt was the first master of the piano transcription, composing more than 50. Busoni continued the tradition into the 20th century with his Bach paraphrases.

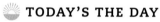

 HALL OF FAME HIT
Ludwig van Beethoven: *Violin Concerto*

Recommended Recording
Isabelle Faust (violin); Orchestra Mozart conducted by Claudio Abbado; Harmonia Mundi HMC 902105

> 'Even Bach comes down to the basic suck, blow, suck, suck, blow.'
>
> **LARRY ADLER, HARMONICA PLAYER**

10
FEBRUARY

🎵 BIRTHS & DEATHS

1914 American harmonica player Larry Adler is born in Baltimore.

1927 American soprano Leontyne Price is born in Mississippi.

1929 American composer Jerry Goldsmith is born in Los Angeles.

🎵 FIRST PERFORMED

1744 George Frideric Handel's opera *Semele* is premiered at Covent Garden in London.

1749 George Frideric Handel's oratorio *Susanna* receives its first performance, also at Covent Garden in London.

1794 Joseph Haydn's *Symphony No. 99* is premiered at the King's Theatre in London.

1881 Jacques Offenbach's opera *The Tales of Hoffmann* is premiered at the Opéra-Comique in Paris, following the composer's death.

1882 Nikolai Rimsky-Korsakov's opera *The Snow Maiden* receives its first performance in St Petersburg.

🌅 TODAY'S THE DAY

1922 The first complete symphony concert on radio, featuring the Detroit Symphony Orchestra conducted by Ossip Gabrilovich, was broadcast on the American station WWJ.

1945 Benjamin Britten completes the full score of his opera *Peter Grimes*.

1948 The Soviet Central Committee issues a decree about how music should sound, in effect censoring what composers could write. Many of the big names of Russian music, including Shostakovich and Prokofiev, fell foul of the authorities over the years.

COMPOSER PROFILE:

Jacques Offenbach

Offenbach started his musical career in 1833 at the age of 14, when his father took him to Paris and got him admitted as a cello student at the Conservatoire. After completing his studies, Offenbach became a cello virtuoso, before turning to conducting and becoming a prime mover in the development of operetta (he wrote more than 100 of them). In the process, he cemented his position as one of the most popular composers of the 19th century, churning out crowd-pleasing music with memorable tunes.

🎵 HALL OF FAME HIT
Tomaso Albinoni: *Adagio in G minor*

Recommended Recording
I Solisti Veneti conducted by Claudio Scimone; Erato 2292 45557 2

11

> 'It's sobering to consider that when Mozart was my age, he had already been dead for a year.'
>
> TOM LEHRER, SATIRIST

 **BIRTHS & DEATHS**

1926 Scottish conductor Alexander Gibson is born in Motherwell.

FIRST PERFORMED

1785 Wolfgang Amadeus Mozart's *Piano Concerto No. 20* is premiered in Vienna, with the composer himself as the soloist.

TODAY'S THE DAY

1785 Joseph Haydn becomes a Freemason.

1855 Future conductor of the Strauss Orchestra, Eduard Strauss, makes his debut performance with the ensemble, as one of the harpists.

1916 The Baltimore Symphony Orchestra gives its first performance, with Gustav Strube conducting.

1949 The London Mozart Players give their first concert, at the Wigmore Hall in London.

ORCHESTRA FOCUS:
London Mozart Players

The London Mozart Players have become famous for being very good at doing one thing: playing a particular repertoire – the music of Haydn, Mozart, Beethoven, Schubert and their contemporaries – and doing it very well. The orchestra was founded in 1949 by the violinist Harry Blech, who set out to take the finest conductors, soloists and players to regional concert halls and small-scale venues in out-of-the-way places right around the country. The music directors who followed on from Blech – Jane Glover, Matthias Bamert, Andrew Parrott and Gérard Korsten – have each continued in this tradition. They have also maintained the purity of the London Mozart Players' central philosophy of performing only music from the Classical period. In a crowded market of London orchestras, this has given the LMP a very clear point of difference.

Composer's notes

The most expensive musical manuscript ever to be sold at auction was a collection of nine of Mozart's symphonies, which went under the hammer in 1987 for £2.58 million. Sixteen years later, the second most expensive musical score was auctioned off. Its buyer paid £2.13 million for a 575-page manuscript of Beethoven's *Symphony No. 9*.

 **HALL OF FAME HIT**

Gabriel Fauré: *Cantique de Jean Racine*

Recommended Recording

Accentus; Members of the Orchestre National de France conducted by Laurence Equilbey; Naïve V 5137

> 'I believe in Bach, the Father, Beethoven, the Son, and Brahms, the Holy Ghost of music.'
>
> **HANS VON BÜLOW, CONDUCTOR AND PIANIST**

BIRTHS & DEATHS

1894 German conductor Hans von Bülow dies in Cairo.
1915 French composer, pianist and conductor Emile Waldteufel dies in Paris.

FIRST PERFORMED

1797 Joseph Haydn's *Emperor String Quartet in C, Op. 76 No. 3*, is given its first performance. Nicknamed the '*Emperor*', it celebrates the birthday of the Austrian Emperor Franz Joseph II.
1924 George Gershwin's *Rhapsody in Blue* is premiered in New York.

TODAY'S THE DAY

1778 Leopold Mozart writes a letter to his son, ordering the young composer to move to Paris. Mozart would rather have gone to Italy. It heralded an unhappy period for the young Wolfgang. His mother, who was travelling with him, died during their time in the French capital.
1812 Pianist Carl Czerny gives the Vienna premiere of Beethoven's *Piano Concerto No. 5* (the '*Emperor*'). It actually received its first performance three months earlier in Leipzig.

COMPOSER PROFILE:

Leopold Mozart

Undoubtedly, Leopold Mozart's greatest musical creation was his son Wolfgang. A composer and violinist, Leopold was a member of the orchestra belonging to the Prince-Archbishop of Salzburg. In 1762, he was promoted to the post of court composer. As a child, his daughter Marie Anna (known to the family as Nannerl) often performed alongside her brother Wolfgang. They were quite an act, and Leopold spent a good deal of time and effort promoting the young duo both as a money-making enterprise and also as a means of gaining access to the palaces of the nobility right across Europe.

Don't judge a book by its cover

The Austrian pianist, composer and teacher, Carl Czerny, is seen today as having been something of an expert on the art of the piano, writing many books on the subject. However worthwhile the text on the inside of the book, he didn't seem to have the knack for coming up with that pithy best-selling title to go on the front cover. His book *Letters to a Young Lady on the Art of Playing the Pianoforte from the Earliest Rudiments to the Highest State of Cultivation* is a particular favourite.

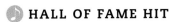

HALL OF FAME HIT

Bedřich Smetana: *Má Vlast*

Recommended Recording
Prague Symphony Orchestra conducted by Tomáš Netopil; FOK 00001-2

13

'The music teacher came twice a week to bridge the awful gap between Dorothy and Chopin.'

GEORGE ADE, HUMORIST

FEBRUARY

 BIRTHS & DEATHS

1883 German composer Richard Wagner dies in Venice.
1870 American (originally Polish) pianist and composer Leopold Godowsky is born in Vilnius.
1946 English composer Colin Matthews is born in London.
1969 American mezzo-soprano Joyce DiDonato is born in Kansas City.

FIRST PERFORMED

1961 Leonard Bernstein's *Symphonic Dances from 'West Side Story'* is premiered by the New York Philharmonic in Carnegie Hall at a concert entitled 'Valentine for Leonard Bernstein'.

 TODAY'S THE DAY

1585 Composer Giovanni Gabrieli becomes the organist at the Scuola Grande di San Rocco, one of the most prestigious roles in Italian church music at the time. He was to hold the job for more than a quarter of a century.
1727 George Frideric Handel writes to the House of Lords asking for permission to become a naturalised English citizen.
1751 George Frideric Handel realises that his eyesight is beginning to fail, as he works on his oratorio *Jephtha*.
1816 The Teatro San Carlo in Naples is wrecked by fire.
1839 Frédéric Chopin leaves Palma by cargo boat.
1888 Gustav Mahler is appointed music director of the Budapest Opera.
1901 Eduard Strauss disbands the Strauss Orchestra at the end of a gruelling tour of the USA, which saw 229 performances in 132 different towns and cities in a single three-month period.
1985 The Dresden Opera House re-opens exactly 40 years after being destroyed in an Allied bombing raid.

Unusual travelling companions

Frédéric Chopin's departure from Palma, with his lover George Sand, her children and his piano, was accompanied by around a hundred pigs. Chopin had been staying on Majorca, but had become progressively more seriously ill with tuberculosis and by the time he was on the boat he was coughing 'basins of blood'. His time on Majorca had not been altogether unproductive though, as he composed his *Prelude No. 15* which has the nickname '*Raindrop*'. He is said to have been inspired by the wet weather on the island.

 HALL OF FAME HIT
George Gershwin: *Rhapsody in Blue*

Recommended Recording
Jean-Yves Thibaudet (piano); Baltimore Symphony Orchestra conducted by Marin Alsop; Decca 478 2189

'Sad. Sad. Sad! Wagner is dead! When I read the news yesterday I may say that I was crushed! It is a great individual who has disappeared! A name that leaves a powerful imprint on the history of art!'

COMPOSER GIUSEPPE VERDI, IN A LETTER DATED 14 FEBRUARY 1883, TO HIS PUBLISHER

14
FEBRUARY

🕐 BIRTHS & DEATHS

1959 American soprano Renée Fleming is born in Indiana.

1987 Russian composer Dmitri Kabalevsky dies in Moscow.

☀ TODAY'S THE DAY

1697 George Frideric Handel's father dies. This is possibly more significant for classical-music history than might first appear to be the case, as Handel's father had been vehemently opposed to his son making a living as a musician. With Handel's twelfth birthday approaching, he is now free to follow the career pathway he desires.

1738 Handel finishes composing his opera *Xerxes*.

1792 The inventor of the nocturne, Irish composer John Field, makes his first public performance at the piano. He's just nine years old and his audience at the concert in Dublin is made up of other children.

1818 Two of the big composing names of the time, Ludwig van Beethoven and Antonio Salieri write articles recommending that other composers use the newly invented metronome, to help them keep tempo.

1847 Hector Berlioz, not exactly renowned for his reliability, heads off from Paris to St Petersburg without letting his lover, Marie Recio, know anything about it. She must have forgiven him though, eventually becoming his wife.

1948 The Russian government officially bans the performance of much of the music of Sergei Prokofiev and Dmitri Shostakovich.

COMPOSER PROFILE:

Hector Berlioz

Berlioz was the son of a doctor who only grudgingly allowed him to become a musician. Initially, Berlioz followed in his father's footsteps and began medical training. But the lure of music was too strong to resist and he switched careers, studying at the Paris Conservatoire. A musical maverick, he pushed down every barrier he came across. His works were often massive, requiring a great number of players. He also used huge forces when putting on concerts of other people's works. On one legendary occasion, he conducted a performance of Beethoven's *Symphony No. 5* with no fewer than 36 double-basses in the orchestra.

🎵 HALL OF FAME HIT

Pyotr Ilyich Tchaikovsky: *Symphony No. 6 ('Pathétique')*

Recommended Recording

Kirov Orchestra conducted by Valery Gergiev; Philips E4565 802

15

FEBRUARY

'Making music is like making love: the act is always the same, but each time is different.'

ARTHUR RUBINSTEIN, PIANIST

 BIRTHS & DEATHS

1797 The piano-maker Heinrich Steinweg (later Steinway) is born in Langelsheim, Germany.
1857 Russian composer Mikhail Glinka dies in Berlin.
1899 French composer Georges Auric, later to be member of 'Les Six', is born in Lodève.
1947 American composer John Adams is born in Massachusetts.
1958 Swedish trombonist Christian Lindberg is born in Danderyd.

 FIRST PERFORMED

1867 Johann Strauss Junior's *By the Beautiful Blue Danube* is first performed, in Vienna.
1947 Erich Korngold's *Violin Concerto* is given its first performance, by the St Louis Symphony with Jascha Heifetz as the soloist.

TODAY'S THE DAY

1779 The funeral of the Master of the King's Musick, William Boyce, is held at St Paul's Cathedral. He had quite a musical send-off, with the choirs of Westminster Abbey and the Chapel Royal joining the St Paul's home team.
1998 Elgar's *Symphony No. 3* is premiered at the Royal Festival Hall in London. The symphony is based on sketches written by Elgar, developed by composer Anthony Payne into a full-length work.

INSTRUMENT FOCUS:

Trombone

Descended from an early English instrument called the 'shagbolt' (or sackbut), the trombone is a length of brass tubing whose notes are changed by lengthening the tube with a slide. Mozart used trombones to great effect in his opera *Don Giovanni*, but their first ever use in a symphony occurred when Beethoven chose to include them in his *Symphony No. 5*. They possess a stout and, let's not deny it, loud sound, useful for its ability to penetrate, but equally at home in a proud, perhaps tragic mode, such as in the *Tuba mirum* from Mozart's *Requiem*.

Anagrams

An anagram of 'Gustav Mahler' is 'M. Ravel's a thug' and if you jumble up the letters of 'Robert Schumann', you arrive at 'Brahms *Nocturne*'.
Mix up the component parts of 'Claude Achille Debussy' and you get 'Delius had a blues cycle'.
In a different order, the letters of 'Gabriel Fauré', who is known for his *Requiem*, form 'Grief, be aural'.

 HALL OF FAME HIT
Sergei Prokofiev: *Romeo and Juliet*

Recommended Recording
Royal Philharmonic Orchestra conducted by Vladimir Ashkenazy; Decca 436 0782

'In my opinion, Berlioz is one of the most remarkable composers of our time.'

FELLOW COMPOSER MIKHAIL GLINKA, AFTER HEARING BERLIOZ CONDUCT A CONCERT IN PARIS, TODAY IN 1845

BIRTHS & DEATHS

1709 English composer Charles Avison is baptised in Newcastle-upon-Tyne.

1829 French composer François-Joseph Gossec dies in Paris.

FIRST PERFORMED

1892 Jules Massenet's opera *Werther* is premiered in Vienna.

1928 The original version of Modest Mussorgky's opera *Boris Godunov* is premiered in Leningrad. It had been composed more than half a century earlier, but had to be extensively revised after being vetoed by the state censor.

TODAY'S THE DAY

1764 Eight-year-old Wolfgang Amadeus Mozart very nearly chokes to death in Paris, but he recovers from his 'violent sore throat and catarrh' a few days later.

1848 Frédéric Chopin makes his final concert performance in Paris, at La Salle Pleyel.

1848 Hector Berlioz conducts a concert at London's Drury Lane Theatre in front of Queen Victoria and Prince Albert.

1882 The Prince of Wales writes to the composer Charles Villiers Stanford to ask him to meet at St James's Palace later in the month to discuss the founding of a new Royal College of Music in London.

1883 The Czech composer Leoš Janáček is accused of 'nationalist fanaticism giving an impression of madness' by his boss. It turns out that Janáček is in the middle of a messy divorce from the boss's daughter and the accusations against him are dropped.

MUSICAL TERM:

Suite

A suite is a collection of instrumental pieces intended to be played together at one sitting. The original French meaning of suite is 'things that follow', so therefore it came to mean music that was played in succession. Over the years it has varied in make-up. A Baroque suite has several dances, almost all featuring an allemande, sarabande, gigue and courante. It often also included any number of variations of the following: gavotte, minuet, passepied and rigaudon. Each dance has its own rules. Later, with the symphony replacing the suite in popularity, it became common to use the suite as a means of gathering together a composer's best moments from an opera or play, sometimes to prevent them slipping into obscurity if the stage work they came from flopped. Sometimes, this job was done by other composers: as in the case of Bizet's two *Carmen* suites.

HALL OF FAME HIT

Dmitri Shostakovich: *The Gadfly* (*Romance*)

Recommended Recording

Nicola Benedetti; Bournemouth Symphony Orchestra conducted by Kirill Karabits; Decca 478 3529

17

FEBRUARY

'Beethoven and Liszt have contributed to the advent of long hair.'

LOUIS MOREAU GOTTSCHALK, PIANIST, COMPOSER AND CONDUCTOR

 BIRTHS & DEATHS

1653 Italian composer Arcangelo Corelli is born in Fusignano.

1925 English composer Ron Goodwin is born in Plymouth.

1944 Welsh composer Karl Jenkins is born in Swansea.

 FIRST PERFORMED

1792 Joseph Haydn's *Symphony No. 93* – the first of his 'London' symphonies – receives its first performance at the Hanover Square Rooms in London.

1855 Franz Liszt's *Piano Concerto No. 1* – which has taken the composer 26 years to complete – is premiered in Weimar, with Liszt at the piano and Hector Berlioz conducting.

1872 The second version of Tchaikovsky's *Romeo and Juliet* is performed for the first time, in St Petersburg.

1904 Giacomo Puccini's *Madam Butterfly* is premiered in Milan.

 TODAY'S THE DAY

1911 Edward Elgar agrees to take over from Hans Richter as the principal conductor of the London Symphony Orchestra.

1943 Sergei Rachmaninov performs in his final concert in Knoxville, Tennessee, before being struck down by illness, from which he never recovers.

COMPOSER PROFILE:

Karl Jenkins

Wales' most successful living classical composer hails from Swansea. He studied at the University of Wales and at the Royal Academy of Music in London. Initially, he played the oboe in a ground-breaking jazz group called Nucleus, winning the 1970 Montreux Jazz Festival Prize. Next he joined the 'prog rock' band Soft Machine, which was a mainstay of the 'Canterbury Sound' of the 1970s. Eventually, composing took over and he enjoyed a highly successful career writing music for television commercials. Jenkins expanded many of these tunes into full-blown classical works and is today a popular and much sought-after composer. In 2000, he premiered *The Armed Man: A Mass for Peace*; his *Requiem* was first performed in 2005 and his *Stabat Mater* in 2008. His ear for a tune is second to none and he has proven time and time again that he has the ability to write modern classical music that strikes a chord with 21st-century listeners.

 HALL OF FAME HIT

Johann Sebastian Bach: *Toccata and Fugue in D minor*

Recommended Recording

Simon Preston (organ); Deutsche Grammophon 427 6682

‘Why should the devil have all the good tunes?’

ROWLAND HILL, ENGLISH EVANGELIST

18 FEBRUARY

BIRTHS & DEATHS

1850 British (originally German) baritone, pianist, conductor and composer George Henschel is born in Breslau.
1997 Eric Fenby, Frederick Delius’s amanuensis, dies in Scarborough, North Yorkshire.

FIRST PERFORMED

1743 George Frideric Handel’s oratorio *Samson* is premiered at Covent Garden in London.

TODAY’S THE DAY

1807 Ludwig van Beethoven’s *Piano Sonata No. 23* (‘*Appassionata*’) is published.
1825 The Mendelssohn family buys a grand new home at 3 Leipziger Strasse in Berlin. It quickly becomes a fashionable destination, at which the city’s artistic and intellectual elite gathers.
1883 Composer Richard Wagner is buried at his home near Bayreuth.
1904 Béla Bartók makes his UK concert debut, with a performance in Manchester.

GENRE FOCUS:

Oratorio

The word oratorio comes from the Latin *oratio* (prayer). Today, oratorio indicates a work for chorus, soloists and orchestra, usually, though not always, with a religious text and intended to be performed in church or in a concert hall. What is generally reckoned to be the first true oratorio, Emilio de’ Cavalieri’s ‘sacred opera’ *Rappresentatione di anima et di corpo*, dates from 1600, though the story is 50 years or so older. St Filippo Neri, an Italian priest, had the idea of what can best be described as moral musical entertainments. He won the backing of the Jesuits for his notion.

After de’ Cavalieri, Giacomo Carissimi, another Italian, developed the form; one of his pupils, Marc-Antoine Charpentier, took it to France. In Germany, Heinrich Schütz was the oratorio’s foremost pioneer. George Frideric Handel was chiefly known as a composer of Italian-style operas when he wrote his first oratorio in 1707. From that point on, he became a master of the genre. His most famous work, *Messiah* – written for a 1742 Dublin premiere – is just the tip of the iceberg. Handel wrote 29 oratorios on religious and secular subjects, ranging from *Saul* and *Solomon* to *Susanna* and *Samson*. Felix Mendelssohn’s two oratorios, *St Paul* and *Elijah*, are still in the repertoire today; he was also at the forefront of an oratorio revival in the 19th century. Meanwhile, Elgar was also a leading oratorio composer, penning *The Dream of Gerontius*, *The Apostles*, *The Kingdom* and *The Light of Life*.

HALL OF FAME HIT

Wolfgang Amadeus Mozart: *The Marriage of Figaro*

Recommended Recording

Various soloists; Scottish Chamber Orchestra and Chorus conducted by Charles Mackerras; Telarc 3CD 80725

19

FEBRUARY

'We're not worried about writing for posterity. We just want it to sound good right now.'

DUKE ELLINGTON, COMPOSER

BIRTHS & DEATHS

1743 Italian composer Luigi Boccherini is born in Lucca.
1941 Irish composer Hamilton Harty dies in Brighton.
1971 American violinist Gil Shaham is born in Illinois.
1977 Italian tenor Vittorio Grigolo is born in Arezzo.

FIRST PERFORMED

1881 The first complete public performance of Franz Schubert's *Symphony No. 3* is given at London's Crystal Palace, some 66 years after the composer had finished writing it.

1923 Jean Sibelius's *Symphony No. 5* is premiered in Helsinki, with the composer conducting.
1947 Heitor Villa-Lobos's *Bachianas Brasileiras No. 3* receives its first performance, in New York, with the composer conducting.

TODAY'S THE DAY

1790 The violinist George Bridgetower, highly regarded for both his solo and chamber performances during the 19th century, makes his London debut at the Theatre Royal, Drury Lane. He is just 12 years old.

1850 Hector Berlioz conducts the first concert of the Société Philharmonique in Paris. Berlioz was keen on the formation of the society as a means of promoting his own work.
1903 Giacomo Puccini is badly hurt in a car crash.
1927 Sergei Prokofiev and Dmitri Shostakovich, two Russian composing greats, meet for the first time in the interval of a concert in Leningrad.
1934 Composer George Gershwin becomes a radio presenter, with a programme on the New York radio station WJZ. It's called *Music by Gershwin*.

COMPOSER PROFILE:

Luigi Boccherini

Boccherini made a big splash in Vienna as a cellist when he was 15, going on to make a name for himself as a composer. In his early twenties, he toured around Italy and visited France and England, before settling in Madrid. The later years of his life were tough, as he struggled to make ends meet. He outlived two wives and three daughters, all of whom died tragically young. This did not help his mental state, and his money worries were increased by his French publisher, who constantly forced down Boccherini's fees. He was penniless when he died at the age of 62 in a small house in Madrid. The middle finger of his left hand was said to be inflamed beyond belief – due to a lifetime's cello playing. He left two priceless Stradivari cellos in his will.

HALL OF FAME HIT
Giuseppe Verdi: *Nabucco*

Recommended Recording
Various soloists; Philharmonia Orchestra conducted by Riccardo Muti; EMI Classics 456 4472

> 'I have wept only three times in my life: the first time when my earliest opera failed, the second time when, with a boating party, a truffled turkey fell into the water, and the third time when I first heard Paganini play.'

GIOACHINO ROSSINI, COMPOSER

20
FEBRUARY

🎵 BIRTHS & DEATHS

1626 English composer John Dowland is buried in London.

1790 Holy Roman Emperor Joseph II dies. One of the most important patrons in classical music, he was a particularly influential supporter of Mozart.

1888 Marie Rambert, founder of the Rambert Dance Company, is born in Warsaw.

1940 German conductor Christoph Eschenbach is born in Breslau.

1948 English conductor Barry Wordsworth is born in Surrey.

1953 Italian conductor Riccardo Chailly is born in Milan.

1961 Australian composer and pianist Percy Grainger dies in New York.

🎵 FIRST PERFORMED

1816 Gioachino Rossini's opera *The Barber of Seville* is premiered in Rome.

1823 Franz Schubert's song '*Gretchen at the Spinning Wheel*' is given its first performance, in Vienna.

1827 Felix Mendelssohn's *Overture to A Midsummer Night's Dream* is premiered in Stettin.

1897 The first and third of Erik Satie's three *Gymnopédies*, in orchestrations by Claude Debussy, are given their first performance in Paris.

1937 Sergei Prokofiev's *Lieutenant Kijé* is premiered in Paris with the composer conducting.

☀️ TODAY'S THE DAY

1727 George Frideric Handel becomes a naturalised British citizen, following an Act of Parliament. (This was the only way for citizenship status to be changed in those days.)

1788 The renowned clarinettist Anton Stadler performs in public on the 'Bass-Klarinet' (now known as a basset clarinet) for the first time. He'd invented the instrument himself, adding two extra keys to the design of a conventional clarinet, enabling it to play lower notes.

1867 The New England Conservatory of Music opens at the Music Hall in Boston.

1875 The librettist W. S. Gilbert shares the libretto to the operetta *Trial by Jury* with the composer Arthur Sullivan. The latter thought it was very funny, saying, 'I was screaming with laughter the whole time.'

🎵 HALL OF FAME HIT
Frédéric Chopin: *Piano Concerto No. 1*

Recommended Recording
Ingrid Fliter (piano); Scottish Chamber Orchestra conducted by Jun Märkl; Linn CKD 455

21

FEBRUARY

'Modern music is as dangerous as cocaine.'

PIETRO MASCAGNI, COMPOSER

 BIRTHS & DEATHS

1791 Austrian pianist and composer Carl Czerny is born in Vienna.

1836 French composer Léo Delibes is born in St Germain du Val.

1844 French composer Charles-Marie Widor is born in Lyons.

1881 English composer Kenneth J. Alford is born in London.

1893 Spanish guitarist Andrés Segovia is born in Linares.

1991 English ballet dancer Margot Fonteyn dies in Panama City.

 FIRST PERFORMED

1891 Pyotr Ilyich Tchaikovsky's incidental music to *Hamlet* is performed for the first time, in St Petersburg.

1907 Frederick Delius's *A Village Romeo and Juliet* is premiered in Berlin.

 TODAY'S THE DAY

1772 Sixteen-year-old Wolfgang Amadeus Mozart finishes work on his *Symphony No. 15* in Salzburg.

1816 Ludwig van Beethoven gains a court order stopping his sister-in-law from visiting her son Karl at boarding school. It was part of a bitter and long-running dispute between the two over how Beethoven's nephew was to be brought up following his father's death.

1818 Franz Schubert is said to have composed the song 'Die Forelle' ('The Trout') today. History suggests that a good deal of red wine aided him with the composition process.

1874 Charles Villiers Stanford is given the job of organist at Trinity College, Cambridge. But he's allowed time off to study in Leipzig.

1890 Pietro Mascagni receives a telegram informing him that his one-act opera *Cavalleria Rusticana* is a finalist in a composing competition in Milan.

1911 Despite being told not to by his doctor, Gustav Mahler insists on conducting the New York Philharmonic at Carnegie Hall. It is his last performance.

1944 New York City Opera opens with a performance of Puccini's *Tosca*.

Bogey at the 18th

It's said that Kenneth J. Alford got the idea for the tune 'Colonel Bogey' while on the golf course. When his golf partner teed off, he would always whistle two notes to warn anyone on the fairway. The notes stuck in his head, all the way round, and became the first two notes of the now world-famous tune.

 HALL OF FAME HIT

Edvard Grieg: *Peer Gynt Suite No. 1*

Recommended Recording

City of Birmingham Symphony Orchestra conducted by Sakari Oramo; Erato 8573 829172

> 'Music gives a soul to the universe, wings to the mind, flight to the imagination, and life to everything.'
>
> **PLATO, GREEK PHILOSOPHER**

22
FEBRUARY

🎵 BIRTHS & DEATHS

1972 Mexican tenor Rolando Villazón is born in Mexico City.
1983 English conductor Adrian Boult dies in London.

🎵 FIRST PERFORMED

1874 Pyotr Ilyich Tchaikovsky's *Symphony No. 4* is premiered in Moscow.
1881 Max Bruch's *Scottish Fantasy* is given its first performance, with the Liverpool Philharmonic Orchestra and soloist Joseph Joachim, in Liverpool.
1910 Frederick Delius's opera *A Village Romeo and Juliet* has its London premiere at Covent Garden, conducted by Thomas Beecham.

🌅 TODAY'S THE DAY

1810 Composer Carl Maria von Weber has money troubles, with debts three times the size of his assets. He agrees to a repayment plan and his creditors agree to him being released from custody.
1835 Eleven-year-old César Franck wins first prize in a piano competition at the Royal Conservatoire of Liège.
1871 Modest Mussorgsky's opera *Boris Godunov* is banned in St Petersburg because it doesn't contain a big enough role for a female singer. The composer sets about making major revisions.

COMPOSER PROFILE:

Carl Maria Von Weber

It is easy to see how, with a father who was both a musician and a theatrical impresario, Weber was always going to be obsessed by the world of opera. He was taught by Haydn's brother, Michael, in Salzburg and also studied for a time in Vienna. A productive period in Stuttgart was halted by seemingly false charges of financial fraud, although he did appear to get himself into debt. After this was resolved, he embarked on a period of short-term conducting jobs in Darmstadt, Munich, Prague and Dresden. It was in Dresden that Weber wrote the opera *Der Freischütz*, which made him an overnight sensation in Germany. It established a new breed of German opera, which was to prove influential for years to come. *Euryanthe* followed, but it was while rehearsing his *Oberon* for its premiere at Covent Garden that he died in London, from tuberculosis, aged just 39. His two concertos and a concertino for the clarinet are among his most popular works today.

🎵 HALL OF FAME HIT
Carl Orff: *Carmina Burana*

Recommended Recording
Various soloists; Berlin Philharmonic Orchestra and the Berlin Radio Choir, conducted by Simon Rattle; EMI 557 8882

23

FEBRUARY

> 'I loathe divas, they are the curse of true music and musicians.'
>
> **HECTOR BERLIOZ, COMPOSER**

 BIRTHS & DEATHS

1685 British (originally German) composer George Frideric Handel is born in Halle.

1931 Australian soprano Nellie Melba dies in Sydney.

1934 English composer and conductor Edward Elgar dies at home in Worcester.

1983 English composer Herbert Howells dies in London.

 TODAY'S THE DAY

1819 Johann Nepomuk Hummel signs up as Kapellmeister for Grand Duke Carl August of Saxe-Weimar-Eisenach.

1831 Richard Wagner enrols at Leipzig University to study music.

1873 Richard Strauss performs as a conductor for the first time, in Munich.

1891 Catalan cellist Pablo Casals makes his debut performance in Barcelona.

1897 Gustav Mahler is baptised into the Roman Catholic Church in Hamburg.

1914 A memorial statue of Jules Massenet is unveiled at the Monte Carlo Opera.

COMPOSER PROFILE:

George Frideric Handel

Handel was the son of a barber-surgeon, who was firmly against his boy following a career in music. Instead, Handel was encouraged to study law at Halle University and was able to follow his musical dream only once his father had died. By 1702, he was composing and playing the organ in Halle Cathedral. In 1703, he travelled to Hamburg, where he played violin in the opera house orchestra. He also started to compose operas. There was nowhere better to perfect this craft than Italy and so he packed his bags once again.

His opera *Agrippina* was immensely popular and he ended up working as court conductor to the Elector of Hanover (later England's King George I). Despite the steady income that this gave him, Handel hankered for something more and was granted an extended sabbatical to allow him to ply his operatic trade in London. There, he soon became a sensation: operas such as *Rinaldo*, *Il pastor fido* and *Amadigi* made him a star. He composed his enduringly popular *Water Music* for George I and wrote the anthem '*Zadok the Priest*' for the Coronation of George II. He also produced a series of oratorios, including *Messiah* and *Solomon*. When he died in 1759, Handel was a national figure and was buried in Westminster Abbey.

 HALL OF FAME HIT

Johann Sebastian Bach:
Brandenburg Concertos

Recommended Recording

European Brandenburg Ensemble conducted by Trevor Pinnock; Avie AV 2119

> 'It reeks of cow turds.'
>
> **COMPOSER EDVARD GRIEG ABOUT HIS OWN INCIDENTAL MUSIC TO PEER GYNT**

24

BIRTHS & DEATHS

1704 French composer Marc-Antoine Charpentier dies in Paris.

1766 English organist and composer Samuel Wesley is born in Bristol.

1842 Italian composer and librettist Arrigo Boito is born in Padua.

1967 American (originally German) composer Franz Waxman dies in Los Angeles.

1972 Russian pianist Arcadi Volodos is born in Leningrad.

FIRST PERFORMED

1607 Claudio Monteverdi's opera *La favola d'Orfeo* receives its first performance, at the ducal palace in Mantua.

1711 George Frideric Handel's opera *Rinaldo* is premiered at the Queen's Theatre, London.

1876 Edvard Grieg's incidental music to Ibsen's play *Peer Gynt* is given its first performance, in Oslo.

TODAY'S THE DAY

1666 English composer Nicholas Lanier is buried in Greenwich.

1788 Wolfgang Amadeus Mozart finishes working on his *Piano Concerto No. 26* in Vienna.

1809 London's Theatre Royal, Drury Lane burns down. It was the third theatre on the site. The first also burned to the ground, while the second was demolished.

1818 Seven-year-old Frédéric Chopin makes his first public performance at the piano in Warsaw.

1825 Hector Berlioz's father cuts off his allowance after hearing news of a disastrous concert some two months before, which had to be called off because the orchestra's parts were filled with musical errors.

1835 Berlioz takes up his pen as regular music critic for the *Journal des Débats*.

1848 While the French Revolution flares up outside, five-year-old Jules Massenet's mother gives him his first music lesson.

1901 After conducting two separate concerts, Gustav Mahler suffers severe bleeding due to haemorrhoids. The bleeding becomes so serious that a leading surgeon has to be called to stem the flow.

Eine kleine cool music

When Mozart came to London on tour, he stayed at 20 Frith Street, lodging with one Thomas Williamson. There's a plaque on the wall of the house and, today, fans of a different kind of music stand and stare at it – it's directly opposite Ronnie Scott's Jazz Club.

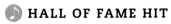

HALL OF FAME HIT
George Frideric Handel: *Solomon*

Recommended Recording
Various soloists; Monteverdi Choir and English Baroque Soloists, conducted by John Eliot Gardiner; Philips 475 7561

25

FEBRUARY

'I am not interested in having an orchestra sound like itself. I want it to sound like the composer.'

LEONARD BERNSTEIN, CONDUCTOR AND COMPOSER

BIRTHS & DEATHS

1845 Belgian conductor Eugène Goossens is born in Bruges.

1873 Italian tenor Enrico Caruso is born in Naples.

1890 English pianist Myra Hess is born in London.

1940 Spanish conductor Jesús López-Cobos is born in Toro.

1948 Welsh tenor Dennis O'Neill is born in Pontarddulais.

FIRST PERFORMED

1877 Pyotr Ilyich Tchaikovsky's symphonic fantasy *Francesca da Rimini* is premiered in Moscow.

1905 Serge Koussevitzky's *Doublebass Concerto* receives its first performance, in Moscow, with the composer as the soloist.

1922 Camille Saint-Saëns' *Carnival of the Animals* is given its first performance, in Paris. The composer had been so worried that the work would leave him open to ridicule that he banned it from being performed in public while he was still alive. His will made it clear that the restriction was removed once he was dead.

1953 Leonard Bernstein's musical *Wonderful Town* is given its premiere, in New York.

1973 Stephen Sondheim's musical *A Little Night Music* opens, in New York.

TODAY'S THE DAY

1723 George Frideric Handel is appointed Composer of Music for His Majesty's Chapel Royal.

1776 The Regio Ducal Teatro in Milan is destroyed by fire.

1828 Muzio Clementi gives his last public performance, on the piano, at a concert put on by London's Philharmonic Society.

1871 A new concert society for the promotion of music by living French composers is founded in Paris. Georges Bizet, Gabriel Fauré, César Franck, Jules Massenet and Camille Saint-Saëns are among the Société Nationale de Musique's prime movers.

1906 Sergei Rachmaninov steps down as conductor of Moscow's Bolshoi Theatre.

COMPOSER PROFILE:

Leonard Bernstein

Born in the USA in 1918 to Russian émigré parents, Bernstein demonstrated his prodigious musical talents from a very early age. His compositions ranged from the serious and reflective, such as his *Kaddish Symphony* and *Chichester Psalms*, through to his wildly successful musicals, *On the Town* and *West Side Story*. He was a virtuoso pianist and had a larger-than-life presence on stage as a conductor, most notably of the New York Philharmonic. Bernstein was also one of the first major classical-music stars of the television age, presenting a long-running series of televised concerts for children.

HALL OF FAME HIT

Giuseppe Verdi: *Requiem*

Recommended Recording

Various soloists; NBC Symphony Orchestra and the Robert Shaw Chorale, conducted by Arturo Toscanini; Regis RRC 1372

> 'You have one of the most upright, moral, and, in music, most eminent of men for a son. I love him just as you do.'
>
> **JOSEPH HAYDN WRITES A LETTER TODAY IN 1792 TO COMPOSER JAN DUSSEK, ABOUT THE LATTER'S SON JAN LADISLAV DUSSEK, WHO WAS ALSO A COMPOSER**

26

FEBRUARY

🏛 BIRTHS & DEATHS

1770 Italian composer Giuseppe Tartini dies in Padua.
1879 English composer Frank Bridge is born in Brighton.
1949 English soprano Emma Kirkby is born in Camberley.

🎻 FIRST PERFORMED

1752 George Frideric Handel's oratorio *Jephtha* is premiered, at London's Covent Garden.
1877 Alexander Borodin's *Symphony No. 2* receives its first performance, in St Petersburg.

☀ TODAY'S THE DAY

1810 Composer Carl Maria von Weber and his father are banished from Württemberg because of the scale of their debts.
1832 Frédéric Chopin makes his concert debut in Paris, in the Salle Pleyel. He plays his *Piano Concerto No. 2* (actually written before his *Piano Concerto No. 1*). Franz Liszt and Felix Mendelssohn are in the audience.
1855 Bedřich Smetana makes his first appearance as a conductor at a concert in Prague. He had previously performed only as a pianist, but this evening also shows off his credentials as a composer.
1885 Arthur Sullivan conducts a Philharmonic Society concert in London for the first time.
1934 Edward Elgar is buried next to his wife at St Wulstan's Church in Little Malvern.

COMPOSER PROFILE:

Giuseppe Tartini

Born in what was then part of northern Italy but is now Slovenia, Tartini intended to become a monk, but he had to rethink this after eloping with the bishop's daughter while studying theology at Padua University. Having married, the couple evaded the bishop's arrest warrant for three years, before Tartini was forced to leave town and his wife was sent to a convent. The composer took the opportunity to hole himself away in a monastery and perfect his amazing violin technique, returning to Padua, now pardoned, and staying there as head of the Cappello del Santo for the rest of his life. His compositions naturally reflect his virtuosity as a violinist.

🔊 HALL OF FAME HIT
Pyotr Ilyich Tchaikovsky: *Swan Lake*

Recommended Recording
Royal Liverpool Philharmonic Orchestra conducted by Vasily Petrenko; Avie AV 2139

27

FEBRUARY

'Nothing is more odious than music without hidden meaning.'

FRÉDÉRIC CHOPIN, COMPOSER

BIRTHS & DEATHS

1848 English composer Hubert Parry is born in Bournemouth.

1887 Alexander Borodin dies in St Petersburg.

1947 Russian violinist Gidon Kremer is born in Riga.

2003 English conductor John Lanchbery dies in Melbourne.

2013 American pianist Van Cliburn dies in Fort Worth, Texas.

FIRST PERFORMED

1919 Gustav Holst's *The Planets* receives its first performance, at the Queen's Hall in London (although without *Venus* and *Neptune*). The composer is stuck on a Greek island nursing a broken foot, so he cannot attend.

1930 The first performance in England of Mahler's *Symphony No. 9,* by the Hallé Orchestra under the baton of Hamilton Harty.

TODAY'S THE DAY

1814 Ludwig van Beethoven's *Symphony No. 8* is performed in Vienna. Fellow composer Louis Spohr plays in the violin section.

1824 Gioachino Rossini signs a contract with the French government agreeing to create new operas to be staged in Paris over the next twelve months. He inks the deal at the home of the French ambassador in London.

1827 A seriously ill Beethoven has a fourth operation to drain fluids from his abdomen.

1832 The inventor of the nocturne, John Field, performs for the first time in England after a gap of thirty years.

1838 Felix Mendelssohn's sister Fanny performs a public piano solo for the only time, in Berlin. She plays her brother's *Piano Concerto No. 1.*

1854 Robert Schumann, by now suffering serious mental illness, throws himself from a bridge into the River Rhine. He is rescued, against his will, by fishermen.

1901 The bodies of Giuseppe Verdi and his wife Giuseppina, who had predeceased him by four years, are transferred to the Casa di Riposo in Milan, a home for retired musicians established by Verdi himself. More than 300,000 people attend the funeral, including fellow composers Leoncavallo, Pietro Mascagni and Giacomo Puccini. Leading conductor Arturo Toscanini directs a massive choir in singing 'Va pensiero' from Verdi's opera *Nabucco.*

1909 Claude Debussy and Jean Sibelius meet for the first time after a concert at the Queen's Hall in London.

1972 American President Richard Nixon ends his six-day visit to China, which is to become the subject of the opera *Nixon in China* by John Adams some 15 years later.

HALL OF FAME HIT

Charles-Marie Widor: *Organ Symphony No. 5*

Recommended Recording

William McVicker (organ); Sony Essential Masterworks 8869 7707362

'I know two kinds of audience only – one coughing and one not coughing.'

ARTUR SCHNABEL, PIANIST

TODAY'S THE DAY

1581 Giovannni Pierluigi da Palestrina marries his second wife, eight months after the death of his first. His new wife comes from a moneyed family; this enables him to live in a style to which he has not previously been accustomed.

1763 Leopold Mozart is promoted to deputy Kapellmeister by the Archbishop of Salzburg.

1840 Robert Schumann is awarded a doctorate by the University of Jena.

1882 The Prince of Wales convenes a meeting of artistic and political leaders at St James's Palace to discuss founding a new Royal College of Music in London.

1896 The Pittsburgh Symphony Orchestra gives its first concert.

ERA FOCUS:

The Baroque period

Originally an architectural term, Baroque translates literally from the French as 'bizarre', although the Portuguese word *barocco*, meaning 'a rare, funny-shaped pearl', is its true ancestor. In music, it covers the period spanning, roughly, the 150 years between 1600 and 1750. Baroque music must have seemed somewhat bizarre to the musical old guard. Its intricacies, particularly those of its harmonies, became more and more complex over the years. In early music (the period preceding Baroque), harmony developed fairly slowly; its tunes possessed an inner simplicity all of their own. In the Baroque period, the notion of harmonic change just took off, while melodies became positively hyperactive (just listen to a fast movement of any of Bach's *Brandenburg Concertos* to prove this point).

Another development was music's ability to picture something of real life, whether in terms of emotions and feelings or even musical representations of landscapes and weather patterns. This change was increasingly possible because music was moving out of its traditional church setting and into the homes and palaces of the nobility. Instrumental music, so long fought by the Church, was developing fast, with the coming of the sonata, the suite and the concerto grosso. The major composers of the Baroque period in terms of musical heritage are J. S. Bach, Handel and Vivaldi. However, many more, such as Corelli, Rameau, Domenico Scarlatti and Purcell, were equally important at the time.

HALL OF FAME HIT

George Frideric Handel: *Coronation Anthems*

Recommended Recording

Choir of King's College, Cambridge; English Chamber Orchestra conducted by David Willcocks; EMI 264 3382

29

FEBRUARY

> 'It is only that which cannot be expressed otherwise that is worth expressing in music.'
>
> **FREDERICK DELIUS, COMPOSER**

 BIRTHS & DEATHS

1792 Italian composer Gioachino Rossini is born in Pesaro.

 TODAY'S THE DAY

1764 Johann Christian Bach and Karl Friedrich Abel perform for the first time together in London. Their joint concerts are to become a major part of the city's cultural activities.

COMPOSER PROFILE:

Gioachino Rossini

Believe it or not, his parents originally intended Rossini to become a blacksmith, despite his having a singer for a mother and a wayward horn player as a father. At the age of 14, however, he was enrolled in the Music Academy in Bologna. Four years later, he wrote his first full-scale opera, one of the staggering total of 39 he composed during his career. Though he wrote sacred and chamber music as well, it is as a masterful operatic composer that he is best known.

Once Rossini had started, he could not stop. Year after year, the operas poured from his pen. Initially, *Tancredi*, a tragedy based on a play by Voltaire, and the sparkling comedy *The Italian Girl in Algiers* were his greatest successes. By the time he was 23, he had signed a contract to produce two operas a year, one for each of the two opera houses in Naples. It was for Rome, however, that he created *The Barber of Seville*, perhaps his greatest comic opera of all.

Rossini married the soprano Isabella Colbran when he was 30, after which he began to travel more. He met Beethoven in Vienna and visited Britain. He settled, though, in Paris, where he composed *William Tell*, his grandest and longest operatic work. By now, he had made so much money out of opera that he wrote nothing more for the stage. After returning home to Italy for a while, he eventually went back to the French capital, where he devoted the rest of his life to fine living and dining.

 **HALL OF FAME HIT**

Richard Strauss: *Four Last Songs*

Recommended Recording

Jessye Norman (soprano); Leipzig Gewandhaus Orchestra conducted by Kurt Masur; Philips Originals 475 8507

March

01

> 'I may not be a first-rate composer, but I am a first-class second-rate composer.'
>
> **RICHARD STRAUSS, COMPOSER**

MARCH

🕐 BIRTHS & DEATHS

1810 Polish composer Frédéric Chopin is born near Warsaw.

1954 American soprano Lorraine Hunt Lieberson is born in San Francisco.

1958 English mezzo-soprano Yvonne Howard is born in Stafford.

1971 English composer Thomas Adès is born in London.

☀️ TODAY'S THE DAY

1751 Austrian composer Karl Ditters von Dittersdorf begins playing in the orchestra of Prince Joseph Friedrich von Sachsen-Hildburghausen in Vienna. He also has to do menial tasks to earn his keep.

1809 When three local noblemen discover that Beethoven plans to move from Vienna they guarantee him a pension for life, so long as he remains in the city.

1830 The Philharmonic Society moves to the King's Theatre in London after its original home is destroyed by fire. It's to be the society's base for the next 38 years.

1875 Richard Wagner invents his own version of the tuba and the instrument is heard for the first time today in Vienna. The sound goes down a storm with the audience.

1916 George Gershwin signs up with a music publisher for the first time. He is 17 years old.

1919 Richard Strauss is given a new job as director of Austria's State Opera company, but the musicians and singers are upset, saying he is being paid too much.

1929 Frederick Delius is made a Companion of Honour.

INSTRUMENT FOCUS:

Tuba

This benevolent-sounding brass instrument comprises a cup-shaped mouthpiece, around 18 feet of coiled tuning and, usually, four valves (there can be anything from three to six). Despite being principally a bass instrument – it can reach nearly an octave lower than the standard bass singing voice – it also possesses an impressive upper register stretching into the high male-tenor range. This versatility has made it an extremely useful instrument for composers since its introduction in around 1835. Vaughan Williams wrote his *Tuba Concerto* in 1954 for the London Symphony Orchestra's then principal tuba, Philip Catelinet. It soon became one of the composer's surprise hits.

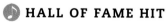

🎵 HALL OF FAME HIT

Giacomo Puccini: *Madam Butterfly*

Recommended Recording

Various soloists; Orchestra dell'Accademia Nazionale di Santa Cecilia conducted by Antonio Pappano; EMI 456 2152

> 'You can chase a Beethoven symphony all your life and not catch up.'
>
> ANDRÉ PREVIN, CONDUCTOR AND COMPOSER

BIRTHS & DEATHS

1824 Bohemian composer Bedřich Smetana is born in Litomyšl.

1900 German composer Kurt Weill is born in Dessau.

1910 English violinist and conductor Harry Blech, the founder of the London Mozart Players, is born in London.

1944 Finnish conductor Leif Segerstam is born in Vaasa.

2003 Australian composer and Master of the Queen's Music, Malcolm Williamson, dies in Cambridge.

FIRST PERFORMED

1792 Joseph Haydn's *Symphony No. 98* receives its first performance, at the Hanover Square Rooms in London, with the composer conducting.

1795 Joseph Haydn's *Symphony No. 103* (*'Drumroll'*) is premiered at the King's Theatre in London, again with the composer conducting.

TODAY'S THE DAY

1759 George Frideric Handel supervises his final Lent oratorio season in London.

1786 Wolfgang Amadeus Mozart finishes work on his *Piano Concerto No. 23* in Vienna.

1795 Ludwig van Beethoven performs for the first time in Vienna. He is a big success.

1798 Bad news for Luigi Boccherini, with the new King of Prussia turning him down for a job as a court composer, despite his having performed the role for the previous king for some 22 years.

1806 John Field performs for the first time in Moscow to great acclaim. He ends up living in Russia for the next few years.

1867 Pyotr Ilyich Tchaikovsky makes his conducting debut in St Petersburg.

1874 Nikolai Rimsky-Korsakov makes his conducting debut, also in St Petersburg.

1884 Frederick Delius sails from Liverpool to New York, before travelling on to work on an orange grove in Florida in which his father has a business interest.

1903 Gabriel Fauré takes up his pen as a music critic for the French newspaper *Le Figaro*.

Ladies first

Originally set up in 1945 by the record company executive Walter Legge as a recording orchestra for EMI, the Philharmonia was the first London orchestra to admit female members. The orchestra has had only five principal conductors in its near-70-year history, the latest of whom is Esa-Pekka Salonen. The Prince of Wales is the orchestra's Patron, but the royal connections don't stop there: an Indian prince, the Maharajah of Mysore, was the Philharmonia's first President.

HALL OF FAME HIT

Felix Mendelssohn: *Hebrides Overture* (*'Fingal's Cave'*)

Recommended Recording

City of Birmingham Symphony Orchestra conducted by Edward Gardner; Chandos CHSA 5132

03

'If anyone has conducted a Beethoven performance, and then doesn't have to go to an osteopath, then there's something wrong.'

SIMON RATTLE, CONDUCTOR

MARCH

🕐 BIRTHS & DEATHS

1869 English conductor Henry Wood is born in London.
1950 French pianist Katia Labèque is born in Hendaye.

🎵 FIRST PERFORMED

1783 Wolfgang Amadeus Mozart's *Symphony No. 35* (*'Haffner'*) is performed for the first time, in Vienna.
1794 Joseph Haydn's *Symphony No. 101* (*'Clock'*) is premiered at London's Hanover Square Rooms.
1842 Felix Mendelssohn's *Symphony No. 3* (*'Scottish'*) is given its first performance, in Leipzig, with the composer conducting.

1875 Georges Bizet's *Carmen* is premiered at the Opéra-Comique, Paris.
2004 In one of the more unusual premieres in this book, Peter Sculthorpe's *Requiem for chorus, didgeridoo and orchestra* has its first public performance, in Adelaide.

☀ TODAY'S THE DAY

1766 Joseph Haydn takes over as Kapellmeister for the Esterházy family. It provides him with a financial base from which to operate for the rest of his career.
1772 Karl Ditters von Dittersdorf gets married to Nicolina Trink, a Hungarian soprano.

1782 Wolfgang Amadeus Mozart performs his *Piano Concerto No. 5* in Vienna to great critical acclaim.
1802 Ludwig van Beethoven's *Piano Sonata No. 14* – better known today as the *'Moonlight'* Sonata – is published.
1854 Johannes Brahms travels to Düsseldorf to help Clara Schumann look after her ailing husband Robert.
1875 Georges Bizet is made a Chevalier of the Légion d'Honneur.
1931 *'The Star-Spangled Banner'* becomes the national anthem of the United States of America.

OPERA FOCUS:

Carmen

Georges Bizet's biggest hit in his own lifetime was his opera *The Pearl Fishers*, which features the incredibly popular duet *'Au fond du Temple Saint'*. But his greatest operatic achievement was *Carmen*, the story of a gypsy girl who, eventually, is murdered outside the bullring in Seville by the lover she has abandoned. It is packed full of wonderful tunes and has a violent, sexually charged story. After its

premiere proved unsuccessful, Bizet lost faith in his own work, branding it 'a definite and hopeless flop'. He retired to his bed and died from a heart attack just after its 33rd performance. Now regarded as one of the greatest operas of all time, it is still being performed in opera houses around the world, getting on for a century and a half later.

🎵 HALL OF FAME HIT

Wolfgang Amadeus Mozart:
The Magic Flute

Recommended Recording

Various soloists; Academy for Ancient Music, Berlin, and the RIAS Kammerchor conducted by René Jacobs; Harmonia Mundi HMC 902068/70

'If that was music, I no longer understand anything about the subject.'

HANS VON BÜLOW, CONDUCTOR AND PIANIST, ABOUT MAHLER'S SYMPHONY NO. 2

04

MARCH

BIRTHS & DEATHS

1678 Antonio Vivaldi is born in Venice.

1920 American harp maker Victor Salvi is born in Chicago.

1929 Dutch conductor Bernard Haitink is born in Amsterdam.

1946 American cellist Ralph Kirshbaum is born in Texas.

1947 Norwegian saxophonist Jan Garbarek is born in Mysen.

FIRST PERFORMED

1877 Tchaikovsky's *Swan Lake* is premiered at the Bolshoi Theatre in Moscow.

1916 Claude Debussy's *Cello Sonata* receives its first performance, in London.

TODAY'S THE DAY

1791 Wolfgang Amadeus Mozart makes his final public performance in Vienna with the premiere of his *Piano Concerto No. 27*.

1895 The first and third movements of Gustav Mahler's *Symphony No. 2* ('Resurrection') are performed by the Berlin Philharmonic with the composer conducting.

1901 Gustav Mahler has his third haemorrhoid operation, in Vienna.

INSTRUMENT FOCUS:

Harp

This is an instrument that has been in existence since ancient times and has developed in many different shapes and sizes over the years. The modern concert harp usually has 46 or 47 strings, which gives it a range of six-and-a-half octaves. That is not quite as much as a piano, but is still pretty wide-ranging: it means that a harp can play notes as deep as a double-bass and as high as a piccolo. Harps also have pedals, which the harpists press once to raise the string up one note and then press again to raise it up another note. The need for simultaneous hand and foot co-ordination makes it an incredibly hard instrument to play, while keeping a harp in tune is almost a full-time job in itself.

The Prince of Wales has recently re-established the position of court harpist. The first holder of the title was Catrin Finch, with Jemima Phillips, Claire Jones and Hannah Stone succeeding her. On the Prince's sixtieth birthday, a concert was given at London's Royal Opera House featuring no fewer than 60 harps. Tuning for the instruments began in the early hours of the morning, to ensure that they were all in top condition come the time of the performance.

HALL OF FAME HIT

Claude Debussy: *Suite Bergamasque*

Recommended Recording

Ji Liu (piano); Classic FM CFMD 33

05

MARCH

'. . . such science, dexterity, harmony and proper attention to rhythm that even the greatest connoisseurs were astounded.'

HAMBURG NEWSPAPER'S REVIEW OF A CONCERT GIVEN TODAY IN 1771 IN ROME BY WOLFGANG AMADEUS MOZART, WHEN HE WAS 15 YEARS OLD

🎵 BIRTHS & DEATHS

1778 English composer Thomas Arne dies in London.

1887 Brazilian composer Heitor Villa-Lobos is born in Rio de Janeiro.

1948 English conductor Richard Hickox is born in Buckinghamshire.

1953 Russian composer Sergei Prokofiev dies in Moscow.

1984 Italian baritone Tito Gobbi dies in Rome.

🎵 FIRST PERFORMED

1841 Franz von Suppé's first complete operatic score is given its debut performance in Vienna. It is the nattily titled *Jung lustig, im Alter traurig, oder Die Folgen der Erziehung*.

1942 Dmitri Shostakovich's *Symphony No. 7* ('*Leningrad*') receives its first performance, in Kuybyshev.

☀ TODAY'S THE DAY

1695 The state funeral of Queen Mary is held, with music composed by Henry Purcell.

1729 Wilhelm Friedmann Bach registers for studies at Leipzig University.

1856 The Covent Garden Opera House in London is destroyed by fire – for the second time.

1884 Antonín Dvořák travels to England for the first time.

COMPOSER PROFILE:

Heitor Villa-Lobos

Born in Rio de Janeiro, Heitor Villa-Lobos studied music with his father until he was 12 years old, at which point he became a guitarist in a Brazilian street band – something that he would later commemorate in his *Chôros*. From the age of 16 onwards, he made his money playing the cello in a theatre orchestra, but at the same time he began to study his country's folk music. He was funded by the government to study in Paris, returning as a music educator and composer when he was 43, and going on to found the Brazilian Academy of Music. For the last two decades of his life, he benefited from the championship of the conductor Leopold Stokowski, who was instrumental in bringing his music to a wider audience. Today his most enduring works outside his home country are his *Bachianas Brasileiras*, a fusion of Bach and Brazil.

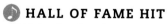

🎵 HALL OF FAME HIT

Frédéric Chopin: *Piano Concerto No. 2*

Recommended Recording

Lise de la Salle (piano); Staatskapelle Dresden conducted by Fabio Luisi; Naïve V5215

'I played over the music of that scoundrel Brahms. What a giftless bastard! It annoys me that this self-inflated mediocrity is hailed as genius.'

PYOTR ILYICH TCHAIKOVSKY, COMPOSER

🕐 BIRTHS & DEATHS

1842 Soprano Constanze Mozart (née Weber), wife of Wolfgang Amadeus, dies in Salzburg.

1930 American conductor Lorin Maazel is born in Neuilly, France.

1932 American composer John Philip Sousa dies in a hotel in Reading, Pennsylvania.

1944 New Zealand soprano Kiri Te Kanawa is born in Gisborne.

1951 Welsh composer, librettist and pianist Ivor Novello dies in London.

1952 French pianist Marielle Labèque is born in Bayonne.

1967 Hungarian composer Zoltán Kodály dies in Budapest.

🎵 FIRST PERFORMED

1853 Giuseppe Verdi's opera *La traviata* is premiered in Venice.

1885 Pyotr Ilyich Tchaikovsky's *Concert Fantasia* for piano and orchestra is given its first performance, in Moscow.

1934 Benjamin Britten's *A Simple Symphony* receives its first performance, in Norwich.

☀️ TODAY'S THE DAY

1844 Nikolai Rimsky-Korsakov finishes composing *The Flight of the Bumblebee*.

1934 Arnold Schoenberg and Albert Einstein meet after the former gives a lecture at Princeton University.

1937 Benjamin Britten meets the tenor Peter Pears at a lunch. They are to become lifelong partners.

1947 The New Zealand National Orchestra (now New Zealand Symphony Orchestra) performs its first concert.

COMPOSER PROFILE:

John Philip Sousa

Sousa was born in Washington DC to a family of Portuguese descent. From singing and violin-playing during his childhood, Sousa moved via theatre orchestras to directing first the Marine Band and then his own group of musicians. From the age of 38, he toured his band with amazing success across the USA, Europe and much of the rest of the world (wherever you are in the UK, you are never very far from a former Sousa concert date). Sousa composed more than 130 marches, becoming known as 'The March King' and creating his own marching bass brass instrument, the Sousaphone, in the process. He wrote his 'Stars and Stripes Forever' on Christmas Day 1896, and played it at pretty much every concert he gave for the next 36 years of his life. By the time he died in 1932, it had become the USA's national march.

HALL OF FAME HIT

Franz Schubert: *Piano Quintet ('Trout')*

Recommended Recording
Nash Ensemble; Virgin 4820042

07

'I am convinced that the soul and spirit of Mozart have passed into the body of young Liszt.'

REVIEW OF A CONCERT GIVEN TODAY IN 1824 BY FRANZ LISZT IN PARIS

MARCH

🎵 BIRTHS & DEATHS

1663 Italian composer Tomaso Antonio Vitali is born in Bologna.

1875 French composer Maurice Ravel is born in Ciboure.

1976 New Zealand bass-baritone Jonathan Lemalu is born in Dunedin.

🎵 FIRST PERFORMED

1711 George Frideric Handel's opera *Rinaldo* is premiered in London.

1904 Ralph Vaughan Williams' *Symphonic Rhapsody* receives its first performance, in Bournemouth.

☀ TODAY'S THE DAY

1785 King Ferdinando IV of Naples gives composer Giovanni Paisiello an annual pension of 1,200 ducats for the rest of his life, so long as he composes an opera annually for the Teatro San Carlo and performs various other musical duties.

1820 Ten-year-old Felix Mendelssohn starts to write down his earliest musical compositions, just as his elder sister Fanny had begun doing a few days before.

1842 Mikhail Glinka appears in the divorce courts in St Petersburg.

1866 Part of Berlioz's *Les Troyens* is performed at a concert in Paris. The composer isn't given a free ticket, so he buys one for three francs towards the back of the auditorium. When the rest of the audience realises that he is there, the crowd goes wild.

1897 Johannes Brahms attends his last concert featuring his own music. The Viennese audience applauds each movement of his *Symphony No. 4* conducted by Hans Richter.

1901 Hubert Parry gives his first lecture as a professor at Oxford University. It proves to be so popular that university officials are forced to move it to the Town Hall, to enable as many people as possible to attend.

1915 Sergei Prokofiev performs his *Piano Concerto No. 2* in Rome – the first time he has given a concert outside of Russia.

Symphonic variation

Mozart wrote 41 symphonies but you could go to Jupiter and back before you find his symphony number 37. It doesn't actually exist. The symphony that was erroneously labelled Mozart's 'symphony No. 37' was actually composed by someone else. Mozart had copied it out for his friend.

🎵 HALL OF FAME HIT

Wolfgang Amadeus Mozart: *Flute and Harp Concerto*

Recommended Recording

Emmanuel Pahud, Marie-Pierre Langlamet (soloists); Berlin Philharmonic Orchestra conducted by Claudio Abbado; EMI Classics 5571282

'It is possible to be as much of a musician as Saint-Saëns; it is impossible to be more of one!'

FRANZ LISZT ON MEETING FELLOW COMPOSER CAMILLE SAINT-SAËNS IN PARIS, TODAY IN 1866

08

MARCH

🕐 BIRTHS & DEATHS

1714 German composer Carl Philipp Emanuel Bach is born in Weimar.

1857 The Italian composer who surely has the longest name in classical music is born in Naples: Ruggero Giacomo Maria Giuseppe Emmanuele Raffaele Comenico Vincenzo Francesco Donato Leoncavallo.

1869 French composer Hector Berlioz dies in Paris.

1911 American composer Alan Hovhaness is born in Somerville, Massachusetts.

1939 Welsh tenor Robert Tear is born in Barry, Glamorgan.

1958 English choral director Simon Halsey is born in London.

1961 English conductor Thomas Beecham dies in London.

1961 English tenor Mark Padmore is born in London.

1983 English composer William Walton dies on the Italian island of Ischia.

🕐 FIRST PERFORMED

1898 Richard Strauss's *Don Quixote* is premiered in Cologne.

1902 Jean Sibelius's *Symphony No. 2* receives its first performance, in Helsinki, with the composer conducting.

1905 Edward Elgar's *Introduction and Allegro for Strings* and *Pomp and Circumstance March No. 3* are premiered at the Queen's Hall in London, with the composer conducting.

☀ TODAY'S THE DAY

1813 The Philharmonic Society stages its first concert at the Argyll Rooms in London's Regent Street. The composer Muzio Clementi is at the piano.

1827 In Vienna, Johann Nepomuk Hummel visits Ludwig van Beethoven, who is dying.

1832 At the end of a massive 140-date UK concert tour, Niccolò Paganini heads to Le Havre on a ship from Southampton.

1845 Giuseppe Verdi's *Ernani* becomes the first of his operas to be staged in England.

1891 Sergei Rachmaninov has his first performance as a conductor at the Moscow Conservatoire.

1911 Contract negotiations between conductor Gustav Mahler and the New York Philharmonic Society break down.

1928 Maurice Ravel writes to Nadia Boulanger, renowned composer, conductor and piano teacher, to ask her to take George Gershwin as a pupil, but she turns down the opportunity.

Piano duel

In the winter of 1781–82, Mozart was challenged to a keyboard duel by Muzio Clementi. It was officially a tie, but while Clementi was graciously wowed by Mozart's abilities, Mozart's views on the event verged on the catty. He said that Clementi was 'mechanical' and played with 'no feeling'.

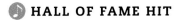

♪ HALL OF FAME HIT

Giacomo Puccini: *La bohème*

Recommended Recording

Various soloists; Bavarian Radio Symphony Orchestra conducted by Bertrand de Billy; Deutsche Grammophon 477 7949

09

MARCH

BIRTHS & DEATHS

1706 German composer Johann Pachelbel is buried in Nuremberg.

1910 American composer Samuel Barber is born in West Chester, Pennsylvania.

1950 English pianist and conductor Howard Shelley is born in London.

FIRST PERFORMED

1842 Giuseppe Verdi's opera *Nabucco* is premiered in Milan.

1844 Giuseppe Verdi's opera *Ernani* is premiered in Venice.

1849 Otto Nicolai's opera *Merry Wives of Windsor* is premiered in Berlin.

TODAY'S THE DAY

1831 Hector Berlioz meets Felix Mendelssohn in Rome.

1831 Italian violinist Niccolò Paganini performs in Paris for the first time. The crowds love him.

1871 Gabriel Fauré is discharged from the Imperial Guard. He had enlisted during the Franco-Prussian war. His first job after leaving the army is as a church organist.

1880 Richard Wagner and Engelbert Humperdinck meet for the first time in Naples.

1902 Gustav Mahler marries Alma Schindler in Vienna.

1918 The Commissar of Public Education steps in to prevent Alexander Glazunov's flat from being confiscated by the Russian government.

1931 Sergei Rachmaninov's music is banned from being performed or studied in the Soviet Union. The ban stays in place until 1933.

COMPOSER PROFILE:

Samuel Barber

Barber's music contrasts sharply with that of his contemporaries Schoenberg, Webern and Berg. While they championed the new atonal sound, Barber's music remained lyrical and heartfelt in style. Although still modern in feel, it achieved popular success by being massively approachable. Barber joined Philadelphia's Curtis Institute when he was only 14 to study composition and singing. Even though he lived into his seventies, he did not produce a great amount of music. Indeed, he stopped composing altogether for the last 20 years of his life after his opera *Antony and Cleopatra*, which was commissioned to mark the opening of the new home for New York's Metropolitan Opera, received a drubbing from the critics. Probably best known for his tuneful *Adagio for Strings*, he rearranged it as an equally stunning choral work, *Agnus Dei*, in 1967.

HALL OF FAME HIT

Wolfgang Amadeus Mozart: *Ave Verum Corpus*

Recommended Recording

Tenebrae; Chamber Orchestra of Europe conducted by Nigel Short; Apex 2564 660707

'It is clear that the first specification for a composer is to be dead.'

ARTHUR HONEGGER, COMPOSER, I AM A COMPOSER (1951)

10
MARCH

🎵 BIRTHS & DEATHS

1749 Birth of Italian librettist Lorenzo da Ponte near Venice.

1832 English (originally Italian) composer, pianist and piano manufacturer Muzio Clementi dies in Evesham.

1844 Spanish composer and violinist Pablo de Sarasate is born in Pamplona.

1870 Bohemian pianist and composer Ignaz Moscheles dies in Leipzig.

1892 Swiss composer Arthur Honegger is born in Le Havre, France.

1915 English conductor Charles Groves is born in London.

1947 English conductor Andrew Parrott is born in Walsall.

🎵 FIRST PERFORMED

1785 Wolfgang Amadeus Mozart's *Piano Concerto No. 21* is given its first performance, in Vienna.

1867 The instrumental version of Johann Strauss Junior's waltz *'By the Beautiful Blue Danube'* is premiered in Vienna.

1877 Alexander Borodin's *Symphony No. 2* is given its first performance, in St Petersburg.

2000 John Tavener's *The Lord's Prayer* is given its first performance, by the Tallis Scholars, in Guildford.

☀️ TODAY'S THE DAY

1834 Felix Mendelssohn is made the founding director of the Düsseldorf Theatrical Association, with opera a big part of his remit.

1915 Maurice Ravel is pronounced fit for duty for the French army.

1924 Sergei Rachmaninov gives a concert at the White House in Washington DC for President Coolidge.

MUSICAL TERM:

Libretto

This Italian word translates as 'little book' in English. Put simply, it is the book of words used for the sung or spoken parts of an opera. Among the most successful librettists of operatic history was Lorenzo da Ponte, who collaborated with Mozart on *The Marriage of Figaro*, *Don Giovanni* and *Così fan tutte*, while Arrigo Boito, himself also a composer, wrote the libretti for Verdi's *Otello* and *Falstaff*. It is by no means an absolute rule that a composer has to work with a librettist, though. Probably the best example of a man who did it all for himself is Wagner, although this was possibly because no librettist would ever be able to match his incredibly high opinion of his own abilities.

🎵 HALL OF FAME HIT
Jean Sibelius: *Symphony No. 5*

Recommended Recording
Finnish Radio Symphony Orchestra conducted by Jukka-Pekka Saraste; RCA Classical Masters 8869 7715212

11
MARCH

'Rigoletto lacks melody. This opera has hardly any chance of being kept in the repertoire.'

GAZETTE MUSICALE DE PARIS, REVIEWING VERDI'S OPERA RIGOLETTO SHORTLY AFTER ITS PREMIERE

BIRTHS & DEATHS

1914 English composer William Lloyd Webber is born in London.

1921 Argentinian composer Ástor Piazzolla is born in Mar del Plata.

1943 English mezzo-soprano Sarah Walker is born in Cheltenham.

1947 English composer Victor Hely-Hutchinson dies in London.

1959 English composer Haydn Wood dies in London.

FIRST PERFORMED

1791 The first season of annual concerts arranged by Joseph Haydn and Peter Salomon begins in London's Hanover Square Rooms, including the premiere of Haydn's *Symphony No. 92* ('Oxford').

1851 Giuseppe Verdi's opera *Rigoletto* is premiered at Teatro La Fenice, Venice.

1867 Giuseppe Verdi's opera *Don Carlos* is premiered by the Paris Opéra.

1886 The first performance of Pyotr Ilyich Tchaikovsky's *Manfred Symphony* is given in Moscow.

1915 Maurice Ravel's *Mother Goose* is premiered in Paris.

1917 Ottorino Respighi's *The Fountains of Rome* received its first performance, in Rome.

TODAY'S THE DAY

1816 A concert by Niccolò Paganini and Charles Philippe Lafont in Milan becomes something of a duel, as each attempts to outdo the other's musical showmanship.

1829 For the first time in nearly a hundred years, J. S. Bach's *St Matthew Passion* is performed in Berlin. Felix Mendelssohn conducts, using a baton for the first time. The audience is ecstatic.

1848 In Hamburg, Johannes Brahms witnesses a stunning performance of Beethoven's *Violin Concerto* by one of the major musical stars of the day, 16-year-old Joseph Joachim.

1860 Emperor Napoleon III gives the order for Richard Wagner's opera *Tannhäuser* to be staged at the Paris Opéra the following year, allowing the composer to return to the French capital after being exiled for eleven years.

1869 Hector Berlioz's funeral takes place in Paris. He is buried in Montmartre next to his two wives, Harriet Smithson and Marie Recio.

1876 Seventeen-year-old Giacomo Puccini walks for seven hours to Pisa to see Verdi's opera *Aida*. He manages to blag his way into the theatre to avoid buying a ticket and hides inside until the opera begins.

1967 Zoltán Kodály's funeral takes place in Budapest.

HALL OF FAME HIT
Jules Massenet: *Thaïs*

Recommended Recording
Nicola Benedetti (violin); London Symphony Orchestra conducted by Daniel Harding; Deutsche Grammophon 987 0577

'I'm not handsome, but when women hear me play, they come crawling to my feet.'

NICCOLÒ PAGANINI, VIOLINIST AND COMPOSER

BIRTHS & DEATHS

604 Pope Gregory I, who gave his name to Gregorian chant, dies in Rome.

1710 English composer Thomas Arne is born in London.

1890 Russian ballet star Vaslav Nijinsky is born in Kiev.

1928 English trumpeter Philip Jones is born in Bath.

1937 French composer and organist Charles-Marie Widor dies in Paris.

1985 American (originally Hungarian) conductor Eugene Ormandy dies in Philadelphia.

1999 American violinist and conductor Yehudi Menuhin dies in Berlin.

2008 Welsh composer Alun Hoddinott dies in Swansea.

FIRST PERFORMED

1857 Giuseppe Verdi's opera *Simon Boccanegra* is premiered in Venice.

1859 Richard Wagner's *Prelude to 'Tristan and Isolde'* receives its first performance, in Prague, conducted by Hans von Bülow, who provides a new ending.

1943 Aaron Copland's *Fanfare for the Common Man* is given its first performance, in Cincinnati.

TODAY'S THE DAY

1770 Wolfgang Amadeus Mozart performs at a gala concert in Milan. He impresses enough to be asked to provide the first opera for the following year's season.

1829 Niccolò Paganini calls by to meet Felix and Fanny Mendelssohn at home in Berlin.

1891 Clara Schumann gives her final performance at the piano, in Frankfurt.

1917 Sergei Rachmaninov donates his fee from a concert to help political prisoners recently released from jail.

1926 Ten-year-old Yehudi Menuhin performs Lalo's *Symphonie Espagnole* with the San Francisco Symphony Orchestra.

1945 The Vienna State Opera is totally destroyed by an American bombing raid.

1956 Dmitri Shostakovich is told that the revised version of his *Lady Macbeth of the Mtsensk District*, now known as *Katerina Izmaylova*, will be banned by the censors.

COMPOSER PROFILE:

Charles-Marie Widor

Widor studied with his organ-builder father and later in Brussels before landing one of the most prestigious posts in France – organist at St Sulpice, Paris. Later as organ and then composition professor at the Paris Conservatoire, Widor devoted his efforts to furthering the cause of the organ. His greatest legacy is his body of ten symphonies for the solo organ, in which he put the instrument through its paces, keen to show that it was capable of emulating the entire orchestra.

HALL OF FAME HIT

Wolfgang Amadeus Mozart: *Solemn Vespers*

Recommended Recording

Various soloists; London Symphony Orchestra and Chorus conducted by Colin Davis; Philips 475 7058

13

MARCH

> 'I've been told that Wagner's music is better than it sounds.'
>
> MARK TWAIN, WRITER

 FIRST PERFORMED

1845 Felix Mendelssohn's *Violin Concerto* is given its first performance, in the Leipzig Gewandhaus.

1861 Richard Wagner's opera *Tannhäuser* is premiered in Paris.

1944 The orchestrated version of Heitor Villa-Lobos's *Bachianas Brasileiras No. 7* receives its first performance, in Rio de Janeiro, with the composer conducting.

 TODAY'S THE DAY

1833 Felix Mendelssohn finishes work on his *Symphony No. 4 ('Italian')*.

1869 Arthur Sullivan, of Gilbert and Sullivan fame, is formally presented to Queen Victoria at Buckingham Palace.

1884 Antonín Dvořák conducts his *Stabat Mater* at London's Royal Albert Hall during his first visit to England.

1915 Percy Grainger makes his debut as a pianist with the New York Philharmonic, playing Grieg's *Piano Concerto*.

1918 French composer Erik Satie narrowly avoids death following a German air raid in the Place de la Concorde in Paris.

COMPOSER PROFILE:

Percy Grainger

Grainger challenges Erik Satie for the title of 'most eccentric composer' in this book. Australian born, he married his 'Nordic Princess' Ella Viola Ström in front of thousands at the Hollywood Bowl. He was nicknamed 'the Jogging Pianist' because he often used to run to piano concerts and rush up on stage at the last minute. Not only did he make his own clothes, but he also designed early prototypes of the women's sports bra. A good friend of both Edvard Grieg and Frederick Delius, he was a great collector of folk tunes. He spent the latter part of his life inventing complicated musical formats using early electronic instruments.

Handel's blindness

George Frideric Handel had great trouble with his sight towards the end of his life. Today, in 1751, after hearing him perform at a concert in London, a member of the audience wrote, 'Noble Handel hath lost an eye, but I have the Rapture to say that St Cecilia makes no complaint of any defect in his Fingers.'

 HALL OF FAME HIT

Ludwig van Beethoven: *Symphony No. 3 ('Eroica')*

Recommended Recording

London Symphony Orchestra conducted by Bernard Haitink; LSO Live 0080

'I have never heard anything so profoundly Shakespearean in my life.'

HECTOR BERLIOZ, WRITING A LETTER TODAY IN 1846 TO FELIX MENDELSSOHN, AFTER HEARING THE LATTER'S INCIDENTAL MUSIC TO A *MIDSUMMER NIGHT'S DREAM*

BIRTHS & DEATHS

1681 German composer Georg Philipp Telemann is born in Magdeburg.

1804 Austrian composer Johann Strauss Senior is born in Vienna.

FIRST PERFORMED

1824 Franz Schubert's *String Quartet No. 13 ('Rosamunde')*, the only chamber work published by the composer during his lifetime, is given its first performance, in Vienna.

1847 Giuseppe Verdi's opera *Macbeth* is premiered in Florence, with the composer conducting.

1885 Arthur Sullivan's and W. S. Gilbert's operetta *The Mikado, or The Town of Titipu* is premiered at the Savoy Theatre in London.

2002 André Previn's *Violin Concerto* receives its first performance, in Boston, with the composer conducting and his future wife, Anne-Sophie Mutter, as soloist.

TODAY'S THE DAY

1840 Franz Liszt and Robert Schumann arrive in Dresden – the former to perform; the latter to review the former's performance.

1904 London's Royal Opera House hosts a three-day festival of the music of Edward Elgar – a rare honour for a living composer.

MUSICAL TERM:

Leitmotiv

Literally translated as 'leading motif', this is a collection of notes, a musical theme, that signifies a particular person, place or idea in an opera. So, a certain tune might be intended to represent a particular character. The theme can sometimes be repeated exactly as it has been heard before, or on other occasions it can be altered, although it remains recognisable. It is very useful for giving the audience a clue about what exactly is going on. It is particularly associated with the operas of Wagner, although many other composers use the device and it is present in the popular musicals of today.

ENSEMBLE FOCUS:

Sinfonia Cymru

Founded in 1996, Sinfonia Cymru set out to do two things: to assist young musicians as they embark upon their careers and to ensure that great classical music is heard in concert halls right across Wales. Its music director is Gareth Jones and the orchestra regularly performs with artists as wide-ranging as conductor Carlo Rizzi, harpist Catrin Finch and violinist Bartosz Woroch.

 HALL OF FAME HIT

Wolfgang Amadeus Mozart: *Eine Kleine Nachtmusik*

Recommended Recording

Chamber Players of Canada; ATMA Classique ACD 22532

15
MARCH

'The opera house is an institution differing from other lunatic asylums only in the fact its inmates have avoided official certification.'

ERNEST NEWMAN, MUSIC CRITIC

🕐 BIRTHS & DEATHS

1835 Austrian composer Eduard Strauss is born in Vienna.
1842 Italian composer Luigi Cherubini dies in Paris.
1853 Italian music publisher Giovanni Ricordi dies in Milan.
1918 French composer Lili Boulanger dies in Mézy.
1961 Italian violinist and conductor Fabio Biondi is born in Palermo, Sicily.
1977 Chinese guitarist Xuefei Yang is born in Beijing.

🎻 FIRST PERFORMED

1807 Ludwig van Beethoven's *Symphony No. 4* receives its first performance.
1886 The orchestrated version of Edvard Grieg's *Holberg Suite* is given its first performance, in Bergen, conducted by the composer.
1897 Sergei Rachmaninov's *Symphony No. 1* receives its first performance.
1908 Maurice Ravel's *Rapsodie Espagnole* is premiered in Paris.

☀ TODAY'S THE DAY

1630 Jacopo Peri prepares his will after suffering a bout of serious illness. He actually lives on for another three years.
1778 Thomas Arne is buried at St Paul's Church in London's Covent Garden. It would have been his 41st wedding anniversary.
1825 Gaetano Donizetti is given the job of maestro di cappella at the Teatro Carolino in Palermo.
1838 The Emperor of Austria gives 18-year-old piano sensation Clara Wieck (later Schumann) the title 'Royal and Imperial Virtuosa'.
1847 Hector Berlioz performs in the first of five concerts in St Petersburg. They are a roaring success and he is paid 12,000 French francs.
1866 Bedřich Smetana finishes orchestrating his comic opera *The Bartered Bride*.
1895 Twenty-two-year-old tenor Enrico Caruso makes his operatic debut in Naples.

1918 Edward Elgar has his tonsils taken out in a London hospital. While he's recovering, he begins work on his *Cello Concerto*.
1941 Sergei Prokofiev moves out of the family home and takes up residence with his mistress Mira Abramovna in Leningrad.
1960 Aaron Copland sets off from the USA to Russia to take part in a cultural-exchange programme between the two countries.
1962 Tenor Luciano Pavarotti makes his first major appearance in an operatic role, playing the Duke in *Rigoletto*, in Palermo.
1978 The Russian citizenship of the cellist Mstislav Rostropovich is revoked, after the Russian government accuses him of 'anti-Soviet activity'.

🎵 HALL OF FAME HIT
Gustav Mahler: *Symphony No. 2* ('Resurrection')

Recommended Recording
Miah Persson, Christianne Stotijn (soloists); Chicago Symphony Orchestra and Chorus conducted by Bernard Haitink; CSO Resound CSOR 901914

'Music will express any emotion, base or lofty. She is absolutely unmoral.'

GEORGE BERNARD SHAW, WRITER AND CRITIC

16
MARCH

🎵 BIRTHS & DEATHS

1736 Italian composer Giovanni Battista Pergolesi dies near Naples.

1934 English conductor Roger Norrington is born in Oxford.

🎵 FIRST PERFORMED

1870 Pyotr Ilyich Tchaikovsky's overture-fantasy *Romeo and Juliet* is premiered in Moscow.

1894 Jules Massenet's opera *Thaïs* is premiered in Paris. Although it is branded 'immoral' by some critics, it becomes a popular success.

1904 Edward Elgar's overture *In the South* is given its first performance, at the Royal Opera House in London.

☀ TODAY'S THE DAY

1653 Jean-Baptiste Lully becomes court composer in Paris.

1781 Wolfgang Amadeus Mozart arrives in Vienna to take part in the celebrations to mark Emperor Joseph II's accession, but he isn't happy there, having been feted in Munich, where he had been staying previously. He complains bitterly about being treated like a servant.

1827 Johann Nepomuk Hummel is made a Chevalier of the Légion d'Honneur.

1828 Niccolò Paganini arrives in Vienna to give his first concerts there.

1833 Felix Mendelssohn is appointed director of the Lower Rhine Festival.

1840 Robert Schumann listens to a performance by Franz Liszt in Dresden, before the pair head off to Leipzig.

1842 Mikhail Glinka sends the score of his opera *Russlan and Ludmilla* to the director of Imperial Theatres in St Petersburg in the hope that it will go into production. Even though the libretto isn't finished, it gets the green light.

1857 Bedřich Smetana makes his debut as conductor of Gothenburg's Harmonic Society.

1877 To mark the 50th anniversary of Beethoven's death, Franz Liszt performs Beethoven's *Choral Fantasy* and *Piano Concerto No. 5* ('Emperor'). A 16-year-old Gustav Mahler is in the audience.

1891 The audience at the Hungarian Opera in Budapest protests over the departure of conductor Gustav Mahler, who has fallen out with the Opera's administrative boss.

1905 Edward Elgar gives a lecture in Birmingham entitled 'A Future for English Music'. He is less than complimentary about some of his contemporaries, resulting in frosty relations developing between him and some of his composer friends.

1905 Nadia Boulanger makes her public concert debut at the piano in Paris.

1933 Benjamin Britten's *Sinfonietta* is performed at the Royal College of Music, where the 19-year-old is a student. It's the only piece by him publicly performed there while he is studying.

1942 Benjamin Britten and Peter Pears leave New York for England on the Swedish cargo ship *Axel Johnson*. It is the height of the Second World War and American Customs officers are concerned that some of the music Britten has with him might be coded messages for the Germans, so they are confiscated. In fact, they are sketches for a clarinet concerto and the choral *Hymn to St Cecilia*.

HALL OF FAME HIT
Pyotr Ilyich Tchaikovsky: *Symphony No. 5*

Recommended Recording
Bavarian Radio Symphony Orchestra conducted by Mariss Jansons; BR Klassik 900105

17

MARCH

'Brass bands are all very well in their place – outdoors and several miles away.'

THOMAS BEECHAM, CONDUCTOR

BIRTHS & DEATHS

1938 Russian ballet dancer Rudolf Nureyev is born in Irkutsk.
1944 English pianist John Lill is born in London.

FIRST PERFORMED

1749 George Frideric Handel's oratorio *Solomon* is premiered in London.
1830 Frédéric Chopin's *Piano Concerto No. 2* receives its first performance, with the composer as soloist. It is his official public debut in Warsaw. The piece was in fact the first piano concerto that he wrote, but it was published after his *Piano Concerto No. 1* – hence the numbers being the wrong way around.

TODAY'S THE DAY

1712 Historians believe the earliest instructions on how to dance the *fandango* are found in a letter written today by a Spanish priest, Martín Martí.
1763 Johann Christian Bach dedicates his first set of harpsichord concertos to George III's wife Charlotte, Queen of Great Britain and Ireland.
1784 Wolfgang Amadeus Mozart gives his first public performance of a piano concerto in Vienna. Music historians believe that he played his *Piano Concerto No. 14*.
1835 Mikhail Glinka gets engaged to Maria Petrovna Ivanovana.
1839 The great violinist Joseph Joachim makes his public performance debut in Pest in Hungary.
1862 Anton Rubinstein becomes the first director of the St Petersburg Conservatoire.
1913 Béla Bartók returns home from a fortnight's trip collecting Romanian folk tunes in Transylvania.
1919 Sergei Rachmaninov makes his first ever recordings, laying down nine piano rolls for the American Piano Company.
1951 Soprano Victoria de los Ángeles makes her American debut at New York's Metropolitan Opera in Gounod's *Faust*.

INSTRUMENT FOCUS:

Brass

Brass instruments do not have to be made of brass, just as woodwind instruments do not have to be made of wood. Their common feature is a cupped mouthpiece, which looks like a small fat chalice. It is plugged into one end of the instrument. When players blow into the mouthpiece, they vibrate their lips across it to produce a sound. Heroes of the brass family include: in the higher registers, the trumpet, cornet and bugle; in the middle register, the French horn; and in the lower registers, the trombones, bass trombones and tuba. Over the years, there have been other members of the family, including the bass horn, invented in the 1970s by brass legend Robert Bobo; the natural horn, which is the devil's own instrument to master; and the ophicleide, the forerunner of the tuba, which looks a bit like a brass bassoon, only fatter.

HALL OF FAME HIT
Jean Sibelius: *Karelia Suite*

Recommended Recording
Vienna Philharmonic Orchestra conducted by Lorin Maazel; Australian Eloquence 480 6568

'Violinist: a man who is always up to his chin in music.'

ANON

18
MARCH

🎵 BIRTHS & DEATHS

1844 Russian composer Nikolai Rimsky-Korsakov is born near St Petersburg.

🎵 FIRST PERFORMED

1842 Gioachino Rossini's *Stabat Mater* has its first performance, in Bologna, conducted by fellow composer Gaetano Donizetti, with Rossini in the audience.

1902 Arnold Schoenberg's *Verklärte Nacht* is premiered in Vienna.

1927 Sergei Rachmaninov's *Piano Concerto No. 4* receives its first performance, at the Academy of Music in Philadelphia.

1953 William Walton's *Orb and Sceptre* march has its first performance, at London's Kingsway Hall, as part of a recording session conducted by the composer.

☀️ TODAY'S THE DAY

1768 Leopold Mozart is told that if he fails to turn up at the Archbishop of Salzburg's office before the beginning of April he will no longer be paid.

1840 Franz Liszt cancels a concert in Leipzig, after suffering an attack of 'violent shuddering'.

1902 Enrico Caruso records ten arias for the Gramophone Company in a Milan hotel room. He is paid $5,000.

1903 Leoš Janáček finishes writing his opera *Jenůfa*.

1905 Béla Bartók meets Zoltán Kodály for the first time in Budapest. They become firm friends with a shared interest in collecting and preserving folk tunes.

COMPOSER PROFILE:

Jean-Baptiste Lully

Although he was Italian by birth, Lully is thought of as being a great French composer. A self-taught violinist, he worked as a servant from the age of 14, before becoming a dancer. In 1653 he began working for Louis XIV as a composer of ballet music. He was quickly promoted, each job slightly more important than the last, and each with a slightly grander title: Leader of the King's Violins; Instrumental Composer to the King; Superintendent of Music; Music Master to the Royal Family. The King even granted him the exclusive rights to present all opera in Paris. This gave him an enormous amount of power over all music in France. Able to hire and fire musicians at will, he took advantage of his grip on the country's music-making to insist on the staging of his own operas and ballets.

🎵 HALL OF FAME HIT

Johann Sebastian Bach: *St Matthew Passion*

Recommended Recording

Various soloists; Cantate Domino Schola Cantorum, Collegium Vocale and Collegium Vocale Orchestra conducted by Philippe Herreweghe; Harmonia Mundi HMC 901676/78

19

MARCH

'I am sitting in the smallest room of my house. I have your review before me. In a moment it will be behind me.'

MAX REGER, COMPOSER, RESPONDING TO A CRITIC

BIRTHS & DEATHS

1873 German composer Max Reger is born in Brand, Bavaria.

1944 Korean (later American) cellist Myung-Wha Chung is born in Seoul.

FIRST PERFORMED

1799 Joseph Haydn's oratorio *The Creation* is given its first performance, in Vienna.

1859 Charles Gounod's opera *Faust* is premiered in Paris.

1892 Pyotr Ilyich Tchaikovsky's *Nutcracker Suite*, comprising eight numbers from the ballet, receives its first performance in St Petersburg, with the composer conducting.

1896 Antonín Dvořák's *Cello Concerto* is first performed, at the Queen's Hall in London, conducted by the composer.

1944 Michael Tippett's oratorio *A Child of Our Time* is given its first performance, at the Adelphi Theatre, London.

1991 John Adams' opera *The Death of Klinghoffer* is premiered in Brussels.

TODAY'S THE DAY

1827 Franz Schubert and Ludwig van Beethoven meet for the first time, in sad circumstances. Schubert is among a group of Viennese musicians paying tribute to Beethoven, who is in his final days.

1842 More than 2,000 people take part in Luigi Cherubini's funeral in Paris.

1884 Pyotr Ilyich Tchaikovsky is made a member of the Order of St Vladimir (4th class) by Tsar Alexander III in St Petersburg.

1903 Igor Stravinsky meets Nikolai Rimsky-Korsakov for the first time at the latter's 59th birthday party.

1907 Edward Elgar enjoys his first professional engagement in New York, as conductor of his oratorio *The Apostles*, in Carnegie Hall.

Russian ballet

During the 19th century, the centre of the ballet world gradually shifted away from France, with Russia emerging as the powerhouse for great new works. *Swan Lake, Nutcracker* and *The Sleeping Beauty*, Tchaikovsky's three full-length ballets, were written between 1876 and 1892. They soon became cornerstones of the repertoire, a position they maintain to this day, often still employing the original choreography of one of the world's masters, Marius Petipa. When Sergei Diaghilev's Ballets Russes produced Stravinsky's three major ballets between 1910 and 1913 (*The Firebird, Petrushka* and *The Rite of Spring*), the company was touring Europe and the rest of the world as one of the biggest paying attractions of the day. The combination of Stravinsky's unconventional music and Nijinsky's iconoclastic choreography for *The Rite of Spring*, in particular, caused an infamous riot on the occasion of its premiere in Paris.

HALL OF FAME HIT

Aram Khachaturian: *Spartacus*

Recommended Recording

Bournemouth Symphony Orchestra conducted by Kirill Karabits; Onyx 4063

> 'We shall never become musicians unless we understand the ideals for temperance, fortitude, liberality and magnificence.'

PLATO, GREEK PHILOSOPHER

BIRTHS & DEATHS

1812 Bohemian composer Jan Ladislav Dussek dies in St Germain-en-Laye.

1915 Russian pianist Sviatoslav Richter is born in Zhitomir in the Ukraine.

FIRST PERFORMED

1914 George Butterworth's *The Banks of Green Willow* receives its first performance, in London.

TODAY'S THE DAY

1734 Newcastle-based composer Charles Avison's music is performed in Hickford's Rooms, London, in a concert that comes right at the start of his professional career.

1807 A fire at a building belonging to instrument makers and music publishers Clementi & Co. in London's Tottenham Court Road causes £40,000 worth of damage. Composer Muzio Clementi was one of the main investors in the firm.

1836 Felix Mendelssohn is made an honorary Doctor of Philosophy by the University of Leipzig.

1843 Fourteen-year-old pianist Anton Rubinstein makes his debut at a concert in St Petersburg. Tsar Nicholas I is in the audience.

1864 Hector Berlioz retires as the music critic of the *Journal des débats*.

1948 The television network CBS transmits a concert by the Philadelphia Orchestra, under the baton of Eugene Ormandy. It's the first symphony orchestra concert to be televised in the USA. Just an hour and a half later, NBC broadcasts the country's second televised live symphony orchestra concert, with Arturo Toscanini conducting the NBC Symphony Orchestra in New York's Carnegie Hall.

1952 The Russian Communist Party's Committee for Artistic Affairs asks the Party's ruling Central Committee to grant an ailing Sergei Prokofiev a monthly pension.

ORCHESTRA FOCUS:

New York Philharmonic

The USA's oldest symphony orchestra was founded in 1842 – almost 40 years before the next-oldest American ensemble. For a period from today in 1928, it was known as the Philharmonic-Symphony Society Orchestra of New York, following a merger between the New York Symphony Society and the New York Philharmonic Society. This mouthful was soon reduced, with the orchestra becoming the New York Philharmonic that we know and love today. The role of the New York Philharmonic's music director is among the most coveted in classical music, with previous holders of the post including Gustav Mahler, Arturo Toscanini, John Barbirolli, Leopold Stokowski, Leonard Bernstein, Pierre Boulez, Zubin Mehta, Kurt Masur and Lorin Maazel. The current music director is Alan Gilbert.

HALL OF FAME HIT

Maurice Ravel: *Boléro*

Recommended Recording

London Symphony Orchestra conducted by Valery Gergiev; LSO Live 0693

21

MARCH

'So long as the human spirit thrives on this planet, music in some living form will accompany and sustain it and give it expressive meaning.'

AARON COPLAND, COMPOSER

BIRTHS & DEATHS

1685 German composer Johann Sebastian Bach is born in Eisenach.

1839 Russian composer Modest Mussorgsky is born in Karevo.

1914 French cellist and conductor Paul Tortelier is born in Paris.

1935 American conductor Erich Kunzel is born in New York.

1936 Russian composer Alexander Glazunov dies in Paris.

1942 Welsh conductor Owain Arwel Hughes is born in Cardiff.

FIRST PERFORMED

1825 Ludwig van Beethoven's *Symphony No. 9 ('Choral')* is given its first performance, in London.

1826 Ludwig van Beethoven's *String Quartet No. 13 in B flat major, Op. 130*, is first performed, in Vienna.

1839 Franz Schubert's *Symphony No. 9 ('Great')*, the score of which had been discovered by Robert Schumann during a visit to Schubert's brother, receives its first performance, in Leipzig, conducted by Felix Mendelssohn.

TODAY'S THE DAY

1605 Orlando Gibbons is formally sworn in as a Gentleman of the Chapel Royal (a member of the choir).

1764 William Boyce is sacked from his job in All Hallows the Great and the Less Parish.

1816 Felix Mendelssohn, along with his two sisters and brother, is baptised into the Lutheran faith.

1831 Giacomo Meyerbeer holds a dinner party for Niccolò Paganini. Around the table are fellow composers Luigi Cherubini and Gioachino Rossini.

1839 Nineteen-year-old pianist Clara Wieck (later Schumann) makes her Paris debut. Her arrival is greeted as a 'sensation'.

1843 Composer, conductor and violinist Joseph Lanner gives his last concert, three weeks before his death at the age of 42.

1846 Adolphe Sax applies for a patent in France for 'a new system of wind instruments, called the saxophone'.

1873 Charles Villiers Stanford is offered the role of assistant organist at Trinity College, Cambridge.

1905 Carl Nielsen resigns from Denmark's Royal Chapel Orchestra after being told that he wasn't being promoted from the second violins to a conducting role, despite a period working as a deputy conductor. He decides to concentrate on composing instead.

1910 Gustav Mahler conducts his farewell performance at New York's Metropolitan Opera.

HALL OF FAME HIT
Jean Sibelius: *Symphony No. 2*

Recommended Recording
Helsinki Philharmonic Orchestra conducted by Leif Segerstam; Ondine ODE 11152

> 'When I heard Liszt for the first time . . . I was overwhelmed and sobbed aloud, it so shook me.'
>
> **CLARA WIECK IN A LETTER DATED TODAY IN 1840 TO ROBERT SCHUMANN**

BIRTHS & DEATHS

1687 French (originally Italian) composer Jean-Baptiste Lully dies in Paris.

1842 German violinist Carl Rosa is born in Hamburg.

1868 Scottish composer and conductor Hamish McCunn is born in Greenock.

1920 English pianist, teacher and competition administrator Fanny Waterman is born in Leeds.

1925 English (originally German) composer and musical comedian Gerard Hoffnung is born in Berlin.

1930 American composer Stephen Sondheim is born in New York.

1948 English composer Andrew Lloyd Webber is born in London.

1979 English impresario and recording executive Walter Legge dies in Cap Ferrat.

TODAY'S THE DAY

1839 Camille Saint-Saëns composes his first piece of music, for piano. He is three years old (that is not a misprint).

1868 Pyotr Ilyich Tchaikovsky appears in print for the first time, with a critique of Rimsky-Korsakov's *Fantasia on Serbian Themes*.

1884 Antonín Dvořák conducts his *Scherzo Capriccioso* at London's Crystal Palace. On the back of the concert, his fame in England rockets skywards.

1894 Richard Strauss gets engaged to Pauline de Ahna.

1944 The Great Opera House in Frankfurt is destroyed in an Allied air raid.

1980 The first compact disc system is put on sale by RCA.

COMPOSER PROFILE:

Nikolai Rimsky-Korsakov

A hugely influential Russian composer, orchestrator and teacher (of, among others, Stravinsky), Rimsky-Korsakov came from a rich, aristocratic family. Like generations of his family before him, he wanted to be a sailor, becoming a sea cadet at the age of 12. He took time out for piano lessons along the way and it was his piano teacher who introduced him to the composer Balakirev; he then met Cui, Mussorgsky and Borodin. These composers were to become known as 'The Five' or 'The Mighty Handful'. It was Balakirev, in particular, who inspired Rimsky-Korsakov to take up composition seriously. While still serving in the navy, he was made professor of composition and orchestration at the St Petersburg Conservatoire at the spectacularly early age of 27. Later, he was able to combine his two passions when he became Inspector of Naval Bands, a post specially created for him by the Russian Admiralty. Hugely influenced by Wagner's operas, he latterly devoted much of his time to writing for the stage. He was also a fine orchestrator of other people's music – particularly that of Mussorgsky and Borodin.

HALL OF FAME HIT

Pyotr Ilyich Tchaikovsky:
Violin Concerto

Recommended Recording

Valeriy Sokolov (violin); Tonhalle Orchestra of Zurich conducted by David Zinman; Virgin Classics 642 0170

23

MARCH

'Nothing primes inspiration more than necessity, whether it be the presence of a copyist waiting for your work, or the prodding of an impresario tearing his hair.'

GIOACHINO ROSSINI, COMPOSER

🛈 BIRTHS & DEATHS

1917 Northern Irish tenor Josef Locke is born in Derry/Londonderry.

1944 English composer Michael Nyman is born in London.

🎵 FIRST PERFORMED

1731 Johann Sebastian Bach's *St Mark Passion* is first performed on Good Friday, in Leipzig.

1784 Parts of Wolfgang Amadeus Mozart's *Serenade for 13 wind instruments* are given their first performance, at the Burgtheater in Vienna.

1792 Joseph Haydn's *Symphony No. 94* ('Surprise') is first performed, in London.

1828 Ludwig van Beethoven's *String Quartet No. 16 in F, Op. 135*, the last substantial work written before the composer's death, receives its first performance.

1886 Pyotr Ilyich Tchaikovsky's *Manfred Symphony* is given its first performance, in Moscow. Sergei Rachmaninov, aged 12, is in the audience.

1899 Samuel Coleridge-Taylor's *Hiawatha's Wedding Feast* is premiered, in Brooklyn, New York.

☀ TODAY'S THE DAY

1687 The funeral of Jean-Baptiste Lully is held in Paris.

1703 Antonio Vivaldi is ordained as a priest in Venice.

1729 Johann Sebastian Bach performs music at the funeral of his former employer, Prince Leopold.

1743 When Handel's oratorio *Messiah* is performed in London, King George II stands at the start of the 'Hallelujah Chorus'. The tradition continues at many performances of the work more than two-and-a-half centuries later.

1784 Wolfgang Amadeus Mozart puts on a wildly successful concert in Vienna's Burgtheater. On the bill: his *Symphony No. 35* ('Haffner') and *Piano Concerto No. 13*, as well as improvised *Variations on a Theme of Gluck*, who was himself in the audience.

1827 Seriously ill, Ludwig van Beethoven signs his will, leaving his entire estate to his nephew Karl.

1841 Eleven-year-old Anton Rubinstein gives his first major performance at the piano, in Paris.

1856 The fair copy of Richard Wagner's *Das Rheingold* is completed.

1864 Richard Wagner gives his Viennese creditors the slip, by heading to Munich and then on to Switzerland.

1950 Aaron Copland wins an Oscar for his score to the movie *The Heiress*.

1965 Benjamin Britten is awarded the Order of Merit.

🎵 HALL OF FAME HIT
Johannes Brahms: *Violin Concerto*

Recommended Recording
Vadim Repin (violin); Leipzig Gewandhaus Orchestra conducted by Riccardo Chailly; Deutsche Grammophon 477 7470

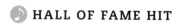

> 'Do it big or stay in bed.'
> LARRY KELLY, AMERICAN OPERA PRODUCER

24
MARCH

BIRTHS & DEATHS

1654 German composer Samuel Scheidt dies in Halle.

1911 Spanish conductor Enrique Jorda is born in San Sebastian.

1916 Spanish composer Enrique Granados drowns in the English Channel.

1937 English baritone Benjamin Luxon is born in Redruth.

FIRST PERFORMED

1784 Wolfgang Amadeus Mozart's *Piano Concerto No. 15* is given its first performance, with the composer as the soloist, in Vienna.

1820 Gioachino Rossini's *Messa di Gloria* is premiered in Naples.

1881 The revised version of Giuseppe Verdi's opera *Simon Boccanegra* is premiered at the Teatro alla Scala in Milan.

1924 Jean Sibelius's *Symphony No. 7* receives its first performance, with the composer conducting, in Stockholm.

1934 Dmitri Shostakovich's *Jazz Suite No. 1* receives its first performance, in Leningrad.

TODAY'S THE DAY

1721 Johann Sebastian Bach finishes his six concertos dedicated to Margrave Ludwig of Brandenburg (the *Brandenburg Concertos*).

1792 Nine-year-old John Field makes his official debut

performance in a concert at the Rotunda Assembly Rooms in Dublin.

1852 Hector Berlioz conducts the first performance of the New Philharmonic Society, in Exeter Hall, London.

1864 Louis Moreau Gottschalk gives a concert in Washington, with President Lincoln in the audience.

1875 Harvard University allows the granting of a PhD in music, although it will be another three decades before anyone actually gets one.

1889 Pyotr Ilyich Tchaikovsky meets fellow composer Jules Massenet in Paris.

COMPOSER PROFILE:
Enrique Granados

After studying in Paris and Barcelona, Granados went on to found his own concert season and piano school in the Spanish city. In his day, he was a pianist first and a composer second. He was especially highly regarded as a performer of his own piano works. His music is unquestionably Spanish in style and this has ensured his enduring popularity in his homeland. Granados and his wife were both drowned when the *Sussex*, the boat on which they were travelling from Liverpool to Dieppe, was torpedoed by a German submarine on this day in 1916. Classical music was robbed of a talent who would have continued to even greater things.

HALL OF FAME HIT
Jean Sibelius: *Violin Concerto*

Recommended Recording
Frank Peter Zimmermann (violin); Helsinki Philharmonic Orchestra conducted by John Storgårds; Ondine ODE 11472

25

MARCH

'After I die I shall return to earth as the doorkeeper of a bordello and I won't let one of you in.'

ARTURO TOSCANINI, CONDUCTOR, TO MEMBERS OF HIS ORCHESTRA, WHO WERE NOT PERFORMING WELL

BIRTHS & DEATHS

1867 Italian conductor Arturo Toscanini is born in Parma.

1881 Hungarian composer Béla Bartók is born in Nagyszentmiklós.

1882 English composer Haydn Wood is born in Slaithwaite.

1918 French composer Claude Debussy dies in Paris.

1977 English cellist Natalie Clein is born in Poole.

FIRST PERFORMED

1875 Gilbert and Sullivan's operetta *Trial By Jury* is premiered at the Royalty Theatre in London.

1911 Claude Debussy's orchestrated *Children's Corner* is given its first performance, with the composer conducting, in Paris.

TODAY'S THE DAY

1563 William Byrd becomes organist and Master of the Choristers at Lincoln Cathedral.

1851 Hundreds of people in Paris are left without a job after the Pleyel piano factory is destroyed by fire.

1886 Charles Villiers Stanford makes his concert debut as conductor of the Bach Choir.

1901 Serge Koussevitzky makes his debut as principal double-bass player in the Bolshoi Theatre Orchestra.

1906 Claude Debussy and Richard Strauss meet for the only time.

1944 A special concert featuring four London orchestras, to celebrate conductor Henry Wood's 75th birthday, is given at the Royal Albert Hall, with the Queen in attendance.

2001 Tan Dun wins an Oscar for his score to the movie *Crouching Tiger, Hidden Dragon*.

INSTRUMENT FOCUS:

Double-bass

Big in size and big in sound, the double-bass is the largest string instrument in the orchestra – and it reaches down to the lowest notes among the strings. Although not always the case, it is usually played with a bow in an orchestral setting. In the jazz world, it tends to be plucked and provides much the same role as a bass guitar does in a rock band. Usually relegated to the back of the orchestra, it does very occasionally get to be the star of the show. The Austrian composer Karl Ditters von Dittersdorf wrote two concertos for the double-bass.

HALL OF FAME HIT

Johann Strauss Junior: *By the Beautiful Blue Danube*

Recommended Recording

Vienna Philharmonic Orchestra conducted by Mariss Jansons; Deutsche Grammophon 477 5566

'Last night the band played Beethoven. Beethoven lost.'
ANON

26
MARCH

BIRTHS & DEATHS

1827 German composer Ludwig van Beethoven dies in Vienna, with a thunderstorm raging overhead.

1918 Russian composer César Cui dies in Petrograd.

1925 French composer and conductor Pierre Boulez is born in Montbrison.

1948 Korean violinist Kyung-Wha Chung is born in Seoul.

1973 English composer and lyricist Noël Coward dies in Blue Harbour, Jamaica.

FIRST PERFORMED

1723 Johann Sebastian Bach's *St John Passion* was first performed on Good Friday, in Leipzig.

TODAY'S THE DAY

1778 Seven-year-old Ludwig van Beethoven makes his first concert appearance in Cologne.

1791 The Prince of Wales attends the official reopening of the King's Theatre, rebuilt after being destroyed by fire, in London.

1811 Beethoven finishes composing his *'Archduke' Trio*.

1821 The nickname *'Jupiter'* is first appended to Mozart's *Sympony No. 41* in a Philharmonic Society of London concert programme.

1828 The first concert comprised completely of music composed by Franz Schubert is performed in Vienna. It is timed to coincide with the first anniversary of Beethoven's death.

1848 The Opéra-Nationale closes down after revolution breaks out on the streets of Paris.

1885 The new Leipzig Gewandhaus building opens.

1943 Gravely ill in Los Angeles, Sergei Rachmaninov enters a coma.

1972 The last of Leonard Bernstein's Young People's Concerts is broadcast on American television. In total, he presented 53 of them.

2000 John Corigliano wins an Oscar for his score for the movie *The Red Violin*.

Beethoven's nicknames

Many of Beethoven's works have gained nicknames over the years, but his best-known work for solo piano, the *'Moonlight' Sonata,* wasn't given the name by Beethoven himself. It acquired the title from a critic, who thought that the piece evoked an image of the moon over Lake Lucerne. And then there's his *Bagatelle in A minor*, which he dedicated to 'Elise' – although his handwriting was so bad that musicologists believe he actually intended to dedicate it to Therese Malfatti, the wife of his doctor.

His publisher misread the dedication, so one of the most famous of all Beethoven's works ended up being a musical love letter to an 'Elise' who never actually existed. There was little doubt about the dedication for his *Symphony No. 3*, though. It was originally for Napoleon Bonaparte, but when the composer heard that his hero had crowned himself 'Emperor', he ran to his manuscript and crossed out the dedication. In its place he put 'Eroica' – 'the hero' – adding the words 'to the *memory* of a great man'.

HALL OF FAME HIT
Jay Ungar: *The Ashokan Farewell*

Recommended Recording
Major J. R. Perkins; Band of Her Majesty's Royal Marines; Classic FM CFMCD4

27

MARCH

'He worked out [a fugue theme] for more than an hour with such science, dexterity, harmony and proper attention to rhythm that even the greatest connoisseurs were astounded.'

REVIEW, PUBLISHED TODAY IN 1771, OF A CONCERT IN VENICE GIVEN BY THE 15-YEAR-OLD WOLFGANG AMADEUS MOZART

🕐 BIRTHS & DEATHS

1851 French composer Vincent d'Indy is born in Paris.

1867 English conductor Alfred Mellon dies in London.

1924 English composer and organist Walter Parratt dies in Windsor.

1927 Russian cellist and conductor Mstislav Rostropovich is born in Baku.

1950 American soprano Maria Ewing is born in Detroit.

1975 English composer and Master of the Queen's Music, Arthur Bliss, dies in London.

🎻 FIRST PERFORMED

1897 Sergei Rachmaninov's *Symphony No. 1* is first performed, in St Petersburg, conducted by Alexander Glazunov. The performance goes incredibly badly, leaving the composer utterly distraught. Sources suggest that the conductor might have been a little the worse for wear.

1914 Ralph Vaughan Williams' *Symphony No. 2* ('*A London Symphony*') receives its first performance, at the Queen's Hall in London.

1917 Giacomo Puccini's *La Rondine* is premiered at the Monte Carlo Opera.

☀️ TODAY'S THE DAY

1709 Jean-Philippe Rameau signs a six-year contract to take over from his father as organist at Notre Dame in Dijon.

1806 *La Clemenza di Tito* becomes the first of Mozart's operas to be performed in London.

1808 Joseph Haydn makes his final public appearance at a performance of his oratorio *The Creation* in Vienna. Antonio Salieri is conducting, and Ludwig van Beethoven is in the audience.

1841 Eleven-year-old Anton Rubinstein is in the audience for a concert in Paris by piano legend Franz Liszt.

1843 The Leipzig Conservatoire opens for business.

1883 Gabriel Fauré marries Marie Fremiet; time would show him not to be a loyal husband.

1898 Pietro Mascagni makes a well-received debut as a symphonic conductor in a major venue at La Scala, Milan.

1943 A group of Russian composers sends a telegram to Sergei Rachmaninov's home in Beverly Hills, congratulating him on his 70th birthday. However, it is a milestone that he will not reach.

1949 Dmitri Shostakovich performs in front of 18,000 people in New York's Madison Square Garden, as a musical finale to the Waldorf Peace Conference.

1958 CBS Laboratories announce the invention of a new stereophonic long-playing record.

1979 The Emerson String Quartet makes its debut performance, in New York.

🎵 HALL OF FAME HIT

Pyotr Ilyich Tchaikovsky: *Nutcracker*

Recommended Recording

Berlin Philharmonic Orchestra conducted by Simon Rattle; EMI Classics 50999 64212227

> 'Music is enough for a lifetime – but a lifetime is not enough for music.'
>
> SERGEI RACHMANINOV, COMPOSER

28
MARCH

🏛 BIRTHS & DEATHS

1881 Russian composer Modest Mussorgsky dies in St Petersburg.

1943 Russian composer Sergei Rachmaninov dies at his home in Beverly Hills, four days short of his 70th birthday.

🎻 FIRST PERFORMED

1800 Joseph Haydn's *Trumpet Concerto* is first performed, in Vienna.

1801 Ludwig van Beethoven's ballet *The Creatures of Prometheus* is premiered in Vienna. Joseph Haydn is in the audience.

1916 Hubert Parry's setting of William Blake's *'Jerusalem'* is given its first performance, at the Queen's Hall in London.

☀ TODAY'S THE DAY

1785 Domenico Cimarosa is given the job of second organist at the Royal Chapel in Naples, getting a salary for the first time.

1837 Felix Mendelssohn marries Cécile Jeanrenaud in Frankfurt am Main.

1862 King Johann of Saxony issues a pardon to Richard Wagner, allowing him to enter the country after being in exile for 13 years.

1884 Composer Arthur Sullivan writes to the promoter Richard D'Oyly Carte to inform him that he can no longer work with the librettist W. S. Gilbert.

1918 Claude Debussy is buried in Paris.

1942 The organ in Lübeck, to which Johann Sebastian Bach walked more than 250 miles to hear his hero Dietrich Buxtehude play in 1705, is destroyed in an Allied bombing raid.

COMPOSER PROFILE:

Modest Mussorgsky

One of the group of five Russian nationalist composers known as 'The Mighty Handful', Mussorgsky started out his adult life as an army officer, but eventually he turned to a musical career, combining composing with working as a low-grade civil servant. A lifelong drinker, he became an alcoholic and, probably for this reason, seemed to lack the ability to finish many of his compositions.

He is famous for his orchestral study *A Night on the Bare Mountain* and also for his piano work *Pictures at an Exhibition*; however, we have his great friend Rimsky-Korsakov to thank for re-orchestrating the former, while the French composer Maurice Ravel turned the latter into the orchestral showpiece that tends to be played today.

🎵 HALL OF FAME HIT
Johann Sebastian Bach: *Mass in B minor*

Recommended Recording
Collegium Vocale Gent conducted by Philippe Herreweghe; PHI LPH 004

29

MARCH

'No man is complete without a feeling for music and an understanding of what it can do for him.'

ZOLTÁN KODÁLY, COMPOSER

BIRTHS & DEATHS

1788 Clergyman and hymn writer Charles Wesley dies in London.

1888 French composer and pianist Alkan (pseudonym of Charles Henri Valentin Morhange) dies in Paris.

1902 English composer William Walton is born in Oldham.

1924 Irish composer Charles Villiers Stanford dies in London.

1936 English composer Richard Rodney Bennett is born in Broadstairs.

1982 German composer Carl Orff dies in Munich.

2011 English tenor Robert Tear dies in London.

FIRST PERFORMED

1795 Ludwig van Beethoven's *Piano Concerto No. 2* is first performed, at the Burgtheater in Vienna, with Beethoven as soloist, making his Viennese performance debut. He receives immediate critical and popular acclaim.

1806 The revised version of Beethoven's opera *Fidelio* is premiered in Vienna. It goes down far better than the original.

1874 Antonín Dvořák's *Symphony No. 3* is given its first performance, in Prague.

1879 Pyotr Ilyich Tchaikovsky's opera *Eugene Onegin* is premiered, in Moscow.

1882 Alexander Glazunov's *Symphony No. 1* receives its first performance, in St Petersburg. The composer is 16 years old.

1892 The first movement of Sergei Rachmaninov's *Piano Concerto No. 1* is first performed, at the Moscow Conservatoire, with the composer at the keyboard.

TODAY'S THE DAY

1792 Luigi Cherubini is made music director of the Opéra-Comique in Paris.

1827 Ludwig van Beethoven is buried in Vienna. Fellow composers Franz Schubert, Johann Nepomuk Hummel and Carl Czerny are among the thousands of people who line the streets to pay their respects.

1832 The funeral is held for Muzio Clementi at Westminster Abbey.

1871 The Royal Albert Hall, named after the Prince Consort, opens in London. Queen Victoria attends the opening ceremony.

1891 Gustav Mahler makes his debut as principal conductor at the Stadttheater in Hamburg.

1894 A memorial service is held for the conductor Hans von Bülow in Hamburg, with Gustav Mahler among the mourners.

1896 Anton Bruckner makes his last public appearance, at a concert in Vienna.

1899 Queen Victoria is charmed by a performance by Ruggero Leoncavallo of music from his *La bohème* and *Pagliacci*.

1905 Police and striking students clash at the St Petersburg Conservatoire.

1913 Igor Stravinsky finishes composing *The Rite of Spring*.

1972 Prime Minister Edward Heath holds a dinner to celebrate William Walton's 70th birthday. Guests include both the Queen and the Queen Mother, as well as fellow composers Benjamin Britten, Arthur Bliss and Herbert Howells.

 HALL OF FAME HIT
Giuseppe Verdi: *La traviata*

Recommended Recording
Various soloists; Orchestra e Coro del Teatro Regio di Parma conducted by Yuri Temirkanov; Tutto Verdi 723 704

> 'The notes I handle no better than many pianists. But the pauses between the notes – ah, that is where the art resides.'
>
> ARTUR SCHNABEL, PIANIST

30
MARCH

🗓 BIRTHS & DEATHS

1764 Italian composer Pietro Antonio Locatelli dies in Amsterdam.

1959 German clarinettist Sabine Meyer is born in Crailsheim.

1980 British (originally Italian) violinist and orchestra leader Annunzio Paolo Mantovani dies in Tunbridge Wells.

🎵 FIRST PERFORMED

1725 The second version of Johann Sebastian Bach's *St John Passion* receives its first performance, on Good Friday in Leipzig. The first version received its premiere in the same place on Good Friday 1724.

1899 Frederick Delius's *Koanga* is premiered, in the Elberfeld Stadttheater.

☀ TODAY'S THE DAY

1773 Seventeen-year-old Wolfgang Amadeus Mozart finishes composing his *Symphony No. 26*.

1836 A performance of Richard Wagner's opera *Das Liebesverbot* is cancelled after fighting breaks out on stage among the cast before the curtain goes up.

1881 Modest Mussorgsky is buried in St Petersburg. Alexander Borodin, César Cui, Mily Balakirev and Nikolai Rimsky-Korsakov are among the mourners.

1886 Isaac Albéniz is made assistant professor of piano at the Real Conservatorio in Madrid.

1889 Richard Strauss is appointed Kapellmeister in Weimar.

1904 Antonín Dvořák, well known for his love of trainspotting, catches a cold after spending the day at Prague railway station.

1905 Striking students cause damage at the St Petersburg Conservatoire, even letting off a stink bomb inside.

1920 The Juilliard Musical Foundation is registered in New York City.

1932 Thirteen-year-old Leonard Bernstein makes his public debut at the piano, in Boston.

1943 Sergei Rachmaninov's funeral is held in the Los Angeles Russian Orthodox Church. He is buried at the Kensico Cemetery near Valhalla, New York.

INSTRUMENT FOCUS:

Clarinet

A member of the woodwind family, the clarinet is a single-reed instrument. It originated around 1690, but the version we know today came into being only towards the middle of the 19th century. Mozart was the first composer to use the clarinet in a symphony. Clarinets come in a whole host of different varieties, so it is important to know which one is which. The clarinet that appears in most orchestral settings is usually pitched in the key of B flat – which means that when it plays a written C in the music, it actually sounds as a B flat, one note lower. There is also a range of other clarinets in, variously, A, E flat, D and F – as well as a bass clarinet – each of which plays its sounded notes differently from its written notes.

🎵 HALL OF FAME HIT

Modest Mussorgsky: *Pictures at an Exhibition*

Recommended Recording

(orchestrated by Maurice Ravel) Kirov Orchestra conducted by Valery Gergiev; Classic FM FW 060

31

MARCH

'Three farts and a raspberry.'

JOHN BARBIROLLI, CONDUCTOR, ABOUT CONTEMPORARY MUSIC

🎵 BIRTHS & DEATHS

1732 Austrian composer Joseph Haydn is born in Rohrau.
1872 Russian ballet master Sergei Diaghilev is born in Selischi.
1901 English composer John Stainer dies in Verona.

🎭 FIRST PERFORMED

1784 Wofgang Amadeus Mozart's *Piano Concerto No. 16* is first performed, in Vienna.
1794 Joseph Haydn's *Symphony No. 100* ('Military') is given its first performance, at the Hanover Square Rooms in London. It's the composer's 62nd birthday.
1901 Antonín Dvořák's *Rusalka* is premiered at the National Theatre in Prague.

1961 Jean Françaix's *The Flower Clock* is first performed by the Philadelphia Orchestra, conducted by Eugene Ormandy.

☀️ TODAY'S THE DAY

1780 France's King Louis XVI bans Italian comic opera from the Théâtre-Italien. Instead, he wants to see only home-grown comic opera on the French stage.
1795 Ludwig van Beethoven performs at a concert in aid of Mozart's widow, Constanze.
1837 Franz Liszt holds a charity piano duel with Sigismond Thalberg in Paris. The result is declared a draw.
1841 Clara Schumann, who has achieved superstar status as a performer, makes her first onstage appearance since her wedding to Robert Schumann in a concert at the Leipzig Gewandhaus.
1878 Richard Wagner comes to a formal financial agreement with those to whom he owes money over the building of his specially designed theatre in Bayreuth.
1905 Enrique Granados makes his concert debut in Paris at the relatively late age of 37.
1909 Despite feeling considerably under the weather with a nasty bout of flu, Gustav Mahler makes his debut as the conductor of the New York Philharmonic.

MUSICAL TERM:

Score

A score is a printed or handwritten copy of a piece of music, which shows all the parts necessary for a complete performance, arranged on different staves. A full orchestral score is a mass of around 30 or so separate lines, each allowing the conductor to see the music played by a certain instrument or group of instruments of the orchestra. Scores often come in reduced formats, one of the most common being a piano score, where the full orchestral part has been reduced down to be playable by a pianist, a task often undertaken by the composer himself.

🎵 HALL OF FAME HIT

Edward Elgar: *The Dream of Gerontius*

Recommended Recording

Various soloists; London Symphony Orchestra and Chorus conducted by Colin Davis; LSO Live 0083

April

01

APRIL

'I love Wagner, but the music I prefer is that of a cat hung up by its tail outside a window and trying to stick to the panes of glass with its claws.'

CHARLES BAUDELAIRE, POET

🕐 BIRTHS & DEATHS

1866 Italian composer Ferruccio Busoni is born near Florence.

1873 Russian composer Sergei Rachmaninov is born in Novgorod.

1917 American composer Scott Joplin dies in New York.

1959 German conductor Christian Thielemann is born in Berlin.

🎵 FIRST PERFORMED

1747 George Frideric Handel's oratorio *Judas Maccabeus* is premiered at Covent Garden in London.

1894 Sergei Rachmaninov's symphonic poem *The Rock* is given its first performance, in Moscow, on the composer's 21st birthday.

☀ TODAY'S THE DAY

1765 Karl Ditters von Dittersdorf is appointed Kapellmeister to the Bishop of Grosswardein, taking over from Michael Haydn (Joseph's brother).

1770 In Florence, 14-year-old Wolfgang Amadeus Mozart meets the man who will become Emperor Leopold II.

1804 Johann Nepomuk Hummel is appointed Konzertmeister to Prince Nikolaus Esterházy. Joseph Haydn is still the Kapellmeister, but this is now more of an honorary position, with Hummel doing most of the day-to-day work.

1825 Two teenage prodigies meet in Paris, when 16-year-old Felix Mendelssohn hears 13-year-old Franz Liszt play piano for the first time.

1837 Richard Wagner is given the job as music director of the city theatre in Königsberg.

1849 Richard Wagner conducts his last concert, in Dresden, with a programme including Beethoven's *Symphony No. 9.*

1865 Edvard Grieg makes his public conducting debut, in Copenhagen.

1888 Alkan is buried in Montmartre Cemetery.

1901 Claude Debussy takes up his pen as a music critic, under the pseudonym 'Monsieur Croche'.

1923 At his house near Vienna, Arnold Schoenberg explains the principles of his new twelve-tone method of composing music to Alban Berg.

1938 Hitler bans recordings of music by Jewish musicians and composers in Germany.

1969 The New York Philharmonic invites Pierre Boulez to take over as music director, but he fears it is an April Fool's joke.

🎵 HALL OF FAME HIT
Richard Wagner: *Tannhäuser*

Recommended Recording
Various soloists; Staatskapelle Berlin; Choir of the German State Opera conducted by Daniel Barenboim; Warner Classics 2564 680207

> 'The Artistic Temperament is a disease that afflicts amateurs.'
> G. K. CHESTERTON, WRITER

BIRTHS & DEATHS

1703 Johann Christoph Bach is buried in Eisenach.

1805 Danish writer and librettist Hans Christian Andersen is born in Odense.

1851 Russian violinist Adolph Brodsky is born in Taganrog.

1946 English classical music impresario Raymond Gubbay is born in London.

FIRST PERFORMED

1798 Joseph Haydn's oratorio *The Creation* is premiered in Vienna.

1800 Ludwig van Beethoven's *Symphony No. 1* is given its first performance, at the Burgtheater in Vienna with the composer conducting.

1911 The first suite from Maurice Ravel's *Daphnis and Chloe* receives its first performance, in Paris.

1958 Ralph Vaughan Williams' *Symphony No. 9* is first performed, at the Royal Festival Hall in London.

TODAY'S THE DAY

1720 The first season of the original Royal Academy of Music opens in London.

1768 Carl Philipp Emanuel Bach takes over as Kapellmeister in Hamburg.

1770 Leopold Mozart and his son Wolfgang Amadeus perform in the presence of Duke Leopold in Florence.

1785 Christoph Willibald von Gluck signs his last will and testament, leaving his estate to his wife.

1826 Alkan makes his public performance debut at the piano, in Paris.

1833 Frédéric Chopin and Franz Liszt perform the latter's *Sonata for Four Hands* as a fundraiser for the actress (and later wife of Hector Berlioz) Harriet Smithson.

1842 The USA's oldest symphony orchestra, the New York Philharmonic, is founded.

1844 The new Glasgow Musical Association (subsequently the Glasgow Choral Union) gives the first performance of Handel's *Messiah* in the city.

1915 Alexander Scriabin makes his final public appearance in St Petersburg, to great critical acclaim. He was to die within a fortnight.

1956 Leonard Bernstein signs his first contract with Columbia Records.

Anonymous

Alongside 'Traditional', 'Anonymous' is among the most prolific of all composing credits in classical music. It covers the tunes for which, thanks to the passage of time and the lack of documentation, the composer is unknown. The further back in musical history we go, the more anonymous music there is – largely due to the fact that before printing presses were invented, the dissemination of musical manuscripts depended heavily on monks copying out every single note by hand. Many tunes that we consider to be 'folk' music were never written down at all. Instead, successive generations learned the music by heart and passed it on to those who followed them.

HALL OF FAME HIT
Richard Wagner: *Die Walküre*

Recommended Recording
Various soloists; Bayreuth Festival Orchestra and Choir conducted by Daniel Barenboim; Teldec 2564 677140

03

> 'If there is anyone here whom I have not insulted, I beg his pardon.'
>
> JOHANNES BRAHMS, COMPOSER, ON HIS WAY OUT OF A PARTY

APRIL

BIRTHS & DEATHS

1897 German composer Johannes Brahms dies in Vienna.

1901 Richard D'Oyly Carte, English producer of Gilbert and Sullivan's operettas, dies in London.

1950 German (latterly American) composer Kurt Weill dies in New York.

1986 English tenor Peter Pears dies in Aldeburgh.

FIRST PERFORMED

1815 Luigi Cherubini's *Overture in G* is first performed, with the Royal Philharmonic Society in London.

1869 Edvard Grieg's *Piano Concerto* receives its first performance, in Copenhagen.

1911 Jean Sibelius's *Symphony No. 4* is given its first performance, in Helsinki.

TODAY'S THE DAY

1775 Pianist Muzio Clementi makes his London debut at the city's Hickford's Rooms.

1781 Wolfgang Amadeus Mozart is back on the concert platform in Vienna for the first time since he was a boy. Emperor Joseph II is in the audience.

1827 Mozart's *Requiem* is performed at a memorial service for Ludwig van Beethoven in Vienna.

1843 Felix Mendelssohn's dream of opening a conservatoire in Leipzig becomes a reality.

1860 Anton Bruckner passes a correspondence course in advanced counterpoint. At the age of 35, he is something of a latecomer to music theory.

1880 Gilbert and Sullivan's *The Pirates of Penzance* opens in London. Its official premiere was in the USA four months earlier, in an attempt to prevent unofficial American performances of the new operetta. A lack of copyright protection for foreigners in the USA meant that anyone could stage a production, with no royalties flowing to the composer and librettist.

1886 A 75th birthday party is thrown for Franz Liszt at Westwood House in Sydenham, South London.

1924 Charles Villiers Stanford's funeral is held in Westminster Abbey.

1930 Gustav Holst is presented with the Royal Philharmonic Society's Gold Medal.

1933 A performance by the Berlin Philharmonic conducted by Richard Strauss is cancelled after a large proportion of the audience return their tickets, outraged that Strauss has agreed to replace Bruno Walter as conductor. The latter has been removed from the concert because he is Jewish.

1982 Carl Orff is buried in Andechs.

HALL OF FAME HIT

Richard Wagner: *Tristan and Isolde*

Recommended Recording

Various soloists; Staatskapelle Dresden conducted by Carlos Kleiber; Deutsche Grammophon 413315

> 'Since the war began he [Saint-Saëns] has composed music for the stage, melodies, an elegy and a piece for the trombone. If he'd been making shell-cases instead it might have been all the better for music.'

MAURICE RAVEL, COMPOSER, WHO HIMSELF WORKED AS AN AMBULANCE DRIVER DURING THE FIRST WORLD WAR

🎵 BIRTHS & DEATHS

1843 Hungarian conductor Hans Richter is born in Raab.

1922 American composer Elmer Bernstein is born in New York.

1957 English organist Thomas Trotter is born in Birkenhead.

1960 English soprano Jane Eaglen is born in Lincoln.

1972 Russian conductor Vladimir Jurowski is born in Moscow.

🎵 FIRST PERFORMED

1739 Handel's oratorio *Israel in Egypt* is premiered at the King's Theatre in London.

1779 Wolfgang Amadeus Mozart's *'Coronation' Mass in C* is given its first performance, in Salzburg Cathedral.

1838 Excerpts from Mikhail Glinka's *Russlan and Ludmilla* are performed for the first time, in St Petersburg.

1861 Johann Strauss Junior's *Perpetuum Mobile* receives its first performance, in Vienna.

1867 Camille Saint-Saëns' *Violin Concerto No. 1* is premiered, in Paris.

1875 Bedřich Smetana's *Vltava*, from *Má Vlast*, is given its first performance, in Prague. By now, Smetana is deaf and so does not hear his own work. A young Leoš Janáček is in the audience.

1977 Henryk Górecki's *Symphony No. 3* ('Symphony of Sorrowful Songs') is premiered, in Royan.

☀ TODAY'S THE DAY

1900 Antonín Dvořák makes his final conducting appearance, with the Czech Philharmonic in Prague.

1905 Alexander Glazunov walks out of his job as a professor at the St Petersburg Conservatoire in disgust at the sacking of Nikolai Rimsky-Korsakov.

INSTRUMENT FOCUS:

Organ

The organ is a monster of an instrument, often employing up to five keyboards (known as manuals), a pedal board and sometimes more than a hundred stops. Although born in ancient Greece (where water was often used to create the necessary pressure), it was in the sixth and seventh centuries that an air-bellowed version of the organ began to come into its own. By J. S. Bach's time, a golden age of organ building had led to a mass of complex music being written for what was then regarded as a high-tech instrument. Two organs to 'name-drop' in conversation: the Royal Albert Hall's organ, with 147 stops and an amazing 9,997 pipes; and Westminster Abbey's organ, with 5 manuals and 109 stops, first used at the Coronation of George VI.

🎵 HALL OF FAME HIT

Léo Delibes: *Lakmé*

Recommended Recording

Various soloists, Chœur du Capitole de Toulouse; Orchestre National du Capitole de Toulouse conducted by Michel Plasson; EMI Highlights 094 8482

05

‘What's the difference between God and Herbert von Karajan? God doesn't think He's a conductor.’

JOKE ATTRIBUTED TO ONE OF VON KARAJAN'S MUSICIANS

APRIL

BIRTHS & DEATHS

1784 German composer Louis Spohr is born in Brunswick.

1908 Austrian conductor Herbert von Karajan is born in Salzburg.

1959 English pianist Julius Drake is born in London.

FIRST PERFORMED

1803 Ludwig van Beethoven's *Symphony No. 2* and *Piano Concerto No. 3* are given their first performances, with the composer as soloist for the concerto, in Vienna.

1811 Carl Maria von Weber's *Clarinet Concertino* is first performed, in Munich. King Maximilian, who was in the audience, liked it so much that he ordered Weber to compose two more clarinet concertos.

1874 Johann Strauss Junior's operetta *Die Fledermaus* is premiered in Vienna.

1902 Maurice Ravel's *Jeux d'eau* and *Pavane pour une infante défunte* receive their first performances, in Paris.

1913 Erik Satie's *Veritable Flabby Preludes (for a dog)* are premiered, in Paris.

1987 Philip Glass's *Violin Concerto* is given its first performance, in New York.

TODAY'S THE DAY

1717 Composer Domenico Zipoli sails from Cadiz to train as a Jesuit missionary in South America.

1801 An official government report published in Venice into the death of Domenico Cimarosa shows that, contrary to rumours at the time, he did not die of poisoning but most probably cancer.

1833 Robert Schumann writes to a friend, telling him that he has broken one of his fingers – hardly good news for a professional musician.

1903 Gabriel Fauré is made an officer of France's Légion d'Honneur.

1960 Leonard Bernstein conducts a special performance by the New York Philharmonic at the White House in the presence of President Eisenhower. Gershwin's *Rhapsody in Blue* goes down particularly well with the President.

COMPOSER PROFILE:

Louis Spohr

Spohr was a violin prodigy who became one of the most successful composers of his day. He toured Russia and Germany as both violinist and conductor. Several visits to the UK (at the behest of the Royal Philharmonic Society) not only made him famous here but also prompted the vogue for conducting with a baton, which has been standard practice ever since. Alongside the popularisation of the baton among conductors, he is also credited with the introduction of the chin-rest for violinists, so he was quite the classical music revolutionary.

HALL OF FAME HIT

Giuseppe Verdi: *Aida*

Recommended Recording

Various soloists; Orchestra e Coro del Teatro Dell'Opera di Roma conducted by Georg Solti; Urania Records 204

'The music of the zither, the flute and the lyre enervates the mind.'

OVID, GREEK POET

BIRTHS & DEATHS

1929 American (originally German) composer, pianist and conductor André Previn is born in Berlin.

1951 French pianist Pascal Rogé is born in Paris.

1953 Scottish composer Patrick Doyle is born in Birkenshaw.

1971 Russian composer Igor Stravinsky dies in New York.

TODAY'S THE DAY

1768 Twelve-year-old Wolfgang Amadeus Mozart and his elder sister Maria Anna perform at the wedding celebrations in Vienna for Archduchess Maria Carolina and King Ferdinando of Naples.

1774 Wolfgang Amadeus Mozart finishes work on his *Symphony No. 29* in Salzburg.

1785 Leopold Mozart joins a Freemasons' lodge in Vienna.

1826 Carl Maria von Weber is made the first honorary member of the Royal Philharmonic Society.

1847 London's Covent Garden Theatre reopens after being converted into an opera house with a production of Rossini's *Semiramide*.

1856 Alexander Borodin passes his exams to become a medical doctor, working at a military hospital, where he meets the teenage soldier Modest Mussorgsky.

1886 Franz Liszt presents a cheque for £1,100 to the Royal Academy of Music, to establish a scholarship there in his name.

1897 Johannes Brahms is buried in Vienna, not far from where Beethoven and Schubert had been laid to rest.

COMPOSER PROFILE:

Alexander Borodin

The illegitimate son of a Russian prince, Borodin was a talented chemist who opted for science over music as a full-time career. He studied medicine in St Petersburg before eventually becoming a professor of chemistry. However, he continued to compose – he described himself as a 'Sunday composer'. His *Symphony No. 1* was eventually premiered when he was 36 years old, after which it took him roughly seven years to produce another. Its tardy appearance was not helped by his losing part of the manuscript and having to write it again. At the age of 54, he died in national costume, dressed in full-length Cossack boots, a big red shirt and baggy blue trousers, having suffered a heart attack at a dance. He left behind an incomplete opera, *Prince Igor*, which he had worked on intermittently for 18 years. It was finished by his great friends Rimsky-Korsakov and Glazunov.

HALL OF FAME HIT
Franz Schubert: *String Quintet D956*

Recommended Recording
Janine Jansen (violin); Boris Brovtsyn (violin); Maxim Rysanov (viola); Torleif Thedéen (cello); Jens Peter Maintz (cello); Decca 478 3551

07

APRIL

'I love to play for people . . . sometimes when I sit down to practise and there is no one else in the room, I have to stifle an impulse to ring for the elevator man and offer him money to come and hear me.'

ARTHUR RUBINSTEIN, PIANIST

🕐 BIRTHS & DEATHS

1820 English conductor Alfred Mellon is born in London.

1970 Norwegian pianist Leif Ove Andsnes is born in Karmøy.

🎭 FIRST PERFORMED

1786 Wolfgang Amadeus Mozart's *Piano Concerto No. 24* is first performed, in Vienna, with the composer as the soloist.

1805 Ludwig van Beethoven's *Symphony No. 3 ('Eroica')* has its first public airing, in Vienna, after a private performance the previous year.

☀ TODAY'S THE DAY

1768 William Boyce resigns from his job at St Michael's, Cornhill, after suggestions that his organ playing isn't up to scratch.

1805 The librettist Lorenzo da Ponte, who wrote the words to some of Mozart's most famous operas, jumps on a ship to America, to get away from his creditors.

1886 Franz Liszt performs in a private concert for Queen Victoria at Windsor Castle.

1917 Sergei Rachmaninov performs a mammoth three concerts (with music by himself, Tchaikovsky and Liszt) in Moscow's Bolshoi Theatre.

1920 Edward Elgar's wife Alice dies in his arms at their London home.

1933 As anti-Semitism worsens in Germany, all Jewish musicians are banned from playing for state-run orchestras and from holding professorships at German universities.

COMPOSER PROFILE:

Franz Liszt

Taught by the composers Salieri and Czerny, Liszt was quickly singled out for his prodigious talent. He gave his first piano recital at the age of nine and was playing for kings and queens by the time he was 12. Just two years later, his first opera was produced. As an adult, he was a friend of Chopin and Berlioz. He was something of a ladies' man and was a flamboyant and highly gifted performer on stage, often playing his own piano transcriptions of other people's works. Despite his colourful private life, he took holy orders when he was nearly 50, although this did not seem to curb his appetite for romance wherever he travelled. As a composer, he was a major influence on other significant Romantic musicians, such as Wagner and Richard Strauss.

🎵 HALL OF FAME HIT

Henryk Górecki: *Symphony No. 3 ('Symphony of Sorrowful Songs')*

Recommended Recording

Dawn Upshaw; London Sinfonietta conducted by David Zinman; Nonesuch 7559 792822

> 'Two skeletons copulating on a tin roof in a thunderstorm.'
>
> **THOMAS BEECHAM, CONDUCTOR, DESCRIBING THE SOUND OF A HARPSICHORD**

🎵 BIRTHS & DEATHS

1692 Italian composer Giuseppe Tartini is born in Pirano, Istria (now in Slovenia).

1810 Italian castrato Venanzio Rauzzini dies in Bath.

1848 Italian composer Gaetano Donizetti dies in Bergamo.

1889 English conductor Adrian Boult is born in Chester.

1921 Czech composer Jan Novák is born in Nová Říše.

🎵 FIRST PERFORMED

1708 George Frideric Handel's *The Resurrection* is first performed, in Rome, with Arcangelo Corelli conducting.

1781 Wolfgang Amadeus Mozart's *Violin Sonata No. 27* and *Rondo in C for violin and orchestra* gain their first public airings.

1876 Amilcare Ponchielli's opera *La Gioconda* is premiered at the La Scala in Milan.

☀ TODAY'S THE DAY

1778 The possessions of composer Thomas Arne are sold, following his death. They include a harpsichord, two guitars and a mandolin.

1781 Wolfgang Amadeus Mozart misses out on a huge payday, when his boss Archbishop Colloredo of Salzburg bans him from performing for Emperor Joseph II. Instead, Mozart performs for the Archbishop.

1805 Joseph Haydn, by now in his seventies, hears Mozart's 14-year-old son Franz Xaver Mozart make his public debut. The veteran composer is full of praise.

1820 As part of a protracted custody battle, Ludwig van Beethoven is made guardian for his nephew Karl. The decision overturns a previous court ruling in favour of the boy's mother.

1878 Composer Charles Villiers Stanford marries a singer, Jennie Wetton. His parents are not impressed.

1897 Newspapers report that Gustav Mahler has been hired as a conductor at the Vienna Opera.

1904 Composer Ruggero Leoncavallo accompanies the tenor Enrico Caruso in a Gramophone and Typewriter Company recording of his '*Mattinata*' at the Grand Hotel in Milan. The song was written especially for the occasion.

🎵 HALL OF FAME HIT
Georges Bizet: *Carmen*

Recommended Recording
Various soloists; Berlin Philharmonic Orchestra and the Choir of the German State Opera conducted by Simon Rattle; EMI Classics 440 2852

09

'Let me tell you, you have the talent for it.'

FRANZ LISZT TO EDVARD GRIEG, AFTER PLAYING THROUGH THE LATTER'S PIANO CONCERTO

BIRTHS & DEATHS

1898 American bass Paul Robeson is born in Princeton.
1906 Hungarian (later American) conductor Antal Dorati is born in Budapest.

FIRST PERFORMED

1977 A suite from Leonard Bernstein's musical *Candide* is given its first performance, in Tel Aviv.

TODAY'S THE DAY

1765 A London newspaper carries an advertisement stating that Wolfgang Amadeus Mozart (who is nine years old) and his sister Maria Anna will be available to show off their musical ability at home for two hours from noon every day. Their father, Leopold, knows that the city's chattering classes only have to hear the youngsters perform for them to be bowled over by their talent.
1835 Franz Liszt collapses after performing at a concert with Hector Berlioz in Paris.

1886 Enrique Granados performs his debut piano concert, in Barcelona.
1898 Richard Strauss signs up for a one-year contract with the Berlin Opera.
1940 Carnegie Hall in New York is the venue for a demonstration by Bell Laboratories of stereo music on film.
1941 The Berlin State Opera is destroyed in an Allied bombing raid.

MUSICAL TERM:

Authentic performance

This term is not a reference to the provenance of a piece of music – proving that it has been written by a certain composer. Instead, it is all about the manner in which music is played. When we say that something is an 'authentic performance' we are confirming that what we are hearing today is genuinely what the composer would have expected to hear when the work was written. Often, this means that the performers have to play on instruments that were around at the time of composition, without any modern tweaks.
Top exponents of this style of performance include the Orchestre Révolutionnaire et Romantique, founded by John Eliot Gardiner, and Les Musiciens du Louvre, formed in 1984 by Marc Minkowski.

HALL OF FAME HIT

Edward Elgar: *Pomp and Circumstance Marches*

Recommended Recording

London Philharmonic Orchestra conducted by Adrian Boult; Heritage HTGCD 250

'Music is a science that would have us laugh and sing and dance.'

GUILLAUME DE MACHAUT, COMPOSER

10

🎵 BIRTHS & DEATHS

1955 English soprano Lesley Garrett is born in Doncaster.

1958 Israeli-American pianist Yefim Bronfman is born in Tashkent.

1979 Italian composer Nino Rota dies in Rome.

1987 New Zealand soprano Hayley Westenra is born in Christchurch.

🎵 FIRST PERFORMED

1820 Louis Spohr's *Symphony No. 2* is given its first performance at a Philharmonic Society concert in London, with the composer conducting the orchestra with his violin bow – an innovation.

1853 Charles Gounod's '*Ave Maria*' is first performed, in Paris.

1868 Part of Johannes Brahms' *A German Requiem* receives its first performance, in Bremen Cathedral, with the composer conducting and Clara Schumann, Max Bruch and the celebrated violinist Joseph Joachim in the star-studded audience.

1935 Ralph Vaughan Williams' *Symphony No. 4* is first performed, at the Queen's Hall, London, with Adrian Boult conducting.

☀️ TODAY'S THE DAY

1602 Claudio Monteverdi is granted citizenship of Mantua.

1764 Leopold, Wolfgang and Maria Anna Mozart leave Paris for London, as their European tour continues.

1770 The Mozart family arrives in Rome. It was on this visit that Wolfgang Amadeus is believed to have written out the whole of Allegri's *Miserere* from memory, after hearing it performed in the Vatican.

1859 Franz Liszt is inducted into the Order of the Iron Crown by Emperor Franz Joseph II. The honour entitles Liszt to request a knighthood from the Emperor.

1861 Eighteen-year-old Arthur Sullivan receives his diploma from Leipzig Conservatoire.

1865 Despite the fact that, only hours beforehand, his wife had given birth to Richard Wagner's child (the two having pursued an affair for some time), Hans von Bülow conducts the opening rehearsal for Wagner's opera *Tristan and Isolde*.

1904 Erik Satie is taken away by police after fighting with a critic during a Beethoven concert in Paris.

🎵 HALL OF FAME HIT
Thomas Tallis: *Spem in Alium*

Recommended Recording
Tallis Scholars conducted by Peter Phillips; Gimell CDGIM 203

‘Music hath charms to soothe the savage beast, but I'd try a revolver first.’

JOSH BILLINGS, HUMORIST

APRIL

BIRTHS & DEATHS

1819 English (originally German) conductor Charles Hallé is born in Hagen.

FIRST PERFORMED

1689 Henry Purcell's opera *Dido and Aeneas* is first performed, at Josias Priest's School for Young Ladies in Chelsea.

1727 Johann Sebastian Bach's *St Matthew Passion* receives its first performance, in Leipzig.

1814 Ludwig van Beethoven's *'Archduke' Piano Trio* is premiered in Vienna, with the composer at the piano. Fellow composer Louis Spohr commented that the piano was out of tune, but Beethoven failed to realise because of his deafness.

1919 Maurice Ravel's *Le tombeau de Couperin* is given its first performance, in Paris.

TODAY'S THE DAY

1668 Dietrich Buxtehude is appointed the organist at the Marienkirche in Lübeck.

1759 George Frideric Handel updates his will to include a bequest of £1,000 to the 'Society for the Support of Decay'd Musicians'.

1789 Ten-year-old English violinist George Bridgetower makes his debut in Paris.

1830 Nineteen-year-old Robert Schumann hears Niccolò Paganini give a performance on the violin for the first time, in Frankfurt.

1844 After taking Vienna and Paris by storm, a polka is performed for the first time in London, on the stage of Her Majesty's Theatre.

1844 Niccolò Paganini's remains are finally allowed to be buried on church ground, three years after his death. It followed rumours that his violin virtuosity was so great that it could have been achieved only through a pact with the Devil himself.

1848 The funeral is held for Gaetano Donizetti in Bergamo.

1858 Franz Liszt becomes a monk. There is little evidence of him adopting the monastic existence that usually comes with the job.

1888 The Royal Concertgebouw opens in Amsterdam.

1906 Edvard Grieg makes a piano-roll recording of six of his works in Leipzig.

1922 Beethoven's *'Coriolan' Overture* becomes the first recording for the New York Philharmonic.

1942 It's announced that Dmitri Shostakovich is the winner of the Stalin Prize for his *Symphony No. 7*.

1958 Van Cliburn performs Rachmaninov's *Piano Concerto No. 3* at the Tchaikovsky International Piano Competition in Moscow, setting himself on the pathway to becoming a global superstar.

HALL OF FAME HIT

George Frideric Handel: *Water Music Suites*

Recommended Recording

Les Musiciens du Louvre conducted by Marc Minkowski; Naïve V 5234

> 'So perfect a band was never before heard on this side of the Channel.'
>
> **REVIEW IN THE MORNING POST, TODAY IN 1838, ABOUT THE JOHANN STRAUSS ORCHESTRA**

12

APRIL

BIRTHS & DEATHS

1684 Italian violin-maker Niccolò Amati dies in Cremona.

1801 Austrian composer and dance master Joseph Lanner is born in Vienna.

1933 Spanish soprano Montserrat Caballé is born in Barcelona.

FIRST PERFORMED

1919 A revised version of Igor Stravinsky's *Firebird Suite* is first performed, in Geneva.

1955 The film *The Gadfly*, with a soundtrack by Dmitri Shostakovich, is first shown.

TODAY'S THE DAY

1781 Wolfgang Amadeus Mozart is told in no uncertain terms by his boss Archbishop Colloredo to return to Salzburg from Vienna in ten days' time. Mozart fails to comply with the order.

1813 Ludwig van Beethoven's brother, who is seriously ill, makes the composer the official guardian of his son, Karl, on his death.

1838 Johann Strauss Senior arrives in London at the start of a UK tour that will last for the next 33 weeks.

1838 In a letter dated today, Franz Liszt proves that everyday sexism was alive and well in the 19th century, when he writes about the 18-year-old Clara Schumann, 'Her compositions are truly most remarkable, especially for a woman.'

1846 Felix Mendelssohn performs Beethoven's *'Moonlight' Sonata* in Leipzig. In the same concert he performs with soprano Jenny Lind, violinist Ferdinand David and in piano duets with Clara Schumann.

1853 Gioachino Rossini is appointed a Commander of the Légion d'Honneur by Emperor Napoleon III.

1854 Eleven-year-old Arthur Sullivan joins the choir of the Chapel Royal.

1858 Hector Berlioz finishes three years of toil on his masterpiece *Les Troyens*.

1950 Soprano Maria Callas makes her performance debut at La Scala, Milan, taking the title role in *Aida*.

1961 Russian cosmonaut Yuri Gagarin sings *'My homeland hears, my homeland knows where in the skies her son soars on'* to a tune written by Dmitri Shostakovich. It is the first time that music created by a human being can be described as literally 'out of this world'.

HALL OF FAME HIT

Antonín Dvořák: *Cello Concerto*

Recommended Recording

Mario Brunello (cello); Orchestra dell'Accademia Nazionale di Santa Cecilia conducted by Antonio Pappano; EMI Classics 914 1022

13

'He composes by splashing ink over his manuscript paper; the result is as chance wills it.'

HECTOR BERLIOZ ON FELLOW COMPOSER FRÉDÉRIC CHOPIN

APRIL

BIRTHS & DEATHS

1377 French composer Guillaume de Machaut dies in Reims.

1816 English composer William Sterndale Bennett is born in Sheffield.

1910 German piano-maker Julius Blüthner dies in Leipzig.

1941 Welsh soprano Margaret Price is born in Gwent.

1946 Welsh soprano Della Jones is born in Neath.

FIRST PERFORMED

1742 George Frideric Handel's *Messiah* is premiered in Dublin.

1896 Jean Sibelius's *The Swan of Tuonela* is given its first performance, in Helsinki, with the composer conducting.

TODAY'S THE DAY

1829 The father of 19-year-old Frédéric Chopin writes to the Polish government to request financial help for his son in studying music abroad. The plea is declined as it is seen as a waste of public money.

1845 Richard Wagner completes the full score of his opera *Tannhäuser*.

1958 In Moscow, the Tchaikovsky International Piano Competition jury votes to give the first prize to Van Cliburn. The 23-year-old is the first American to win the competition.

1991 Composer John Tavener undergoes heart surgery at a London hospital.

Musical nationalism

While it is true to say that nationalism has been around for as long as there have been nations, the main period during which it flourished was the 19th century, often alongside, and as a bi-product of, political movements for change. In the music world, it is often pithily labelled 'patriotism in music'. It is the desire by composers to reflect audibly, to varying extents, the nations within which they were born. The idea is that the listeners will be able to hear the nationality in the music. Sometimes this is achieved by the use of traditional folk songs, tunes and rhythms, which are incorporated into the music. On other occasions, composers simply write their own material in the style of their country's traditional music. Russian, Scandinavian and Czech nationalism are all particularly strongly represented in classical music.

HALL OF FAME HIT

George Butterworth: *The Banks of Green Willow*

Recommended Recording

English String Orchestra conducted by William Boughton; Nimbus NI5068

> 'As a musician I tell you that if you were to suppress adultery, fanaticism, crime, evil, the supernatural, there would no longer be the means for writing one note.'
>
> **GEORGES BIZET, COMPOSER**

BIRTHS & DEATHS

1759 George Frideric Handel dies at his home in Brook Street, London.

1843 Austrian composer and dance master Joseph Lanner dies in Oberdöbling.

1859 Austrian piano-maker Ignaz Bösendorfer dies in Vienna.

1929 Finnish conductor Paavo Berglund is born in Helsinki.

1949 Scottish trumpeter and former Principal of the Royal Conservatoire of Scotland, John Wallace, is born in Methihill, Fife.

1951 English cellist Julian Lloyd Webber is born in London.

1956 American soprano Barbara Bonney is born in Montclair, New Jersey.

1957 Russian pianist and conductor Mikhail Pletnev is born in Arkhangelsk.

1982 American cellist Alisa Weilerstein is born in Rochester, New York.

2013 English conductor Colin Davis dies in London.

FIRST PERFORMED

1883 Léo Delibes' opera *Lakmé* is premiered in Paris.

TODAY'S THE DAY

1775 Wolfgang Amadeus Mozart finishes work on his *Violin Concerto No. 1* in Salzburg.

1831 In one of the more unlikely stories in classical music history, Hector Berlioz receives a letter from his fiancée's mother suggesting that his girlfriend is about to marry another man. He sets off from Florence to Paris, planning to kill both mother and daughter, while disguised as a maid. Thankfully, he doesn't follow through with the plot.

1849 Fifteen-year-old Johannes Brahms performs his second piano recital, in Hamburg, to critical acclaim.

1856 Clara Schumann plays for the first time for London audiences, with a performance of Beethoven's '*Emperor*' Concerto, at the Hanover Square Rooms.

1998 George Gershwin receives a posthumous award from the Pulitzer Committee to mark his contribution to American music, commemorating a century since he was born.

Encore

The French word for 'again' is shouted by audiences at the end of a concert, to encourage the performers to play a little bit more. It is also the name for the pieces that are played after the official end of the concert and which are often designed to show off a performer's talents at their very best. Some performers become as famous for their encores as they are for playing the main body of their concerts. Although they are made to look spontaneous, most encores are prepared in advance. An interesting footnote: although 'encore' is a French word, it is not what concertgoers in France shout when they want more from a performer. Perplexingly, the French for encore is *bis*, which translates into English as 'twice'.

 HALL OF FAME HIT
Gabriel Fauré: *Pavane*

Recommended Recording
Orchestre de Paris; Chœur de l'Orchestre de Paris conducted by Paavo Järvi; Virgin 070 9212

15

APRIL

'An opera begins long before the curtain goes up and ends long after it has come down. It starts in my imagination, it becomes my life, and it stays part of my life long after I've left the opera house.'

MARIA CALLAS, SOPRANO

BIRTHS & DEATHS

1924 English conductor and violinist Neville Marriner is born in Lincoln.

1948 American composer Michael Kamen is born in New York.

FIRST PERFORMED

1738 George Frideric Handel's opera *Xerxes* is premiered at the King's Theatre, London.

2009 Tan Dun's *Internet Symphony No. 1* is given its first performance, at Carnegie Hall in New York, conducted by the composer. The work was commissioned by Google and YouTube and featured performers from all over the world, who were chosen on the basis of recordings of their own performances that they had uploaded online.

TODAY'S THE DAY

1770 Pope Clement XIV grants Leopold and Wolfgang Amadeus Mozart an audience at the Vatican.

1898 Richard Strauss signs up to become the conductor of the Berlin Court Opera.

ORCHESTRA FOCUS:

Academy of St Martin in the Fields

Founded by the violinist Neville Marriner in 1958, the Academy of St Martin in the Fields is based in a church of the same name just off Trafalgar Square in London. It is among the most recorded of all orchestras, with more than 500 discs to its name, and had a particularly busy period in the recording studio with the advent of CDs in the 1980s. Initially, it was formed by the musicians on a collegiate basis, without a conductor. But a couple of years after its launch, Marriner laid down his violin and took up the conductor's baton. The orchestra varies in size from chamber to symphonic strength.

Young talent

Some of the greatest composers didn't hang around when it came to making music in public. The Spanish composer Isaac Albéniz had his first professional engagement at just four years old. Felix Mendelssohn was nine years old when he first appeared before an audience. Wolfgang Amadeus Mozart was six when he went on his first tour, way ahead of César Franck – he didn't go on the road for the first time until the relatively advanced age of 11.

HALL OF FAME HIT

Pyotr Ilyich Tchaikovsky: *Romeo and Juliet*

Recommended Recording

Swedish Chamber Orchestra conducted by Thomas Dausgaard; BIS 1959

> 'The truth is, that within limits, any music can be made to fit any situation.'
>
> RALPH VAUGHAN WILLIAMS, COMPOSER

16
APRIL

BIRTHS & DEATHS

1924 American composer Henry Mancini is born in Cleveland.

FIRST PERFORMED

1735 George Frideric Handel's opera *Alcina* is premiered at London's Covent Garden Theatre.

1791 A revised version of Wolfgang Amadeus Mozart's *Symphony No. 40* receives its first performance, in Vienna, conducted by Antonio Salieri. This version is tweaked to include two clarinets.

1937 William Walton's march *Crown Imperial* is first performed, at an HMV recording session.

TODAY'S THE DAY

1632 Claudio Monteverdi enters the priesthood.

1779 William Boyce's music library is up for sale at the auctioneers Christie and Ansell.

1786 The New Musical Fund is set up to give financial help to musicians who have fallen on hard times, as well as to their widows and children. Uniquely for the time, musicians who live outside London qualify for grants.

1847 Felix Mendelssohn is in England to ensure all goes well with four performances of his oratorio *Elijah* in London and a further two in Manchester. Queen Victoria and Prince Albert will be among the audience members.

1850 Richard Wagner writes to his wife, telling her that he is separating from her. His latest dalliance is with the wife of a French wine merchant.

1895 Antonín Dvořák sets sail from New York, returning back home to Europe.

1917 The schoolboy Dmitri Shostakovich sees Lenin arrive at the Finland Station and make a historic speech.

1938 Sergei Prokofiev returns home to Russia from the USA.

MUSICAL TERM:

Harmony

The best way of explaining harmony in music is to borrow some thinking from the world of mathematics. Think of a graph with a horizontal x axis and a vertical y axis. A musical score works in much the same way. If we take one note and keep playing it, we are hearing it 'horizontally', so to speak. Putting other notes before or after it allows a tune, or melody to give it its correct name, to proceed horizontally. But, if we take that original note and simultaneously add other notes above and below it, then we have a chord. More than one note, sounded vertically on our axis, is harmony.

 HALL OF FAME HIT
Camille Saint-Saëns: *Carnival of the Animals*

Recommended Recording
Orchestral Ensemble of Paris; Mirare MIR 108

17

APRIL

'I always make sure that the lid over the keyboard is open before I start to play.'

ARTUR SCHNABEL, PIANIST, WHEN ASKED TO REVEAL THE SECRET OF PLAYING THE PIANO

BIRTHS & DEATHS

1790 American statesman and inventor of the glass harmonica Benjamin Franklin dies in Philadelphia.

1882 Austrian pianist Artur Schnabel is born in Lipnil.

1950 Brazilian pianist Cristina Ortiz is born in Bahia.

TODAY'S THE DAY

1831 Hector Berlioz nearly drowns, after falling into the sea at Genoa, while he is on the way to Florence to tackle his fiancée over her unfaithfulness.

1837 Tsar Alexander II approves the production of Modest Mussorgsky's opera *Boris Godunov*.

1849 Louis Moreau Gottschalk makes his professional performance debut at the piano in Paris.

1906 Enrico Caruso stars as Don José in a Metropolitan Opera production of Bizet's *Carmen* in San Francisco, shortly before a serious earthquake causes widespread damage in the city.

INSTRUMENT FOCUS:

Piano

The invention of the piano solved a problem that faced many 18th-century keyboard players: the lack of the ability of the clavichord and harpsichord to play loudly and quietly. A harpsichord is basically a box of strings that the player plucks via its keys. A clavichord is different because it hits its strings with metal blades called tangents, which stay in position until the keys are released. The volume produced depends on how hard a player can strike the keys. Either way, there was no sense of light and shade in the playing of both instruments.

The man who changed all that was an Italian called Bartolomeo Cristofori. He was born in Padua in 1655 and was possibly a cello- or violin-maker. While working in Florence for Duke Ferdinand de' Medici, he produced a keyboard with an action using hammers that allowed the string either to resonate or not, depending on whether the player wanted it to. The hammers then returned to a prone position, ready to be used again. This gave the new instrument both agility and volume. That unique selling point – the '*nuova invention che fa'il piano e il forte*', as Cristofori put it at the time – led to the instrument gaining the name 'Pianoforte', which translates as 'quiet loud'. Today, this has been shortened simply to 'piano'.

HALL OF FAME HIT

Wolfgang Amadeus Mozart: *Così fan tutte*

Recommended Recording

Various soloists; Concerto Cologne conducted by René Jacobs; Harmonia Mundi HMC 901663/65

> 'You don't need any brains to listen to music.'
> LUCIANO PAVAROTTI, TENOR

18

BIRTHS & DEATHS

1819 Austrian composer Franz von Suppé is born in Split.

1882 American conductor Leopold Stokowski is born in London.

1936 Italian composer Ottorino Respighi dies in Rome.

1944 British/Australian pianist Penelope Thwaites is born in Chester.

FIRST PERFORMED

1682 Jean-Baptiste Lully's opera *Perseus* is premiered in Paris.

1800 Ludwig van Beethoven's *Horn Sonata* is given its first performance, in Paris.

TODAY'S THE DAY

1831 Hector Berlioz is still on his way back to Paris to do away with both his fiancée and her mother. However, he takes the opportunity today to stop off for a month in Nice.

1838 Franz Liszt takes part in a charity fundraiser to help flood victims in Pest. As usual, he is the star of the show.

1842 Richard Wagner calls in to see Robert Schumann at his home in Leipzig.

1885 Pyotr Ilyich Tchaikovsky sends a letter to fellow composer Nikolai Rimsky-Korsakov, giving him the chance to become director of the Moscow Conservatoire.

1891 Pyotr Ilyich Tchaikovsky sets sail for New York from Le Havre.

1919 Sergei Rachmaninov undertakes his first gramophone recording session, which lasts for six days.

1999 The Three Tenors perform in Pretoria, South Africa.

COMPOSER PROFILE:

Franz von Suppé

Born in the then Dalmatian city of Spalato (now Split in Croatia), von Suppé's musical talent was first spotted by the local bandmaster and choirmaster. When von Suppé moved to Vienna, aged 16, he was determined to study music, despite false starts in law and medicine. He soon became not only an opera conductor, but also a singer, composing a huge number of stage works along the way and becoming a rival to Johann Strauss Junior for the title of 'the Viennese Offenbach'. However, the overtures to his operettas *Poet and Peasant* and *Morning, Noon and Night in Vienna* fare better these days than do the operas themselves.

♪ HALL OF FAME HIT
Camille Saint-Saëns: *Danse macabre*

Recommended Recording
Orchestre de Paris conducted by Daniel Barenboim; Deutsche Grammophon 474 6122

19

> 'Singers have the most marvellous breath control and can kiss for about ten minutes.'
>
> JILLY COOPER, NOVELIST

APRIL

BIRTHS & DEATHS

1836 American industrialist and founder of the illustrious New York music school that bears his name Augustus D. Juilliard is born on board a ship.

1876 English composer Samuel Sebastian Wesley dies in Gloucester.

1892 French composer Germaine Tailleferre is born in Pau-St Maur.

1935 English pianist and actor Dudley Moore is born in London.

1947 French conductor and violinist Yan-Pascal Tortelier is born in Paris.

1947 American pianist Murray Perahia is born in the Bronx, New York.

1963 English composer Graham Fitkin is born in Cornwall.

1965 French soprano Natalie Dessay is born in Lyons.

1966 French soprano Véronique Gens is born in Orléans.

1986 Swedish composer Dag Wirén dies in Stockholm.

FIRST PERFORMED

1897 Edward Elgar's *Imperial March* is first performed, at London's Crystal Palace, during Queen Victoria's Diamond Jubilee celebrations.

TODAY'S THE DAY

1768 Carl Philipp Emanuel Bach takes up his new job as Hamburg's main director of music.

1770 Leopold and Wolfgang Amadeus Mozart meet Bonnie Prince Charlie while staying in Rome.

1853 Nineteen-year-old Johannes Brahms begins a concert tour of cities near his home in Hamburg.

1871 Richard Wagner takes a look at the opera house in Bayreuth, but he is disappointed with the size of the stage. Undeterred, he opts to replace it with a new building.

1899 Sergei Rachmaninov appears on the London stage for the first time, as both conductor and soloist, at the Queen's Hall.

PROFILE:

Guido d'Arezzo

One of the earliest personalities to appear in this book, we have a lot to thank this Italian monk for. Born a few years before the turn of the first millennium, he invented a system called 'solmisation', which he used to help other monks learn chants very quickly. By giving names to musical notes, he enabled people to work out where they were on the scale – the same principle used by Julie Andrews' Maria to teach the von Trapp children in *The Sound of Music*. Guido wrote about it in *Micrologus*, which was published around the year 1025, earning him widespread fame across Italy. Today, he is widely regarded as the father of modern notation.

HALL OF FAME HIT

Johannes Brahms: *A German Requiem*

Recommended Recording

Anna Lucia Richter; Stephan Genz; Leipzig MDR Radio Symphony Chorus and Orchestra conducted by Marin Alsop; Naxos 8572996

'What a man, what a violin, what an artist.'

FRANZ LISZT AFTER WITNESSING NICCOLÒ PAGANINI PERFORMING IN PARIS TODAY, IN 1832

20

APRIL

BIRTHS & DEATHS

1943 English conductor John Eliot Gardiner is born in Dorset.

2001 Italian conductor Giuseppe Sinopoli dies in Berlin.

FIRST PERFORMED

1910 The original version of Maurice Ravel's *Mother Goose,* a piano duet written for two young girls, is first performed, in Paris.

TODAY'S THE DAY

1759 George Frideric Handel is buried at Westminster Abbey, in accordance with his wishes. More than 3,000 mourners attended the funeral service.

1770 Fourteen-year-old Wolfgang Amadeus Mozart performs in front of the great and the good in Rome.

1792 Johann Nepomuk Hummel makes his concert debut in London, with a performance of Haydn's *Piano Trio in A flat.*

1807 Ludwig van Beethoven signs a contract with the music publisher Muzio Clementi, giving him the right to distribute in Britain a group of his works, including his *Symphony No. 4, Piano Concerto No. 4* and *Violin Concerto.*

1862 Nikolai Rimsky-Korsakov graduates from naval college in St Petersburg.

1882 The first students are admitted to the new Royal College of Music after going through a rigorous selection process.

1904 Gustav Holst takes over from Ralph Vaughan Williams as a singing teacher at James Allen's Girls' School in London.

1936 Ottorino Respighi's funeral is held in Rome.

1986 Aged 82, pianist Vladimir Horowitz returns home to give a concert at the Moscow Conservatoire. It has been six decades since he was last on Russian soil.

COMPOSER PROFILE:

Gustav Holst

While he was studying at the Royal College of Music, Holst began a lifelong friendship with his contemporary Ralph Vaughan Williams. During the holidays, Holst played trombone in a seaside band and after leaving the college he played professionally as a trombonist for the Scottish Orchestra (now the Royal Scottish National Orchestra). In 1919, after a period as a school teacher, he was made Professor of Music at the University of Reading and also worked as a professor at his alma mater. Holst's first major success was *The Planets,* an impressive orchestral suite; it remains his best-known work. Aside from composing, he was also a keen cyclist – even going on a biking holiday to Algiers.

HALL OF FAME HIT

Karl Jenkins: *The Armed Man: A Mass for Peace*

Recommended Recording

Guy Johnston (cello); National Youth Choir of Great Britain; London Philharmonic Orchestra conducted by Karl Jenkins; EMI Classics 50999 21729621

21

‘Music, being identical with heaven, isn’t a thing of momentary thrills, or even hourly ones. It’s a condition of eternity.’

GUSTAV HOLST, COMPOSER

APRIL

🎵 BIRTHS & DEATHS

1991 Austrian conductor and violinist Willi Boskovsky dies in Visp.

🎵 FIRST PERFORMED

1749 George Frideric Handel’s *Music for the Royal Fireworks* is premiered in London, although the composer is unhappy because the premiere is not supposed to happen for another six days. However, more than 12,000 people turn up to listen to the rehearsal in Vauxhall Gardens, completely jamming up London Bridge in the process.

1918 Sergei Prokofiev’s *Symphony No. 1 ('Classical')* is given its first performance, in Petrograd, with the composer conducting.

1948 Ralph Vaughan Williams’ *Symphony No. 6* receives its first performance, at the Royal Albert Hall in London.

☀️ TODAY'S THE DAY

1783 The National Theatre in Prague opens. It will play host to the premieres of many of Wolfgang Amadeus Mozart’s major operas.

1829 Felix Mendelssohn arrives in London for the first time. Bad weather delays his journey by sea from Hamburg.

1890 Librettist W. S. Gilbert is outraged by the expenses he is being charged by producer Richard D’Oyly Carte for the production of his operetta *The Gondoliers*.

1900 Antonín Dvořák begins work composing the score to *Rusalka*.

1920 Sergei Rachmaninov signs an exclusive recording contract with the Victor Talking Machine Company for the next 5 years. In fact, he ends up staying with the record label for the next 22 years.

1923 Gustav Holst leaves English shores for New York. His conducting engagements in America include the University of Michigan.

1926 Dmitri Shostakovich passes his undergraduate exams at the Leningrad Conservatoire and signs up to be a postgraduate student.

1939 Leonard Bernstein makes his conducting debut at Harvard University.

MUSICAL TERM:

Arranger

An arranger is not the person who makes sure that a group of musicians gets bookings – in musical parlance, he or she is a ‘fixer’. Instead, arrangers take a tune, which they may or may not have written, and make it work for a particular combination of instruments, a certain-sized choir, a full orchestra or even a solo performer. One great example of this is the Classic FM favourite *The Ashokan Farewell*. The original piece was a waltz, written by the American composer Jay Ungar. It was arranged for the Band of Her Majesty’s Royal Marines by Major John Perkins – and it is this version that became a hit.

🎵 HALL OF FAME HIT

Ludwig van Beethoven: *Romance No. 2*

Recommended Recording

Maxim Vengerov (violin); London Symphony Orchestra conducted by Mstislav Rostropovich; EMI Classics 336 4032

> 'Music begins where the possibilities of language end.'
> JEAN SIBELIUS, COMPOSER

22
APRIL

🕐 BIRTHS & DEATHS
1858 English composer Ethel Smyth is born in Sidcup.

1892 French composer Edouard Lalo dies in Paris.

1906 English composer (and Frederick Delius's amanuensis) Eric Fenby is born in Scarborough.

1912 English contralto Kathleen Ferrier is born in Higher Walton.

1916 American violinist Yehudi Menuhin is born in New York.

1944 American pianist, conductor and composer Joshua Rifkin is born in New York.

1956 Finnish conductor Jukka-Pekka Saraste is born in Heinola.

🎵 FIRST PERFORMED
1827 Beethoven's *String Quartet No. 13* is first performed with a new ending, in Vienna.

1885 Dvořák's *Symphony No. 7* is premiered at St James's Hall, London.

☀ TODAY'S THE DAY
1723 Johann Sebastian Bach is appointed music director at the St Thomas Church in Leipzig.

1761 Prince Paul Anton Esterházy becomes aware of the brilliance of the music of Joseph Haydn during a concert. When he finds out that Haydn is already one of his servants, he orders him to dress like a maestro and from then on the composer is always seen dressed in a courtier's wig.

1785 Leopold Mozart is appointed a Master Mason in Vienna.

1789 Wolfgang Amadeus Mozart gives a free concert on the organ in Leipzig's St Thomas Church. As usual, the crowd loves it.

1821 The Musical Fund Society – the USA's oldest music society still in existence – gives its first concert. Its aim is to raise money for 'the relief of decayed musicians and the cultivation of skill and diffusion of taste in music'.

1845 Adolphe Sax throws down the gauntlet to the French Minister of War, suggesting that a military band made up of instruments he has designed would help to improve the standards of French military music. A public contest is held, with Sax's instruments winning, giving him a huge contract to supply French military instruments.

1872 Richard Wagner moves house to Bayreuth, so that he can personally supervise the building of the Festspielhaus.

1885 Pietro Mascagni leaves the Milan Conservatoire to take up the job of assistant conductor of the Castagnetta-Forlì opera company.

1885 Edvard Grieg and his wife Nina move to their new home on the edge of Lake Nordås. It is named 'Troldhaugen', which translates as 'Troll Hill'.

1952 Joseph Stalin signs a decree giving Sergei Prokofiev a pension of 2,000 roubles per month.

1959 Aram Khachaturian wins the Lenin Prize.

2000 The Three Tenors perform their 22nd concert, in Las Vegas.

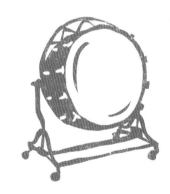

🔊 HALL OF FAME HIT
Johann Sebastian Bach: *Cantata No. 147*

Recommended Recording
English Baroque Soloists; Monteverdi Choir conducted by John Eliot Gardiner; Deutsche Grammophon 478 4231

'He is an artist whom one must hear and see for oneself.'

PIANIST CLARA WIECK ABOUT FRANZ LISZT TO ROBERT SCHUMANN IN A LETTER DATED TODAY IN 1838

BIRTHS & DEATHS

1564 English writer William Shakespeare, whose plays inspired countless classical music works, is born in Stratford-upon-Avon.

1891 Russian composer Sergei Prokofiev is born in Sontsovka.

1960 Northern Irish pianist Barry Douglas is born in Belfast.

2005 Canadian composer Robert Farnon dies on Guernsey.

TODAY'S THE DAY

1764 Leopold, Wolfgang Amadeus and Maria Anna Mozart all arrive in London from Paris. They stay at the White Bear in Piccadilly.

1843 Felix Mendelssohn performs in a concert at the Leipzig Gewandhaus to mark the unveiling of a memorial to J. S. Bach in front of the St Thomas Church.

1863 Pyotr Ilyich Tchaikovsky becomes a full-time student at the St Petersburg Conservatoire, leaving behind him a life of form-filling at the Russian Ministry of Justice.

1884 After showing signs of serious mental illness, Bedřich Smetana is committed to an asylum in Prague.

1946 Arturo Toscanini arrives to conduct at La Scala, Milan. Before he picks up his baton he demands that all Jewish musicians who lost their jobs during the Second World War, as well as those who were sacked for opposing fascism, are reinstated.

ORCHESTRA FOCUS:

Leipzig Gewandhaus Orchestra

The German city of Leipzig was one of the most influential places in classical music history. The Gewandhaus was originally a drapers' hall, which became a concert hall way back in 1781. A new hall was built in 1884, but it was damaged by Allied bombing in 1944 and was knocked down in 1968, finally being replaced in 1981. The orchestra's conductors over the years have included Felix Mendelssohn from 1835 to 1847, Wilhelm Furtwängler from 1922 to 1928, Kurt Masur from 1970 to 1996, and Riccardo Chailly since 2005 – Chailly took over the music directorship of the Leipzig Opera at the same time.

HALL OF FAME HIT

Hector Berlioz: *Symphonie Fantastique*

Recommended Recording

Royal Concertgebouw Orchestra conducted by Colin Davis; Philips 475 7557

> 'A creative artist works on his next composition because he was not satisfied with his previous one.'
>
> DMITRI SHOSTAKOVICH, COMPOSER

BIRTHS & DEATHS

1706 Italian composer Giovanni Martini is born in Bologna.

1939 English composer John Foulds dies in Calcutta, India.

1941 Australian guitarist John Williams is born in Melbourne.

1980 Welsh harpist Catrin Finch is born in Llanon, Ceredigion.

FIRST PERFORMED

1801 Joseph Haydn's oratorio *The Seasons* is first performed, at the Schwarzenberg Palace in Vienna; Haydn had finished composing it only earlier in the day.

TODAY'S THE DAY

1862 A letter from Giuseppe Verdi appears in *The Times* complaining that the organisers of the London Exhibition have rejected one of his works, even though they commissioned it.

1871 Anton Bruckner wins a competition to represent Austria in a series of demonstration concerts for the new organ in London's Royal Albert Hall.

1876 Ernest Chausson passes his law degree in Paris.

1876 Anton Bruckner delivers his first lecture in his new honorary role as lecturer in harmony and counterpoint at Vienna University.

1915 Crowds gather outside the Moscow apartment of Alexander Scriabin as news travels that he is dying.

1934 Laurens Hammond files a patent application for the electric organ that would take his name.

1948 Dmitri Shostakovich makes a speech to the First All-Union Congress of Soviet Composers, where he accepts the government's edict on how music should sound, agreeing to place Russian folk melodies at the centre of his future compositions.

INSTRUMENT FOCUS:

Guitar

Although the guitar is a stringed instrument, and a classical music instrument at that, it is not usually considered as being a stringed instrument in the orchestral sense – mainly because, unlike the violin, viola, cello and double bass, it is never played with a bow. The guitar that we know today is actually a member of the lute family. It has six strings, which are tuned to E, A, D, G, B and E. The back and sides of a good classical guitar are usually made of Brazilian rosewood; the neck is cedar; the fingerboard is ebony, and the face is spruce. Over the years composers such as Boccherini, Berlioz and Paganini have composed for the instrument. A pinnacle of the guitar concerto repertoire was composed by the Spaniard Joaquín Rodrigo – the *Concierto de Aranjuez*. It became a staple for two great guitar virtuosos in the latter part of the 20th century: the Englishman Julian Bream and the Australian John Williams.

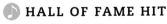

HALL OF FAME HIT

Antonio Vivaldi: *Gloria RV589*

Recommended Recording

Gemma Bertagnoli; Anna Simboli; Concerto Italiano conducted by Rinaldo Alessandrini; Naïve NC 40017

25

'Here, death triumphed over art.'

ARTURO TOSCANINI, CONDUCTOR, AT THE PREMIERE OF *TURANDOT* ON THIS DAY IN 1926.
HE STOPPED PLAYING AT EXACTLY THE POINT WHERE PUCCINI STOPPED COMPOSING
THE WORK, IGNORING THE NEW ENDING PENNED BY ANOTHER COMPOSER

APRIL

🎵 BIRTHS & DEATHS

1961 Norwegian cellist Truls Mørk is born in Bergen.

🎵 FIRST PERFORMED

1926 Giacomo Puccini's opera *Turandot* is premiered at La Scala, Milan.

🎵 TODAY'S THE DAY

1785 Leopold Mozart has lunch with his son Wolfgang Amadeus and his daughter-in-law Constanze near Vienna. It is the last time father and son see each other.

1841 Hector Berlioz, Franz Liszt, Jacques Offenbach and an 11-year-old Anton Rubinstein all perform in a charity concert to raise money for the Beethoven monument in Bonn. It isn't a financial success and, according to fellow composer Richard Wagner, who writes a scathing review of the evening, it isn't a critical success either.

1856 Anton Bruckner is given the job as organist in Linz Cathedral on a permanent basis.

1865 Franz Liszt moves into the Vatican after receiving the tonsure – a sign of religious devotion in Catholicism that involves the cutting of hair.

1960 Joan Sutherland makes her debut at the Paris Opéra in the title role in Donizetti's *Lucia di Lammermoor*.

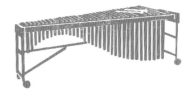

COMPOSER PROFILE:

Giacomo Puccini

Puccini was born into a family steeped in music: his father, grandfather and great-grandfather were all musicians. He studied at the Lucca music school and then in Milan at the Conservatoire, where the young Mascagni was a fellow student. The future king of Italian opera started off his career at the age of 14 as a church organist. It was only after attending a performance of Verdi's *Aida* four years later that he was bitten by the opera bug. Inspired by what he had heard, he eventually entered a competition for a new one-act opera. Not only did Puccini's entry, *Le Villi (The Willies* or *The Fairies)*, fail to win: it was disqualified because the judges said that Puccini's manuscript was illegible. Nevertheless, some of the composer's friends organised a staging at a local theatre in Milan. Giulio Ricordi, who had been Verdi's publisher, heard the opera and was impressed enough by it to put its composer on a retainer. *Edgar*, the first opera that Puccini wrote for Ricordi, was a flop, but *Manon Lescaut*, which followed in 1893, was a smash hit, as were *La bohème* (1896), *Tosca* (1900) and *Madam Butterfly* (1904). Together, they are now regarded as cornerstones of the operatic repertoire.

🎵 HALL OF FAME HIT

Wolfgang Amadeus Mozart:
Clarinet Quintet

Recommended Recording

Romain Guyot (clarinet); members of the Chamber Orchestra of Europe;
Mirare MIR 183

> 'I always said God was against art and I still believe it.'
> EDWARD ELGAR, COMPOSER

26
APRIL

🎵 BIRTHS & DEATHS
1972 Russian pianist Nikolai Lugansky is born in Moscow.

🎵 FIRST PERFORMED
1738 George Frideric Handel's opera *Xerxes* is premiered at the King's Theatre in London's Haymarket.

1830 Niccolò Paganini's *Violin Concerto No. 4* is given its first performance, in Frankfurt.

1835 Frédéric Chopin's *Grande Polonaise Brillante* is first performed, at the Paris Conservatoire, with the composer at the piano.

1899 Jean Sibelius's *Symphony No. 1* (in its original version) receives its first performance, in Helsinki, with the composer conducting.

1929 Antonín Dvořák's *Cello Concerto in A major* is performed in Prague 64 years after its composition. (This is not his famous *Cello Concerto in B minor*, which is more often heard.)

🌅 TODAY'S THE DAY
1763 Christoph Willibald von Gluck is given a pension of 600 gulden by Empress Maria Theresa.

1779 Wolfgang Amadeus Mozart finishes work on his *Symphony No. 32.*

1783 Thirteen-year-old Ludwig van Beethoven becomes a pianist in the court in Bonn.

1847 Queen Victoria and Prince Albert are in the audience to hear Felix Mendelssohn's last concert with the London Philharmonic Society.

1855 An unwell Gioachino Rossini heads for Paris in the hope that French doctors might find a cure for his illness. Sadly, he is never to return home to Florence.

1856 Richard Wagner plays and sings the first act of his opera *Die Walküre* for a group of friends.

1891 Pyotr Ilyich Tchaikovsky arrives in New York after setting off by boat from Le Havre.

1907 Edvard Grieg makes his final concert appearance, in Kiel.

1920 Gabriel Fauré is appointed a Grand Officier de la Légion d'Honneur.

1924 Edward Elgar is offered the position of Master of the King's Music.

Keeping it in the family

The cellist Julian Lloyd Webber might be the most famous of the Lloyd Webber dynasty when it comes to classical music, but that hasn't stopped his big brother Andrew making incursions from musical theatre into the classical world. His *Requiem* was premiered in 1985 and gave us the enduringly popular *Pie Jesu*. It's not really a surprise that both the Lloyd Webbers have done well for themselves in the music business – their father William was himself a prolific and respected composer. Julian Lloyd Webber has spent many years ensuring that his father's music reaches the audience that it deserves.

 HALL OF FAME HIT
Aaron Copland: *Appalachian Spring*

Recommended Recording
London Symphony Orchestra conducted by Aaron Copland; Regis RRC 1404

'Music should strike fire from the heart of man, and bring tears from the eyes of woman.'

LUDWIG VAN BEETHOVEN, COMPOSER

APRIL

🕐 BIRTHS & DEATHS

1812 German composer Friedrich von Flotow is born in Teutendorf.

1915 Russian composer Alexander Scriabin dies in Moscow.

1959 Canadian pianist Louis Lortie is born in Quebec.

2007 Russian cellist Mstislav Rostropovich dies in Moscow.

🎵 FIRST PERFORMED

1926 William Walton's *Façade* is premiered in London.

1982 Philip Glass's music score for the film *Koyaanisqatsi* is heard for the first time at the Santa Fe Film Festival.

☀ TODAY'S THE DAY

1749 George Frideric Handel's *Music for the Royal Fireworks*

receives its official premiere in London's Green Park, despite having already been performed six days previously. The music is an enormous success; the fireworks burn out of control.

1764 Eight-year-old Wolfgang Amadeus Mozart performs with his sister Maria Anna for King George III at Buckingham Palace.

1781 Wolfgang Amadeus Mozart performs for the last time while working for the Archbishop of Salzburg.

1810 Today's date is written on Beethoven's *Bagatelle in A minor* for piano, with the dedication '*Für Elise*', although music historians reckon that it might not actually have been 'for Elise' at all. Blame Beethoven's handwriting, which was never exactly neat.

1845 Franz Liszt is appointed a Chevalier de la Légion d'Honneur.

1850 Hector Berlioz gets a new job, as head librarian at the Paris Conservatoire.

1919 At a fundraising concert in New York, a bid for $1 million is made in auction for an encore by Sergei Rachmaninov. It turns out that the bidder is Ampico, a piano company with a business arrangement with the composer. Publicity stunt or not, it still raises a fortune.

What's in a name?

The literal translation of the first name of Russian cellist Mstislav Rostropovich is 'avenged glory', although he was known by most of his friends as 'Slava', which simply means 'glory'. Have a listen to one of his recordings and you'll quickly hear why the name is so appropriate.

🎵 HALL OF FAME HIT

Max Bruch: *Scottish Fantasy*

Recommended Recording

Tasmin Little (violin); Royal Scottish National Orchestra conducted by Vernon Handley; EMI Classics 085 8832

> 'Inspiration is a guest that does not willingly visit the lazy.'
>
> **PYOTR ILYICH TCHAIKOVSKY, COMPOSER**

BIRTHS & DEATHS

1943 English conductor Jeffrey Tate is born in Salisbury.

1992 French composer Olivier Messiaen dies in Paris.

FIRST PERFORMED

1948 Igor Stravinsky's ballet *Orpheus* is premiered at the New York City Center, with the composer conducting.

TODAY'S THE DAY

1847 Felix Mendelssohn conducts his oratorio *Elijah* in London in front of Queen Victoria and Prince Albert. He will do it again – in front of the same two royal concertgoers – in two days' time.

1848 Richard Wagner finishes work on his opera *Lohengrin* in Dresden.

1892 Sergei Rachmaninov finishes composing a student assignment at the Moscow Conservatoire. His one-act opera *Aleko* is the work that propels him to the forefront of his generation of young Russian composers.

1907 Nikolai Rimsky-Korsakov leaves St Petersburg for Paris, where he will conduct a series of Russian concerts staged by the impresario Sergei Diaghilev. They are key to putting Russian music on the map across Europe – and also make Rimsky-Korsakov a name to be reckoned with.

1878 Richard Wagner's operas *Das Rheingold* and *Die Walküre* are performed in Leipzig over two days. These are their first performances away from Bayreuth.

ORCHESTRA FOCUS:

St Petersburg Philharmonic Orchestra

Russia's oldest symphony orchestra was founded in 1882, originally as the private court orchestra of Tsar Alexander III. Following the Russian Revolution in 1917, it became the State Philharmonic Orchestra of Petrograd before being named the Leningrad Philharmonic Orchestra three years later. It reverted to its original name in 1991. The St Petersburg Philharmonic's success in the 20th century was thanks in the main to conductor Evgeny Mravinsky, who was its music director for an amazing 50 years from 1938 to 1988. Illustrious guest conductors have included Otto Klemperer, Felix Weingartner and Bruno Walter. Prokofiev premiered his piano concertos with the orchestra; it also gave the first performances of eight of Shostakovich's 15 symphonies. The current chief conductor is Yuri Temirkanov.

HALL OF FAME HIT

John Williams: *Schindler's List*

Recommended Recording

Itzhak Perlman (violin); Pittsburgh Symphony Orchestra conducted by John Williams; Sony S2K 51333

29
APRIL

'There is indeed a great dearth of melody, an unclarity and a formlessness, but nonetheless great flashes of genius in conception, in orchestral colouring and in purely musical respects.'

GIACOMO MEYERBEER ON WAGNER'S TANNHÄUSER, TODAY IN 1855

BIRTHS & DEATHS

1879 English conductor Thomas Beecham is born in St Helen's.

1895 English conductor Malcolm Sargent is born in Ashford, Kent.

1936 Indian conductor Zubin Mehta is born in Mumbai.

1948 Australian pianist Leslie Howard is born in Melbourne.

1959 Scottish composer Craig Armstrong is born in Glasgow.

FIRST PERFORMED

1784 Wolfgang Amadeus Mozart's *Violin Sonata No. 32* is given its first performance, in Vienna, with the composer at the keyboard. Emperor Joseph II, in the audience, notices that Mozart appears to be playing the piano part without any notes actually written on the manuscript paper in front of him. It appears that although he has finished writing the music for the violinist, the piano part is largely being made up as he goes along.

1792 Claude-Joseph Rouget de Lisle's '*La Marseillaise*' is performed for the first time by the French National Guard Band in Strasbourg. It's another three years before the piece is adopted as the national anthem of France.

1798 Joseph Haydn's *The Creation* receives a private performance at the Schwarzenberg Palace in Vienna. It doesn't get a full public outing for almost another year.

TODAY'S THE DAY

1863 Alexander Borodin gets married to the daughter of a doctor at Golitsyn Hospital in Moscow. His new bride turns out to be a pretty good piano player.

1915 The funeral of Alexander Scriabin is held in Moscow, with Sergei Rachmaninov among the mourners.

1939 Benjamin Britten and his partner Peter Pears head off from Britain to Canada, living in North America for the next three years.

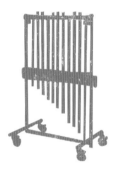

Tonight on solo vacuum cleaner ...

What do composers do when they run out of conventional instruments for which they want to write? Well, often they start to include all manner of weird and wonderful new 'instruments' in their scores. Gershwin put car horns in *An American in Paris*; Luciano Berio included a part for car springs, while the composer of silence, John Cage, once wrote a piece for liquidizer. And Malcolm Arnold really did write a piece for vacuum cleaner. Three vacuum cleaners, in fact. Together with a floor polisher and four rifles.

HALL OF FAME HIT
Ludwig van Beethoven: *Piano Concerto No. 4*

Recommended Recording
Richard Goode (piano); Budapest Festival Orchestra conducted by Iván Fischer; Nonesuch 7559 799283

'The only love affair I have ever had was with music.'

MAURICE RAVEL, COMPOSER

30
APRIL

🎵 BIRTHS & DEATHS

1870 Austro-Hungarian composer Franz Lehár is born in Komárom.

1883 German violinist and founder of the opera company that bears his name, Carl Rosa, dies in Paris.

🎵 FIRST PERFORMED

1849 Johann Strauss Junior's *Alice Polka* is first performed, at Buckingham Palace, in honour of Queen Victoria's six-year-old daughter, Princess Alice.

1902 Claude Debussy's opera *Pelléas et Mélisande* is premiered in Paris. Fellow composer Maurice Ravel is in the audience for all of the first thirty performances.

☀️ TODAY'S THE DAY

1821 Franz Schubert's song *'Gretchen at the Spinning Wheel'* is published. It goes on to be a massive hit.

1885 The Boston Pops Orchestra is founded by Henry Lee Higginson.

1903 Victor Records releases its first recording on the Red Seal label – a recording by the contralto Ada Crossley.

1911 Ten-year-old violinist Jascha Heifetz gives his first public concert performance, in St Petersburg.

1976 89-year-old pianist Arthur Rubinstein gives his final recital in London.

ERA FOCUS:
The Classical period

The word 'Classical' means two very different things in music. Firstly, it is a specific period in music, generally defined as being from around 1750 to 1820, although there may be leakage around the edges. In addition, the word has come to be used as a catch-all for the music from all its fellow periods (and itself) combined. So, Early, Baroque, Romantic and Modern are all often simply referred to as 'classical music'. The practice possibly started after the death of Mozart, when it became fashionable to refer to his music and others as being worthy of comparison with the classical masters. In terms of composers, Haydn and Beethoven provide the backbone of the Classical period, alongside Mozart, but the full cast list would run into the hundreds, with composers such as Salieri and Cherubini being particularly significant. Early pioneers include C. P. E. Bach, Quantz and Gluck. The musical changes in the Classical period came about partly as a reaction to the Baroque period that preceded it, and partly as a consequence of the linear development of musical sound. Mirroring a similar move in architecture, the musicians of the Classical period shifted from the ornate, florid and intricate to the simple, clean and natural – directly reminiscent of the classicists.

🎵 HALL OF FAME HIT
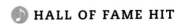
Howard Shore: *The Lord of the Rings*

Recommended Recording
Vienna Philharmonic Orchestra conducted by Ludwig Wicki; Howe Records HWR 1005

May

01

'It is a mistake to think that the practice of my art has become easy to me.'

WOLFGANG AMADEUS MOZART, COMPOSER

MAY

BIRTHS & DEATHS

1904 Czech composer Antonín Dvořák dies in Prague.

1978 Armenian composer Aram Khachaturian dies in Moscow.

FIRST PERFORMED

1769 Wolfgang Amadeus Mozart's opera *La finta semplice* is premiered in Salzburg.

1786 Wolfgang Amadeus Mozart's opera *The Marriage of Figaro* is premiered at the Burgtheater in Vienna, with the composer playing the keyboard.

1815 Luigi Cherubini's *Symphony in D* is first performed, at the Royal Philharmonic Society in London, with the composer conducting.

1886 Pyotr Ilyich Tchaikovsky's fantasy-overture *Romeo and Juliet* receives the first performance of its third version, in Tbilisi.

1871 Charles Gounod's *Gallia* is given its first performance, at the grand opening of the Royal Albert Hall in London.

TODAY'S THE DAY

1753 George Frideric Handel plays the organ at a concert at the Foundling Hospital, London. It is believed to be his last public performance on the organ.

1761 Joseph Haydn is formally given the job of assistant Kapellmeister by Prince Paul Anton Esterházy.

1892 Eleven-year-old Béla Bartók plays in public for the first time, in a charity concert in the Ukrainian town of Vinogradov.

1964 Conductor Pierre Boulez makes his debut in New York.

COMPOSER PROFILE:

Aram Khachaturian

Incredibly, Khachaturian managed to win a place at the Gnesin Music Academy in Moscow to study the cello, even though he had never played the instrument before. He built up his reputation with works such as his *Piano Concerto* and *Violin Concerto*, as well as the ballets *Gayaneh* and *Spartacus*, the latter being his best-known piece. Prokofiev was a fan and Khachaturian held a selection of government-sponsored posts, until he wrote some music that earned the disapproval of the state, at which point he moved to writing film scores. He is seen today as having been the foremost proponent of Armenian folk music.

♪ HALL OF FAME HIT
Erik Satie: *3 Gymnopédies*

Recommended Recording
Jean-Yves Thibaudet (piano); Decca 470 2902

> 'All criticism of him is silenced, as though posterity had already spoken . . . unanimous praise was on everyone's lips.'
>
> **FRANZ LISZT'S REVIEW OF A CONCERT BY FRÉDÉRIC CHOPIN, PUBLISHED TODAY IN 1841**

02
MAY

BIRTHS & DEATHS

1660 Italian composer (and father of the better-known Domenico) Alessandro Scarlatti is born in Palermo.

1864 German composer Giacomo Meyerbeer dies in Paris.

1947 Belgian conductor Philippe Herreweghe is born in Ghent.

1953 Russian conductor Valery Gergiev is born in Moscow.

FIRST PERFORMED

1692 Henry Purcell's opera *The Fairy Queen* is premiered at the Queen's Theatre in London.

1794 Joseph Haydn's *Symphony No. 100 ('Military')* receives its first performance, in London.

1924 Andrey Paschenko's *Symphonic Mystery* for theremin and orchestra, the first orchestral work with the solo played by an electronic instrument, is given its first performance. The theremin solo is performed by the instrument's inventor, Lev Sergeyevich Termen.

1936 Sergei Prokofiev's *Peter and the Wolf* is premiered in Moscow.

TODAY'S THE DAY

1689 King William III cuts the costs of musical entertainment in the royal household, ordering that the 'musicians be presently reduced to 24 and an instrument keeper'.

1776 Joseph Haydn buys a new house in Eisenstadt, after being confirmed in his new job as assistant Kapellmeister.

1781 Wolfgang Amadeus Mozart moves into the Weber family's home in Vienna, where he was to meet his future wife Constanze.

1825 Samuel Wesley is arrested after failing to pay maintenance to his estranged wife.

1835 Twenty-one-year-old Richard Wagner hopes to raise enough money to clear his debts by arranging a concert in Magdeburg, but his finances go from bad to worse, as the performers outnumber the concertgoers.

1848 The *Morning Chronicle* today describes Louis Spohr as 'the first composer of the day, without a possible rival'.

The oldest orchestra

According to the *Guinness Book of World Records*, the very first symphony orchestra was the Gewandhaus Orchestra, which began playing in Leipzig, Germany, in 1743. The Royal Liverpool Philharmonic is the oldest continuously operating professional symphony orchestra in the UK. Although the Liverpool Philharmonic Society dates back to 1840, the orchestral musicians were not permanently contracted until 1853, five years ahead of the launch of the next oldest, the Hallé Orchestra, down the road in Manchester.

HALL OF FAME HIT

Ludwig van Beethoven: *Piano Sonata No. 8 ('Pathétique')*

Recommended Recording

Jean-Efflam Bavouzet; Chandos CHAN 10720(3)

03

'Music, I feel, must be emotional first and intellectual second.'

MAURICE RAVEL, COMPOSER

MAY

🎵 BIRTHS & DEATHS

1844 English impresario Richard D'Oyly Carte is born in London.
1856 French composer Adolphe Adam dies in Paris.
1953 English composer Stephen Warbeck is born in Southampton.
1997 Spanish guitarist Narciso Yepes dies in Murcia.
2002 Russian conductor Yevgeny Svetlanov dies in Moscow.

🎵 FIRST PERFORMED

1792 Joseph Haydn's *Symphony No. 97* is performed for the first time, in London.
1952 Dmitri Shostakovich's music for the film *The Unforgettable Year, 1919* is heard for the first time. It includes the popular *Assault on Beautiful Gorky.*

☀️ TODAY'S THE DAY

1793 The Cologne Privy Council agrees to continue to give a grant to Ludwig van Beethoven.
1845 Nearly five years after his death, with the wrangling about whether Niccolò Paganini was or was not possessed by the Devil now over, the remains of the violinist and composer are buried in Parma.
1864 Goachino Rossini faints in Paris after being told that fellow composer Giacomo Meyerbeer has died.

1866 Edvard Grieg arrives in Berlin and buys Hector Berlioz's book on orchestration.
1883 Arthur Sullivan is offered a knighthood by Prime Minister William Gladstone.
1941 Leonard Bernstein graduates with a conducting diploma from the Curtis Institute of Music in Philadelphia.

Classic BRIT Awards: 3 May 2007

Singer of the Year: Anna Netrebko
Instrumentalist of the Year: Leif Ove Andsnes
Album of the Year: Paul McCartney – *Ecce Cor Meum*
Contemporary Composer of the Year: John Adams – *The Dharma at Big Sur/My Father Knew Charles Ives*
Classical Recording of the Year: Berlin Philharmonic Orchestra conducted by Simon Rattle – *Holst: The Planets*

Soundtrack Composer of the Year: George Fenton – *Planet Earth*
Young British Classical Performer: Ruth Palmer
Critics' Award: Freiburg Baroque Orchestra, RIAS Kammerchor, René Jacobs – *Mozart: La Clemenza di Tito*
Lifetime Achievement: Vernon Handley

🎵 HALL OF FAME HIT

Ludovico Einaudi: *Le Onde*

Recommended Recording

Ludovico Einaudi (piano); Decca 476 4490

> 'To play great music you must keep your eyes on a distant star.'
>
> **YEHUDI MENUHIN, VIOLINIST AND CONDUCTOR**

04

MAY

BIRTHS & DEATHS

1931 Russian conductor Gennadi Rozhdestvensky is born in Moscow.

1937 Spanish harpist Marisa Robles is born in Madrid.

1942 Mexican conductor Enrique Bátiz is born in Mexico City.

1955 Romanian conductor and composer Georges Enescu dies in Paris.

FIRST PERFORMED

1795 Joseph Haydn's *Symphony No. 104* ('*London*') is given its first performance, in London. It is his final symphony and the composer conducts.

TODAY'S THE DAY

1677 Johann Pachelbel becomes the court organist at Eisenach.

1825 Gaetano Donizetti has a nightmare opening performance in his new role as director of opera in Palermo. The orchestra is so far below par that the wonderfully named Superintendent of Public Spectacles demands improvements.

1836 Giuseppe Verdi gets married to Margherita, the daughter of Antonio Barezzi, a grocer who also supports the young composer's work.

1847 The soprano Jenny Lind takes London by storm at her first concert in the city, helped in no small way by Queen Victoria breaking with royal protocol and throwing a wreath at the singer's feet.

1855 Hector Berlioz and Giuseppe Verdi have dinner together in Paris.

1864 King Ludwig II of Bavaria rescues Richard Wagner from his financial problems by paying off his debts and giving him a house and an annual cash sum.

Classic BRIT Awards: 4 May 2006

Singer of the Year: Andreas Scholl
Instrumentalist of the Year: Leif Ove Andsnes
Album of the Year: Katherine Jenkins – *Living a Dream*
Ensemble/Orchestral Album of the Year: Takács Quartet – *Beethoven: The Late String Quartets*
Contemporary Music Award: James MacMillan – *Symphony No. 3 'Silence'*

Soundtrack/Musical Theatre Composer Award: Dario Marianelli – *Pride and Prejudice*
Young British Classical Performer: Alison Balsom
Critics' Award: Royal Opera House Chorus and Orchestra, conducted by Antonio Pappano – *Tristan and Isolde*
Lifetime Achievement: Plácido Domingo

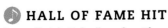

HALL OF FAME HIT

Pyotr Ilyich Tchaikovsky: *The Sleeping Beauty*

Recommended Recording

Berlin Philharmonic Orchestra conducted by Mstislav Rostropovich; Deutsche Grammophon 449 726

MAY 3–4 | 145

05

MAY

🕐 BIRTHS & DEATHS

1932 Russian conductor Mark Ermler is born in St Petersburg.

☀ TODAY'S THE DAY

1723 Johann Sebastian Bach signs a contract to become Kantor in Leipzig. He wasn't the first choice for the position, with the local council preferring Georg Philipp Telemann, who at the time was one of the biggest names in German classical music. Telemann wouldn't teach Latin as part of the job though, and then the second-choice candidate withdrew, so the officials opted for their third choice. Bach agreed to pay for a stand-in to do the Latin teaching for him.

1748 George Frideric Handel begins work on his oratorio *Solomon*.

1774 Wolfgang Amadeus Mozart finishes work on his *Symphony No. 30* in Salzburg.

1842 The family home of eight-year-old Johannes Brahms narrowly escapes being consumed by fire in a massive blaze that rages across Hamburg, destroying around one fifth of the city.

1855 Robert Schumann pens his last letter to his wife Clara from an asylum near Bonn.

1878 In a letter of recommendation to his publisher, Johannes Brahms writes, 'The best that a musician can have, Dvořák has.'

1891 New York's Carnegie Hall opens for business, with a concert that includes Pyotr Ilyich Tchaikovsky conducting his own music.

1904 Antonín Dvořák is buried in Prague.

1917 Claude Debussy gives his final public performance as a pianist in Paris.

1920 Violinist Jascha Heifetz makes his London debut at the Queen's Hall.

1924 Edward Elgar is officially made Master of the King's Music.

1928 Two composers of very different kinds of classical music, George Gershwin and Alban Berg, meet for the first time, in Vienna.

COMPOSER PROFILE:

Edward MacDowell

New York born, MacDowell spent 12 years living in France and Germany from the age of 16. He studied first at the Paris Conservatoire and then with the Swiss composer, Joachim Raff. His composing career really began to take off once his music was championed by Liszt. He returned to his homeland and was hailed as the new hero of American classical music. His *Piano Concerto* went down particularly well and he was appointed the first ever Professor of Music at Columbia University in New York, today in 1896. He struggled to balance the demands of university life with those of being a composer and, not long afterwards, he suffered a mental breakdown from which he never recovered. One little-known fact about MacDowell: he wrote his first few pieces under the pseudonym 'Edgar Thorn'.

🎵 HALL OF FAME HIT

Alexander Borodin: *In the Steppes of Central Asia*

Recommended Recording

Kirov Orchestra conducted by Valery Gergiev; Philips 470 8402

'There was no one near to confuse me, so I was forced to become original.'

JOSEPH HAYDN, COMPOSER

06
MAY

 FIRST PERFORMED

1897 Ruggero Leoncavallo's opera *La bohème* is premiered in Venice. Critics were not keen on the music, and history has judged Puccini's opera of the same name a far bigger success.

1948 William Walton's film score to *Hamlet* is heard for the first time at the film's premiere at the Odeon Cinema in London's Leicester Square, next door to Classic FM's studios.

☀ TODAY'S THE DAY

1637 Venice's first opera house, the Teatro San Cassiano, opens.

1678 Antonio Vivaldi is officially baptised. He had been unofficially baptised on the day he was born a few weeks earlier because medical staff were worried about his survival.

1824 The final rehearsal takes place for Ludwig van Beethoven's *Symphony No. 9*. The composer embraces each of the orchestra and choir members as they prepare to take to the stage.

1846 Ten-year-old Camille Saint-Saëns makes his debut at the piano at the Salle Pleyel in Paris.

1847 Felix Mendelssohn performs in a concert at the Prussian Embassy in London. British Prime Minister William Gladstone is in the audience.

1849 Richard Wagner's opera house in Dresden catches fire as Prussian and Saxon troops march on the city.

1854 After a distinctly lukewarm premiere, a new production of Giuseppe Verdi's opera *La traviata*, featuring different singers and in a different venue, the Teatro San Benedetto in Venice, gets a far warmer reception.

1864 Giacomo Meyerbeer's funeral takes place in Paris, before his body is taken by a special train to Berlin.

1926 Leoš Janáček performs at London's Wigmore Hall, despite the city being in the grip of the General Strike.

Classic BRIT Awards:
6 May 2000

British Artist of the Year: Charlotte Church
Female Artist of the Year: Martha Argerich
Male Artist of the Year: Bryn Terfel
Critics' Award: Ian Bostridge for *The English Songbook*
Album of the Year: Andrea Bocelli – *Sacred Arias*
Best-selling Classical Album: Andrea Bocelli – *Sacred Arias*

Ensemble/Orchestral Album of the Year: Choir of King's College, Cambridge – Rachmaninov: *Vespers*
Young British Classical Performer: Daniel Harding
Outstanding Contribution to Music: Nigel Kennedy

🎵 **HALL OF FAME HIT**
Edvard Grieg: *Holberg Suite*

Recommended Recording
Norwegian Chamber Orchestra conducted by Terje Tønnesen (violin); Simax PSC 1264

07

MAY

'Madam, you have between your legs an instrument capable of giving pleasure to thousands – and all you can do is scratch it.'

THOMAS BEECHAM, CONDUCTOR, TO A FEMALE CELLIST

🕐 BIRTHS & DEATHS

1825 Italian composer Antonio Salieri dies in Vienna.
1833 German composer Johannes Brahms is born in Hamburg.
1840 Russian composer Pyotr Ilyich Tchaikovsky is born in Kamsko-Votkinsk.
1981 English cellist Guy Johnston is born in Harpenden.

🎭 FIRST PERFORMED

1824 Ludwig van Beethoven's *Symphony No. 9 ('Choral')* is premiered in Vienna. At the end of the concert, the composer, by now completely deaf, is oblivious to the audience's rapturous applause. One of the singers gently turns him around, so that he can see the reaction for himself.
1979 More than half a century after the composer's death, Erik Satie's first published works, *Valse-ballet* and *Fantasie-valse* for piano, get their first public airing, in Paris.

☀ TODAY'S THE DAY

1783 Wolfgang Amadeus Mozart writes to his father about a new librettist he has met in Vienna, one Lorenzo da Ponte. In time, they will enjoy a highly successful partnership, with da Ponte writing the words to some of Mozart's most successful operas.
1788 Joseph Haydn maintains that Mozart is the world's greatest composer, after hearing a performance of his *Don Giovanni* in Vienna.
1849 Despite being heavily pregnant, Clara Schumann travels to Dresden to rescue her three youngest children from an artillery barrage in the city.
1855 Clara Schumann gives Johannes Brahms a *Romance in B minor* as a birthday present.
1883 The Prince of Wales officially opens the Royal College of Music in London. While he is there, he announces that Arthur Sullivan is to be knighted.
1889 Giacomo Puccini asks his publisher to obtain the rights for him to turn the play *La Tosca* into an opera. The publisher refuses to help – a decision he will come to regret.

1898 Edward Elgar conducts the inaugural concert of the Worcestershire Philharmonic Orchestra.
1916 Ignacy Jan Paderewski, Fritz Kreisler and Pablo Casals all perform in a memorial concert for composer Enrique Granados at the Metropolitan Opera in New York.
1918 Sergei Prokofiev heads off from Vladivostok to St Petersburg using the trans-Siberian railway.
1936 The first concert in the air takes place when pianist Fritz Wagner performs on the airship *Hindenburg,* while it travels from Hamburg to New York.
1960 Thomas Beecham conducts his final concert, with the Royal Philharmonic Orchestra, at the Guildhall in Portsmouth.
1973 Benjamin Britten goes into hospital for an operation to replace a heart valve. He suffers a small stroke and subsequently movement of his right arm is impaired, ending his performing career as conductor and pianist.
2000 The Three Tenors perform their 23rd concert together, in Washington.

🎵 HALL OF FAME HIT
Antonín Dvořák: *Rusalka*

Recommended Recording
Various soloists; Czech Philharmonic Orchestra and the Kühn Mixed Choir conducted by Charles Mackerras; Decca 460 5682

> 'Don't only practise your art, but force your way into its secrets.'
>
> LUDWIG VAN BEETHOVEN, COMPOSER

08
MAY

BIRTHS & DEATHS

1829 American composer and pianist Louis Moreau Gottschalk is born in New Orleans.

1846 American opera composer Oscar Hammerstein is born in Stettin.

1944 English composer Ethel Smyth dies in Woking.

1945 American composer and pianist Keith Jarrett is born in Allentown.

1947 English soprano Felicity Lott is born in Cheltenham.

TODAY'S THE DAY

1693 Leipzig's first opera house opens during the city's Easter Fair.

1804 Not yet aged 18, Carl Maria von Weber is given the job of Kapellmeister at the theatre in Breslau.

1816 Ludwig van Beethoven writes rather mournfully to a friend in a letter dated today, 'Unfortunately, I have no wife. I found one whom I shall doubtless never possess.'

1822 The Liszt family moves to Vienna so that ten-year-old Franz can continue his study of music at a higher level.

1827 Felix Mendelssohn begins studying at the University of Berlin.

1835 Mikhail Glinka gets married. He is already related to his new wife, but not by blood. She is his sister's brother-in-law's wife's sister. It wasn't a happy union and they split up a few years later.

1838 Frédéric Chopin and George Sand realise they have fallen in love at a dinner party hosted by a French nobleman.

1844 Felix Mendelssohn is back in London on his eighth trip across the English Channel to perform.

1847 Felix Mendelssohn leaves London for the very last time.

1866 Anton Bruckner begins a three-month stay in a sanatorium after suffering a nervous breakdown.

1889 Edward Elgar gets married at Brompton Oratory in London.

1920 Dmitri Shostakovich performs his own music for the first time in public at an art exhibition in St Petersburg.

1945 Aaron Copland wins the Pulitzer Prize for *Appalachian Spring*.

Classic BRIT Awards: 8 May 2008

Male Artist of the Year: Colin Davis
Female Artist of the Year: Anna Netrebko
Young British Classical Performer: Nicola Benedetti
Album of the Year: Blake – *Blake*
Soundtrack of the Year: James Newton Howard – *Blood Diamond*
Critics' Award: Steven Isserlis – *Bach: Cello Suites*
Outstanding Contribution: Andrew Lloyd Webber

HALL OF FAME HIT

Ralph Vaughan Williams: *Fantasia on Greensleeves*

Recommended Recording

London Philharmonic Orchestra conducted by David Parry; LPO 0063

09

MAY

'Imagination creates reality.'

RICHARD WAGNER, COMPOSER

 BIRTHS & DEATHS

1707 German organist and composer Dietrich Buxtehude dies in Lübeck.
1740 Italian Giovanni Paisiello is born in Taranto.
1874 Founder of the Old Vic and Sadler's Wells ballet company Lilian Baylis is born in London.
1955 Swedish soprano Anne Sofie von Otter is born in Stockholm.

 FIRST PERFORMED

1812 Gioachino Rossini's opera *The Silken Ladder* is premiered in Venice.
1893 Sergei Rachmaninov's opera *Aleko* is premiered in Moscow.
1906 The first book of Isaac Albéniz's piano suite *Iberia* receives its first performance, in Paris.
1937 William Walton's *Crown Imperial* is given its premiere in a radio broadcast, ahead of its inclusion in George VI's Coronation.

 TODAY'S THE DAY

1781 Wolfgang Amadeus Mozart has a huge row with his boss, Archbishop Colloredo of Salzburg; he decides he wants to leave to work in Vienna instead.
1786 Mozart's *The Marriage of Figaro* is proving so popular that all of the encores each night cause the performances to drag on too long for Emperor Joseph II's taste. He bans any singer from giving more than one encore per night.
1791 Mozart is given the job of deputy Kapellmeister at St Stephen's Cathedral in Vienna.
1829 Niccolò Paganini performs in Berlin for the first time. Felix Mendelssohn's sister, Fanny, is in the crowd. She loves the performance, but memorably describes the great man as having 'the appearance of an insane murderer, and the movements of an ape'.
1870 Gabriel Fauré is one of the guests in the home of Camille Saint-Saëns in Paris, when Anton Rubinstein gives a performance on the piano.
1939 Benjamin Britten and Peter Pears arrive in Quebec to begin a tour of North America.
1960 As a protest against his impending deportation, an East German refugee sets fire to Beethoven's birthplace in Bonn, destroying two signed manuscripts.
1965 Pianist Vladimir Horowitz performs at New York's Carnegie Hall after taking a 12-year break from the concert platform. The standing ovation at the end is said to have lasted for half an hour.

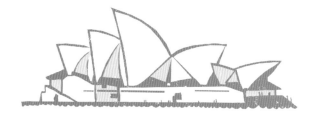

 HALL OF FAME HIT
Arvo Pärt: *Spiegel im Spiegel*

Recommended Recording
Tasmin Little (violin); Martin Roscoe (piano); EMI Classics 565 0312

> 'Competitions are for horses, not artists.'
>
> **BÉLA BARTÓK, COMPOSER**

BIRTHS & DEATHS

1760 French composer Claude-Joseph Rouget de Lisle is born in Lons-le-Saunier.

1770 English composer Charles Avison dies in Newcastle.

1888 American composer Max Steiner is born in Vienna.

1938 Russian conductor and pianist Maxim Shostakovich is born in Leningrad.

1963 English composer Debbie Wiseman is born in London.

1977 Russian trumpeter Sergei Nakariakov is born in Gorky.

FIRST PERFORMED

1893 Arthur Sullivan's *Imperial March* is first performed at the opening by Queen Victoria of the Imperial Institute in London.

1957 Dmitri Shostakovich's *Piano Concerto No. 2* is premiered in Moscow, with the composer's 19-year-old son Maxim at the keyboard.

TODAY'S THE DAY

1781 The Archbishop of Salzburg's chief of staff refuses to allow Wolfgang Amadeus Mozart to leave the Salzburg court to move to Vienna.

1825 Antonio Salieri is buried in Vienna.

1839 Hector Berlioz is appointed a Chevalier of the Légion d'Honneur.

1864 Richard Wagner discovers that his prized piano has been sold off to pay his debts. However, he settles up the money he owes in Vienna and manages to get back some of his other personal items, which were being kept in lieu of payment.

1885 Charles Gounod loses a libel court case in England – although it has little effect on him, as he is at home in France.

1896 Clara Schumann suffers a serious stroke.

ENSEMBLE FOCUS:

The orchestra

The word 'orchestra' did not originally mean a group of people playing music at all. Instead, it was the place where the group stood or sat. In a Greek amphitheatre, the natural slope of the seats was called the 'Loilon'; the backdrop to the stage was known as the 'Scena', and the semi-circular piece of flat ground between the two was the 'Orchestra'. Eventually, it came to mean the people who played there, too. The modern orchestra, like the ancient one before it, was also born in the theatre, originally to accompany plays and operas. The Dresden Staatskapelle is the world's oldest, tracing its routes back as far as 1548. It was soon joined by others, as churches, courts, cities and towns across Europe founded their own orchestras over the next couple of centuries. The virtuoso Mannheim orchestra (run by the local Elector) was particularly important in advancing the cause.

HALL OF FAME HIT
Johann Sebastian Bach: *Cello Suites*

Recommended Recording
Steven Isserlis (cello); Hyperion CDA 67541/2

11

MAY

🕐 BIRTHS & DEATHS

1888 American composer Irving Berlin is born in Tyumen, Russia.
1916 German composer Max Reger dies in Leipzig.
1945 Conductor Ross Pople is born in New Zealand.
1954 British composer Judith Weir is born in Cambridge.

🎵 FIRST PERFORMED

2000 Colin Matthews' *Pluto – The Renewer* received its first performance, in Manchester. The work was composed as an 'extra' planet to add on to Holst's *The Planets*. Pluto hadn't been discovered when Holst wrote the original work. However, it has subsequently turned out that Pluto shouldn't really be classed as a planet, so Holst turned out to be unwittingly right all along.

☀️ TODAY'S THE DAY

1865 Hans von Bülow conducts the final dress rehearsal for Richard Wagner's *Tristan and Isolde* in Munich.
1876 Thousands of people throng to Gilmore's Gardens in New York to hear the first American concert conducted by Jacques Offenbach.
1897 Gustav Mahler makes his Vienna Hofoper conducting debut with an acclaimed performance of Wagner's *Lohengrin*.
1946 The opera house La Scala, Milan, reopens after being bombed in the Second World War.

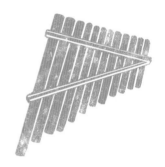

COMPOSER PROFILE:

Gustav Mahler

Mahler's father owned a distillery in Bohemia. The second of 14 children, Gustav owed his early success to a farm manager who heard him playing the piano and recommended him to the Vienna Conservatoire, where he studied from the age of 15. Although he studied composition and continued to play the piano, it was for his conducting that Mahler became best known during his lifetime. He achieved superstardom as a composer only long after his death. During his early thirties, Mahler conducted concerts in all the major European centres of classical music, including Prague, Leipzig and Budapest. After converting from Judaism to Catholicism, he was appointed conductor to the Vienna Court Opera and of the Vienna Philharmonic Orchestra. He made it on the other side of the Atlantic too, as chief conductor of the New York Metropolitan Opera and music director of the New York Philharmonic Orchestra. His workload in America was immense and, in late 1910, he was taken seriously ill. He returned to Vienna, where he died of pneumonia at the age of just 50. It was only after the Second World War that his music – and particularly his nine symphonies – really took off.

🎵 HALL OF FAME HIT

Wolfgang Amadeus Mozart: *Symphony No. 40 in G minor*

Recommended Recording

Scottish Chamber Orchestra conducted by Charles Mackerras; Linn CKD 308

'Mournful and yet grand is the destiny of the artist.'
FRANZ LISZT, COMPOSER

 BIRTHS & DEATHS

1842 French composer Jules Massenet is born in Montaud.
1845 French composer Gabriel Fauré is born in Pamiers.
1884 Bohemian composer Bedřich Smetana dies in Prague.
1931 French composer Eugène Ysaÿe dies in Brussels.

FIRST PERFORMED

1832 Gaetano Donizetti's opera *L'elisir d'amore* is premiered in Milan.
1926 Dmitri Shostakovich's *Symphony No. 1* receives its first performance, in St Petersburg.

TODAY'S THE DAY

1740 The governors of the orphanage employing Antonio Vivaldi agree to pay him to produce 20 new concertos.
1764 Wilhelm Friedemann Bach storms out of his job as organist and music director in Halle, refusing to work out his notice period.
1770 Charles Avison is buried at St Andrew's Church in Newcastle.
1809 Three great composers are in Vienna when the city faces an artillery bombardment from French troops. Ludwig van Beethoven, Franz Schubert and Joseph Haydn are all unscathed by the attack.
1830 Felix Mendelssohn finishes work on his *Symphony No. 5*.

1844 Frédéric Chopin is deeply affected by a letter from Warsaw, telling him of his father's death.
1847 Frédéric Chopin suffers a serious asthma attack, which lasts for four days.
1852 Hector Berlioz is hailed as one of the conducting greats after performing Beethoven's *Symphony No. 9* with the New Philharmonic Society in London's Exeter Hall.
1871 Richard Wagner tells the world that his *Ring Cycle* will be performed in two years' time in Bayreuth. He doesn't let the fact that he neither has an opera house there nor permission to build one get in the way of his grand announcement.
1902 Sergei Rachmaninov marries his cousin at a Moscow chapel.
1902 Fritz Kreisler performs for the first time on his violin in London at a Philharmonic concert with Hans Richter conducting.
1937 The music featured in the Coronation of George VI – including William Walton's *Crown Imperial* – is brought to a television audience for the first time.
1939 Tenor Jussi Björling makes his debut at London's Covent Garden in *Il trovatore*.

Classic BRIT Awards: 12 May 2011

Male Artist of the Year: Antonio Pappano
Female Artist of the Year: Alison Balsom
Newcomer Award: Vilde Frang
Composer of the Year: Arvo Pärt
Critics' Award: Tasmin Little – *Elgar: Violin Concerto*
Artist of the Decade: Il Divo
Album of the Year: André Rieu – *Moonlight Serenade*
Outstanding Contribution to Music: John Barry

 HALL OF FAME HIT

Johannes Brahms: *Piano Concerto No. 2*

Recommended Recording

Nicholas Angelich (piano); Frankfurt Radio Symphony Orchestra conducted by Paavo Järvi; Virgin 266 3492

13

MAY

> 'When I wished to sing of love, it turned to sorrow. And when I wished to sing of sorrow, it was transformed for me into love.'
>
> **FRANZ SCHUBERT, COMPOSER**

🎵 BIRTHS & DEATHS

1842 English composer Arthur Sullivan is born in London.

1949 English conductor Jane Glover is born in Helmsley.

1965 English violinist Tasmin Little is born in London.

🎵 FIRST PERFORMED

1833 Felix Mendelssohn's *Symphony No. 4 ('Italian')* receives its first performance, in London. Niccolò Paganini and Vincenzo Bellini are both in the crowd at Covent Garden.

1868 Camille Saint-Saëns' *Piano Concerto No. 2* is given its first performance, in Paris, with the composer providing the solo and Anton Rubinstein conducting.

☀ TODAY'S THE DAY

1749 The Burgtheater opens in Vienna.

1825 After hearing 15-year-old Frédéric Chopin's keyboard skills for himself while visiting Warsaw, Tsar Alexander I presents the teenager with a diamond ring.

1849 Ducking and diving to avoid his creditors, Richard Wagner arrives in Weimar looking for assistance from Franz Liszt, but he doesn't find him.

1890 The cornerstone of Carnegie Hall is laid in New York.

1893 Johannes Brahms is given the gold medal of the Gesellschaft der Musikfreunde in Vienna.

1932 Dmitri Shostakovich gets married near Leningrad, although neither his nor his new wife's families are told beforehand.

Classic BRIT Awards: 13 May 2010

Male Artist of the Year: Vasily Petrenko
Female Artist of the Year: Angela Gheorghiu
Composer of the Year: Thomas Adès – *The Tempest*
Young British Classical Performer of the Year: Jack Liebeck
Album of the Year: Only Men Aloud – *Band of Brothers*
Soundtrack of the Year: Thomas Newman – *Revolutionary Road*
Critics' Award: Orchestra e Coro dell'Accademia Nazionale di Santa Cecilia, conducted by Antonio Pappano, with Rolando Villazón, Anja Harteros, Sonja Ganassi and René Pape – Verdi: *Requiem*
Lifetime Achievement Award: Kiri Te Kanawa

🎵 HALL OF FAME HIT

Ralph Vaughan Williams: *Five Variants of Dives and Lazarus*

Recommended Recording

New Queen's Hall Orchestra conducted by Barry Wordsworth; Decca 460 3572

> 'Simplicity is the final achievement. After one has played a vast quantity of notes and more notes, it is simplicity that emerges as the crowning reward of art.'
>
> FRÉDÉRIC CHOPIN, COMPOSER

14

MAY

🛈 BIRTHS & DEATHS

1847 German composer, pianist and conductor Fanny Mendelssohn dies after suffering a stroke while conducting a choir rehearsal in Berlin.

1885 German conductor Otto Klemperer is born in Breslau.

🎭 FIRST PERFORMED

1832 Felix Mendelssohn's *Hebrides Overture* (also known as *Fingal's Cave*) is premiered in London.

1897 John Philip Sousa's *'The Stars and Stripes Forever'* is first performed, in Philadelphia at the unveiling of a statue of George Washington.

☀ TODAY'S THE DAY

1719 The Lord Chamberlain commissions George Frideric Handel to visit Europe to contract singers to appear at London's new Royal Academy of Music.

1778 Wolfgang Amadeus Mozart writes home with news that he has been offered the role of organist at Versailles.

1789 Ludwig van Beethoven begins his studies at the University of Bonn.

1831 Niccolò Paganini arrives in London for a series of concerts, to discover a furore over the doubling of ticket prices for his concert series at the King's Theatre. He feigns illness and the prices are quietly reduced for the postponed series, which eventually begins in June.

1849 Franz Liszt agrees to hide Richard Wagner from the authorities at his home in Weimar, before arranging for him to flee to Switzerland.

1901 Antonín Dvořák becomes a member of the Austrian House of Peers.

1902 Italian tenor Enrico Caruso makes his debut at London's Covent Garden, in Verdi's *Rigoletto*.

1931 Arturo Toscanini refuses to open a concert in Bologna with a fascist hymn. He is physically assaulted in the street outside the concert hall.

1959 Leonard Bernstein leads the celebrations of the start of building work on New York's Lincoln Center. President Eisenhower is in attendance.

1965 Cellist Jacqueline du Pré performs for the first time in the USA, playing the Elgar *Cello Concerto*.

1974 Conductor Leopold Stokowski makes his final London performance, at the age of 92, with the New Philharmonia Orchestra.

Classic BRIT Awards: 14 May 2009

Male Artist of the Year: Gustavo Dudamel
Female Artist of the Year: Alison Balsom
Composer of the Year: Howard Goodall – *Eternal Light: A Requiem*
Young Classical Perfomer: Alina Ibragimova
Album of the Year: Royal Scots Dragoon Guards – *Spirit of the Glen*

Soundtrack of the Year: Hans Zimmer and James Newton Howard – *The Dark Knight*
Critics' Award: Scottish Chamber Orchestra conducted by Charles Mackerras – *Mozart Symphonies Nos 38–41*
Lifetime Achievement in Music: José Carreras

HALL OF FAME HIT

Franz Schubert: *Symphony No. 9 ('Great')*

Recommended Recording

Vienna Philharmonic Orchestra conducted by Georg Solti; Decca 448 9272

15

MAY

'I frequently hear music in the heart of noise.'

GEORGE GERSHWIN, COMPOSER

🎵 BIRTHS & DEATHS

1567 Italian composer Claudio Monteverdi is born in Cremona.

1908 Swedish composer Lars-Erik Larsson is born in Akarp.

1923 English arranger and conductor John Lanchbery is born in London.

1945 English composer Kenneth J. Alford (famous for 'Colonel Bogey') dies in Reigate.

🎵 FIRST PERFORMED

1920 Igor Stravinsky's ballet *Pulcinella* is premiered in Paris. None other than Pablo Picasso designs the costumes and sets.

🎵 TODAY'S THE DAY

1728 Domenico Scarlatti gets married in Rome.

1754 A performance of Handel's *Messiah* at the Foundling Hospital in London is thought to be the last time the composer conducts the work.

1848 Queen Victoria, Prince Albert and Kaiser Wilhelm I hear Frédéric Chopin play for the first time in London at a dinner in Lancaster House.

1858 The Royal Opera House in London's Covent Garden opens for the third time, after being destroyed twice by fire.

1865 The premiere of Richard Wagner's opera *Tristan and Isolde* is postponed because the lead soprano is ill. Wagner continues to have money troubles, with bailiffs removing furniture from his home in lieu of money owed.

1872 Nineteen-year-old Charles Villiers Stanford gives his first organ recital, at Trinity College, Cambridge.

1875 Jacques Offenbach sells the Théâtre de la Gaîté to release funds to pay off his debts.

1890 The ending of the partnership between W. S. Gilbert and Arthur Sullivan is now in the public domain, with impresario Richard D'Oyly Carte providing comments on the affair to the newspapers.

1900 Enrique Granados launches a new initiative to drive forward classical music in Barcelona, with the first performance promoted by his Society of Classical Concerts at the city's Teatre Liric.

1914 In his own inimitable style, Erik Satie instructs performers to play his new *Choral inappétissant* 'hypocritically'.

1916 George Gershwin earns his first copyright royalty from the song '*When you want 'em, you can't get 'em, when you've got 'em, you don't want 'em*'.

1920 Maurice Ravel signs a contract to record his music on piano rolls for the Aeolian Company of London.

🎵 HALL OF FAME HIT

Charles Gounod: *Mors et Vita*

Recommended Recording

Various soloists; Orféon Donostiarra; Orchestre National du Capitole de Toulouse conducted by Michel Plasson; EMI 54459

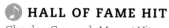

> 'Works of art make rules; rules do not make works of art.'
>
> CLAUDE DEBUSSY, COMPOSER

16
MAY

🕐 BIRTHS & DEATHS

1891 Austrian tenor Richard Tauber is born in Linz.

1953 English violinist Monica Huggett is born in London.

1959 American conductor Andrew Litton is born in New York.

🐘 FIRST PERFORMED

1906 Richard Strauss's opera *Salome* is premiered in Graz. Gustav Mahler is in the audience.

☀ TODAY'S THE DAY

1661 Jean-Baptiste Lully becomes Master of the King's Music in France – a hugely powerful position from which he quickly establishes himself as the dominant force in French music.

1707 German organist Dietrich Buxtehude is buried in Lübeck.

1792 Teatro La Fenice opens in Venice.

1813 Johann Nepomuk Hummel gets married in Vienna.

1849 A warrant for Richard Wagner's arrest is issued in Dresden.

1888 The flat gramophone disc goes on show at the Franklin Institute in Philadelphia.

INSTRUMENT FOCUS:

Violin

The violin is the crowned king of string instruments. Violins make up a third of the modern symphony orchestra, the largest of any section. They are divided into two groups – the first violins and the second violins. As with all the sections of the orchestra, each group of violins has a principal player, who sits at the front of the group. The principal first violinist is usually known as the Leader (occasionally the term 'Concert Master' is used). He or she is the senior regular player in the orchestra and works particularly closely with the conductor. As an instrument, the violin has a fantastic range of around four octaves and, because of its compact size and the way in which it is played,

is capable of amazing agility. It was developed, in the way we know it today, in the 16th century and enjoyed a golden period in the 17th century, a situation that gives rise to the deified status of instruments of the period, notably those made by Stradivari, Guarneri, Amati and Montagnana. Antonio Stradivari, sometimes known by the Latin version of his name (Stradivarius), is considered the greatest of all violin-makers. Known affectionately as 'Strads' and prized for their amazing tone (particularly those made between 1698 and 1725), his violins sell for art-world prices. In 2006, Christie's sold a Stradivarius, nicknamed 'The Hammer', for $3.54 million.

🎵 HALL OF FAME HIT

Giacomo Puccini: *Tosca*

Recommended Recording

Various soloists; New Philharmonia Orchestra and the John Alldis Choir conducted by Zubin Mehta; RCA 82876 707832

17

MAY

'The musician is perhaps the most modest of animals, but he is also the proudest.'

ERIK SATIE, COMPOSER

🛈 BIRTHS & DEATHS

1866 French composer Erik Satie is born in Honfleur.
1918 Swedish soprano Birgit Nilsson is born in Västra Karup.
1921 English horn player Dennis Brain is born in London.
1935 French composer Paul Dukas dies in Paris.
1958 English conductor Ivor Bolton is born in Blackrod.

🎭 FIRST PERFORMED

1864 The Norwegian national anthem gets its first public performance, to celebrate the 50th anniversary of the country's constitution.
1890 Pietro Mascagni's *Cavalleria Rusticana* is premiered in Rome.

To say it is a massive hit would be an understatement – there were no fewer than 30 curtain calls. The composer is an overnight sensation.

☀ TODAY'S THE DAY

1771 Among America's earliest full orchestral performances, a symphony by Johann Christian Bach is played in Boston.
1838 Franz Liszt performs for the Empress of Austria in Vienna.
1847 Fanny Mendelssohn is buried in Berlin.
1876 Arthur Sullivan heads up the new National Training School for Music in London.
1877 Richard Wagner visits Queen Victoria at Windsor Castle.

1884 First performance by Australian soprano Nellie Melba in Melbourne.
1885 Charles Villiers Stanford accepts a new job as conductor of the Bach Choir.
1935 Ralph Vaughan Williams receives a letter from Buckingham Palace asking him if he will accept the Order of Merit.
1969 Leonard Bernstein conducts the New York Philharmonic for the final time as its music director.
1978 The Dutch company Philips Electronics announces the invention of digital sound reproduction from thin metal and plastic 'compact discs'.

COMPOSER PROFILE:

Erik Satie

Although best known for his *Gymnopédies* for piano, Satie was something of an eccentric and had a habit of giving many of his compositions ridiculous names. These include: *Veritable Flabby Preludes (for a dog)*, *Five Grins or Mona Lisa's Moustache*, *Menus for Childish Purposes*, *Three Pear-Shaped Pieces*, *Waltz of the*

Chocolate with Almonds, Sketches and Provocative Gestures of a Big Wooden Fellow. He also wrote a remarkable piano piece called *Vexations*, which is made up of the same few bars of music played again and again and again – a total of 840 times.

🎵 HALL OF FAME HIT

Aaron Copland: *Fanfare for the Common Man*

Recommended Recording

Detroit Symphony Orchestra conducted by Antal Doráti; Decca 478 4585

'I am hitting my head against the walls, but the walls are giving way.'

GUSTAV MAHLER, COMPOSER

18
MAY

🎵 BIRTHS & DEATHS

1909 Spanish composer Isaac Albéniz dies in Cambo-les-Bains.

1911 Bohemian composer Gustav Mahler dies in Vienna.

1919 English ballet dancer Margot Fonteyn is born in Surrey.

1975 American composer Leroy Anderson dies in Woodbury.

2012 German baritone Dietrich Fischer-Dieskau dies in Bavaria.

🎵 FIRST PERFORMED

1897 Paul Dukas' *The Sorcerer's Apprentice* is given its first performance, in Paris.

1925 Leoš Janáček's opera *The Cunning Little Vixen* is premiered in Prague.

🌅 TODAY'S THE DAY

1811 Prince Nikolaus Esterházy sacks Johann Nepomuk Hummel – for the second time.

1843 Gioachino Rossini and Giuseppe Verdi meet for the first time, in Parma.

1865 Anton Bruckner meets Richard Wagner for the first time, in Munich.

1917 The term 'surrealism' is coined by Guillaume Apollinaire in the programme notes to the premiere of Erik Satie's ballet *Parade*, in Paris.

Orchestration

Orchestration is the part of a composer's job that comes after the initial composing itself. Once the central ideas have been created, the art of sorting out who plays what is called 'orchestration'. Many composers consider it a completely separate procedure, and some are thought of as being greater masters of the process than others. Maurice Ravel, Hector Berlioz and Paul Dukas, for example, are all considered experts in the field. Nikolai Rimsky-Korsakov was another such expert, making a habit of superbly orchestrating virtually everything that he laid his hands on. He was already strong in the area of orchestration while he was still at college, writing musical arrangements for the student band. He perfected his craft while he was in the navy, when he made a point of learning how to play just about every instrument of the orchestra.

Richard Wagner is also worthy of a mention. When he could not get quite the right combination of orchestral colours to do justice to the sound that was in his head, he simply invented his own instrument to create it. The 'Wagner Tuba' was the result. It is, in fact, more of a big horn than a tuba. Wagner employed it to great musical effect in his mammoth four-opera cycle, *The Ring*.

🎵 HALL OF FAME HIT

·Felix Mendelssohn: *Symphony No. 4* ('Italian')

Recommended Recording

London Symphony Orchestra conducted by Claudio Abbado; Decca 475 8677

19

MAY

'To achieve great things, two things are needed: a plan, and not quite enough time.'

LEONARD BERNSTEIN, COMPOSER

🕐 BIRTHS & DEATHS

1786 English composer John Stanley dies in London.
1861 Australian soprano Nellie Melba is born in Melbourne. (Her real name is the far less glamorous Helen Porter Mitchell.)
1954 American composer Charles Ives dies in New York.

🎵 FIRST PERFORMED

1886 Camille Saint-Saëns' *Symphony No. 3 ('Organ')* is first performed, at St James's Hall in London, conducted by the composer.

☀ TODAY'S THE DAY

1764 Eight-year-old Wolfgang and 12-year-old Maria Anna Mozart perform for King George III and Queen Charlotte in London.
1773 Wolfgang Amadeus Mozart finishes work on his *Symphony No. 23*, in Salzburg.
1831 Hector Berlioz heads back to Rome after spending a month in Nice, not quite making it as far as Paris, where he had intended to murder his former fiancée and her mother, after he was unceremoniously dumped.

1892 Sergei Rachmaninov is awarded the Gold Medal by the examiners at the Moscow Conservatoire for his one-act student opera *Aleko*.
1976 Samuel Barber is awarded the Gold Medal for Music by the National Institute of Arts and Letters of the United States.

MUSICAL TERM:
Scherzo

The Italian word for joke has given its name to a lively musical work, or a movement of a work (often a symphony). Developed from the 'minuet and trio', it is usually light in style, and sometimes a little fast and furious. Beethoven was one of the first to grab the scherzo by the scruff of the neck and make it his own. In the third movement of his *'Pastoral' Symphony,* he used the trappings of the scherzo to depict 'peasants' merrymaking', complete with dancing and the sound of a country band. Meanwhile, in the scherzo from his incidental music for *A Midsummer Night's Dream,* Mendelssohn took advantage of the jokey nature of the movement to represent the character Puck, who was known for his fondness for pranks.

INSTRUMENT FOCUS:
Harpsichord

This small keyboard was a forerunner of the piano. The main difference between the two instruments is that the harpsichord does not hammer the strings inside its casing as a piano does. Instead, it plucks them with a pin. The inner workings of a harpsichord contain a series of around 48 strings, each with its own pin plucker, and a spruce or cedar soundboard, which helps to amplify the sound. Although harpsichords are still played today, the invention of the piano has rendered them far less popular than they were in Baroque times and they remain an instrument that listeners tend either to love or to hate.

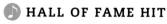

🎵 HALL OF FAME HIT

Alexander Borodin: *Prince Igor*

Recommended Recording

Berlin Philharmonic Orchestra conducted by Herbert von Karajan; Deutsche Grammophon 469 6222

'I detest imitation, I detest hackneyed devices.'

SERGEI PROKOFIEV, COMPOSER

20

MAY

🎵 BIRTHS & DEATHS

1896 German composer and pianist Clara Schumann dies in Frankfurt.

1955 Polish composer Zbigniew Preisner is born in Bielsko-Biala.

1966 English clarinettist Emma Johnson is born in London.

1972 English pianist Paul Lewis is born in Liverpool.

2000 French flautist Jean-Pierre Rampal dies in Paris.

☀ TODAY'S THE DAY

1777 Johann Christian Bach organises a performance by 11-year-old Samuel Wesley in Hickford's Rooms in London.

1785 Wolfgang Amadeus Mozart finishes work on his *Fantasia in C minor*.

1824 Samuel Wesley gets a new job as organist of Camden Chapel.

1842 Felix Mendelssohn listens to the 12-year-old Anton Rubinstein performing at the Hanover Square Rooms in London.

1872 Franz Liszt sends a peace-making letter to Richard Wagner over the latter's relationship with Liszt's daughter Cosima.

1873 Nikolai Rimsky-Korsakov is given a new job that combines his seafaring and musical passions – Inspector of Music Bands of the Russian Navy Department.

1877 Franz Liszt has to take over during a performance of his *St Elisabeth* in Hanover, after the original conductor falls off the podium in a drunken heap.

1884 Librettist W. S. Gilbert sends composer Arthur Sullivan the outline to a new operetta, *The Mikado*.

1910 New York's Metropolitan Opera begins its first European tour.

1958 Crowds of more than 100,000 people come out onto the streets of New York for a tickertape parade for the pianist Van Cliburn.

ORCHESTRA FOCUS:

Chicago Symphony Orchestra

Established in 1891, the USA's third-oldest symphony orchestra is now widely regarded as being America's greatest ensemble. Founded by Theodore Thomas, the orchestra even took his name for an eight-year period following his death. The orchestra's international reputation grew to new heights between 1969 and 1991 under Music Director Georg Solti. On one occasion in the 1970s, the players received so much acclaim on a triumphant tour of Europe that they were given a ticker tape welcome through the city on their return. Solti handed the baton on to Daniel Barenboim in 1991, with the mighty Riccardo Muti becoming only the tenth music director in 2006. It remains an orchestra of enviable standing on the worldwide classical music stage.

🎵 HALL OF FAME HIT

Samuel Barber: *Violin Concerto*

Recommended Recording

Joshua Bell (violin); Baltimore Symphony Orchestra conducted by David Zinman; Classic FM FW 004

21

MAY

'It never seems to occur to people that a man might just want to write a piece of music.'

RALPH VAUGHAN WILLIAMS, COMPOSER

 BIRTHS & DEATHS

1895 Austrian composer Franz von Suppé dies in Vienna.

1931 Swiss oboist, composer and conductor Heinz Holliger is born in Langenthal.

1933 French trumpeter Maurice André is born in Alès.

1949 English soprano Rosalind Plowright is born in Worksop.

FIRST PERFORMED

1892 Ruggero Leoncavallo's opera *Pagliacci* is premiered in Milan.

TODAY'S THE DAY

1729 Italian oboist and composer Giuseppe Sammartini makes his first appearance on stage in London at a concert in Hickford's Rooms. He went down a storm and stayed in London for the rest of his life.

1830 Vincenzo Bellini suffers a nasty case of 'bilious gastric inflammatory fever' in Milan. It's weeks before he recovers.

1862 Edvard Grieg plays three of his *Piano Pieces*, his first published work, in Bergen.

1871 Charles Gounod's wife and son move home to France after the composer begins an affair in London.

1875 Fourteen-year-old Isaac Albéniz performs in San Juan, Puerto Rico.

INSTRUMENT FOCUS:

Celesta

This unusual instrument looks and sounds a little like a baby's piano. Invented in 1886 by Auguste Mustel, it uses metal plates struck by hammers to make its heavenly sound. As soon as he saw the new instrument in Paris, Tchaikovsky was desperate to be the first Russian to use it, and it featured in *'The Dance of the Sugar Plum Fairy'* from his ballet *Nutcracker*. Mahler was the first composer to use the celesta in a symphony (his sixth). It is widely employed by modern-day film composers, such as John Williams, who used its magical sound in *'Hedwig's Theme'* from his *Harry Potter* soundtrack.

 HALL OF FAME HIT

Karl Jenkins: *Adiemus*

Recommended Recording

Mary Carewe; Miriam Stockley; London Philharmonic Orchestra conducted by Karl Jenkins; EMI 095 0582

> 'Extraordinary and precocious musical talent.'

REPORT SENT TODAY IN 1770 FROM ROME TO A HAMBURG NEWSPAPER ABOUT 14-YEAR-OLD WOLFGANG AMADEUS MOZART

BIRTHS & DEATHS

1813 German composer Richard Wagner is born in Leipzig.

1969 English tenor Toby Spence is born in Hertford.

FIRST PERFORMED

1790 Wolfgang Amadeus Mozart's *String Quartets Nos 21 and 22* are first performed at his home in Vienna.

1813 Gioachino Rossini's opera *The Italian Girl in Algiers* is premiered in Venice.

1836 Felix Mendelssohn's oratorio *St Paul* is performed for the first time, in Düsseldorf, with the composer conducting.

1874 Giuseppe Verdi's *Requiem* is given its first performance, in the church of San Marco, Milan, with the composer conducting.

1950 Richard Strauss's *Four Last Songs* are heard for the first time, in London.

TODAY'S THE DAY

1722 Johann Sebastian Bach arrives in Leipzig for his new job as Cantor of St Thomas Church.

1853 Richard Wagner celebrates his 40th birthday with three nights of concerts in Zurich. They are critically acclaimed, but financially ruinous.

1859 Franz Liszt and Arthur Sullivan meet for the first time, in Leipzig.

1864 Richard Wagner is given a new Bechstein piano for his birthday by King Ludwig II, after his previous piano was seized in lieu of payment of his debts.

1872 Richard Wagner lays the cornerstone for the Bayreuth Festspielhaus.

1874 Anton Rubinstein ends a massive 203-concert tour of North America with a final date in New York.

1883 Queen Victoria knights Arthur Sullivan at Windsor Castle.

1911 Gustav Mahler is buried in the Grinzing cemetery in Vienna.

1953 Aaron Copland receives a telegram calling him to appear before Senator Joseph McCarthy's Senate Permanent Subcommittee on Investigations.

Classic BRIT Awards: 22 May 2003

Female Artist of the Year: Renée Fleming

Male Artist of the Year: Simon Rattle

Album of the Year: Andrea Bocelli – *Sentimento*

Best-selling Classical Album: Andrea Bocelli – *Sentimento*

Ensemble/Orchestral Album of the Year: Berlin Philharmonic Orchestra conducted by Simon Rattle – *Mahler: Symphony No. 5*

Contemporary Music Award: Arvo Pärt – *Orient and Occident*

Young British Classical Performer: Chloe Hanslip

Critics' Award: Murray Perahia – *Chopin: Etudes, Op. 10, Op. 25*

Outstanding Contribution to Music: Cecilia Bartoli

HALL OF FAME HIT

Johann Sebastian Bach: *Orchestral Suite No. 3*

Recommended Recording

Academy for Ancient Music, Berlin; Harmonia Mundi HMG 501578/59

23

'Inspiration is an awakening, a quickening of all man's faculties, and it is manifested in all high artistic achievements.'

GIACOMO PUCCINI, COMPOSER

MAY

🛈 BIRTHS & DEATHS

1794 Czech composer Ignaz Moscheles is born in Prague.
1901 English composer Edmund Rubbra is born in Northampton.
1912 French composer Jean Françaix is born in Le Mans.
1934 American composer Robert Moog – inventor of the eponymous synthesizer – is born in New York.

🎼 FIRST PERFORMED

1814 The third version of Ludwig van Beethoven's opera *Fidelio* is premiered in Vienna, to far greater success than the first two outings.

1873 Pyotr Ilyich Tchaikovsky's *The Snow Maiden* is premiered at the Bolshoi Theatre in Moscow.
1894 Claude Debussy's *Arabesque No. 2* receives its first performance, in Paris.
1931 The young Princesses Elizabeth and Margaret watch with their parents, the Duke and Duchess of York (eventually King George VI and Queen Elizabeth, the Queen Mother), as Edward Elgar's *Nursery Suite* is given its first performance, at the HMV Studio in London, with the composer conducting.

☀ TODAY'S THE DAY

1934 Gustav Holst is in hospital for an operation on a duodenal ulcer.
1939 Dmitri Shostakovich is given a new job as a professor at the Leningrad Conservatoire.

Classic BRIT Awards: 23 May 2002

Female Artist of the Year: Cecilia Bartoli
Male Artist of the Year: Colin Davis
Album of the Year: Russell Watson – *Encore*
Ensemble/Orchestral Album of the Year: London Symphony Orchestra conducted by Richard Hickox – *Vaughan Williams: A London Symphony*
Contemporary Music Award: Tan Dun – *Crouching Tiger, Hidden Dragon*

Young British Classical Performer: Guy Johnston
Critics' Award: London Symphony Orchestra conducted by Colin Davis – *Berlioz: Les Troyens*
Biggest-selling Classical Album: Russell Watson – *Encore*
Outstanding Contribution to Music: Andrea Bocelli

🎵 HALL OF FAME HIT

Antonio Vivaldi: *Mandolin Concerto RV425*

Recommended Recording

Il Giardino Armonico; Warner Classics 2564 698542

164 | THE BIG BOOK OF CLASSICAL MUSIC

> 'Music is the social act of communication among people, a gesture of friendship, the strongest there is.'
>
> **MALCOLM ARNOLD, COMPOSER**

24 MAY

BIRTHS & DEATHS

1960 English conductor Paul McCreesh is born in London.

FIRST PERFORMED

1803 Ludwig van Beethoven's *Kreutzer Sonata* is first performed, in Vienna, with the composer at the keyboard and George Bridgetower playing the violin. Beethoven hurriedly finished the sonata so that Bridgetower could perform it, with the latter reading from the composer's handwritten manuscript.

1810 Ludwig van Beethoven's *Egmont Overture* is heard for the first time, in Vienna.

1918 Béla Bartók's opera *Duke Bluebeard's Castle* is premiered at Budapest Opera House.

1939 Aaron Copland's ballet *Billy the Kid* is premiered in New York (for the first time with an orchestra).

1948 Benjamin Britten's *The Beggar's Opera* is premiered in Cambridge.

TODAY'S THE DAY

1829 Tsar Nikolas I presents Niccolò Paganini with a diamond ring following his performance at a grand dinner in Warsaw to mark the Tsar's Coronation as King of Poland.

1852 Swedish superstar soprano Jenny Lind performs the last of 20 concerts in New York, as part of an American tour promoted by the larger-than-life P. T. Barnum.

1861 Franz Liszt hails Georges Bizet as one of the top three pianists in Europe, along with Hans von Bülow and himself.

1872 Richard Wagner hires an architect to design the Bayreuth Festspielhaus.

1875 Desperate to stave off his increasing deafness, Bedřich Smetana submits himself to a month's treatment from a doctor who claims to be able to cure him using all manner of strange therapies. Sadly for Smetana, it is a waste of time and money.

1886 Richard Strauss arrives in Munich, ahead of starting his new job at the Munich Court Opera.

1888 Australian soprano Nellie Melba makes her London debut, at Covent Garden, in Donizetti's *Lucia di Lammermoor*.

1896 Clara Schumann is buried in Bonn, next to her husband Robert. Her close friend Johannes Brahms is among the mourners.

Chart topper

When Salford-born classical-crossover tenor Russell Watson released his first album, *The Voice*, in 2001, it topped the UK's classical music chart for an entire year until the release of his second album, *Encore*, which replaced *The Voice* in the top spot.

 HALL OF FAME HIT
Pyotr Ilyich Tchaikovsky: *Symphony No. 4*

Recommended Recording
London Philharmonic Orchestra conducted by Vladimir Jurowski; LPO Live 0064

25

MAY

'I can't understand why people are frightened of new ideas. I'm frightened of the old ones.'

JOHN CAGE, COMPOSER

 **BIRTHS & DEATHS**
1934 English composer Gustav Holst dies in London.

 **FIRST PERFORMED**
1870 Léo Delibes' ballet *Coppélia* is premiered in Paris.
1878 Gilbert and Sullivan's operetta *HMS Pinafore* is premiered in London, with the composer conducting.

TODAY'S THE DAY
1829 Felix Mendelssohn conducts his *Symphony No. 1* at a Philharmonic Society Concert in London's Argyll Rooms. It is the first time he has been seen in action with the baton in the city.
1869 Wolfgang Amadeus Mozart's *Don Giovanni* is performed at the opening of the new Vienna State Opera House.
1884 Franz Liszt conducts for the final time, in Weimar.
1887 More than 130 people die in a fire at the Théâtre de l'Opéra-Comique in Paris. The blaze takes hold midway through a performance, hence the high death toll.

1903 Béla Bartók plays Liszt's *Rhapsodie Espagnole* as his final examination piece at the Budapest Academy of Music.
1908 The new Teatro Colón opens in Buenos Aires with Verdi's *Aida*.
1939 A crowd of 18,000 is left disappointed after the pianist Ignacy Jan Paderewski pulls out of a recital because of arthritis.

Classic BRIT Awards: 25 May 2005

Female Artist of the Year: Marin Alsop
Male Artist of the Year: Bryn Terfel
Album of the Year: Katherine Jenkins – *Second Nature*
Ensemble/Orchestral Album of the Year: Harry Christophers and The Sixteen – *Renaissance*
Contemporary Music Award: John Adams – *On the Transmigration of Souls*
Soundtrack Composer Award: John Williams – *Harry Potter and the Prisoner of Azkaban* and *The Terminal*
Young British Classical Performer: Natalie Clein
Critics' Award: Stephen Hough – *Rachmaninov Piano Concertos*
Outstanding Contribution to Music: James Galway

 HALL OF FAME HIT
Philip Glass: *Violin Concerto*

Recommended Recording
Gidon Kremer (violin); Vienna Philharmonic Orchestra conducted by Christoph von Dohnanyi; Deutsche Grammophon 437 0912

> 'To send light into the darkness of men's hearts – such is the duty of the artist.'
>
> **ROBERT SCHUMANN, COMPOSER**

BIRTHS & DEATHS

1958 English composer and Classic FM presenter Howard Goodall is born in Bromley.
1973 Czech mezzo-soprano Magdalena Kožená is born in Brno.

FIRST PERFORMED

1916 Leoš Janáček's opera *Jenůfa* is premiered in Prague in a version shortened and re-orchestrated from the original performance in Brno 12 years earlier.

TODAY'S THE DAY

1828 Hector Berlioz puts on his first concert as a promoter, at the Paris Conservatoire.
1833 Felix Mendelssohn conducts Handel's *Israel in Egypt* in Düsseldorf; Mendelssohn's championing of Handel helps to bring the Baroque composer's music to a wider audience in Germany.
1855 Franz Liszt visits Cologne under the pretext of attending a music festival; in reality, it is a cover story for a tryst with a secret lover.

1857 Mikhail Glinka's remains are disinterred in Berlin and taken to his final resting place in St Petersburg.
1935 Frederick Delius's remains are reburied in Limpsfield in Surrey, after having been exhumed from their original burial site in France.
1953 Aaron Copland appears before a private hearing of Senator Joseph McCarthy's Senate Permanent Subcommittee on Investigations. He is told that he will face further questioning in public, but this never takes place.

Classic BRIT Awards: 26 May 2004

Female Artist of the Year: Cecilia Bartoli
Male Artist of the Year: Bryn Terfel
Album of the Year: Bryn Terfel – *Bryn*
Ensemble/Orchestral Album of the Year: Vienna Philharmonic conducted by Simon Rattle: *Beethoven Symphonies*
Contemporary Music Award: Philip Glass – *The Hours*

Young British Classical Performer: Daniel Hope
Critics' Award: Maxim Vengerov, Mstislav Rostropovich and the London Symphony Orchestra – *Britten/Walton Concertos*
Outstanding Contribution to Music: Renée Fleming

HALL OF FAME HIT

Wolfgang Amadeus Mozart: *Piano Concerto No. 23*

Recommended Recording

Daniel Barenboim (piano); English Chamber Orchestra; EMI Classics 575 3652

27

'I should be sorry if I only entertained them.
I wish to make them better.'

GEORGE FRIDERIC HANDEL, COMPOSER

MAY

BIRTHS & DEATHS

1840 Italian composer and violinist Niccolò Paganini dies in Nice.

1959 English conductor Sian Edwards is born in West Chiltington.

2003 Italian composer Luciano Berio dies in Rome.

FIRST PERFORMED

1906 Gustav Mahler's *Symphony No. 6* is given its first performance, in Essen, with the composer conducting.

TODAY'S THE DAY

1762 Johann Christian Bach is granted a one-year sabbatical from his job at Milan Cathedral, to allow him to make the trip to England to compose two operas.

1783 Wolfgang Amadeus Mozart finishes work on his *Horn Concerto No. 2* in Vienna.

1844 Despite the Philharmonic Society not usually allowing child stars to perform, Felix Mendelssohn manages to persuade the powers-that-be to allow 12-year-old violinist Joseph Joachim to make his London debut under the Society's auspices. He performs Beethoven's *Violin Concerto,* with Mendelssohn conducting.

1889 Pietro Mascagni sends the score of his opera *Cavalleria Rusticana* to Milan for entry into a composition competition. The resulting win is life changing for him.

1918 Leoš Janáček is saved from serious injury after being dragged out of the pathway of an oncoming tram in Brno. He had accidentally fallen onto the track.

ARTIST PROFILE:

Niccolò Paganini

Even in a period stuffed with musical prodigies, Paganini appears to have been something of a wonder. The greatest violin virtuoso of the previous generation, Alessandro Rolla, said he could teach the Genoa-born youngster nothing more by the time he had reached the age of 12. Paganini's phenomenal technique had firmly established him as a great solo artist by the time he was 13. He toured first Italy then all around Europe, writing his own concertos to display his amazing skills. When rumours abounded that he must be in league with the Devil to be so accomplished, Paganini himself did little to deny the myth. He commissioned Berlioz to write *Harold in Italy,* though he initially rejected it because he felt that the solo viola part was not showy enough. Later, he apologised and embraced it wholeheartedly. His later life was marred by bad health and ill-judged financial investments.

HALL OF FAME HIT

Gioachino Rossini: *William Tell*

Recommended Recording

Various soloists; National Philharmonic Orchestra conducted by Riccardo Chailly; Decca E417 1542

> 'Every great inspiration is but an experiment.'
>
> **CHARLES IVES, COMPOSER**

28

MAY

🕐 BIRTHS & DEATHS

1787 German composer and violinist Leopold Mozart dies in Salzburg. His best-known artistic creation was his son, Wolfgang Amadeus.

1805 Italian composer Luigi Boccherini dies in Madrid.

1923 Hungarian composer György Ligeti is born in Transylvania.

1925 German baritone and conductor Dietrich Fischer-Dieskau is born in Berlin.

1948 Cypriot violinist Levon Chilingirian, founder of the Chilingirian Quartet, is born in Nicosia.

🎵 FIRST PERFORMED

1904 A revised version of Giacomo Puccini's *Madam Butterfly* is given its first performance, in Brescia.

☀️ TODAY'S THE DAY

1808 The parents of 11-year-old Franz Schubert see an advertisement for boy choristers in the Viennese Imperial and Royal Court Chapel in the *Wiener Zeitung* newspaper.

1840 The Bishop of Nice prevents Niccolò Paganini from being buried on church land.

1878 Tragedy strikes the home of composer Camille Saint-Saëns, when his four-year-old son falls to his death from a fourth-floor window.

1878 Just seven weeks after the death of his previous wife, Johann Strauss Junior remarries.

1934 The first season of opera begins at Glyndebourne, a country house near Lewes in East Sussex. It lasts for two weeks with productions of *The Marriage of Figaro* and *Così fan tutte*.

1942 Benjamin Britten appears before a court to argue the case for allowing him to resist military service, as a conscientious objector. The court ruling does allow him to avoid military service, but still requires him to do non-combat duties. He launches an appeal.

1958 The Soviet leadership loosens the rules on anti-formalism, meaning that composers such as Dmitri Shostakovich are freer to write music in the style that they wish, rather than under a strict government-imposed framework.

1966 Dmitri Shostakovich gives his last performance as a pianist, suffering a heart attack shortly afterwards.

🎵 HALL OF FAME HIT
Igor Stravinsky: *The Rite of Spring*

Recommended Recording
London Philharmonic Orchestra conducted by Kent Nagano; Virgin Virgo 482 0032

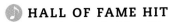

'Without craftsmanship, inspiration is a mere reed shaken in the wind.'

JOHANNES BRAHMS, COMPOSER

MAY

BIRTHS & DEATHS

1860 Spanish composer Isaac Albéniz is born in Camprodón.

1897 American composer Erich Korngold is born in Brno.

1910 Russian composer Mily Balakirev dies in St Petersburg.

1911 English librettist W. S. Gilbert dies in Harrow. He suffers a heart attack after diving into his lake to save a woman to whom he has been giving swimming lessons.

1935 Czech composer Josef Suk dies in Benešov.

1953 American composer Danny Elfman is born in Los Angeles.

FIRST PERFORMED

1801 Joseph Haydn's oratorio *The Seasons* is premiered in Vienna. Ludwig van Beethoven is in the audience.

1912 Claude Debussy's ballet version of *Prélude à l'après-midi d'un faune* is performed for the first time, in Paris, with the choreographer Vaslav Nijinsky taking the part of the faun. It causes quite a stir among the Parisian chattering classes. Twenty years younger than Debussy, composer Igor

Stravinsky is in the crowd. It turns out that he is also not one to shy away from composing ballets that cause outrage.

1913 Igor Stravinsky's ballet *The Rite of Spring* causes an actual riot when it is performed for the first time in Paris. Among those watching are Maurice Ravel and Camille Saint-Saëns, the latter walking out in disgust. Those who debate the rights and wrongs of Stravinsky's way of doing things end up brawling.

TODAY'S THE DAY

1777 Christoph Willibald von Gluck appears before Queen Marie Antoinette, who is a huge fan of his music. He's in Paris for the performance of his opera *Armide*.

1787 Leopold Mozart is buried in Salzburg.

1842 Felix Mendelssohn makes his seventh trip to London, performing his *Symphony No. 3*. On this occasion, he brings his wife with him for the first time.

1855 Samuel Sebastian Wesley gives the first recital on the new organ in St George's Hall, Liverpool.

1872 Fourteen-year-old Edward Elgar finishes working on what is considered to be his first proper musical work. It's a piece for piano called *The Language of Flowers*; he gives it to his sister Lucy, as a birthday present.

1874 The first meeting of the Royal Musical Association takes place in the boardroom of the South Kensington Museum, in London. Its objectives include 'the investigation and discussion of subjects connected with the art, science and history of music'.

HALL OF FAME HIT

Gioachino Rossini: *Overture: The Thieving Magpie*

Recommended Recording

Montreal Symphony Orchestra conducted by Charles Dutoit; Australian Eloquence 460 5902

'I'm an adventurer. I like invention; I like discovery.'

KARLHEINZ STOCKHAUSEN, COMPOSER

 FIRST PERFORMED

1866 Bedřich Smetana's opera *The Bartered Bride* is premiered in Prague, with the composer conducting.

1962 Benjamin Britten's *War Requiem* receives its first performance, in Coventry Cathedral.

TODAY'S THE DAY

1723 The day before his official induction as Cantor at St Thomas Church in Leipzig, J. S. Bach makes his debut in the role, with his *Cantata No. 75* at St Nicholas Church.

1782 Michael Haydn (brother of Joseph) is given Wolfgang Amadeus Mozart's old job as court organist by Archbishop Colloredo of Salzburg, following Mozart's unceremonious departure from the role.

1826 Carl Maria von Weber makes his final public appearance, at a concert in London.

1839 Charles Gounod wins the Prix de Rome.

1844 Felix Mendelssohn visits Queen Victoria at Buckingham Palace. He even accompanies Her Majesty in an impromptu singalong around the piano.

1852 Charles Gounod gets a new job as Director General for Vocal Instruction for Paris's state-run schools.

1855 Clara Schumann hosts Franz Liszt and Joseph Joachim at her home in Düsseldorf.

1875 Georges Bizet is taken ill with what is described as an 'acute rheumatic attack'.

1933 Edward Elgar visits Frederick Delius at his home in France. Both composers are now in their seventies.

GENRE FOCUS:

Overture

Overtures started off life as short pieces played before the opera-house curtain rose on the main business of the evening. In many cases, they were little more than a medley of the tunes that were to appear later in the opera proper. In the Romantic era, the overture developed an existence of its own as a stand-alone piece of orchestral music. Such overtures are occasionally called 'concert overtures' to differentiate them from their pre-dramatic counterparts and are often similar in style to the later 'symphonic poem' or 'tone poem'. From Mozart's opera overtures, through Rossini's and Verdi's and on to the concert overtures by Beethoven, Berlioz, Mendelssohn and Brahms, the overture remains one of the most approachable forms of orchestral music around.

 HALL OF FAME HIT

Dmitri Shostakovich: *Symphony No. 5*

Recommended Recording

London Symphony Orchestra conducted by Maxim Shostakovich; Alto ALC 1067

31

MAY

'I was obliged to be industrious. Whoever is equally industrious will succeed equally well.'

JOHANN SEBASTIAN BACH, COMPOSER

🎵 BIRTHS & DEATHS

1809 Austrian composer Joseph Haydn dies in Vienna.

🎭 FIRST PERFORMED

1817 Gioachino Rossini's opera *The Thieving Magpie* is premiered at La Scala, Milan.

1884 Giacomo Puccini's opera *Le Villi (The Willies* or *The Fairies)* is premiered in Milan.

☀ TODAY'S THE DAY

1625 The court of King Charles I sets out from London to Canterbury. Senior organist Orlando Gibbons is taken seriously ill on the way to the Kent city; he never recovers.

1774 Wolfgang Amadeus Mozart finishes work on his *Sinfonia Concertante* for two violins and orchestra in Salzburg.

1790 Muzio Clementi appears in concert on solo piano for the final time, in London.

1794 Eleven-year-old Niccolò Paganini makes his public concert debut in Genoa.

1810 John Field gets married in the French Catholic Church in Moscow.

1841 Franz Liszt is injured when his coach overturns after a private concert for the Duke and Duchess of Cambridge.

1883 Gustav Mahler agrees the terms for his new job as Royal Music and Choral Director in Kassel.

1889 Jean Sibelius finishes studying at the Helsinki Music Institute.

1917 John Philip Sousa signs up to the US Naval Reserve.

VENUE FOCUS:

Glasgow Royal Concert Hall

'You've got a killer hall here.' So said the violinist Nigel Kennedy, no less, about the Glasgow Royal Concert Hall. It's Scotland's premier classical-music venue and is the place to go for great live concerts in the city. The auditorium holds just shy of 2,500 seats and is often packed to bursting for performances from the Royal Scottish National Orchestra (Classic FM's Orchestra in Scotland). It is also the primary venue for 'Celtic Connections', the world's largest winter music festival, and the Hall hosts more than 400 concerts every year. It hasn't always been in such good shape though. In the autumn of 1962, the then St Andrew's Halls were completely destroyed by fire. For the next 28 years, the city was without a concert hall, until the Glasgow Royal Concert Hall was opened in 1990.

HALL OF FAME HIT

Johann Sebastian Bach: *Goldberg Variations*

Recommended Recording

Glenn Gould (piano); Sony Classical 87703

June

01

'Nothing primes inspiration more than necessity.'
GIOACHINO ROSSINI, COMPOSER

JUNE

🕐 BIRTHS & DEATHS

1804 Russian composer Mikhail Glinka is born in Smolensk.
1826 German piano maker F. W. Bechstein is born in Gotha.
1906 English record company executive Walter Legge, who founded the Philharmonia Orchestra, is born in London.
1942 Spanish flamenco guitarist Paco Peña is born in Cordoba.
1943 American pianist Richard Goode is born in New York.

🎵 FIRST PERFORMED

1853 Franz Liszt's *Hungarian Fantasy* is given its first performance, in Budapest.
1869 A fully revised version of Bedřich Smetana's *The Bartered Bride* is premiered in Prague.

☀ TODAY'S THE DAY

1723 Johann Sebastian Bach becomes Cantor at St Thomas Church in Leipzig.
1728 The original Royal Academy of Music closes.
1750 At the age of 65, George Frideric Handel writes his will; he will amend it four times before his death.

1789 Pianist and composer Jan Ladislav Dussek performs for the first time at London's Hanover Square Rooms. He is to become a big name in the city over the next 11 years.
1791 Joseph Haydn is inspired to think about composing oratorios after hearing a performance of Handel's *Messiah* in Westminster Abbey.
1809 Joseph Haydn is buried in Vienna, although his head was stolen shortly afterwards, so that it could be examined by phrenologists. It will be almost 150 years before Haydn's body and head will be reunited.
1828 Gaetano Donizetti gets married in Rome.
1838 Frédéric Chopin arrives at George Sand's manor house in Nohant, in central France. He will compose some of his most significant music there each summer for the next eight years.
1840 Robert Schumann sues his father-in-law Friedrich Wieck for slander.
1847 Bedřich Smetana branches out on his own, leaving the employment of Count Leopold

Thun, to try his luck as a pianist on tour, across western Bohemia.
1872 Pyotr Ilyich Tchaikovsky meets Antonina Ivanovna Milyukova, the woman who will become his wife, for the first time. Theirs will be a deeply unhappy union.
1873 Jacques Offenbach becomes the manager of the Théâtre de la Gaîté in Paris.
1894 Englebert Humperdinck and Gustav Mahler meet for the first time, in Weimar.
1901 The music publishing company Universal Edition is founded in Vienna.
1918 Sergei Prokofiev arrives in Tokyo, where he performs a series of concerts.
1942 A microfilm containing the score and parts of Dmitri Shostakovich's *Symphony No. 7* (*'Leningrad'*) is taken by plane from Russia to America.
1953 Benjamin Britten is appointed a Companion of Honour.
1966 Tenor Luciano Pavarotti makes his debut at London's Covent Garden. He earns the epithet 'The King of the High Cs'.

🎵 HALL OF FAME HIT
George Frideric Handel: *Xerxes*

Recommended Recording
Renée Fleming; Orchestra of the Age of Enlightenment conducted by Harry Bicket; Decca 478 4446

'There is only one real happiness in life, and that is the happiness of creating.'

FREDERICK DELIUS, COMPOSER

02
JUNE

BIRTHS & DEATHS

1857 English composer Edward Elgar is born near Worcester.
1947 English conductor Mark Elder is born in Hexham.
1987 Spanish guitarist Andrés Segovia dies in Madrid.

FIRST PERFORMED

1896 Camille Saint-Saëns' *Piano Concerto No. 5* receives its first performance, in Paris, at a concert to celebrate his half-century of professional music-making. The composer is at the piano.

1937 Alban Berg's incomplete opera *Lulu* is premiered in Zurich.
1953 William Walton's *Coronation Te Deum* and *Orb and Sceptre* feature in the Coronation of Queen Elizabeth II at Westminster Abbey.

TODAY'S THE DAY

1715 Antonio Vivaldi gets a pay rise because of the standard of the music he is composing for the Pietà orphanage.
1846 Camille Saint-Saëns makes his debut at the piano, in Paris.
1874 Edvard Grieg is given a grant of 1,600 kroner by the Norwegian Parliament.

1967 The Snape Maltings concert hall in Suffolk, home of the Aldeburgh Festival, is opened by the Queen. It is the brainchild of composer Benjamin Britten.

COMPOSER PROFILE:

Edward Elgar

Considered by many as England's greatest ever composer, Edward Elgar was born into a musical family. His father ran a music shop in Worcester and was also the local travelling piano tuner. Although Edward learned piano, violin and organ as a youngster, he started off his working life in a solicitor's office. He hated it; by the time he was 16, he was working as a freelance musician. Elgar did not enjoy expensive private music tuition, nor did he study at a top-rated conservatoire. Much of what he learned he taught himself. By the turn of the 20th century, Elgar was composing extensively, fulfilling a particular need from English festivals and music societies for big choral works. He was still teaching violin to pay the bills, but had enormous success in London with the premiere of his *Enigma Variations*. His most creative period saw him write the choral barnstormers *The Dream of Gerontius*, *The Apostles* and *The Kingdom*, alongside two symphonies, his *Violin Concerto* and his *Introduction and Allegro for Strings*. He is probably most widely known for his *Pomp and Circumstance March No. 1*, to which A. C. Benson added the words of '*Land of Hope and Glory*'.

HALL OF FAME HIT

Wolfgang Amadeus Mozart: *Piano Concerto No. 20*

Recommended Recording

Mitsuko Uchida (piano); Cleveland Orchestra; Decca 478 2596

03

'Time is a great teacher, but unfortunately it kills all its pupils.'

HECTOR BERLIOZ, COMPOSER

JUNE

 BIRTHS & DEATHS

1875 French composer Georges Bizet dies in Paris.

1899 Austrian composer Johann Strauss Junior dies in Vienna.

1956 English soprano Lynne Dawson is born in York.

1965 German oboist Albrecht Mayer is born in Erlangen.

TODAY'S THE DAY

1831 Niccolò Paganini's concert series finally opens in London after controversy in the newspapers about sky-high ticket prices.

1854 The first concert on the new organ at Chichester Cathedral is performed by Samuel Sebastian Wesley.

1869 Georges Bizet gets married in Paris.

1869 Louis Moreau Gottschalk gives his first concert, in Rio de Janeiro. Leading society figures are there to hear him play.

1931 Edward Elgar is given a baronetcy (a hereditary knighthood).

1933 Edward Elgar is appointed a Knight of the Grand Cross of the Royal Victorian Order (GCVO) – an honour in the personal gift of the monarch.

1935 Ralph Vaughan Williams is appointed to the Order of Merit.

COMPOSER PROFILE:

Georges Bizet

Bizet was studying at the Paris Conservatoire by the time he was just nine years old and he had his compositional technique well honed by the time he was 17. His biggest hit in his own lifetime was his opera *The Pearl Fishers*, which features the incredibly popular duet 'Au fond du Temple Saint'. Bizet's greatest operatic achievement was *Carmen*, the story of a gypsy girl who, eventually, is murdered outside the bullring in Seville by the lover she abandoned.

It is packed full of wonderful tunes and has a violent, sexually charged story. After its premiere in 1875 proved unsuccessful, Bizet lost faith in his own work, branding it 'a definite and hopeless flop'. He retired to his bed and died from a heart attack just after the opera's 33rd performance. Now regarded as one of the greatest operas of all time, it is still being performed in opera houses around the world getting on for a century and a half later.

 HALL OF FAME HIT

Felix Mendelssohn: *A Midsummer Night's Dream*

Recommended Recording

Chicago Symphony Orchestra conducted by James Levine; Deutsche Grammophon 445 6052

'If you think you've hit a false note, sing loud. When in doubt, sing loud.'

ROBERT MERRILL, BARITONE

🎵 BIRTHS & DEATHS

1909 American composer and co-founder of the Nordoff–Robbins music-therapy charity Paul Nordoff is born in Philadelphia.

1917 American baritone Robert Merrill is born in New York.

1951 American double bassist and conductor Serge Koussevitzky dies in Boston.

1966 Italian mezzo-soprano Cecilia Bartoli is born in Rome.

☀ TODAY'S THE DAY

1774 Wolfgang Amadeus Mozart finishes work on his *Bassoon Concerto* in Salzburg.

1838 Hector Berlioz signs up to be director of the Théâtre-Italien in Paris.

1877 Pyotr Ilyich Tchaikovsky becomes engaged to Antonina Ivanovna Milyukova.

1894 Anton Rubinstein plays for students at Stuttgart Conservatoire in what is to be his final performance.

1934 Igor Stravinsky is granted French citizenship; it all becomes official on 10 June.

1944 When Allied troops reach the centre of Rome, the Free French forces requisition the Hotel Plaza for their officers. All of the guests are forced to leave, except for Pietro Mascagni and his wife.

INSTRUMENT FOCUS:

Bassoon

This rather large, elongated, wooden instrument sits in the woodwind section of the orchestra. In fact, it is the second lowest of all the woodwind instruments; the lowest being its close relation, the double bassoon, which is also known as the contra-bassoon. It is a 'double reed' instrument, which means that the player makes a sound by blowing through two reeds stuck together, rather than just one on its own. In terms of the bassoon's body, it is basically two conical pieces of wood (usually maple or Brazilian rosewood), connected a 'hairpin' design allowing the tube through which the sound travels to double back on itself. One of the instrument's many claims to fame is that it stars as the musical voice of the grandfather in Prokofiev's *Peter and the Wolf*.

HALL OF FAME HIT

George Frideric Handel: *Music for the Royal Fireworks*

Recommended Recording

Zefiro conducted by Alfredo Bernadini; Deutsche Harmonia Mundi 8869 73679128

05

JUNE

'Music is a pastime, a relaxation from more serious occupations.'

ALEXANDER BORODIN, COMPOSER

 BIRTHS & DEATHS

1625 English composer Orlando Gibbons dies in Canterbury.

1816 Italian composer Giovanni Paisiello dies in Naples.

1826 German composer Carl Maria von Weber dies in London.

1885 British composer and conductor Julius Benedict dies in London.

1941 Argentinian pianist Martha Argerich is born in Buenos Aires.

2004 English conductor and soloist Iona Brown dies in Salisbury.

TODAY'S THE DAY

1764 Eight-year-old Wolfgang Amadeus and 11-year-old Maria Anna Mozart make their London concert debut in the Spring Garden Rooms.

1773 Karl Ditters is allow to append 'von Dittersdorf' to his name by decree of Empress Maria Theresa.

1822 Ludwig van Beethoven writes to the music publisher Peters, offering to compose a string quartet for a fee of 50 ducats.

1824 Twelve-year-old Franz Liszt performs for the first time in London, in the Argyll Rooms.

1833 Felix Mendelssohn arrives in London for his fourth visit to the city. He brings his father with him.

1857 Mikhail Glinka is buried in St Petersburg.

1871 Charles Villiers Stanford becomes the assistant conductor of the Cambridge University Musical Society.

1874 Richard D'Oyly Carte is the new man in charge at the Opera Comique in London. He sees the work of Jacques Offenbach in Paris as the benchmark for success.

1875 Georges Bizet's funeral is held in Paris. Charles Gounod is among the mourners.

1891 Sergei Rachmaninov passes his piano exams at the Moscow Conservatoire, one year ahead of schedule.

1891 Antonín Dvořák is invited to become the director of the National Conservatory of Music in New York.

1907 Gustav Mahler signs up to direct the Metropolitan Opera from the beginning of the following year.

1909 Isaac Albéniz's body arrives at Barcelona's main railway station. Mourners are out in force to mark the occasion.

1925 A service takes place at Canterbury Cathedral to mark the 300th anniversary of the death of Orlando Gibbons; it is the first time a service held there is broadcast on the radio.

1937 An opera is televised in the UK for the first time; Charles Gounod's *Faust* is the chosen work.

1954 Joseph Haydn's skull is finally reunited with his body, almost 150 years after his death.

1970 Snape Maltings concert hall re-opens in time for the Aldeburgh Festival after being destroyed by fire this time the previous year.

1971 Conductor James Levine makes his debut with the Metropolitan Opera in New York.

 HALL OF FAME HIT

Dmitri Shostakovich: *Jazz Suite No. 2*

Recommended Recording

Royal Concertgebouw Orchestra conducted by Riccardo Chailly; Decca 475 9983

> 'If it is art, it is not for all, and if it is for all, it is not art.'
>
> ARNOLD SCHOENBERG, COMPOSER

06
JUNE

 BIRTHS & DEATHS

1840 English composer John Stainer is born in London.

1881 Belgian violinist and composer Henri Vieuxtemps dies in Algeria.

1903 Armenian composer Aram Khachaturian is born in Tblisi.

1926 German conductor Klaus Tennstedt is born in Merseburg.

1934 French pianist and conductor Philippe Entremont is born in Rheims.

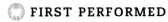 FIRST PERFORMED

1903 Edward Elgar's oratorio *The Dream of Gerontius* is premiered at Westminster Cathedral in London.

1925 Sergei Prokofiev's *Symphony No. 2* receives its first performance, in Paris.

1942 Heitor Villa-Lobos's *Bachianas Brasileiras No. 4* is first performed, in New York, with the composer conducting.

1943 Dmitri Shostakovich's *Piano Sonata No. 2* is given its first performance, in Moscow.

☀ TODAY'S THE DAY

1699 Jeremiah Clarke is appointed a vicar-choral at St Paul's Cathedral in London.

1727 During a performance of Giovanni Battista Bononcini's opera *Astianatte,* under the auspices of the original Royal Academy of Music in London, a simmering feud between the two leading sopranos descends into an unseemly fight on stage. So offended was the Princess of Wales, who was in the audience, that the whole season was abandoned.

1844 Jacques Offenbach performs for Queen Victoria, Prince Albert and assorted European royalty at Windsor Castle.

1882 Edvard Grieg is appointed a Knight of the Royal Norwegian Order of St Olav.

1899 Johann Strauss Junior is buried in Vienna, close to Beethoven, Schubert and Brahms. Gustav Mahler joins the crowd of mourners.

1909 Isaac Albéniz is buried in Barcelona.

VENUE FOCUS:

Wales Millennium Centre

The Wales Millennium Centre – or, to give it its Welsh name, the Canolfan Mileniem Cymru – is a buzzing part of Cardiff's cultural scene, and a destination venue for audiences from miles around. Every year, more than 500 performances of one kind or another take place there and the venue brings in £50 million to the Welsh economy. Performers include the resident Welsh National Opera, as well as visiting orchestras and ensembles from across the globe. When the venue was commissioned, the architects Percy Thomas were instructed to create somewhere that was 'unmistakably Welsh and internationally outstanding'. It opened in 2004 and, along with St David's Hall up the road, the Wales Millennium Centre provides a compelling reason to make a trip to Cardiff for an unforgettable classical-music experience.

HALL OF FAME HIT

Giacomo Puccini: *Turandot*

Recommended Recording

Various soloists; Vienna Philharmonic Orchestra conducted by Herbert von Karajan; Deutsche Grammophon 423 8552

07

'The old idea . . . of a composer suddenly having a terrific idea and sitting up all night to write it is nonsense. Night time is for sleeping.'

BENJAMIN BRITTEN, COMPOSER

JUNE

BIRTHS & DEATHS

1937 Estonian conductor Neeme Järvi is born in Tallinn.

1963 French tenor Roberto Alagna is born in Clichy-sous-Bois.

1967 Finnish pianist Olli Mustonen is born in Helsinki.

FIRST PERFORMED

1945 Benjamin Britten's opera *Peter Grimes* is premiered at Sadler's Wells Theatre in London. Fellow composers Ralph Vaughan Williams, William Walton and Michael Tippett are in the audience.

1958 William Walton's *Façade* is given its first performance, in London.

TODAY'S THE DAY

1856 Louis Moreau Gottschalk plays the last of his 16-date concert run at Dodworth's Hall in New York. He's been such a hit that extra seats were even placed on the stage.

1867 Franz Liszt is awarded the Commander's Cross of the Order of Franz Joseph.

1935 John Cage gets married in Arizona.

1939 Benjamin Britten and Peter Pears arrive in Toronto, as their tour of North America continues.

1969 The Snape Maltings concert hall, home of the Aldeburgh Festival, is destroyed by fire overnight after the opening concert of the annual festival.

COMPOSER PROFILE:

Benjamin Britten

Britten was mentored by the composer Frank Bridge when he was just 11 years old. Later, he studied at the Royal College of Music. He became close friends with the poet W. H. Auden and they collaborated on various projects for the G.P.O. Film Unit, which produced public information films, and concert works. He left Britain for North America at the start of the Second World War with the tenor Peter Pears, for whom he was to write many major operatic roles and song cycles. They eventually returned to the UK in 1942 and moved to the Suffolk town of Aldeburgh in 1947. Britten and his partner Pears are buried in the churchyard on the hill. Britten founded the Aldeburgh Festival in 1948; it is still going strong today. He wrote extensively for the annual event, as well as doing an enormous amount to redefine the English opera scene, penning works such as *Peter Grimes* and *Billy Budd*, which have become a permanent part of the repertoire. His *War Requiem* received rave reviews when it was premiered to celebrate the reconsecration of the rebuilt Coventry Cathedral in 1962.

HALL OF FAME HIT

Wolfgang Amadeus Mozart: *Don Giovanni*

Recommended Recording

Various soloists; Freiburg Baroque Orchestra and Chorus conducted by René Jacobs; Harmonia Mundi HMC 901 96466

'Music has always been transnational; people pick up whatever interests them, and certainly a lot of classical music has absorbed influences from all over the world.'

YO-YO MA, CELLIST

08

JUNE

BIRTHS & DEATHS

1671 Italian composer Tomaso Albinoni is born in Venice.
1810 German composer Robert Schumann is born in Saxony.
1949 American pianist Emanuel Ax is born in Lvov.

FIRST PERFORMED

1912 Maurice Ravel's ballet *Daphnis and Chloe* is premiered in Paris. Igor Stravinsky is in the audience.
1937 Carl Orff's choral work *Carmina Burana* is given its first performance, in Frankfurt.

TODAY'S THE DAY

1781 The Archbishop of Salzburg's chief of staff, Count Arco, tells Wolfgang Amadeus Mozart that he is free to leave the court 'with a kick on the arse, by order of our worthy Prince Archbishop'.
1847 Franz Liszt arrives in Constantinople for five weeks of concerts.
1874 Charles Gounod and his mistress Georgina Weldon finally part at London's Charing Cross railway station, after a stormy three-year affair.

1884 The music publisher Giovanni Ricordi announces that he will publish Giacomo Puccini's *Le Villi (The Willies* or *The Fairies)*.
1945 The Dresden Philharmonic begins giving concerts once again, following the end of the Second World War.

COMPOSER PROFILE:

Charles Gounod

When he was 21 years old, Gounod won the Prix de Rome composition competition and went on to become an organist in Paris – a pathway followed by many of the great French composers. In his thirties, he began to write operas, but success came only in his forties with *Faust*. He spent a good deal of time in England and his oratorio *Mors et Vita,* one particular part of which (the *Judex*) has become something of a hit among Classic FM listeners, was premiered at the Birmingham Festival. He is known to many nowadays for his addition to Bach's *Prelude No. 1* of an overlaying tune, which is now usually referred to as Gounod's *Ave Maria*.

HALL OF FAME HIT

John Williams: *Star Wars*

Recommended Recording
London Symphony Orchestra conducted by John Williams;
Sony SK 61816

09

JUNE

'To copy the truth can be a good thing, but to invent the truth is better, much better.'

GIUSEPPE VERDI, COMPOSER

🎵 BIRTHS & DEATHS

1766 Austrian trumpeter Anton Weidinger is born in Vienna.

1865 Danish composer Carl Nielsen is born in Norre-Lyndelse.

🎵 FIRST PERFORMED

1902 Gustav Mahler's *Symphony No. 3* is performed for the first time, in Krefeld, with the composer conducting. Richard Strauss and Engelbert Humperdinck are in the audience.

🌅 TODAY'S THE DAY

1759 William Boyce gets married in Stepney.

1763 Leopold Mozart leaves Salzburg behind to take his prodigious young children, Wolfgang and Maria Anna, on their first tour of Europe.

1840 Franz Liszt uses the word 'recital' for the first time, to describe a solo piano performance he is giving in the Hanover Square Rooms in London.

1846 A statue of Gioachino Rossini (who is still very much alive at this point) is unveiled at the Paris Opéra.

1876 Jacques Offenbach performs the last of a 30-date concert run in New York.

1879 Edward MacDowell makes his concert debut in Frankfurt, playing the music of Liszt. The composer is there to hear him.

1892 Alexander Scriabin is awarded a diploma from the Moscow Conservatoire.

1904 The London Symphony Orchestra makes its concert debut in the city's Queen's Hall with Hans Richter conducting.

1920 Eighteen-year-old William Walton passes his Bachelor of Music degree. Ralph Vaughan Williams is one of his examiners.

1921 Aaron Copland heads off by ship from New York to France, where he will continue his studies.

1921 After 18 years as *Le Figaro*'s music critic, Gabriel Fauré lays down his pen, with a final review of Hector Berlioz's *Les Troyens*.

1925 Carl Nielsen's 60th birthday is celebrated with a national holiday in his native Denmark.

1994 The Three Tenors sing in their second concert together, in Monte Carlo.

2004 The London Symphony Orchestra celebrates the centenary of its first concert, with Colin Davis conducting Britten's *Peter Grimes*.

🎵 HALL OF FAME HIT
Ennio Morricone: *The Mission*

Recommended Recording
Gilda Butta et al; Sony SK 93456

'The Prelude to *Tristan and Isolde* sounded as if a bomb had fallen in a large music factory and had thrown all the notes into confusion.'

J. STETTENHEIM, REVIEW IN THE BERLIN TRIBUNE TODAY IN 1873

10
JUNE

BIRTHS & DEATHS

1899 French composer Ernest Chausson dies in Limay.
1934 English composer Frederick Delius dies near Fontainebleau in France.
1960 English composer Mark-Anthony Turnage is born in Corringham.

FIRST PERFORMED

1791 Wolfgang Amadeus Mozart's final complete piece of chamber music, his *Adagio and Rondo for Glass Harmonica, Flute, Oboe, Viola and Cello*, is performed for the first time in Vienna.
1865 Richard Wagner's opera *Tristan and Isolde* is premiered in Munich, conducted by Hans von Bülow.

1939 Ralph Vaughan Williams' *Five Variants of Dives and Lazarus* receives its first performance, at Carnegie Hall in New York.

TODAY'S THE DAY

1673 Fourteen-year-old Henry Purcell is given an unpaid job as the assistant to the Keeper of the King's Wind and Keyboard Instruments.
1818 Gioachino Rossini's *The Thieving Magpie* opens the rebuilt opera house in Pesaro.
1855 Queen Victoria opens the Crystal Palace in London. A choir of 1,500 people performs Handel's *Hallelujah Chorus*.
1859 Pyotr Ilyich Tchaikovsky graduates from the School of Jurisprudence in Moscow and

takes up a job with the Ministry of Justice.
1892 Sergei Rachmaninov is awarded his diploma by the Moscow Conservatoire.
1911 Henry Purcell's *The Fairy Queen* has its first performance, at the Royal Victoria Hall in London, since the composer's death more than 200 years earlier. Gustav Holst is the driving force behind the production.
1949 In his last public concert, Richard Strauss conducts part of *Der Rosenkavalier* in Munich as part of the celebrations for his 85th birthday.
1969 Pierre Boulez is confirmed as the replacement for Leonard Bernstein as music director of the New York Philharmonic.

MUSICAL TERM:

Atonal

This term is applied to music that is not in a particular key, meaning that it is unlike almost all of the music played on Classic FM, which is written in a key or series of keys and is therefore 'tonal'. You do not need to have passed your music exams to hear when the progression of musical sounds seems inevitable and harmonious. By contrast, atonal music tends to sound uncomfortable and jarring. One form of atonal music, which has its own internal logic, with all twelve notes of the octave given equal precedence, is known as serial music. Schoenberg is the composer who is largely credited with developing this style of composition.

HALL OF FAME HIT

Claude Debussy: *Prélude à l'après-midi d'un faune*

Recommended Recording

Cleveland Orchestra conducted by Pierre Boulez; Deutsche Grammophon 435 7662

11

'A new language requires a new technique. If what you're saying doesn't require a new language, then what you're saying probably isn't new.'

PHILIP GLASS, COMPOSER

JUNE

🎵 BIRTHS & DEATHS

1864 German composer Richard Strauss is born in Munich.
1955 English conductor Douglas Bostock is born in Cheshire.

🎵 FIRST PERFORMED

1960 Benjamin Britten's opera *A Midsummer Night's Dream* is premiered in Aldeburgh.

☀ TODAY'S THE DAY

1804 Carl Maria von Weber arrives in Breslau ready for his new job as Kapellmeister.

1831 He may only be 21 years old, but today Frédéric Chopin plays in Vienna for the final time.
1845 The Birmingham Festival committee votes to commission Felix Mendelssohn to compose a new oratorio for the next festival and for him to conduct it.
1855 Queen Victoria and Prince Albert are in the audience for one of Richard Wagner's series of seven orchestral concerts in London.
1867 Edvard Grieg gets married to his cousin in Copenhagen.

1892 Edvard Grieg composes *Wedding Day at Troldhaugen* to celebrate his 25th wedding anniversary.
1937 Arnold Bax receives his knighthood at Buckingham Palace.

COMPOSER PROFILE:

Richard Strauss

The son of the principal horn player in the Munich Court Orchestra (now the Bavarian State Orchestra), Strauss grew up as a lover of Wagner's music – a predilection possibly stimulated by his father's antipathy. Having written his first symphony at the age of 16 without any formal composition lessons, he soon became regarded as a musical iconoclast, first as a conductor and then as a composer. His series of symphonic tone poems, starting with *Tod und Verklärung* (*Death and Transfiguration*) and *Macbeth,* continuing with *Also Sprach Zarathustra, Don Juan, Ein Heldenleben* and *Till*

Eulenspiegel made him the hottest musical property in Germany. With the 20th century, Strauss turned to opera, becoming, arguably, the most important operatic composer of his generation. *Salome,* which created a scandal at its first performances because of its racy treatment of a biblical theme, *Elektra* and *Der Rosenkavalier* are towering works, still firmly in the operatic repertoire. His *Four Last Songs* for soprano and orchestra (there were to be five, but the cycle was left incomplete) is one of the most moving swansongs produced by any composer.

🎵 HALL OF FAME HIT

Dmitri Shostakovich: *Jazz Suite No. 1*

Recommended Recording

Royal Concertgebouw Orchestra conducted by Riccardo Chailly; Decca 475 9983

'Creativity is more than just being different. Anybody can play weird – that's easy. What's hard is to be as simple as Bach. Making the simple awesomely simple, that's creativity.'

CHARLES MINGUS, COMPOSER

🏛 BIRTHS & DEATHS

1952 British composer Oliver Knussen is born in Glasgow.
1962 English composer John Ireland dies in Sussex.
1967 German composer Klaus Badelt is born in Frankfurt.
2006 Hungarian composer György Ligeti dies in Vienna.

🎭 FIRST PERFORMED

1923 William Walton's *Façade,* with words by Edith Sitwell, is given its first performance, at the Aeolian Hall in London, with the composer conducting. It does not go down well with many in the first-night crowd.

☀ TODAY'S THE DAY

1766 Wolfgang Amadeus Mozart finishes work on his *Symphony No. 31* in Paris.
1893 Ahead of receiving degrees from Cambridge University, Max Bruch, Pyotr Ilyich Tchaikovsky and Camille Saint-Saëns all conduct a selection of their works in the city.

1905 Gabriel Fauré starts his new job as director of the Paris Conservatoire.
1973 William Walton conducts a 50th-anniversary performance of *Façade* at the Aeolian Hall in London. It is the final time the public sees him conducting.
1976 Benjamin Britten becomes Baron Britten of Aldeburgh in the County of Suffolk; he is the first composer to receive a life peerage.

COMPOSER PROFILE:

Max Bruch

Bruch composed his *Violin Concerto No. 1* when he was just 28 years old. Arguably, he spent the rest of his life trying to emulate that success. He lived his life in the shadow of Brahms, while his conservative outlook on composition might also have held him back. He wrote three operas and achieved some success with his choral works, particularly with the public in his native Germany. Noted for his somewhat grumpy personality, Bruch spent a few bad-tempered years as principal conductor of the Liverpool Philharmonic Orchestra between 1880 and 1883, though, during his time on Merseyside, he did manage to produce his *Kol Nidrei*, a soulful setting for cello and orchestra of a Jewish prayer that is considered one of his best works. He was also in charge of the Scottish Orchestra (now the Royal Scottish National Orchestra) between 1898 and 1900.

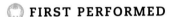

🎵 HALL OF FAME HIT

Ludwig van Beethoven: *Egmont Overture*

Recommended Recording

Philharmonia Orchestra conducted by Vladimir Ashkenazy; Australian Eloquence 480 7722

13

'If a film score comes out uninfluenced by Berlioz, it's no good!'

MALCOLM ARNOLD, COMPOSER

JUNE

BIRTHS & DEATHS

1700 Master of the King's Musick Nicholas Staggins dies in Windsor.

1899 Mexican composer and conductor Carlos Chávez is born in Mexico City.

1963 English mezzo-soprano Sarah Connolly is born in Middlesborough.

FIRST PERFORMED

1784 Wolfgang Amadeus Mozart's *Piano Concerto No. 17* is first performed, in Döbling.

1811 Carl Maria von Weber's *Clarinet Concerto No. 1* receives its first performance, in Munich.

1911 Igor Stravinsky's ballet *Petrushka* is premiered in Paris.

1945 Benjamin Britten's *Four Sea Interludes* from *Peter Grimes* is given its first performance, in Cheltenham, with the composer conducting.

1986 John Adams' *Short Ride in a Fast Machine* is heard for the first time, in Mansfield, Massachusetts.

TODAY'S THE DAY

1748 George Frideric Handel finishes work on his oratorio *Solomon*.

1828 Mikhail Glinka gives up his civil service job in the Office of Communications and sets off on his travels to Italy.

1835 Felix Mendelssohn agrees to direct the following year's Gewandhaus concerts in Leipzig.

1855 Hector Berlioz conducts the New Philharmonic Society at London's Exeter Hall. Once again, the crowd is wowed.

1872 Johann Strauss Junior arrives in New York for a conducting engagement in Boston. As well as his wife and servants, he brings his dog along too.

1886 Richard Wagner's huge personal supporter and benefactor King Ludwig II of Bavaria drowns in Lake Starnberg.

1893 Camille Saint-Saëns, Arrigo Boito, Max Bruch, Edvard Grieg and Pyotr Ilyich Tchaikovsky all receive honorary degrees from Cambridge University, although Grieg is too unwell to pick his up in person.

1905 Gabriel Fauré is given the job of running the Paris Conservatoire.

COMPOSER PROFILE:

Mikhail Glinka

Glinka's parents were fairly wealthy, allowing him the creative freedom to do what he wanted without fear of ever suffering poverty. He studied for a short period with the Irish composer John Field, before travelling to Italy, where he developed a love of opera. His first smash hit was *A Life for the Tsar* and it propelled him to the position of being the first major Russian opera composer. His music virtually defined the Russian Nationalist sound overnight. Glinka's second opera, *Russlan and Ludmilla*. cemented his success outside his homeland. He created unquestionably Russian music for the rest of his life, paving the way for a new generation of Russian composers, all of whom continued to write music that relied heavily on their native folk sounds for its inspiration.

HALL OF FAME HIT

Camille Saint-Saëns: *Samson and Delilah*

Recommended Recording

Various soloists; Orchestra and Chorus of the Bastille Opera conducted by Myung-Whun Chung; EMI 088 1982

> 'Since Mozart's day, composers have learnt the art of making music throatily and palpitatingly sexual.'
>
> **ALDOUS HUXLEY, WRITER**

14
JUNE

🎵 BIRTHS & DEATHS
1982 Chinese pianist Lang Lang is born in Shenyang.
1994 American composer Henry Mancini dies in Beverley Hills.
2005 Italian conductor Carlo Maria Giulini dies in Brescia.

🎵 FIRST PERFORMED
1846 Hector Berlioz's *Le Chant des chemins de fer* is first performed, as part of the opening of Paris's Gare du Nord.
1876 Léo Delibes' ballet *Sylvia* is premiered in Paris.
1921 Ralph Vaughan Williams' *The Lark Ascending* is performed for the first time, in its original orchestral setting, at the Queen's Hall in London.
1942 Benjamin Britten's *A Ceremony of Carols* is given its first performance, in Aldeburgh.
1946 Francis Poulenc's *The Story of Babar the Elephant* is premiered in Paris, with the composer at the keyboard.

🌅 TODAY'S THE DAY
1787 Wolfgang Amadeus Mozart finishes work on his *A Musical Joke*.

1842 Felix Mendelssohn meets Prince Albert at Buckingham Palace for the first time. He is to become a firm favourite with the royals.
1914 Richard Strauss is made a Chevalier of the French Légion d'Honneur.
1918 Gustav Holst passes the medical examination to become a YMCA Music Organiser.
1970 Dmitri Shostakovich's *Symphony No. 14* is heard for the first time outside Russia. Benjamin Britten conducts.

ORCHESTRA FOCUS:

London Philharmonic Orchestra

Thomas Beecham founded the LPO in 1932 and the new orchestra gave its first concert at the Queen's Hall in London that same year. Just seven years later, with the outbreak of the Second World War, it ran into financial difficulties and was saved from bankruptcy only by its players, who took over the administration. It has been self-governing ever since. The LPO's notable international achievements include being the first ever British orchestra to appear in Soviet Russia (in 1956) and being the first Western orchestra to visit China (in 1973). The orchestra is resident at the Royal Festival Hall in London and also spends the summer as the resident orchestra at Glyndebourne – a role it has undertaken since 1964. The LPO is also particularly successful in the cinema, with its soundtrack recordings including *The Lord of the Rings* trilogy, *Lawrence of Arabia* and *The Mission*. After Beecham, its principal conductors have included Adrian Boult, Bernard Haitink, Georg Solti, Klaus Tennstedt, Kurt Masur and the present incumbent Vladimir Jurowski – one of a new generation of young conductors galvanising the British orchestral scene.

🎵 HALL OF FAME HIT

Joseph Haydn: *The Creation*

Recommended Recording
Various soloists; Vienna Philharmonic Orchestra and the Arnold Schoenberg Choir conducted by Nikolaus Harnoncourt; Apex 2564 615932

15
JUNE

'I occasionally play works by contemporary composers, and for two reasons. First, to discourage the composer from writing any more, and second to remind myself how much I appreciate Beethoven.'

JASCHA HEIFETZ, VIOLINIST

BIRTHS & DEATHS

1763 German composer Franz Danzi is born in Mannheim.
1812 Austrian clarinettist Anton Stadler, for whom Mozart wrote his *Clarinet Concerto*, dies in Vienna.
1843 Norwegian composer Edvard Grieg is born in Bergen.
1865 Conductor of the Liverpool Philharmonic, J. Zeugheer Herrmann, dies in Liverpool.
1953 English cellist Raphael Wallfisch is born in London.
1983 German violinist Julia Fischer is born in Munich.

FIRST PERFORMED

1810 Ludwig van Beethoven's *Egmont Overture* is first performed, in Vienna.

1889 John Philip Sousa's march *'The Washington Post'* receives its first performance, at the Smithsonian Institute in Washington DC.

TODAY'S THE DAY

1809 Mozart's *Requiem* is sung at a memorial service in Vienna for Joseph Haydn.
1853 Johannes Brahms meets Franz Liszt, who is more than twenty years his senior. Brahms is too nervous to play any music for the more experienced composer.
1882 Erik Satie is kicked out of the Paris Conservatoire after failing his examination performance of Beethoven's *Piano Sonata No. 12*.

1891 After hearing a celesta played in Paris, Pyotr Ilyich Tchaikovsky immediately places an order for the new instrument.
1899 Gabriel Fauré, Isaac Albéniz and Claude Debussy are among the mourners at the funeral of Ernest Chausson in St François-de-Sales.
1908 42-year-old Erik Satie passes his counterpoint exams at the Schola Cantorum in Paris.
1920 The sound of Nellie Melba singing is broadcast on the Marconi transmitter at Writtle, near Chelmsford.
1928 Alexander Glazunov leaves Leningrad for Vienna, where he is representing Russia in the official commemoration of the centenary of Franz Schubert's death.

The Well-tempered Clavier

This enormous body of work by Johann Sebastian Bach was more than 20 years in the making. It is a collection of 48 preludes and fugues to be played on a keyboard, two in each of the major and minor keys. The first 24 were written in Bach's Cöthen period, with the second being composed while he was in Leipzig. The 'well-tempered' in the title is in reference to the 'temperament', which was a method of tuning an instrument. Bach was something of a trailblazer in this area. In terms of the pieces themselves, the preludes are quite free-roaming, but the fugues are the exact opposite.

HALL OF FAME HIT
Henry Litolff: *Concerto Symphonique No. 4*

Recommended Recording
Peter Donohoe (piano); Bournemouth Symphony Orchestra conducted by Andrew Litton; Hyperion CDA 66889

> 'I almost think that my emotional life and the life of my thoughts have more to say than my artistic life.'
> **COMPOSER PERCY GRAINGER, IN A LETTER WRITTEN ON THIS DAY IN 1917**

16

JUNE

BIRTHS & DEATHS

1909 Austrian conductor Willi Boskovsky is born in Vienna.
1986 French composer Maurice Duruflé dies in Paris.

FIRST PERFORMED

1929 Dmitri Shostakovich's opera *The Nose* is premiered in concert in Leningrad.

TODAY'S THE DAY

1710 George Frideric Handel begins working for the Elector of Hanover, who will ultimately become King George I.
1816 Antonio Salieri is presented with a gold medal as part of the celebrations to mark the 50th anniversary of the composer's arrival in Vienna.
1837 Niccolò Paganini performs for the very last time, in Turin.
1844 Felix Mendelssohn has dinner with the author Charles Dickens, in London.
1891 Antonín Dvořák is awarded a doctorate by Cambridge University.

VENUE FOCUS:

Philharmonic Hall

This is the place to go if you want to hear the Royal Liverpool Philharmonic Orchestra (Classic FM's Orchestra in the North West of England). This Grade II listed building dates from the 1930s. Nowadays, the 1,790-seat Art Deco concert hall is home not just to the Liverpool Phil, but to a huge range of ensembles – from jazz and folk to pop and rock.

The Royal Liverpool Philharmonic gives around 70 concerts a year in this, its home venue, but if you want to hear the orchestra elsewhere in Liverpool, you'll often find it performing in the city's two cathedrals. It also regularly heads further afield, performing across the UK and around the world. While you're in Liverpool, you should also check out St George's Hall, just opposite Lime Street station. It's one of the most beautiful concert halls anywhere in the world and has even been designated a World Heritage Site.

HALL OF FAME HIT

Wolfgang Amadeus Mozart: *Horn Concerto No. 4*

Recommended Recording
Alessio Allegrini (horn); Orchestra Mozart conducted by Claudio Abbado; Deutsche Grammophon 477 8083

17

JUNE

'Writing a tune is like sculpting. You get four or five notes, you take one out and move one around . . . and eventually, as the sculptor says, "In that rock there is a statue, we have to go find it."'

JOHN WILLIAMS, COMPOSER

🕊 BIRTHS & DEATHS

1818 French composer Charles Gounod is born in Paris.
1882 Russian composer Igor Stravinsky in born near St Petersburg.

🎭 FIRST PERFORMED

1919 Manuel de Falla's *Three-Cornered Hat* is first performed, in a concert version, in Madrid.

🌅 TODAY'S THE DAY

1733 After a period when the concert halls in Leipzig fell quiet out of respect for the death of Elector Friedrich August I, performances by Johann Sebastian Bach's Collegium Musicum get back under way.

1783 Wolfgang Amadeus Mozart's wife, Constanze, gives birth to their first child, Raimund Leopold. Sadly, he is one of four of their six children to die in infancy.
1789 A fire quickly takes hold at the King's Theatre in London midway through a rehearsal, destroying the building.
1816 Franz Schubert makes a note in his diary that he has just composed a piece of music for a fee for the very first time.
1858 Modest Mussorgsky gives up life as an army officer, deciding to pursue a career in music instead.
1869 Hans von Bülow agrees to a formal separation from his wife

Cosima. He appears not to know that she has just given birth to Richard Wagner's baby.
1872 Johann Strauss Junior and his orchestra are among the headline acts at the World Peace Jubilee and International Music Festival in Boston.
1914 Jean Sibelius is awarded a doctorate by Yale University.
1997 The Three Tenors sing together in concert for the 15th time, in Modena.

Taking Boney apart

Evidently Napoleon fancied himself as something of a music critic, telling the composer Cherubini, 'My dear Cherubini, you are certainly an excellent musician; but really your music is so noisy and complicated that I can make nothing of it.' Without missing a beat, came the reply from the composer: 'My dear general, you are certainly an excellent soldier, but in regard to music, you must excuse me if I don't think it necessary to adapt my compositions to your comprehension.' Touché.

🎵 HALL OF FAME HIT
Antonio Vivaldi: *Motet in E major*

Recommended Recording
Emma Kirkby (soprano); Academy of Ancient Music conducted by Christopher Hogwood; Decca Virtuoso 478 3615

> 'It is easy to play any musical instrument: all you have to do is touch the right key at the right time and the instrument will play itself.'
>
> **JOHANN SEBASTIAN BACH, COMPOSER**

18

🕐 BIRTHS & DEATHS

1942 English pop singer turned classical composer Paul McCartney is born in Liverpool.
1953 English pianist Peter Donohoe is born in Manchester.

🎵 FIRST PERFORMED

1778 Wolfgang Amadeus Mozart's *Symphony No. 31*, is first performed, in Paris.
1821 Carl Maria von Weber's opera *Der Freischütz* is premiered, in Berlin. 12-year-old Felix Mendelssohn is there to listen and learn.

☀ TODAY'S THE DAY

1770 In a seemingly rare moment away from musical endeavours, during one of their European tours, Leopold and Wofgang Amadeus Mozart travel from Naples to see the volcanic Mount Vesuvius, in Pompeii.
1812 Antonio Salieri takes Franz Schubert as a pupil in Vienna, teaching him counterpoint.
1819 Vincenzo Bellini begins studying at music college in Naples.
1907 Alexander Glazunov is awarded a doctorate by Oxford University.

1929 RCA places an order for 500 theramins – a new electronic musical instrument. The company wants to find out if it can create a market for new invention.
1963 The fiftieth anniversary of the first performance of Igor Stravinsky's *The Rite of Spring* in its original venue in Paris. There is no riot this time.

COMPOSER PROFILE:

Paul McCartney

Having been at the very top of the pop music tree since the 1960s, Paul McCartney successfully made the move into classical music in the 1990s. His first major classical work was the *Liverpool Oratorio*, a collaboration with Carl Davis, to celebrate the Royal Liverpool Philharmonic's 150th anniversary. It received its premiere in Liverpool Cathedral in 1991 and the subsequent album recording features the sopranos Kiri Te Kanawa and Sally Burgess, the tenor Jerry Hadley and the bass-baritone Willard White, performing alongside the Royal Liverpool Philharmonic Orchestra and the choir of Liverpool Cathedral. McCartney's other classical works include: *Standing Stone* (1997), featuring the London Symphony Orchestra conducted by Lawrence Foster, *Working Classical* (1999), a collection of short classical pieces, some of which are based on his earlier pop compositions; and *Ecce Cor Meum* (2006), an oratorio in four movements that won the Best Album category in the 2007 Classic Brit Awards. The title is Latin for 'Behold My Heart'.

🎵 HALL OF FAME HIT

Joseph Canteloube: *Songs of the Auvergne*

Recommended Recording

Véronique Gens; Orchestre National de Lille conducted by Jean-Claude Casadesus; Naxos 8557491

19

Advice to a pianist: 'When a piece gets difficult, make faces.'

ARTUR SCHNABEL, PIANIST

JUNE

 FIRST PERFORMED

1899 Edward Elgar's *Enigma Variations* is given its first performance, at St James's Hall in London.

 TODAY'S THE DAY

1678 Johann Pachelbel is hired as organist at the Protestant Predigerkirche at Erfurt.
1841 Eleven-year-old Anton Rubinstein plays in front of the Dutch King Willem II.
1876 John Philip Sousa is one of the first violins in a concert in Philadelphia conducted by Jacques Offenbach.

ERA FOCUS:

The Romantic period

Even the actual dates of the Romantic period of classical music are frequently disputed, so it is easy to see how a precise definition of the term might be tricky to establish. Romantic music has been claimed to cover any piece of music written from 1815 (some say as late as 1830) onwards to 1900 or 1910, although some composers of the period continued to write Romantic music well beyond the 1930s.

As a definable term, it is possible to get to grips with it only by means of placing it in the context of other musical periods. This way, it can be seen as simply the maturing of the Classical period, which was itself a maturing of – and occasionally a reaction to – the Baroque period. If we accept the argument that the rules of music had been worked out in the Baroque period and then explored in the Classical one, they undoubtedly were now stretched to their limit and broken. As part of a movement in which the same was happening in art and literature – particularly between 1830 and 1850 – Romantic composers shook off the shackles in favour of free-ranging expression. Music was allowed to paint pictures, to evoke poems and to play on the emotions.

 HALL OF FAME HIT
Wolfgang Amadeus Mozart:
Symphony No. 41 ('Jupiter')

Recommended Recording
Scottish Chamber Orchestra conducted by Charles Mackerras;
Linn CKD 308

'I'm a flute player, not a flautist. I don't have a flaut and I've never flauted.'

JAMES GALWAY, FLUTE PLAYER

BIRTHS & DEATHS

1819 French composer Jacques Offenbach is born in Cologne.
1831 The founder of the Bournemouth Symphony Orchestra Dan Godfrey is born in London.
1922 Italian composer Vittorio Monti dies.
1992 English conductor Charles Groves dies in London.

FIRST PERFORMED

1901 Edward Elgar's *Cockaigne Overture (In London Town)* is performed for the first time, at the Queen's Hall in London, with the composer conducting.
1947 Benjamin Britten's opera *Albert Herring* is premiered at Glyndebourne.

TODAY'S THE DAY

1825 Thirteen-year-old Franz Liszt performs at the piano in Manchester. He's also on the bill as a composer, with 'A New Grand Overture, by Master Liszt' advertised to concertgoers.
1852 Composers Giacomo Meyerbeer and Mikhail Glinka meet in Berlin.
1868 Anton Bruckner gets a new job on the teaching staff at the Vienna Conservatoire.
1883 Ernest Chausson gets married in Paris.
1922 A national tribute is held in France in honour of Gabriel Fauré.

Conductors

Conductors are the gods and goddesses of the classical music world. At the highest levels, they command hefty fees (unlike the rank-and-file performers they conduct) and can tell you what they will be doing sometimes many years into the future, so great are the demands on their time. Their role, musically speaking, is not just the obvious one of using their baton or hands to keep time for all the players and/or singers in front of them to see. A conductor also plays an important part as the channel for the overall interpretation of the music. They have a lot of say over how an orchestra makes a particular piece of music sound. Some conductors choose to try to interpret a composer's wishes to the tiniest degree, hoping to bring out every nuance in the music as its writer intended it. Others prefer simply to be a channel for their own unique vision (perhaps audition would be a better word in this case) of the way the music should sound. Often this is done not just by means of time and dynamics, but via something wholly more indefinable: the quality of the conductor's presence on the podium, the rapport already established with the musicians, and even mere movements and gestures of the eyes.

HALL OF FAME HIT
Vincenzo Bellini: *Norma*

Recommended Recording
Maria Callas (soprano); Orchestra and Chorus of La Scala, Milan conducted by Tullio Serafin; EMI 094 8302

21

JUNE

'If something happened where I couldn't write music any more, it would kill me. It's not just a job. It's not just a hobby. It's why I get up in the morning.'

HANS ZIMMER, COMPOSER

BIRTHS & DEATHS

1732 German composer Johann Christoph Friedrich Bach is born in Leipzig.

1899 Czech composer Pavel Haas is born in Brno.

1908 Russian composer Nikolai Rimsky-Korsakov dies in St Petersburg.

1958 American mezzo-soprano Jennifer Larmore is born in Atlanta.

1963 Italian composer Dario Marianelli is born in Pisa.

2000 American composer Alan Hovhaness dies in Seattle.

FIRST PERFORMED

1868 Richard Wagner's opera *Die Meistersinger von Nürnberg* is premiered in Munich, with Hans von Bülow conducting.

1890 Richard Strauss's tone poem *Death and Transfiguration* is given its first performance, in Eisenach, with the composer conducting.

1902 Edward Elgar's 'Land of Hope and Glory' (with words by A. C. Benson) receives its first performance, at the Royal Albert Hall in London.

1980 Peter Maxwell Davies' *Farewell to Stromness* is heard for the first time, at the St Magnus Festival in Orkney, with the composer at the piano.

TODAY'S THE DAY

1824 Twelve-year-old Franz Liszt appears at the keyboard in public in London for the first time, at the Argyll Rooms. Muzio Clementi is in the audience.

1826 Carl Maria von Weber's funeral is held in London. He is buried in Moorfields Chapel.

1856 Confirming his place among the Parisian artistic elite, having previously been seen as something of the 'bad boy of music', Hector Berlioz is elected to the French Institute, filling the vacancy caused by the death of fellow composer Adolphe Adam.

1868 Franz Liszt gives a concert at the Vatican for Pope Pius IX, who is celebrating 22 years as pontiff.

1888 Ludwig van Beethoven's remains are exhumed and moved to the Zentralfriedhof (the main cemetery) in Vienna. Anton Bruckner is among those in attendance.

1907 Gustav Mahler signs up to conduct the Metropolitan Opera in New York for three months per year for the next four years.

1916 Ralph Vaughan Williams is posted to France as an army medic during the First World War.

HALL OF FAME HIT

Joseph Haydn: *Trumpet Concerto*

Recommended Recording

Alison Balsom (trumpet); German Philharmonic Chamber Orchestra of Bremen; EMI 216 2130

> 'The good singer should be nothing but an able interpreter of the ideas of the master, the composer. In short, the composer and the poet are the only true creators.'
>
> GIOACHINO ROSSINI, COMPOSER

22
JUNE

 BIRTHS & DEATHS

1910 English tenor Peter Pears is born in Farnham.

1933 Czech conductor Libor Pešek is born in Prague.

1974 French composer Darius Milhaud dies in Geneva.

FIRST PERFORMED

1810 Louis Spohr's *Clarinet Concerto No. 2* is performed for the first time, in Frankenhausen.

1911 At the Coronation of George V in Westminster Abbey, both Edward Elgar's *Coronation March* and Hubert Parry's *Te Deum in D* are given their first performances. Parry also revises his anthem '*I was glad*', which was first heard at the Coronation of Edward VII.

1943 Aaron Copland's ballet *Rodeo* receives its first performance in an orchestral arrangement, in New York.

 TODAY'S THE DAY

1832 Eighteen-year-old Giuseppe Verdi applies to enter the Milan Conservatoire.

1832 Felix Mendelssohn leaves London to go home to Berlin. It's been another good trip to England: he met Niccolò Paganini and was also given a brand new piano.

1846 Adolphe Sax patents the saxophone.

1857 Fifteen-year-old Arthur Sullivan finds his time as a member of the Chapel Royal drawing to a close, after his voice breaks.

1901 Gustav Holst gets married at Fulham Register Office in London.

1911 The world's largest organ, the Wanamaker Organ, named after the owner of John Wanamaker's Department Store in Philadelphia, is heard in public for the first time today.

1921 Music is broadcast from the Eiffel Tower in Paris for the first time.

1939 Leonard Bernstein graduates from Harvard University.

1940 John Ireland is evacuated from Guernsey because of the serious threat of German occupation of the Channel Islands.

2001 The Three Tenors sing together in concert for the 27th time, in Seoul.

MUSICAL TERM:

Symphony

The word symphony derives from Greek, meaning 'sounding together'. There have been various definitions of what exactly a symphony is over the years, but today it means an extended work for an orchestra. Very often, but not always, this consists of four movements; many consider it the purest form of music a composer can write.

 HALL OF FAME HIT
Franz Schubert: *Symphony No. 5*

Recommended Recording
Royal Concertgebouw Orchestra conducted by Nikolaus Harnoncourt; Teldec 2564 688316

23

JUNE

BIRTHS & DEATHS

1927 Scottish tenor Kenneth McKellar is born in Paisley.
1943 American conductor James Levine is born in Cincinnati.
1950 English conductor Nicholas Cleobury is born in Bromley.

FIRST PERFORMED

1791 Wolfgang Amadeus Mozart's *Ave Verum Corpus* is premiered in Baden, near Vienna.

TODAY'S THE DAY

1755 Giovanni Battista Sammartini gets married for the second time, in Milan.
1758 William Boyce is appointed organist at the Chapel Royal.
1830 The Royal Academy of Music receives its royal charter.
1844 Franz Liszt performs in concert on the piano for the last time, in Paris.
1848 Richard Wagner is in need of cash again; this time he sends a begging letter to Franz Liszt.

1876 Gustav Mahler wins first prize in the piano competition at the Vienna Conservatoire.
1879 Librettist Arrigo Boito talks Giuseppe Verdi through the storyline for *Otello*, while the two are in Milan.
1883 Isaac Albéniz gets married in Barcelona.
2001 The Three Tenors sing together in concert for the 28th time, in Beijing.

Tenor at the movies

When you're famous for one thing, it can seem like a good idea to try your hand at something else, to see if you can become celebrated for that too. So it was, in 1982, for Luciano Pavarotti when he made an ill-fated bid to achieve stardom as a film actor. Pavarotti played the male lead in a romantic comedy with the unlikely title *Yes, Giorgio*. The movie told the tale of an international opera star, by the name of Fini, who suddenly loses his voice. Thanks to the medical expertise and love of a young lady doctor, called Pamela, his vocal cords perk up and all is well in the world. Pavarotti's character is heard to utter a chat-up line that deserves to achieve immortality: 'Pamela, you are a thirsty plant. Fini can water you.' The *New York Times* review of the film notes, '*Yes, Giorgio* is rated PG ("Parental Guidance suggested"). Its sexual innuendoes will not disturb children, although adults may find them alarming.'

HALL OF FAME HIT

Pyotr Ilyich Tchaikovsky: *Capriccio Italien*

Recommended Recording

Los Angeles Philharmonic Orchestra conducted by Zubin Mehta; Australian Eloquence 466 6842

'The only blight on my 80th birthday is the realisation my age will probably keep me from celebrating the funeral of your senile music columnist.'

COMPOSER IGOR STRAVINSKY IN A LETTER TO THE EDITOR OF *THE NEW YORK HERALD TRIBUNE*, PUBLISHED TODAY, 1962

24

JUNE

FIRST PERFORMED

1943 Ralph Vaughan Williams' *Symphony No. 5* is performed for the first time, at London's Royal Albert Hall, with the composer conducting.

TODAY'S THE DAY

1678 As part of his contract as organist of the Protestant Predigerkirche at Erfurt, Johann Pachelbel is required to undergo an examination every year on this day to ensure that his music-making has improved over the preceding 12 months.
1767 Johann Christoph Friedrich Bach applies to succeed Telemann as music director in Hamburg, but he misses out on the job to his brother, Carl Philipp Emanuel Bach.
1806 Because of the quality of his voice, 14-year-old Gioachino Rossini is given a place to study free of charge at the Bologna Accademia Filarmonica.
1835 Twelve-year-old César Franck starts his composition lessons in Paris.
1837 In a sign of the lack of equality between male and female composers, Felix Mendelssohn suggests it would not be the done thing for his sister Fanny to have her musical works published.

1839 Robert Schumann begins the legal process to allow him to marry Clara Wieck, even if her father continues to forbid the union.
1865 Samuel Sebastian Wesley begins work as the organist at Gloucester Cathedral.
1872 A new orchestra school opens in Weimar, to improve training prospects for instrumental musicians.
1876 Less than three months after joining, Isaac Albéniz walks out of the Leipzig Conservatoire.
1886 Johann Strauss Junior becomes a citizen of the Duchy of Saxe-Coburg-Gotha, enabling him to marry his mistress.
1908 The funeral of Nikolai Rimsky-Korsakov is held in St Petersburg.
1934 Ralph Vaughan Williams conducts the music at a service at Chichester Cathedral, where Gustav Holst's ashes are laid to rest.

HALL OF FAME HIT

Gustav Mahler: *Symphony No. 1* ('Titan')

Recommended Recording
London Symphony Orchestra conducted by Valery Gergiev; LSO Live 0663

25

> 'It's not hard to compose, but it is wonderfully hard to let the superfluous notes fall under the table.'
>
> JOHANNES BRAHMS, COMPOSER

JUNE

🎵 BIRTHS & DEATHS

1767 German composer Georg Philipp Telemann dies in Hamburg.

1822 German writer and composer E. T. A. Hoffmann dies in Berlin.

🎵 FIRST PERFORMED

1840 Felix Mendelssohn's *Symphony No. 2* and *Festgesang* for male chorus are first performed, at the Leipzig Festival, with the composer conducting. Eventually, part of *Festgesang* will provide the tune for the Christmas carol 'Hark! The Herald Angels Sing'.

1910 Igor Stravinsky's ballet *The Firebird* is premiered in Paris.

1977 William Walton's *Prelude for Orchestra* is heard for the first time, at St John's Smith Square in London, to mark the Queen's Silver Jubilee.

2000 The Three Tenors sing together in concert for the 24th time, in Cleveland, Ohio.

2004 The redesigned Hollywood Bowl hosts its first concert.

☀️ TODAY'S THE DAY

1708 Johann Sebastian Bach is offered the job of Cantor in Weimar.

1774 Wolfgang Amadeus Mozart finishes work on his *Missa Brevis* in Salzburg.

1799 Ludwig van Beethoven gives his friend Karl Amenda a copy of one of his earliest string quartets as a present.

1855 Hector Berlioz and Richard Wagner have dinner together in London for the third time in as many weeks.

1872 Hubert Parry gets married at St Paul's Church, Knightsbridge.

COMPOSER PROFILE:

Georg Philipp Telemann

One of the most prolific composers ever, Telemann wrote masses of music for more or less every instrumental or vocal combination. He studied law at Leipzig University, following his parents' wishes, but soon switched to music, winning church posts in Leipzig, Eisenach, Frankfurt and Hamburg. At the age of 41, he turned down the offer of a return to Leipzig; the post he rejected was subsequently filled by 37-year-old J. S. Bach. Living to a grand old age, Telemann remained active as a composer into his eighties, a feat made possible by a team of copyists and occasional visits to take the waters at various health spas. His massive catalogue of works was dispersed to various rural libraries in Germany during the Second World War, to avoid destruction.

🎵 HALL OF FAME HIT

Ludwig van Beethoven: *Bagatelle No. 25 (Für Elise)*

Recommended Recording

Vladimir Ashkenazy (piano); Decca 475 6643

> 'I cannot switch my voice. My voice is not like an elevator going up and down.'
>
> **MARIA CALLAS, SOPRANO**

26
JUNE

🕐 BIRTHS & DEATHS

1933 Italian conductor Claudio Abbado is born in Milan.

2007 English clarinettist Thea King dies in London.

🎵 FIRST PERFORMED

1870 Richard Wagner's opera *Die Walküre* is premiered in Munich, although the composer did not want this production to take place. Johannes Brahms and Camille Saint-Saëns are among those in the audience.

1912 Gustav Mahler's *Symphony No. 9* receives its first performance, in Vienna.

1926 Leoš Janáček's *Sinfonietta* is heard for the first time, in Prague.

☀️ TODAY'S THE DAY

1708 Mühlhausen town council agrees to allow Johann Sebastian Bach to leave its employment and move to Weimar.

1786 Wolfgang Amadeus Mozart finishes work on his *Horn Concerto No. 4* in Vienna.

1788 Wolfgang Amadeus Mozart finishes work on his *Symphony No. 39* in Vienna.

1805 Joseph Haydn, now in his seventies, is awarded a membership diploma by the Paris Conservatoire.

1881 The Milan Conservatoire's academic council fines Giacomo Puccini for failing to attend lessons as required.

1898 With a lot of encouragement from Edvard Grieg, the Royal Concertgebouw Orchestra plays a starring role in the first Bergen Music Festival.

1902 Charles Villiers Stanford receives a knighthood in the Coronation honours list.

1906 Anton Webern passes his musicology exam at the University of Vienna.

1919 New York businessman Augustus D. Juilliard leaves millions of dollars in his will to create the Juilliard Music Foundation.

1921 Aaron Copland is among the first students at the Conservatoire Americain in Fontainebleau. Nadia Boulanger signs up as one of the teachers.

1932 Sergei Prokofiev travels to London for his first recording session, at the Abbey Road studios.

1937 George Gershwin is released from hospital in Los Angeles with a diagnosis of 'hysteria'. It turns out his headaches have a far more serious cause.

1945 A cinematic biography of George Gershwin, entitled *Rhapsody in Blue,* is released in Hollywood.

🎵 HALL OF FAME HIT
Domenico Zipoli: *Elevazione*

Recommended Recording
Gordon Hunt (oboe); Norrköping Symphony Orchestra; BIS NLCD 5017

'One should try everything once, except incest and folk-dancing.'

ARNOLD BAX, COMPOSER

BIRTHS & DEATHS

1859 American composer Mildred Hill is born in Louisville, Kentucky. With her younger sister Patty, she wrote *'Happy Birthday to You'*.

1958 Finnish composer and pianist Magnus Lindberg is born in Helsinki.

TODAY'S THE DAY

1592 In Mantua, Claudio Monteverdi dedicates his *Third Book of Madrigals* to Duke Vincenzo.

1757 William Boyce officially takes over as Master of the King's Musick.

1784 Thirteen-year-old Ludwig van Beethoven is given a job as assistant organist by the Elector of Cologne.

2002 The Three Tenors perform together in concert for the 29th time, in Yokohama.

ORCHESTRA FOCUS:

Royal Liverpool Philharmonic Orchestra

It might seem surprising to some that Liverpool is the home of the UK's oldest symphony orchestra. The 'Phil' (as it is known on Merseyside) can trace its origins back to 1840. It became a fully professional band in 1853, five years before the UK's next oldest symphony orchestra – the Hallé in Manchester.

The orchestra was founded by some well-to-do merchants who wanted to ensure that Liverpool's cultural life rivalled that of the capital. They built their own Philharmonic Hall on Hope Street in 1849. It was destroyed by fire in 1933 with a replacement opening in 1939. It is still the orchestra's home. The list of its principal conductors has included Malcolm Sargent, Charles Groves and, in more recent times, the eminent Czech conductor Libor Pešek.

The RLPO has been a prolific recording orchestra. In the days of 78s, there were famous versions of *Messiah* and *The Dream of Gerontius*, both conducted by Sargent. Later, it made pioneering first recordings of English works – notably by Delius and Bax – under the batons of Groves and Vernon Handley. It made a notable cycle of the Beethoven symphonies, conducted by Charles Mackerras, and has recorded all the Shostakovich symphonies, directed by the dynamic young Russian Vasily Petrenko, who is the orchestra's current chief conductor.

 HALL OF FAME HIT

Edward Elgar: *Violin Concerto*

Recommended Recording

Tasmin Little (violin); Royal Scottish National Orchestra conducted by Andrew Davis; Chandos CHSA 5083

'It's always a great thing, to defy expectations.'

THOMAS NEWMAN, COMPOSER

28

JUNE

🕐 BIRTHS & DEATHS

1491 Part-time English composer and full-time king Henry VIII is born in Greenwich.

1712 Swiss composer (and philosopher) Jean-Jacques Rousseau is born in Geneva.

1753 Austrian clarinettist Anton Stadler, for whom Mozart wrote his *Clarinet Concerto*, is born in Bruck an der Leitha.

1831 Hungarian violinist Joseph Joachim is born in Kittsee.

1902 American composer Richard Rodgers is born in New York.

1955 American baritone Thomas Hampson is born in Indiana.

🎭 FIRST PERFORMED

1841 Adolphe Adam's ballet *Giselle* is premiered in Paris.

☀️ TODAY'S THE DAY

1698 Marc-Antoine Charpentier is appointed Master of Music at the Sainte-Chapelle in Paris's Palais de Justice.

1774 Johann Christian Bach is among the music impresarios who buy a building in London's Hanover Square; they plan to build a new concert hall.

1839 Niccolò Paganini is fined for non-payment of debts by a Paris court; he's threatened with a ten-year jail sentence if he fails to pay up.

1840 Niccolò Paganini's body remains unburied, as the Bishop of Nice rejects an appeal requesting that he be allowed a full Catholic burial.

1904 A charter is granted to the Institute of Musical Art in New York; it will become the Juilliard School.

1905 Edward Elgar is awarded an honorary doctorate by Yale University.

INSTRUMENT FOCUS:

Cor anglais

Translated literally as 'English horn', this member of the woodwind family of instruments is neither English nor a horn. It is actually a tenor version of the oboe. According to one theory, it got its rather strange name because early tenor oboe audiences thought that it sounded like angels. The German word for 'angel' is *Engel*, but somehow the true meaning was lost in translation and it ended up being called 'English horn'. Funnily enough, we always refer to it in French, just to confuse matters further. It looks just like an oboe, except that it is slightly bigger with a bulbous bell. It has a particularly alluring sound.

🎵 HALL OF FAME HIT
Robert Schumann: *Piano Concerto*

Recommended Recording
Alfred Brendel (piano); Philharmonia Orchestra conducted by Kurt Sanderling; Philips 462321.

29

JUNE

'Opera is when a guy gets stabbed in the back and, instead of bleeding, he sings.'

ED GARDNER, AMERICAN RADIO PERSONALITY

BIRTHS & DEATHS

1908 American composer and conductor Leroy Anderson is born in Cambridge, Massachusetts.

1911 American composer Bernard Herrmann is born in New York.

1914 Czech-Swiss conductor Rafael Kubelík is born near Býchory.

1941 Polish politician, composer and pianist Ignacy Jan Paderewski dies in New York. He is buried at the Arlington National Cemetery, by order of President Roosevelt.

1963 German violinist Anne-Sophie Mutter is born in Rheinfelden.

1980 Welsh mezzo-soprano Katherine Jenkins is born in Neath.

FIRST PERFORMED

1830 Ludwig van Beethoven's *Missa Solemnis* receives its first complete performance, in Bohemia.

1888 Richard Wagner's *The Fairies* is premiered in Munich.

1889 Alexander Glazunov's *Symphony No. 2* is given its first performance, in Paris.

1894 Hubert Parry's *Lady Radnor's Suite* is first performed, at St James's Hall in London.

☀ TODAY'S THE DAY

1669 Johann Pachelbel begins studying at the university at Altdorf. Despite taking a job as an organist to help pay the bills, he is forced to leave after a year because of money worries.

1767 Georg Philipp Telemann is buried in St John's churchyard in Hamburg.

1801 Ludwig van Beethoven mentions his deafness in a letter, saying, 'I shall, if it is at all possible, challenge my fate, although there will be moments when I shall be God's most unhappy creature.'

1831 Johann Nepomuk Hummel and Niccolò Paganini perform before King William IV at St James's Palace in London.

1848 The critics love Hector Berlioz's second concert in London and his fame is secured.

1992 The body of former Polish prime minister and renowned concert pianist Ignacy Jan Paderewski arrives in Poland from the USA, more than half a century after his death. Previously, the Polish communist government had refused to accept the return of his remains, on political grounds.

1996 The Three Tenors perform together in concert for the fourth time, in Tokyo.

ORCHESTRA FOCUS:

Scottish Chamber Orchestra

A relative newcomer in musical circles, the Scottish Chamber Orchestra was founded in 1974. It performs throughout Scotland, touring the Highlands and Islands as well as the southern part of the country each year. Further commitments to the Edinburgh, East Neuk and St Magnus Festivals have ensured that it is heard by a wide fan base. Conductors have included Jukka-Pekka Saraste and its Conductor Laureate, Charles Mackerras. The orchestra's present principal conductor is London-born Robin Ticciati.

HALL OF FAME HIT

Christoph Willibald von Gluck: *Orpheus and Euridice*

Recommended Recording

Various soloists; Ambrosian Opera Chorus; Philharmonia Orchestra conducted by Riccardo Muti; EMI 948 2702

> 'Before I compose a piece, I walk around it several times, accompanied by myself.'
>
> **ERIK SATIE, COMPOSER**

30
JUNE

🕐 BIRTHS & DEATHS

1861 Russian composer Anton Arensky is born in Novgorod.

1931 Scottish conductor James Loughran is born in Glasgow.

1954 English conductor Stephen Barlow is born in Melbourne.

1958 Finnish conductor Esa-Pekka Salonen is born in Helsinki.

☀️ TODAY'S THE DAY

1702 Jean-Philippe Rameau signs a 6-year contract to be organist at Clermont Cathedral, in the Auvergne.

1859 Antonín Dvořák graduates from the Prague Organ School.

1923 Heitor Villa-Lobos sets sail on board a ship from Brazil to find fame and fortune in Europe.

1933 Nadia Boulanger conducts her first entire public concert in Paris.

COMPOSER PROFILE:

Antonín Dvořák

A great composer, Dvořák was a man who had interests in life aside from music. He was also a fanatical trainspotter, a dedicated pigeon fancier and even had a passion for steamships. He spent his childhood helping in the family's butcher's shop in a small Czech village. After studying music, he was a viola player in a Prague orchestra that was conducted by the great Czech composer Bedřich Smetana, before switching to concentrate his efforts on teaching and composing full time.

Antonín Dvořák's music is undoubtedly nationalist in style and he remained very proud of his homeland, even though he travelled extensively. His music became popular in Britain and he made nine visits to the country, with some of his works receiving their premiere performances in cities such as Birmingham, London and Leeds. In 1892, he took up a job in the USA as director of the National Conservatoire of Music in New York. While he was in America, he became a great fan of African-American spirituals and used some of these melodies in his *Symphony No. 9 ('From the New World')*, which remains his most widely recognised work today. The slow movement of this piece became famous as the background music to the Hovis television adverts. When he returned to Prague, Dvořák mentored a new generation of Czech composers, including Suk and Novak.

🎵 HALL OF FAME HIT

Giacomo Puccini: *Gianni Schicchi*

Recommended Recording

Aleksandra Kurzak (soprano); Orchestra de la Comunitat Valenciana conducted by Omar Meir Wellber; Decca 478 2730

July

01

'I don't know much about classical music. For years I thought the Goldberg Variations were something Mr and Mrs Goldberg tried on their wedding night.'

WOODY ALLEN, FILM ACTOR AND DIRECTOR, STARDUST MEMORIES (1980)

JULY

🕐 BIRTHS & DEATHS

1784 German composer Wilhelm Friedemann Bach dies in Berlin.

1925 French composer Erik Satie dies in Paris.

1955 Russian pianist Nikolai Demidenko is born in Anisimovo.

1958 English conductor Paul Daniel is born in Birmingham.

1973 The American inventor of the Hammond organ, Laurens Hammond, dies in Cornwall, Connecticut.

🎵 FIRST PERFORMED

1889 Hubert Parry's *Symphony No. 4* is performed for the first time, in London.

1997 Tan Dun's *Heaven Earth Mankind* is premiered at the ceremony reuniting Hong Kong with mainland China.

☀ TODAY'S THE DAY

1716 Domenico Zipoli joins the Society of Jesus, in readiness to become a Jesuit missionary in Paraguay.

1763 Johann Christian Bach commits to staying in London at the behest of Queen Charlotte, rather than returning to Italy.

1859 A monument to George Frideric Handel is unveiled in the marketplace of the German town of Halle, where Handel was born. Franz Liszt is there to see the statue being dedicated.

1877 Alexander Borodin and Franz Liszt meet in Weimar; it's the first of half a dozen meetings between the two composers this month.

1885 Gustav Mahler moves on from his conducting job in Kassel.

1894 Giacomo Puccini is held by the authorities in Malta for a few hours, after being seen photographing a military installation.

1945 Orchestral concerts begin again in Hamburg, following the ending of the Second World War.

1959 George Gershwin's *Porgy and Bess* is released on film.

1975 Dmitri Shostakovich suffers a heart attack near Moscow and is taken to hospital.

1961 Olivier Messiaen gets married in Paris, but the composer tries to keep it largely a secret.

COMPOSER PROFILE:

Domenico Zipoli

Domenico Zipoli was an organist, choirmaster and composer – or at least he was for the first 28 years of his short life. Born in Prato near Florence, where he studied, he began his successful career as a composer there, later working in Milan and Rome. Then, in 1716, he became a Jesuit missionary, sailing to Córdoba, Argentina, where he spent three years studying theology. He was part of the same so-called 'Jesuit Reductions' – an attempt to convert the local tribes to Christianity – that featured in the 1986 Roland Joffe movie *The Mission* (in which Father Gabriel soothes the locals with his exquisite oboe playing). As well as his magnum opus – a collection of sonatas, which he wrote in 1716 – his popularity blossomed from the early 1990s onwards with the revival of his *Elevazione,* a piece for oboe and strings he wrote to mark the raising of the Host during Mass.

🎵 HALL OF FAME HIT

Francisco Tárrega: *Memories of the Alhambra*

Recommended Recording

Miloš Karadaglić (guitar); Deutsche Grammophon 477 9693

'Rossini would have been a great composer if his teacher had spanked him enough on the backside.'

LUDWIG VAN BEETHOVEN, COMPOSER

02

JULY

BIRTHS & DEATHS

1714 German composer Chistoph Willibald von Gluck is born in Erasbach.

1778 Swiss-French composer (and philosopher) Jean-Jacques Rousseau dies in Ermenonville.

FIRST PERFORMED

1900 Jean Sibelius's *Finlandia,* in its final form, is performed for the first time, in Helsinki (although the work is currently called *Suomi*).

TODAY'S THE DAY

1685 Nicholas Staggins is appointed the first professor of music at Cambridge University.

1835 Felix Mendelssohn performs in concert for the final time as Düsseldorf's music director, after two years in the job.

1881 Franz Liszt is out of action for the next eight weeks, after injuring himself falling down the stairs in his home in Weimar.

1941 Dmitri Shostakovich applies to join the Red Army for a second time, after his first application was rejected.

COMPOSER PROFILE:

Jean Sibelius

Alongside the piano, Sibelius's first love was violin. He longed to be a concert violinist, although he also studied composition from books. When he was 20, he started studying law at Helsinki University, but soon switched both venues and subject, enrolling to study music at the city's conservatoire a year later.

Gradually composition became the dominant factor in Sibelius's musical life. He took lessons in Berlin and Vienna, before returning to teach in Helsinki. When he was 27, he composed *En Saga,* a tone poem, and *Kullervo,* a nationalist choral symphony. Just five years later, the Finnish state awarded him an annual pension to allow him to do nothing but compose. Two years after that, the government's faith in him paid off when he wrote another tone poem, this time called *Finlandia*. It was to become the country's unofficial national anthem.

The composition of *Finlandia* also coincided, more or less, with Sibelius's first foray into symphonies, which, from then on, were to form the backbone of his musical output. He consoled the violinist inside himself by writing a violin concerto when he was 38. Much like Rossini, Sibelius practically stopped composing for the last 26 years of his life, resting on the laurels of the legendary status he had gained in his homeland; Sibelius stamps were even issued in his honour.

 HALL OF FAME HIT

Ralph Vaughan Williams: *English Folksongs Suite*

Recommended Recording

Royal Liverpool Philharmonic Orchestra conducted by James Judd; Naxos 857 2304

03

> 'How wonderful the opera world would be if there were no singers.'
>
> **GIOACHINO ROSSINI, COMPOSER**

JULY

🎵 BIRTHS & DEATHS

1854 Czech composer Leoš Janáček is born in northern Moravia.

1860 Scottish composer and writer William Wallace is born in Greenock.

1927 British film director Ken Russell, celebrated for his films on Delius, Debussy, Elgar and Strauss, is born in Southampton.

1930 German conductor Carlos Kleiber is born in Berlin.

2006 American mezzo-soprano Lorraine Hunt Lieberson dies in Santa Fe.

☀ TODAY'S THE DAY

1749 William Boyce is presented with both Bachelor and Doctor of Music degrees at Cambridge University.

1778 Wolfgang Amadeus Mozart's mother dies in Paris, while she is travelling with him.

1795 Instead of a pay rise, Luigi Cherubini negotiates copyright ownership for all his future compositions for the Théâtre Feydeau.

1823 An early violin concerto by Felix Mendelssohn, who is still only 14 years old, is performed in Berlin.

1832 Giuseppe Verdi scores badly in his entrance test to the Milan Conservatoire – particularly in his piano exam.

1900 The music of Jean Sibelius reaches a far wider audience outside his native Finland after the Helsinki Philharmonic Orchestra embarks on a major international tour around Europe.

COMPOSER PROFILE:

Leoš Janáček

This Czech composer was virtually unknown outside his homeland for most of his life. He worked as a composer, conductor, organist and teacher. His masterpiece is the opera *Jenůfa*, which was first performed when he was 50 years old. It was a success in Brno, where it was premiered, but because Janáček had fallen out with the head of the Prague Opera, it took another 12 years for the work to reach the Czech capital. When it was finally performed there, the opera was incredibly warmly received, with the result that Janáček, now aged 62, became an overnight success. This spurred him on to compose other acclaimed works, such as *The Cunning Little Vixen,* another opera, and his *Glagolitic Mass.* The conductor Charles Mackerras was a leading champion of his music.

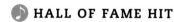

🎵 HALL OF FAME HIT

John Williams: *Harry Potter*

Recommended Recording

Royal Liverpool Philharmonic Orchestra conducted by Carl Davis; Naxos 857 0505

> '[His music] opens up to us the kingdom of the gigantic and the immeasurable.'

WRITER E. T. A. HOFFMAN ABOUT BEETHOVEN'S SYMPHONY NO. 5, PUBLISHED ON THIS DAY IN 1810

BIRTHS & DEATHS

1623 English composer William Byrd dies in Stondon Massey.
1963 German singer, actress and dancer Ute Lemper is born in Münster.

FIRST PERFORMED

1923 Ralph Vaughan Williams' *English Folksongs Suite* is first performed, at the Royal Military School of Music.

TODAY'S THE DAY

1743 George Frideric Handel finishes work on his oratorio *Semele*, just days after suffering a stroke.
1856 Fourteen-year-old Arthur Sullivan wins a scholarship entitling him to a year's free tuition at the Royal Academy of Music.
1857 Georges Bizet wins the Prix de Rome composition competition in Paris.

ORCHESTRA FOCUS:

Vienna Philharmonic Orchestra

Formed in 1842 by the composer Otto Nicolai, the Vienna Philharmonic is one of Europe's supreme orchestras. Its founding principles of autonomy and democracy still hold true today. It selects its own conductors and the players are all chosen from the Vienna State Opera orchestra. The Vienna Philharmonic is resident in Vienna's amazing, gilded Musikverein concert hall and its seasons are often oversubscribed. Bookings for the famous New Year's Day concert sometimes have to be made a couple of years in advance. The orchestra has been directed by an illustrious line of great conductors, including Gustav Mahler, Wilhelm Furtwängler and Herbert von Karajan.

COMPOSER PROFILE:

William Byrd

Along with Thomas Tallis, Byrd made up the great double act of Elizabethan music. Byrd was organist first at Lincoln Cathedral and then, jointly with Tallis, at the Chapel Royal. Elizabeth I granted the pair the licence to print music in England. Of huge value, this gave them a monopoly over all printed music, no matter by whom it was composed. It was little wonder that when Byrd and Tallis published their *Cantiones Sacrae* in 1575 they dedicated it to the Queen. Much of the detail of Byrd's life has been lost, but it is known that he was allowed to mix in the highest echelons of society despite his Roman Catholicism – a denomination that at the time was definitely frowned upon in the royal court.

HALL OF FAME HIT

Richard Addinsell: *Dangerous Moonlight (Warsaw Concerto)*

Recommended Recording

Daniel Adni (piano); Bournemouth Symphony Orchestra conducted by Kenneth Alwyn; EMI 352 3922

05

'After playing Chopin, I feel as if I had been weeping over sins that I had not committed.'

OSCAR WILDE, WRITER

BIRTHS & DEATHS

1942 Swiss conductor Matthias Bamert is born in Ersigen.

1945 Russian conductor Alexander Lazarev is born in Moscow.

1992 Argentinian composer Astor Piazzolla dies in Buenos Aires.

TODAY'S THE DAY

1770 Wolfgang Amadeus Mozart is told that the Pope is appointing him to the Order of the Knight of the Golden Spur.

1866 Giuseppe Verdi is distraught to learn that Austria has given Venetia to France rather than Italy. For a while, it completely throws him off his stride while composing his opera *Don Carlos*.

1867 Modest Mussorgsky finishes composing *A Night on the Bare Mountain*.

1904 Edward Elgar is knighted by King Edward VII at Buckingham Palace.

1913 Lili Boulanger becomes the first woman to win the Prix de Rome for music.

1965 Soprano Maria Callas makes her last operatic appearance, as Tosca, at London's Covent Garden.

1996 The Three Tenors perform together in concert, for the 5th time, in London. The concert is broadcast by Classic FM.

ARTIST PROFILE:

Maria Callas

Arguably the greatest soprano of the 20th century, Callas lived her life in the glare of publicity. Incredibly talented, with an unforgettable voice and great acting ability, her glamour made her a worldwide star. American-born of Greek parents, she made her debut at La Scala, Milan, aged 27 and at the Royal Opera House in London's Covent Garden two years later, quickly becoming the most talked about soprano of her day. She looked and behaved every inch the diva and became known for her fiery temperament and a tendency to cancel her scheduled performances if she felt that she was not on top form. The myth and hype that grew up around her is second to none, but the recordings she left behind testify to her unique abilities. Her fans nicknamed her La Divina – 'the divine one'.

HALL OF FAME HIT

John Rutter: *Requiem*

Recommended Recording

Polyphony; Bournemouth Sinfonietta conducted by Stephen Layton; Hyperion CDA 30017

> 'Wagner has lovely moments, but awful quarters of an hour.'
>
> GIOACHINO ROSSINI, COMPOSER

06

JULY

BIRTHS & DEATHS

1937 Russian pianist and conductor Vladimir Ashkenazy is born in Gorky.

1965 English violinist Anthony Marwood is born in London.

1973 German conductor and composer Otto Klemperer dies in Zurich.

1999 Spanish composer Joaquín Rodrigo dies in Madrid.

☀ TODAY'S THE DAY

1811 Muzio Clementi gets married for the third time, at St Pancras' Church in London.

1812 Ludwig van Beethoven writes his famous letter to his 'Immortal Beloved'. Over the years, musical historians have debated the identity of the mysterious recipient of the composer's affections. Many believe that she was Antonie Brentano, a married Viennese aristocrat.

1842 Less than a year old, Antonín Dvořák is rescued by his father from their burning home – an inn a few miles north of Prague.

1901 Antonín Dvořák takes up a new role as director of the Prague Conservatoire, although he avoids having to do any of the administrative duties normally associated with the job.

1925 Erik Satie is buried in Arcueil. Maurice Ravel is among the many mourners from the world of music.

ARTIST PROFILE:

Vladimir Ashkenazy

Born in Russia in 1937, Ashkenazy became a piano wonder, specialising in the music of Chopin. He won the second ever Tchaikovsky Piano Competition, sharing the prize with John Ogdon. Ashkenazy defected from the former USSR in 1963 and settled in Britain, taking Icelandic nationality before moving to Switzerland. Over the years, he successfully made the leap into conducting, and was appointed to a host of major positions, including chief conductor of the Czech Philharmonic Orchestra and music director of the NHK Symphony Orchestra in Tokyo and of the European Union Youth Orchestra. He is conductor laureate of the Philharmonia Orchestra.

HALL OF FAME HIT

Franz Schubert: *Symphony No. 8* ('*Unfinished*')

Recommended Recording

Swedish Chamber Orchestra conducted by Thomas Dausgaard; BIS SACD 1656

07

'Film composing is a splendid discipline, and I recommend a course of it to all composition teachers.'

RALPH VAUGHAN WILLIAMS, COMPOSER

JULY

BIRTHS & DEATHS

1860 Austrian composer Gustav Mahler is born in Kališt.

1911 Italian-American composer and conductor Gian Carlo Menotti is born in Cadegliano.

1976 Russian conductor Vasily Petrenko is born in St Petersburg.

FIRST PERFORMED

1994 John Williams' *Cello Concerto* is first performed, in Tanglewood, with Yo-Yo Ma as soloist and the composer conducting the Boston Symphony Orchestra.

TODAY'S THE DAY

1700 Jeremiah Clarke is sworn in as a Gentleman-extraordinary of the Chapel Royal.

1720 The funeral of J. S. Bach's first wife takes place.

1759 Composer of '*Rule, Britannia!*', Thomas Arne, is awarded a doctorate by Oxford University.

1775 Highwaymen rob composer Johann Christian Bach and painter Thomas Gainsborough as they return to London from Bath by coach.

1791 Joseph Haydn is awarded a doctorate by Oxford University; he conducts his *Symphony No. 92* in Oxford to celebrate.

1837 Frédéric Chopin visits London, although the heavy soot in the air doesn't agree with his asthma.

1878 Tragedy strikes the family of Camille Saint-Saëns once again; only weeks after the death of his four-year-old son, his baby son dies of an infant illness.

1949 Sergei Prokofiev suffers a stroke in Moscow, from which he recovers, although he remains unwell for much of the rest of his life.

1990 The first of the Three Tenors concerts takes place in Rome as part of the Italia '90 football World Cup. It is an enormous success and an international phenomenon is born, with Luciano Pavarotti, José Carreras and Plácido Domingo performing together no fewer than 31 times over the next 13 years. *The Three Tenors Live in Concert*, recorded at this original concert in Rome, remains the biggest-selling classical CD of all time.

COMPANY FOCUS:

Scottish Opera

Founded in 1962 by the conductor Alexander Gibson, Scottish Opera originally presented seasons in Edinburgh and Aberdeen (even travelling as far afield as Newcastle). The company moved into the newly refurbished Theatre Royal, Glasgow, in 1975. In 1980, the Orchestra of Scottish Opera was founded. Having achieved notable successes with premieres, such as *Ines de Castro* by James MacMillan, it continues to champion the widest range of opera, of the highest standard, in front of the largest possible audience right across Scotland.

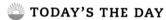

HALL OF FAME HIT

Hans Zimmer: *Gladiator*

Recommended Recording

Lyndhurst Orchestra conducted by Gavin Greenaway; Decca 131 922

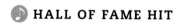

'He knows everything but lacks . . . inexperience!'

HECTOR BERLIOZ AFTER HEARING SAINT-SAËNS' SYMPHONY NO. 1

🕐 BIRTHS & DEATHS

1882 Australian composer Percy Grainger is born in Melbourne.
1992 English pianist Benjamin Grosvenor is born in Southend-on-Sea.

☀ TODAY'S THE DAY

1588 John Dowland graduates from Christ Church, Oxford, with a Bachelor of Music degree.
1770 Pope Clement XIV receives 14-year-old Wolfgang Amadeus Mozart at a private audience at the Palazzo Santa Maria Maggiore.
1799 King Ferdinando IV sacks Giovanni Paisiello as royal maestro di camera because of the composer's republican sympathies.
1879 Camille Saint-Saëns visits Queen Victoria at Windsor Castle; he visits her again on the same day the following year.

COMPOSER PROFILE:

Camille Saint-Saëns

French composer Camille Saint-Saëns was an early developer. He gave his first piano recital when he was aged only 10 and entered the Paris Conservatoire just two years later. There, his dazzling talents won him the admiration of Gounod, Rossini, Berlioz and Liszt – the latter hailing his lifelong friend as the finest organist in the world. As a church organist, Saint-Saëns started off at a small church on the rue Saint Martin, before moving on in 1857 to the prestigious La Madeleine, where he remained until 1877. For some of the time, he also taught piano, the young Fauré being his favourite pupil. Later, he was instrumental in the founding of the Société Nationale de Musique, an association for the promotion of new French music.

Composing was always Saint-Saëns' first love. As well as his symphonies – the *Third*, the so-called *'Organ' Symphony,* is a real Romantic monster of a work – he turned out symphonic poems, concertos, chamber music, church music and 13 operas, though only one of these, *Samson and Delilah,* is much performed today. His best-known composition is probably *Carnival of the Animals.* At least in its composer's lifetime, it had a chequered career. Concerned that the piece – a suite with 14 short movements – was too frivolous and so likely to damage his reputation as a serious composer, Saint-Saëns forbade its public performance. He allowed only one movement of it, *The Swan,* to be published while he was still alive.

🎵 HALL OF FAME HIT

Johann Strauss Senior: *Radetzky March*

Recommended Recording

Vienna Philharmonic Orchestra conducted by Georges Prêtre; Decca 478 2113

09

JULY

'Mine was the kind of piece in which nobody knew what was going on – including the composer, the conductor and the critics. Consequently I got pretty good critics.'

OSCAR LEVANT, PIANIST AND COMPOSER

🕐 BIRTHS & DEATHS

1879 Italian composer Ottorino Respighi is born in Bologna.

1963 English tenor John Mark Ainsley is born in Cheshire.

☀ TODAY'S THE DAY

1687 Arcangelo Corelli becomes the Master of Music for Cardinal Pamphili in Rome.

1779 Wolfgang Amadeus Mozart finishes work on his *Symphony No. 33* in Salzburg.

1839 Richard Wagner is on the run to avoid paying his debts once again – this time from Riga to Paris.

1842 Felix Mendelssohn visits Queen Victoria and Prince Albert at Buckingham Palace. He admits that one of 'his' songs is actually composed by his sister Fanny.

1846 Fanny Mendelssohn writes to her brother Felix to tell him that she is going to publish her music after all, despite his advice against so doing.

1886 Anton Bruckner is awarded the Knight Cross of the Order of Franz Joseph.

1937 Despite being able to play the piano at home in the morning, by this evening George Gershwin is in hospital in a coma.

1951 The decidedly risqué content in Constant Lambert's ballet *Tiresias* is edited ahead of its gala performance in front of Queen Elizabeth.

COMPOSER PROFILE:

Ottorino Respighi

Respighi studied first in his hometown of Bologna, becoming a proficient violinist, before taking lessons in composition in Russia with Rimsky-Korsakov, and, briefly, in Berlin with Bruch. As well as playing in a string quintet, he became the director of the Academy of St Cecilia in Rome before giving up the position to allow himself more time to compose. He is best remembered today for his orchestral 'pictures' – studies such as *Fountains of Rome* and *Pines of Rome*, as well as *The Birds*, which replicates authentic bird-calls. Respighi was much admired by Mussolini, though he claimed not to reciprocate the Italian dictator's feelings.

🎵 HALL OF FAME HIT

Johannes Brahms: *Symphony No. 4*

Recommended Recording

Orchestre Révolutionnaire et Romantique conducted by John Eliot Gardiner; Soli Deo Gloria SDG 705

> 'Learning music by reading about it is like making love by mail.'
>
> ISAAC STERN, VIOLINIST

10

BIRTHS & DEATHS

1690 Italian composer Domenico Gabrieli dies in Bologna.

1835 Polish violinist and composer Henryk Wieniawski is born in Lublin.

1895 German composer Carl Orff is born in Munich.

1936 American conductor David Zinman is born in New York.

1969 German tenor Jonas Kaufmann is born in Munich.

FIRST PERFORMED

1733 George Frideric Handel's oratorio *Athalia* is premiered in Oxford.

1825 Hector Berlioz's *Messe Solennelle* is first performed, in the Church of St Roch.

2001 Leonard Bernstein's *West Side Story Suite* is given its first performance, with violinist Joshua Bell playing alongside the New York Philharmonic in the city's Central Park.

TODAY'S THE DAY

1713 The *Worcester Postman* reports a performance of Henry Purcell's *Te Deum* at what is to be a forerunner of the Three Choirs Festival.

1721 Georg Philipp Telemann is offered the job of music director of the city of Hamburg; he accepts.

1762 A monument to George Frideric Handel is unveiled in Westminster Abbey.

1832 Samuel Sebastian Wesley becomes organist at Hereford Cathedral.

1843 King Friedrich Wilhelm IV of Prussia tells Felix Mendelssohn he wants him to direct two oratorios and orchestral concerts each year, as well as being responsible for religious music on the main holy days.

1860 Bedřich Smetana gets married for a second time, near Prague.

1890 After his first year as a student, Maurice Ravel wins second prize in the Paris Conservatoire piano competition.

1900 The trademark 'His Master's Voice' is registered in the USA. The image, belonging to the Victor Recording Company, features Nipper the dog listening to a gramophone.

1998 The Three Tenors sing together in their 17th concert, in Paris.

MUSICAL TERM:

Barcarolle

Barcarolles are based on the songs of Venice's gondoliers. They tend to have a hypnotic rhythm that goes 'dum . . . dum dum . . . dum dum'. This is intended to suggest the gentle rocking of a gondola on a canal. The most famous barcarolle of all features in Offenbach's opera *The Tales of Hoffmann* – less well known is the fact that the composer lifted it from *Die Rheinnixen*, another of his operas. Perhaps the fact that it was a goblin's song in its first incarnation might have had something to do with the earlier opera's failure.

HALL OF FAME HIT
George Frideric Handel: *Sarabande*

Recommended Recording
Ensemble Instrumental de France; Disque Dom FOR 16527

11

JULY

'Definition of a true musician: one who, when he hears a lady singing in the bathtub, puts his ear to the keyhole.'

MOREY AMSTERDAM, ACTOR AND COMEDIAN

 BIRTHS & DEATHS

1925 Swedish tenor Nicolai Gedda is born in Stockholm.
1937 American composer George Gershwin dies in Los Angeles.
1953 English conductor Bramwell Tovey is born in Ilford.
1967 Australian guitarist Craig Ogden is born in Perth.

TODAY'S THE DAY

1804 Carl Maria von Weber begins a new job as the conductor at the theatre in Breslau.

1825 Johann Strauss Senior gets married. His new wife, Maria Anna, is already pregnant with their son, Johann Strauss Junior.
1839 Nine-year-old pianist Anton Rubinstein makes his debut in Moscow.
1863 Pope Pius IX visits Franz Liszt, who is staying at a monastery near Rome.
1884 Composer Edward MacDowell gets married in New York.
1885 The Boston Pops Orchestra gives its first concert, in the city's

music hall – although, at this stage, the band is known as the Boston Promenade Orchestra.
1886 Pyotr Ilyich Tchaikovsky writes his will, after a period of illness. He actually lives for another seven years.
1922 The Los Angeles Philharmonic performs for the first time at the Hollywood Bowl.
1941 Leonard Bernstein makes his professional conducting debut with the Boston Pops Orchestra.

VENUE FOCUS:

Royal Albert Hall

Of all the venues featured in this book, this is the one that probably needs the most minimal of introductions. Even if you've never been to the Royal Albert Hall, it's likely that it's already very much on your musical radar. The creation of the venue stretches back to the days of Queen Victoria – or more specifically to her husband Prince Albert, who was a great lover of all things cultural. He believed that London needed a centre to promote greater recognition and appreciation of the arts and sciences. Fast forward to the 21st century and you'll find a venue that hosts an eclectic and hugely enjoyable range of events – from Classic FM Live concerts and the Classic BRIT Awards to the Music for Youth Schools Proms, via all manner of other rock, pop, classical and jazz gigs.

 HALL OF FAME HIT
Richard Wagner: *Siegfried* (orchestral highlights from the opera)

Recommended Recording
Berlin Philharmonic Orchestra conducted by Lorin Maazel; RCA 7432 1687172

'Music is an agreeable harmony for the honour of God and the permissible delights of the soul.'

JOHANN SEBASTIAN BACH, COMPOSER

12

JULY

🕮 BIRTHS & DEATHS

1861 Russian composer Anton Arensky is born in Novgorod.
1885 English composer George Butterworth is born in London.
1895 American lyricist Oscar Hammerstein II is born in New York.
1934 American pianist Van Cliburn is born in Louisiana.
1945 English pianist Roger Vignoles is born in Cheltenham.

🔔 FIRST PERFORMED

1900 Gabriel Fauré's *Requiem* is premiered in Paris.

☀ TODAY'S THE DAY

1782 Carl Philipp Emanuel Bach and Jan Ladislav Dussek meet in Hamburg.
1789 Wolfgang Amadeus Mozart sends one of many begging letters to his friend Michael Puchberg, asking for cash.
1872 Nikolai Rimsky-Korsakov gets married; Modest Mussorgsky is his best man.

COMPOSER PROFILE:

George Butterworth

Butterworth is quite possibly the composer who could claim the title of being the least prolific in this book, due to his hugely self-critical nature and to his life being tragically cut short in the First World War. His entire output numbers just 11 works, almost all of which were composed in the 4 years just before he joined the army. Had he lived, he would surely have been destined for greatness.

Butterworth was an avid collector of folk songs, through which he became friendly with Vaughan Williams. Rather more surprisingly, he was also an enthusiastic folk dancer. He was awarded the Military Cross after his death in the trenches on the Somme. Vaughan Williams dedicated his *London Symphony* to his memory. Butterworth is best known today for his wonderfully evocative *The Banks of Green Willow*.

🎵 HALL OF FAME HIT
William Walton: *Crown Imperial*

Recommended Recording
City of Birmingham Symphony Orchestra conducted by Louis Frémaux; EMI Classics CDM 764 2012

13

> 'If she can strike a low G or F like a death-rattle and high F like the shriek of a little dog when you step on its tail, the house will resound with acclamations.'
>
> **HECTOR BERLIOZ, COMPOSER, ABOUT A SOPRANO**

JULY

🕐 BIRTHS & DEATHS

1951 Austrian composer Arnold Schoenberg dies in Los Angeles.

2004 German conductor Carlos Kleiber dies in Konjsica, Slovenia.

🐾 FIRST PERFORMED

1909 Edward Elgar's *Elegy* is performed for the first time, at Mansion House in London.

☀ TODAY'S THE DAY

1842 Gaetano Donizetti finds out that he has a new job as Hofkapellmeister to the Emperor of Austria.

1858 Arthur Sullivan finishes his time studying at the Royal Academy of Music with an *Overture in D minor*.

1862 Bedřich Smetana makes his debut as chorus master of the Hlahol Choral Society in Prague.

1881 Leoš Janáček gets married in Brno.

1885 Gustav Mahler arrives in Prague ready to take over as the city's Kapellmeister.

1892 Seventeen-year-old Gustav Holst makes the journey from Cheltenham to London to witness Gustav Mahler conducting Wagner's *Götterdämmerung* at Covent Garden.

1898 Hubert Parry receives his knighthood from Queen Victoria at Windsor Castle.

1997 The Three Tenors sing together in their 16th concert, in Barcelona.

COMPOSER PROFILE:

Hubert Parry

Charles Hubert Hastings Parry was very much a man of his age. After Eton and Oxford (he completed his music degree at the age of 18 while still at Eton), he became an underwriter at Lloyds of London. Following seven years in the City, studying music in his spare time, he gave up business for composition – earning extra money writing articles for the august *Grove's Dictionary of Music and Musicians,* the first volume of which was published in 1878. Parry taught successfully for many years, his star pupils including Vaughan Williams and Holst. His own compositions rapidly put him at the head of the musical establishment and his large-scale choral works, notably '*I Was Glad*' and '*Blest Pair of Sirens*', are still staples of the repertoire. He is probably best known, however, for his *Jerusalem*. In 1916, he set Blake's visionary poem to music for 'Fight for the Right', a women's suffrage movement. Some years later, Elgar re-orchestrated the piece and it is this version that is still sung at the Last Night of the Proms every year. When he heard it, George V is said to have remarked that he wished it could take the place of the national anthem.

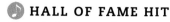

🎵 HALL OF FAME HIT

Edward Elgar: *Symphony No. 1*

Recommended Recording

London Philharmonic Orchestra conducted by Vernon Handley; LPO Live 0046

'Here lyes Henry Purcell Esq., who left this life and is gone to that blessed place where only his harmony can be exceeded.'

INSCRIPTION ON HENRY PURCELL'S TOMB IN WESTMINSTER ABBEY

 BIRTHS & DEATHS

1901 English composer Gerald Finzi is born in London.
2010 Australian conductor Charles Mackerras dies in London.

TODAY'S THE DAY

1682 Henry Purcell becomes a Gentleman of the Chapel Royal.
1795 'La Marseillaise' becomes the French national anthem.
1898 Richard Strauss writes a letter to more than 150 fellow German composers, arguing for a change in the country's copyright laws, to enable them to earn more from their music.

COMPOSER PROFILE:

Henry Purcell

Henry Purcell was born into a long line of musicians in Westminster in 1659. Details of his early life are somewhat sketchy, but he was probably just four years old when his father died and he became a 'child of the Chapel Royal'. As a result he would almost certainly have been taught by John Blow and Pelham Humphrey – both hugely successful composers in their day. Purcell remained a member of the Chapel Royal until his voice broke, when he was around 14. Instead of being dismissed – the usual fate of boy choristers who could no longer sing high notes – Purcell was kept on, no doubt because of his other musical talents. He was given a job as Assistant to the Instrument Tuner and spent the next few years looking after the Westminster Abbey organ and copying out music. Eventually he was appointed a court composer, before succeeding John Blow as organist of the Abbey itself.

Purcell was a prolific composer. Even by the time he became Westminster Abbey's organist, he had already written a large number of anthems (many with orchestral accompaniment), songs, funeral music, sacred part-songs and music for consorts of viols (viols of various sizes were the precursors of modern stringed instruments). In the 1680s, he premiered *Dido and Aeneas* at Josias Priest's School for Young Ladies in Chelsea. It is an early landmark in the story of English opera, although Purcell himself referred to it simply as a 'dramatic entertainment'.

HALL OF FAME HIT
Richard Wagner: *Lohengrin*

Recommended Recording
Various soloists; Staatskapelle Berlin; Choir of the German State Opera conducted by Daniel Barenboim; Warner Classics 2564 678994

15

JULY

'There's only two ways to sum up music: either it's good or it's bad. If it's good you don't mess about with it – you just enjoy it.'

LOUIS ARMSTRONG, TRUMPETER

🎵 BIRTHS & DEATHS

1857 Austrian composer Carl Czerny dies in Vienna.

1910 English composer Ronald Binge is born in Derby.

1933 English guitarist Julian Bream is born in London.

1934 English composer Harrison Birtwistle is born in Accrington.

1941 English composer Geoffrey Burgon is born in Hambleton.

🎵 FIRST PERFORMED

1777 A *Te Deum* by 16-year-old Luigi Cherubini is given its first performance, in Florence.

1965 Leonard Bernstein's *Chichester Psalms* is premiered in New York, conducted by the composer.

☀ TODAY'S THE DAY

1556 The first book of music printed in the Americas is *The Latin Ordinary Mass*, published by Mexican printer Juan Pablos.

1822 Mikhail Glinka leaves St Petersburg University Boarding School, playing Hummel's *Piano Concerto No. 2* at the graduation ceremony.

1830 For the fourth time, Hector Berlioz is selected as a finalist for the Prix de Rome composition competition.

1877 Pyotr Ilyich Tchaikovsky tells Nadezhda von Meck, the financial patron whom he has vowed never to meet, that he is getting married in three days' time.

1937 The funeral of George Gershwin takes place in New York.

COMPOSER PROFILE:

Hildegard of Bingen

It is hard not to come to the conclusion that classical music is primarily a man's world. Certainly, the number of successful composers over the years is weighted heavily in favour of men. However, one of the earliest composers whom we play on Classic FM is, in fact, a woman. Hildegard lived for 81 years, during which time she founded nunneries and wrote major theological works, plays and music. She was also an expert on politics, poetry and medicine. One of the most prominent individuals of her day, she corresponded with many other leading figures. Musically, she was a mistress of plainchant, writing pieces to honour the saints and the Virgin Mary.

🎵 HALL OF FAME HIT

Edward Elgar: *Chanson de Matin*

Recommended Recording

New Zealand Symphony Orchestra conducted by James Judd; Naxos 8557577

'Composing is like driving down a foggy road towards a house. Slowly, you see more details . . . the colour of the slates and bricks, the shape of the windows. The notes are the bricks and mortar of the house.'

BENJAMIN BRITTEN, COMPOSER

BIRTHS & DEATHS

1858 Belgian composer, violinist and conductor Eugène Ysaÿe is born in Liège.

1896 English music publisher Alfred Novello dies in Genoa.

1948 Israeli violinist Pinchas Zukerman is born in Tel Aviv.

1959 English pianist Joanna MacGregor is born in London.

1959 Scottish composer James MacMillan is born in Kilwinning.

1989 Austrian conductor Herbert von Karajan dies in Anif.

FIRST PERFORMED

1782 Wolfgang Amadeus Mozart's opera *The Abduction from the Seraglio* is premiered in Vienna.

TODAY'S THE DAY

1782 Wolfgang Amadeus Mozart decides to get married to Constanze Weber.

1839 Robert Schumann asks the court of appeal for permission to marry Clara Wieck, despite the entrenched opposition of her father.

1883 Giacomo Puccini ends his time at the Milan Conservatoire.

1899 Granville Bantock organises a concert celebrating the music of Edward Elgar as part of his highly popular series at New Brighton on the Wirral. The two men become firm friends as a result.

1994 The Three Tenors sing together in their 3rd concert, in Los Angeles.

1996 The Three Tenors sing together in their 6th concert, in Vienna.

COMPOSER PROFILE:

Clara Schumann

Clara Schumann must have been a formidable woman. She resolutely fought her father when it came to her marriage to Robert, and stuck by her husband until his sad end. At this point, she became the chief interpreter of his music, bringing it to as wide an audience as possible, while holding his memory dear enough to stave off the advances of Schumann's last protégé, the young Brahms. After her husband died, in 1856, Clara continued to tour for more than 30 years. She also found time to be head of piano studies at the conservatoire in Frankfurt, as well as, eventually, caring for a number of her grandchildren and children (tragically, her son Ludwig ended his days suffering from severe mental illness, as did his father). Her own compositions have become increasingly popular in recent years, a fitting turnaround for someone whose music played second fiddle to that of her husband during her lifetime.

 HALL OF FAME HIT

Niccolò Paganini: *Violin Concerto No. 1*

Recommended Recording

Hilary Hahn (violin); Swedish Radio Symphony Orchestra conducted by Eiji Oue; Detusche Grammophon 477 6232

17

JULY

'Music with dinner is an insult both to the cook and the violinist.'

G. K. CHESTERTON, WRITER

🎵 BIRTHS & DEATHS

1960 American soprano Dawn Upshaw is born in Nashville.

🎭 FIRST PERFORMED

1717 George Frideric Handel's *Water Music* is performed for the first time, on a barge on the River Thames in London.

☀ TODAY'S THE DAY

1776 Joseph Haydn's house in Eisenstadt is badly damaged in a fire.

1807 Carl Maria von Weber arrives in Stuttgart, ready to take up his new job as private secretary to Duke Ludwig, the brother of King Frederick I of Württemberg.

1858 The French government sets up a commission to define 'universal pitch'. Hector Berlioz will become the major force behind the commission's work, supported by a cast of famous composers, including Gioachino Rossini and Giacomo Meyerbeer.

1865 Richard Wagner starts work on his autobiography.

1877 The Vienna Philharmonic Orchestra performs in Salzburg on its first concert tour. This is a forerunner of the annual Salzburg Festival, which is established in 1925.

1880 Claude Debussy is given the first prize in accompaniment at the Paris Conservatoire.

1999 The Three Tenors sing together in their 20th concert, in Detroit.

MUSICAL TERM:

Incidental music

Most of the incidental music composed today is commissioned for cinema or television, as soundtracks to films or TV dramas. This was not always the case. Long before movies came along, most major composers from the 1800s onwards had the odd commission for incidental music under their belts, so it is important to draw a distinction between what is and what is not classed as incidental music. Although operas, operettas and even sometimes oratorios are written to be performed as staged works, the music for these is not thought of as being 'incidental' – instead, it is part of the main event, if you like. On the other hand, music written either to accompany dialogue in a play, or to fill in between scenes (such as entr'actes and interludes), very firmly does fall into the incidental music camp. Two famous examples are the music written by Mendelssohn for Shakespeare's *A Midsummer Night's Dream* and by Grieg for Ibsen's *Peer Gynt*.

🎵 HALL OF FAME HIT

Ludwig van Beethoven: *Piano Concerto No. 3*

Recommended Recording

Leif Ove Andsnes (piano); Mahler Chamber Orchestra; Sony Classical 8872 5420582

> 'Artists who say they practise eight hours a day are liars or asses.'
>
> ANDRÉS SEGOVIA, GUITARIST

18

JULY

BIRTHS & DEATHS

1927 German conductor Kurt Masur is born in Brzeg, Poland.
1949 Czech composer Vitezslav Novak dies in Skute.
1959 English composer Jonathan Dove is born in London.

FIRST PERFORMED

2003 *The Evening That Was Lit Up by the Embers,* a piano piece by Claude Debussy, discovered two years ago in a church in Sweden, is given its first performance. Composed in 1917, during the First World War, it was given to the composer's coal supplier by way of thanks for keeping his house warm.

TODAY'S THE DAY

1763 Seven-year-old Wolfgang Amadeus Mozart plays the keyboard for local nobility near Mannheim.
1806 Emperor Napoleon appoints Giovanni Paisiello a member of the French Légion d'Honneur.
1870 Anton Bruckner formally leaves his jobs in Linz, although he has actually been working in Vienna for the past two years.
1870 Hans von Bülow's divorce petition is granted in Berlin.
1872 Despite being a success as a composer, Mily Balakirev takes up a job as a railway clerk.

1877 Pyotr Ilyich Tchaikovsky gets married in Moscow.
1890 Camille Saint-Saëns attends the opening of a museum in Dieppe dedicated to his life and music.
1956 The Gulbenkian Foundation, a Portuguese charity set up by Calouste Sarkis Gulbenkian, is established to fund arts and education projects. Many musicians and musical organisations will benefit from its generous grants in the years to come.

COMPOSER PROFILE:

Anton Bruckner

An organist by trade, Bruckner is remembered today for his massive orchestral symphonies. Listening to one is like bathing under a waterfall of sound. Bruckner's musical style and his championship of Wagner won him no friends among the more conservative critics of his day. Although his symphonies are numbered only up to 9, he actually wrote 11 of them. He gave his *Symphony in D minor* the title '*Die Nullte*', which means it tends to be catalogued as *No. 0*. Bizarrely, he wrote a further *Symphony in F minor* before he finally got going with his *Symphony No. 1 in C minor*. This often appears in lists of his works as *Symphony No. 00*.

 HALL OF FAME HIT
Hamish MacCunn: *The Land of the Mountain and the Flood*

Recommended Recording
Royal Scottish National Orchestra conducted by Alexander Gibson; Chandos CHAN 8379

19

JULY

> 'Composers tend to assume that everyone loves music. Surprisingly enough, everyone doesn't.'
>
> **AARON COPLAND, COMPOSER**

 BIRTHS & DEATHS

1960 Italian conductor Carlo Rizzi is born in Milan.

1964 English conductor Mark Wigglesworth is born in Sussex.

1965 Scottish percussionist Evelyn Glennie is born in Aberdeenshire.

1987 Scottish violinist Nicola Benedetti is born in West Kilbride.

 FIRST PERFORMED

1987 Henryk Górecki's *Totus Tuus* is given its first performance, in Warsaw.

1996 John Williams' *Summon the Heroes* is premiered in Atlanta, for the Olympic Games.

 TODAY'S THE DAY

1812 Ludwig van Beethoven and poet Johann Wolfgang von Goethe meet for the first time while taking the waters at Teplice.

1841 Eleven-year-old Anton Rubinstein makes his piano debut in Germany with a concert in Cologne.

1886 Franz Liszt performs on the piano in public for the final time, at the Luxembourg Casino.

1942 Arturo Toscanini conducts the American premiere of Dmitri Shostakovich's *Symphony No. 7* (*'Leningrad'*). It is broadcast on the radio by NBC; Igor Stravinsky is among those who listen at home.

COMPOSER PROFILE:

Henryk Górecki

Originally a primary school teacher, Górecki switched to studying music and started to make his name after his *Beatus Vir* was performed during Pope John Paul II's visit to Poland in 1979. His writing was influenced by avant-garde composers such as Stockhausen but, in the end, he became known for composing chants with simple, rich harmonies. His success in the UK will be forever tied to the launch of Classic FM, with his *Symphony No. 3* (subtitled 'A *Symphony of Sorrowful Songs*') becoming a sensational hit during the station's first year of existence, despite the fact that it had actually been composed, and received its premiere, some 15 years earlier.

MUSICAL TERM:

Requiem

Strictly speaking, a Requiem is a Roman Catholic Mass for the Dead, containing the following sections: *Requiem aeternam, Dies irae, Domine Jesu Christe, Sanctus, Agnus Dei, Lux aeterna* and finally the *Libera me*. However, many composers down the centuries have added extra liturgical sections and also used secular words. Fauré added the *In Paradisum* to his *Requiem*, for example, while Howard Goodall featured English poetry in his *Eternal Light*. Other well-known requiems include those by Mozart, Duruflé, Berlioz, Verdi, Rutter, Jenkins and Britten.

 HALL OF FAME HIT

Sergei Prokofiev: *Symphony No. 1* (*'Classical'*)

Recommended Recording

London Symphony Orchestra conducted by Valery Gergiev; Philips 475 7655

> "'Is there meaning to music?' My answer to that would be, 'Yes.' And, 'Can you state in so many words what the meaning is?' My answer to that would be, 'No.'"
>
> **AARON COPLAND, COMPOSER**

20
JULY

BIRTHS & DEATHS

1803 Swiss conductor of the Liverpool Philharmonic, J. Zeugheer Herrmann, is born in Zurich.

TODAY'S THE DAY

1831 Frédéric Chopin leaves Vienna for Munich. Ultimately, he wants to reach Paris.

1925 George Gershwin is the cover star for *Time* magazine – the first American-born musician to be accorded the honour.

1942 Today's *Time* magazine front cover features a picture of Dmitri Shostakovich in a fireman's helmet – a reference to the struggles back home in Leningrad, told in music in his *Symphony No. 7 ('Leningrad')*.

1983 A memorial service for William Walton is held in Westminster Abbey, where a memorial stone is unveiled in Musicians' Corner.

1996 The Three Tenors sing together in their 7th concert, in New York.

COMPOSER PROFILE:

William Walton

Although musical, William Walton's parents were not well off. Aged 10, Walton won a choral scholarship to Christ Church Cathedral School, Oxford, where his early aspirations to become a composer were fostered. Despite eventually failing his degree, Walton met the poets Edith Sitwell and Siegfried Sassoon while an undergraduate, later becoming part of their London social set.

Having explored the mixing of classical music and jazz in works such as *Façade* and also having composed his *Symphony No. 1* and choral pieces such as *Belshazzar's Feast*, Walton was excused military service in the Second World War in order to continue to compose. Patriotic scores, such as his *Spitfire Prelude and Fugue* and his music for Laurence Olivier's film of *Henry V,* were the result. After the war, he moved to Ischia, an island off the Italian coast, where he concentrated on operas, such as *Troilus and Cressida*. Thankfully, his temporary post-war reputation of being old fashioned has been re-assessed since his death in 1983.

 HALL OF FAME HIT
Alexander Borodin: *String Quartet No. 2*

Recommended Recording
Borodin String Quartet; ONYX 4002

21

'Too many pieces of music finish too long after the end.'

IGOR STRAVINSKY, COMPOSER

JULY

 BIRTHS & DEATHS

1920 American violinist Isaac Stern is born in Kremenets, Ukraine.

1934 English theatre and opera director Jonathan Miller is born in London.

2004 American composer Jerry Goldsmith dies in Beverley Hills.

2010 English tenor Anthony Rolfe Johnson dies in London.

 FIRST PERFORMED

1776 Wolfgang Amadeus Mozart's *Serenade No. 7* ('*Haffner*') is performed for the first time, at a wedding in Salzburg.

 TODAY'S THE DAY

1829 Frédéric Chopin sets off for Vienna after finishing his exams at the Warsaw Conservatoire.

1841 César Franck wins the second prize in organ at the Paris Conservatoire.

1862 Work starts on building the new Paris Opéra.

1876 Camille Saint-Saëns becomes the music critic of the Paris newspaper *Le Bon Sens*.

1884 Edvard Grieg buys a piece of land near Bergen, where he plans to build a new home.

1930 Opera star Jussi Björling makes a very early appearance at the Royal Swedish Opera as the Lamplighter in *Manon Lescaut*, although this small role is not generally recognised as his debut, which comes a month later.

COMPOSER PROFILE:

César Franck

One of Belgium's greatest classical music exports, Franck was touring by the age of 11 and had moved with his family to Paris to study at the Conservatoire. Until relatively late in his life, his music failed to capture the imagination of the French public. He worked as an organist and rose to fame for his playing – and particularly for his improvisations. At the age of 50, he became a professor at the Conservatoire. Gradually, his works were performed more and more. His pleasant demeanour and general good nature led to him being nicknamed 'Père Franck' by those who knew him.

King of recycling

For Rossini, recycling was not about taking his empties to the bottle bank or bundling up old piles of paper. He was shameless about how he recycled his own music. The overture for his opera *Aureliano in Palmira* was used again as the overture for his subsequent opera *Elizabeth Queen of England*, and then he had no pang of conscience about using it all over again as the overture to *The Barber of Seville*. This time, it became a smash hit and we normally think of it as being attached to this opera, rather than to either of the other two.

🎵 **HALL OF FAME HIT**
Peter Maxwell Davies: *Farewell to Stromness*

Recommended Recording
Peter Maxwell Davies (piano); Unicorn Kanchana DKPCD 9070

> 'I always think that when something is currently very trendy, it's already very old.'
>
> **ENNIO MORRICONE, COMPOSER**

22

JULY

🕐 BIRTHS & DEATHS

1953 English composer Nigel Hess is born in Somerset.

🐾 FIRST PERFORMED

1919 Manuel de Falla's ballet *The Three-Cornered Hat* is premiered in London.

☀ TODAY'S THE DAY

1822 Gioachino Rossini leaves Vienna and heads off to Verona.

1829 Felix Mendelssohn leaves London to visit Edinburgh.

1970 John Tavener begins recording *The Whale* for Apple Records, after being discovered by Ringo Starr.

2000 The Three Tenors sing together in their 21st concert, in São Paulo.

COMPOSER PROFILE:

Manuel de Falla

This Spanish composer spent his twenties studying piano and composition and started to receive recognition for his music only when he had almost turned 30. He moved to Paris in 1907 and became friends with the French composers Debussy, Ravel and Dukas. He also met the Russian composer Stravinsky and the impresario Diaghilev. After the First World War, he went back to Spain. Diaghilev commissioned de Falla to write the score for the ballet *The Three-Cornered Hat*, which had its premiere at the Alhambra Theatre in London's Leicester Square, next door to where Classic FM's studios are based. Becoming disillusioned with his homeland because of the Spanish Civil War, he spent the last seven years of his life in Argentina.

COMPOSER PROFILE:

John Tavener

John Tavener was a classmate of fellow composer John Rutter at Highgate School in London. His early school compositions were instrumental in winning him a scholarship to the Royal Academy of Music when he was 18. Here he met and was influenced by Stravinsky (who, it is said, read through the score of his *John Donne Sonnets* and simply wrote 'I know!' on the first page). His early student oratorio *The Whale* won him a wider audience when it was recorded by the Beatles' Apple record label. Aged 34, he joined the Russian Orthodox Church and much of his subsequent music, such as the *Liturgy of St John Chrysostom*, reflects this faith. From 2000 onwards, he broadened his religious and musical scope; his *Requiem* (2009) sets Sanskrit, Hebrew and Islamic texts alongside the traditional Latin.

🎵 HALL OF FAME HIT

Edward Elgar: *Introduction and Allegro for Strings*

Recommended Recording

London Philharmonic Orchestra conducted by Vernon Handley; EMI 433 2872

23

JULY

'Gee! That'll make Beethoven.'

WALT DISNEY, HAVING ADAPTED THE FIRST MOVEMENT OF BEETHOVEN'S SYMPHONY NO. 6 FOR HIS ANIMATED FILM *FANTASIA*

 BIRTHS & DEATHS

1757 Italian composer Domenico Scarlatti dies in Madrid.

1944 Portuguese pianist Maria João Pires is born in Lisbon.

1983 French composer Georges Auric dies in Paris.

 FIRST PERFORMED

1896 Edward Elgar's *Serenade for Strings* is performed in full for the first time, in Antwerp.

1912 Ralph Vaughan Williams' *The Wasps* suite is given its first performance, in Queen's Hall, London, with the composer conducting.

 TODAY'S THE DAY

1839 Nine-year-old Anton Rubinstein makes his piano debut in Moscow.

COMPOSER PROFILE:

Ralph Vaughan Williams

A great landscape painter who worked in tones and semitones rather than oils or watercolours, Vaughan Williams was born in the Gloucestershire village of Down Ampney and went to school at Charterhouse, where he was in the orchestra. Having composed from a young age, he went early to the Royal College of Music, and then Cambridge, before returning to the RCM, where Holst was a fellow student. He then had lessons, albeit briefly, with Bruch in Berlin.

Shortly after the turn of the 20th century, Vaughan Williams became hooked on folk-song collecting, alongside Cecil Sharp, Percy Grainger and others, and was responsible for the survival of numerous folk gems. Following more time studying, this time with Ravel in Paris, he returned to England to write *On Wenlock Edge* and incidental music to *The Wasps* (for a Cambridge student production). This was also the time of successes such as *Fantasia on a Theme by Thomas Tallis* and *A London Symphony*.

Vaughan Williams went on to live through the two world wars – he was a stretcher-bearer in the first, but a respected veteran composer during the second – and came to be regarded as one of Britain's finest symphonic writers. A late crop of works towards the end of the 1940s and during the early 1950s underlined his pre-eminence. He was a familiar figure at his famous White Gates house in Dorking (where you will find his statue).

 HALL OF FAME HIT

Igor Stravinsky: *The Firebird*

Recommended Recording

Columbia Symphony Orchestra conducted by Igor Stravinsky; Sony 88/6 5442692

"'"When you write the music for a film, do you know whether the film will be a great success?" I tell them, "No, I was mainly concerned about finishing the music in time."'

MAURICE JARRE, COMPOSER

🕐 BIRTHS & DEATHS

1803 French composer Adolphe Adam is born in Paris.

1949 English clarinettist and Principal of the Royal College of Music Colin Lawson is born in Saltburn-by-the-Sea in Yorkshire.

🎭 FIRST PERFORMED

1828 Niccolò Paganini's *Violin Concerto No. 3* is first performed, in Vienna, with the composer as soloist.

☀ TODAY'S THE DAY

1662 Jean-Baptiste Lully gets married in Paris.

1765 Leopold, Wolfgang Amadeus and Maria Anna Mozart leave London for France, travelling through Kent via Canterbury.

1792 Joseph Haydn, returning to Vienna after a trip to England, stops in Bonn, where he meets 21-year-old Ludwig van Beethoven for the second time.

1933 Arnold Schoenberg returns to the Jewish faith in Paris, having embraced Christianity some 35 years earlier.

Haydn's symphonies

Joseph Haydn wrote his first symphony in 1757 and his last in 1795. The first 30 followed the old-fashioned Italian style, with three movements, the first and last of which were fast, with a slow section sandwiched in the middle. From *Symphony No. 31* onwards, all of his symphonies were in four movements (usually fast–slow–fast–fast). Many of them were given nicknames, for example:

Symphony No. 22	The Philosopher
Symphony No. 55	The Schoolmaster
Symphony No. 60	The Distracted
Symphony No. 82	The Bear
Symphony No. 83	The Hen
Symphony No. 94	Surprise
Symphony No. 100	Military
Symphony No. 101	Clock
Symphony No. 103	Drumroll
Symphony No. 104	London

🏛 HALL OF FAME HIT

Henry Purcell: *Dido and Aeneas*

Recommended Recording

Various soloists; Les Arts Florissants conducted by William Christie; Erato 2564 659880

25

JULY

> 'To listen is an effort, and just to hear has no merit. A duck hears also.'
>
> **IGOR STRAVINSKY, COMPOSER**

 FIRST PERFORMED

1976 Philip Glass's opera *Einstein on the Beach* is premiered in Avignon.

 TODAY'S THE DAY

1762 Joseph Haydn gets a pay rise from his new boss, Prince Nikolaus Esterházy.

1788 Wolfgang Amadeus Mozart finishes work on his *Symphony No. 40*, in Vienna.

1880 Richard Wagner finishes dictating his autobiography 15 years after starting – it is four volumes long.

1886 Gustav Mahler is in Leipzig ready to start his new job as opera conductor.

COMPOSER PROFILE:

Richard Wagner

Like him or loathe him, there is no disputing the fact that Wagner was a colossus among composers. Through his operas, he revolutionised music. Obsessed with opera from the start, Wagner was given lessons in his mid-teens. He took various jobs conducting at Würzburg, Magdeburg and then in Riga. Forced to flee from his creditors, he took refuge in Paris, where he wrote the operas *Rienzi* and *The Flying Dutchman*. Successful productions of both works in Dresden a few years later brought him instant fame, as did *Tannhäuser*, which followed shortly after. Wagner's good fortune soon ran out. He left Germany to escape arrest following his involvement in the unsuccessful 1849 revolution, finally ending up in Switzerland.

It was there that he wrote not only *Das Rheingold* and *Die Walküre* (the first two operas of the mammoth

Ring Cycle), but *Tristan and Isolde* into the bargain. King Ludwig of Bavaria became his patron, helping the composer to raise the money he needed to build his own opera house in Bayreuth. The first performance of the now complete *Ring Cycle* (adding *Siegfried* and *Götterdämmerung* to the first two) took place there in 1876. He completed *Parsifal*, his last opera, in 1882.

Wagner's stormy career ended in triumph, but, for much of it, he was his own worst enemy. His extravagance meant that he was always short of funds, often spending as much time dodging his creditors as he did composing. Nor were his personal relationships better managed. Convinced of his own destiny, he possessed deeply unpleasant views, and was racist, egotistical and often completely amoral.

 HALL OF FAME HIT

Antonín Dvořák: *Symphony No. 8*

Recommended Recording

Philharmonic Orchestra conducted by Charles Mackerras; Signum SIGCD 183

'The tuba is certainly the most intestinal of instruments – the very lower bowel of music.'

PETER DE VRIES, WRITER

BIRTHS & DEATHS

1782 Irish composer John Field is born in Dublin.
1874 American (originally Russian) conductor and double-bass player Serge Koussevitzky is born in Vyshny Volochyok.
1958 Canadian pianist Angela Hewitt is born in Ottawa.

FIRST PERFORMED

1882 Richard Wagner's opera *Parsifal* is premiered in the Bayreuth Festspielhaus. Anton Bruckner is in the audience.

TODAY'S THE DAY

1812 Franz Schubert gives his last performance as a chorister at the Imperial Chapel; his voice has broken.
1829 Felix Mendelssohn arrives in Edinburgh for a three-day trip that includes watching a bagpipe competition.
1859 Jules Massenet wins first prize in piano at the Paris Conservatoire.
1871 Nikolai Rimsky-Korsakov accepts a job teaching orchestration and composition at the St Petersburg Conservatoire.

1876 Jules Massenet is appointed to the French Légion d'Honneur.
1877 Pyotr Ilyich Tchaikovsky and his new wife return to Moscow; the cracks in their relationship are already starting to show.
1888 Conductor Charles Hallé gets married.
1996 The Three Tenors sing together in their eighth concert, in Gothenburg.

COMPOSER PROFILE:

John Field

Field was already wowing the crowds in his home city of Dublin by the time he was 10 years old. So much so, that his father took him off to London to seek his fame and fortune. There, he studied with the piano genius Muzio Clementi and just got better and better. Field always saw himself as a pianist who composed, rather than purely as a composer. He travelled around Europe playing Clementi's compositions, ultimately settling in St Petersburg. He developed a series of short pieces for the piano, which he called *Nocturnes*. The idea was taken on and developed by Chopin, who became famous for them, but it was actually Field who invented them in the first place.

 HALL OF FAME HIT

Dmitri Shostakovich: *The Unforgettable Year 1919*

Recommended Recording
English Chamber Orchestra conducted by Jerzy Maksymiuk; EMI 382 2342

'He was incessantly sidling about caressing everybody like an old bogey at a witches' Sabbath who had got hold of all the pretty rascals he liked best.'

HUBERT PARRY ON SEEING FRANZ LISZT AT A PARTY, TODAY IN 1882

 BIRTHS & DEATHS

1741 Italian composer Antonio Vivaldi dies in Vienna.
1867 Spanish composer Enrique Granados is born in Lleida.
1924 Italian composer Ferruccio Busoni dies in Berlin.

TODAY'S THE DAY

1733 Johann Sebastian Bach asks the new Elector of Saxony for an upgrade in his job title; it is more than three years in coming.
1782 Wolfgang Amadeus Mozart writes to his father Leopold, asking for his permission to marry Constanze Weber.
1824 Twelve-year-old Franz Liszt plays the piano for King George IV at Windsor.
1856 Clara Schumann sees her ill husband Robert for the first time in more than two years. He does not communicate with her.
1870 Cosima von Bülow gets confirmation that her marriage to conductor Hans von Bülow is now officially over.

COMPOSER PROFILE:

Antonio Vivaldi

At the stage in musical history when J. S. Bach was composing in Germany, Handel was making music in England and François Couperin was writing in France, Vivaldi was doing the same in Italy. The composer of *The Four Seasons* was born in Venice, a sickly child of a violinist in the St Mark's Orchestra. He learned the violin in childhood, accompanying his father on some of his musical trips. When he was 15 years old, he began studying for the priesthood, being ordained 10 years later. The same year, Vivaldi joined the La Pietà orphans' institute as head of the violins – the orphanage had an impressive orchestra and chorus – remaining there, on and off, in various posts until he was 38. During this time, he wrote many great instrumental works, including his now famous concertos and sonatas.

Between the ages of 38 and 50, he worked variously out of Mantua and Rome, concentrating on opera, although he still composed 'by post' for La Pietà. He then ventured further afield – to Vienna and Prague – before returning to La Pietà as maestro di capella. Late in life, he moved to Vienna in pursuit of more opera commissions, but he died, aged 63, in relative poverty.

 HALL OF FAME HIT
John Williams: *Saving Private Ryan*

Recommended Recording
Boston Symphony Orchestra; Tanglewood Festival Chorus conducted by John Williams; Dreamworks DRD 50046

'The prospect of having to sit through one of his extended symphonies or piano concertos tends, quite frankly, to depress me.'

AARON COPLAND ON HIS FELLOW COMPOSER SERGEI RACHMANINOV

 BIRTHS & DEATHS

1750 German composer Johann Sebastian Bach dies in Leipzig.

1796 Founder of the Austrian firm of piano makers, Ignaz Bösendorfer is born in Vienna.

1925 English conductor Kenneth Alwyn is born in London.

1941 Italian conductor Riccardo Muti is born in Naples.

TODAY'S THE DAY

1741 Antonio Vivaldi's funeral takes place in Vienna; his status accords him only a pauper's burial.

1828 Niccolò Paganini offers to pay off his mistress if she will abandon their relationship, but allow their young son to stay with him.

1851 Camille Saint-Saëns wins the first prize in organ at the Paris Conservatoire.

1856 Clara Schumann and Johannes Brahms begin a round-the-clock vigil outside Robert Schumann's room, as his illness worsens.

1865 Gabriel Fauré wins the top prizes for composition, fugue and counterpoint as he leaves the Ecole Niedermeyer.

1867 Anton Rubinstein resigns as director of the St Petersburg Conservatoire.

1867 Arthur Sullivan announces his engagement. His prospective mother-in-law is outraged, banning him from her house.

1874 Bedřich Smetana exhibits the early signs of syphilis, having trouble hearing and suffering from giddy spells.

1944 Henry Wood conducts a performance of Beethoven's *Symphony No. 7* in Bedford; it is his last time on the concert podium.

COMPOSER PROFILE:

Gabriel Fauré

A whizz at the organ and a great composer in his own right, Fauré was also responsible for passing on his expertise to a whole new generation of French composers during the 15-year period that he was director of the Paris Conservatoire. He himself studied with Saint-Saëns, and his pupils included Maurice Ravel and Nadia Boulanger; the latter was responsible for giving his *Requiem* a wider hearing. Fauré had written it to be performed at his local church and, despite Boulanger's best efforts, it still took until after the end of the Second World War before it was widely recognised as the masterpiece that it surely is. It also took him quite a while to get noticed outside France. Towards the end of his life he became deaf. It didn't stop him from giving composition advice right to the end – not least to Les Six, the group of young French composers that included Satie and Poulenc.

 HALL OF FAME HIT

Gerald Finzi: *Eclogue*

Recommended Recording

Peter Donohoe (piano); Royal Northern Sinfonia conducted by Howard Griffiths; Naxos 855 5766

'A lot of my friends didn't know what to do with their lives. But I always had this very strong idea of what I wanted.'

NICOLA BENEDETTI, VIOLINIST

 BIRTHS & DEATHS

1856 German composer Robert Schumann dies near Bonn.
1963 Russian mezzo-soprano Olga Borodina is born in Leningrad.
1970 British conductor and cellist John Barbirolli dies in London.
1992 Welsh composer William Mathias dies in Menai Bridge, Anglesey.

 TODAY'S THE DAY

1710 Giuseppe Tartini gets married in Padua.
1846 Sixteen-year-old Hans von Bülow meets Richard Wagner, who is composing his opera *Lohengrin*.
1871 Anton Bruckner arrives in London ready to play the organ as a representative of his country at the International Exhibition.
1910 Gustav Mahler discovers that his wife Alma is having an affair, after opening a letter to her from her lover.

Russian nationalist music

In Russia, musical nationalism was fathered by Mikhail Glinka, one of the first Russian composers to achieve any sort of fame outside his own country. He was born into a wealthy, land-owning family and first discovered his latent nationalism when he was abroad, homesick in Italy. When he returned, he wrote *A Life for the Tsar*, the first major Russian opera, which, according to one commentator, 'marked the boundary between the past and the future of Russian music'.

A group of younger composers, based in St Petersburg, continued where Glinka left off. Dubbed 'The Five' or 'The Mighty Handful', they were led by Balakirev (the group's other members were Cui, Mussorgsky, Rimsky-Korsakov and Borodin). They were largely self-taught, and their works, often infused with folk music, served to make Russia a thriving centre of the 19th-century musical universe. Borodin's *Prince Igor*, Mussorgsky's *A Night on the Bare Mountain* and Rimsky-Korsakov's *Scheherazade* are all great examples of their work. Interestingly, though, Tchaikovsky, the other great Russian composer at the time, preferred to stand apart. Indeed, 'The Five' did not consider him to be a nationalist. Despite this, many of his compositions – the opera *Eugene Onegin*, the orchestral *Marche Slave* and the *1812 Overture*, for instance – sound hugely nationalistic to our ears today.

 HALL OF FAME HIT

Maurice Ravel: *Pavane pour une infante défunte*

Recommended Recording

Artur Pizarro (piano); Linn CKD 315

'I want to write and feel the drama. Music is essentially an emotional language, so you want to feel something from the relationships and build music based on those feelings.'

HOWARD SHORE, COMPOSER

BIRTHS & DEATHS

1751 Austrian pianist Maria Anna 'Nannerl' Mozart, the elder sister of Wolfgang Amadeus, is born in Salzburg.

1955 English conductor and violinist Christopher Warren-Green is born in Gloucestershire.

TODAY'S THE DAY

1612 Claudio Monteverdi is sacked from his job in Mantua.

1779 Christoph Willibald von Gluck suffers a stroke, from which he will recover.

1792 Around 500 French national guards arrive in Paris from Marseille, singing a song composed by Claude-Joseph Rouget de Lisle. It quickly becomes known as '*La Marseillaise*' and is ultimately adopted as the French national anthem.

1829 Felix Mendelssohn visits Holyrood House in Edinburgh, where the ideas behind his '*Scottish*' *Symphony* begin to take shape in his mind.

1830 Robert Schumann writes to his mother to tell her that he is turning his back on studying law. He wants to be a pianist instead.

1836 Fanny Mendelssohn writes to her brother Felix, telling him that she would 'cease being a musician tomorrow if you thought I was not good at that any longer'.

1853 Robert Schumann suffers a stroke while visiting Bonn.

1892 A special concert is held in honour of John Philip Sousa on the White House lawn, in the presence of President Benjamin Harrison. It marks Sousa leaving the marines.

1904 Sixteen-year-old Nadia Boulanger is awarded the first prizes in organ, piano accompaniment and fugue at the Paris Conservatoire.

Up in smoke

Liverpool's original Philharmonic Hall was opened in 1849 and burned to the ground in 1933. The current art deco building, home to the Royal Liverpool Philharmonic Orchestra, was opened in 1939. If you're there, make sure you allow time to nip into the Gents of the Philharmonic pub opposite. The red marble urinals are listed and have become a big attraction for visitors to the city – something of an inconvenience if you happen to be availing yourself of the convenience at the moment when a coach party drops in for a peek.

HALL OF FAME HIT

Richard Strauss: *Der Rosenkavalier*

Recommended Recording

Various soloists; Vienna Philharmonic Orchestra conducted by Silvio Varviso; Australian Eloquence 480 3149

31

JULY

'I play every gig as if it could be my last, then I enjoy it more than ever.'

NIGEL KENNEDY, VIOLINIST

🕐 BIRTHS & DEATHS

1886 Hungarian composer Franz Liszt dies in Bayreuth.
1919 English conductor and composer Norman Del Mar is born in London.

🎭 FIRST PERFORMED

1820 Carl Maria von Weber's *Der Freischütz Overture* is given its first performance, in Halle. The rest of the opera will be heard once Berlin's new opera house has been built.

🌅 TODAY'S THE DAY

1795 A benefit concert for 12-year-old Niccolò Paganini is put on in Genoa.
1808 Giovanni Paisiello is given an annual pension of 1,000 francs by Emperor Napoleon, backdated to 23 September 1804.
1829 Frédéric Chopin arrives in Vienna; it is his first trip to the city.
1845 Adolphe Sax, the inventor of the saxophone, first sells his instrument to French army bands.
1856 Robert Schumann is buried in Bonn. Johannes Brahms and Joseph Joachim are among the mourners.

COMPOSER PROFILE:

Claudio Monteverdi

He might have been born well over 400 years ago, but Monteverdi was one of a group of composers who were quietly revolutionary in the way that they wrote their music. They broke many of the accepted rules of the time and did much to develop the way in which music was composed.

History has judged Monteverdi to have been particularly influential in the development of opera, although he began by composing madrigals. He was a master at bringing emotion into his music and also at creating a sense of drama around what he wrote. Arguably, he was among the first composers to ensure that the music he wrote matched the words being sung, making his songs more natural in their style than many of those that had been written before. His first opera was *La favola d'Orfeo*, featuring a score written for a full-size orchestra, which was unusual at the time.

🎵 HALL OF FAME HIT

Ludwig van Beethoven: *Piano Concerto No. 1*

Recommended Recording

Martha Argerich (piano); Philharmonia Orchestra conducted by Giuseppe Sinopoli; Deutsche Grammophon 445 5042

Augus

01

'Just love what you are doing, and try to play more.'
LANG LANG, PIANIST

AUGUST

 BIRTHS & DEATHS
1989 English pianist John Ogdon dies in London.
1997 Russian pianist Sviatoslav Richter dies in Moscow.

 FIRST PERFORMED
1740 Thomas Arne's 'Rule, Britannia!' receives its first performance, at Cliveden in Buckinghamshire.

 TODAY'S THE DAY
1777 Wolfgang Amadeus Mozart writes to his boss Archbishop Colloredo to ask if he can leave his service.
1824 Gioachino Rossini arrives in Paris to take up the role of director of the Théâtre-Italien. He is also contracted by the Royal Household to write two new operas.

1829 Felix Mendelssohn begins a three-week walking tour of the Scottish highlands.
1840 In one of the youngest debuts in this book, four-year-old Camille Saint-Saëns performs in public at the keyboard for the first time, in Paris.
1841 Felix Mendelssohn moves to Berlin.
1844 Hector Berlioz leads more than a thousand performers for the premiere of his *Hymne à la France*. He is taken unwell at half-time, with a doctor diagnosing typhoid.
1886 Richard Strauss begins a 3-year contract to work as one of the conductors at the Munich Court Opera.

1892 John Philip Sousa leaves the US Marine Corps Band, to form his own private-sector version.
1897 Gustav Mahler becomes interim director of the Vienna Opera.
1908 Carl Nielsen begins work as the conductor of the Royal Danish Orchestra in Copenhagen.
1913 Nineteen-year-old Lili Boulanger signs as an exclusive recording artist with the Ricordi Company.
1938 Leonard Bernstein gives his first full-length piano recital, in Massachusetts.
2002 Composer and pianist André Previn and violinist Anne-Sophie Mutter get married in New York.

The name game

Stanley Myers' *Cavatina* is often known as 'the theme from *The Deer Hunter*'. But things could have been different. It would be fair also to call it 'the theme from *The Walking Stick*'. Myers wrote it originally for a 1970 film called *The Walking Stick* and simply reused it eight years later in *The Deer Hunter*.

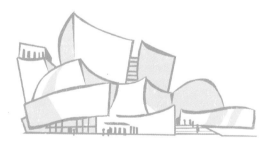

 HALL OF FAME HIT
Frederick Delius: *The Walk to the Paradise Garden* (from *A Village Romeo and Juliet*)

Recommended Recording
Royal Liverpool Philharmonic Orchestra conducted by John Wilson; Avie AV2194

> 'When one is a composer for films, it's day and night. One needs to be in great physical condition!'
>
> **ALEXANDRE DESPLAT, COMPOSER**

 BIRTHS & DEATHS

1891 English composer Arthur Bliss is born in London.

1916 Scottish composer Hamish MacCunn dies in London.

1921 Italian tenor Enrico Caruso dies in Naples.

1936 English composer Anthony Payne is born in London.

1945 Italian composer Pietro Mascagni dies in Rome.

 FIRST PERFORMED

1774 The French version of Christoph Willibald von Gluck's *Orpheus and Euridice* is premiered in Paris.

1990 Patrick Doyle's *The Thistle and the Rose* is given its first performance, in the ballroom at Buckingham Palace, for the 90th birthday of the Queen Mother.

TODAY'S THE DAY

1768 Many of Joseph Haydn's possessions and manuscripts are destroyed in a large fire in his local area.

1834 Richard Wagner makes his debut as an opera conductor, with Mozart's *Don Giovanni*.

1838 César Franck is given the first prize for piano at the Paris Conservatoire.

1875 Richard Wagner listens to an orchestra performing for the first time at his new Bayreuth Festspielhaus.

1905 Claude Debussy gets divorced.

1946 Arnold Schoenberg nearly dies from a heart attack at his home in Los Angeles.

1947 Maria Callas appears in Ponchielli's *La Gioconda* in Verona. Her performance catapults her to stardom and she begins to be seen in big roles in opera houses across Europe.

COMPOSER PROFILE:

Hamish MacCunn

Something of a 'one-hit wonder', Hamish MacCunn was born in Greenock and studied at the Royal College of Music, where he went on to take a teaching post when he was barely out of his teens. He tasted success early with his concert overture *The Land of the Mountain and the Flood* when he was just 21 years old. From then on, he never quite composed anything to rival it in the public's affections, but that did not stop him from working, and he was much in demand as an opera conductor. He conducted the Carl Rosa Opera Company and later frequently stood in for Thomas Beecham. He was a particularly ardent advocate of Scottish music. In his forties, he was appointed Head of Composition at the Guildhall School of Music. Gradually, his health deteriorated, not helped by his heavy workload of conducting, composing and teaching, and he died when he was just 48 years old.

 HALL OF FAME HIT
Johannes Brahms: *Symphony No. 1*

Recommended Recording
Swedish Chamber Orchestra conducted by Thomas Dausgaard; BIS 1756

03

> 'Those who have achieved all their aims probably set them too low.'
>
> HERBERT VON KARAJAN, CONDUCTOR

AUGUST

BIRTHS & DEATHS

1784 Italian composer Giovanni Battista Martini dies in Bologna.
1952 English pianist Martin Roscoe is born in Halton.
1959 English baritone Simon Keenlyside is born in London.
1998 Russian composer Alfred Schnittke dies in Hamburg.
2006 German soprano Elisabeth Schwarzkopf dies in Schruns.

FIRST PERFORMED

1829 Gioachino Rossini's opera *William Tell* is premiered in Paris.
1960 Ralph Vaughan Williams' *Four Last Songs* is heard for the first time, broadcast by the BBC Home Service.

TODAY'S THE DAY

1668 German composer and organist Dietrich Buxtehude gets married in Lübeck. As was the custom, his wife was the daughter of the retiring organist.

1778 Milan's opera house La Scala opens with a performance of Salieri's *L'Europa Riconosciuta*.
1795 The Paris Conservatoire is founded, following the merger of two singing and instrumental colleges.
1863 Jules Massenet is awarded the First Grand Prize in the Prix de Rome scholarship contest.
1886 Franz Liszt is buried in the Bayreuth city cemetery.
1910 Zoltán Kodály gets married to fellow composer Emma Sándor.

ORCHESTRA FOCUS:

London Symphony Orchestra

Widely acknowledged as being among the greatest orchestras in the world, the LSO is a self-governing orchestra, which came into being in 1904 after a group of players fell out with the conductor Henry Wood and resigned en masse from his Queen's Hall Orchestra. The new orchestra was owned and governed by the players, along the lines of the Berlin Philharmonic, which had come into existence around 20 years earlier. The LSO's first conductor was the legendary Hans Richter. In the years since, the orchestra has been conducted by a *Who's Who* of top baton-wavers, including Thomas Beecham, Richard Strauss, John Barbirolli, Benjamin Britten, Leonard Bernstein, André Previn, Leopold Stokowski, Claudio Abbado, Colin Davis, Michael Tilson Thomas and Valery Gergiev. The orchestra has mounted extensive international tours ever since it became the first British orchestra to tour abroad, to Paris, in 1906. Six years later, the LSO was the first British orchestra to visit the USA, narrowly avoiding travelling on the *Titanic*. In 1956, it was the first British orchestra to visit South Africa and, in 1963, it was the first to visit Japan. The LSO's first world tour was in 1964, taking in Israel, Turkey, Iran, India, Hong Kong, Korea, Japan and the USA. For many people, the LSO has become synonymous with film soundtracks – it has provided the musical accompaniment to all of the *Star Wars* movies.

HALL OF FAME HIT

Ludwig van Beethoven: *Triple Concerto*

Recommended Recording

Sviatoslav Richter (piano); David Oistrakh (violin); Mstislav Rostropovich (cello); Berlin Philharmonic Orchestra conducted by Herbert von Karajan; EMI 955 9782

> 'The earth has music for those who listen.'
> **WILLIAM SHAKESPEARE, PLAYWRIGHT**

BIRTHS & DEATHS

1960 American soprano Deborah Voigt is born in Chicago.

1965 Australian violinist, composer and conductor Richard Tognetti is born in Canberra.

TODAY'S THE DAY

1756 Thirteen-year-old Luigi Boccherini makes his concert debut in Lucca, playing the cello.

1764 Luigi Boccherini debuts in his new role as Lucca's town cellist.

1782 Wolfgang Amadeus Mozart gets married to Constanze Weber in St Stephen's Cathedral in Vienna.

1828 Niccolò Paganini wins custody of his son Achille, following a legal battle.

1877 Charles Gounod is appointed a commander of the Légion d'Honneur.

1879 The name 'Mr D'Oyly Carte's Opera Company' is born, midway through a production of Gilbert and Sullivan's *HMS Pinafore*.

1886 Anton Bruckner is one of the performers at a Requiem Mass in honour of Franz Liszt in Bayreuth.

1945 200,000 people turn out on to the streets of Rome for Pietro Mascagni's funeral.

VENUE FOCUS:

Sage Gateshead

This stunning venue provides ample reason to get off at Newcastle if you're ever journeying up or down the East Coast mainline. If you already live in the North East of England, then you've really got no excuse for not having visited. The building is a marvel. Designed by Norman Foster (his first performing arts venue, as it happens), Sage Gateshead cost £70 million to construct. Most of the 3,858 tonnes of steel are hidden from view down in the foundations; more than 11,000 steel piles were drilled into the ground to support the massive structure; and more than 18,000 cubic metres of concrete were poured into the foundations of the building. That's enough concrete to fill twenty-three 50-metre swimming pools.

Inside, you will find an incredible range of music-making – from pensioners' workshops to parents' and babies' sessions – but if you're looking for an orchestral concert, you should make your way to Hall One for a performance from the Royal Northern Sinfonia, Classic FM's Orchestra in the North East of England.

HALL OF FAME HIT

Tomaso Albinoni: *Oboe Concerto Op. 9 No. 2*

Recommended Recording
Albrecht Mayer (oboe); New Seasons Ensemble; Decca 478 0313

05

AUGUST

'It appears to me that it is the special province of music to move the heart.'

CARL PHILIPP EMANUEL BACH, COMPOSER

BIRTHS & DEATHS

1397 Franco-Flemish composer Guillaume Dufay is born near Brussels.

1891 English composer Henry Litolff dies in Bois-Colombes.

1916 English composer George Butterworth dies in action on the Somme.

1944 English composer Christopher Gunning is born in Cheltenham.

FIRST PERFORMED

1814 Ludwig van Beethoven's *Elegiac Song* ('Gentle as you lived') is given its first performance, in Vienna.

TODAY'S THE DAY

1717 Johann Sebastian Bach gets a new job as Kapellmeister to Prince Leopold in Cöthen.

1735 Antonio Vivaldi returns to the Pietà orphanage as orchestra conductor.

1764 Leopold Mozart, on a visit to London, goes out to Chelsea (at this time, regarded as being 'the country') to recover from a throat infection.

1805 Louis Spohr takes up the role of Concert Master in Gotha; he is the youngest person with the title in Germany.

1884 Claude Debussy wins the Prix de Rome.

1937 The Boston Symphony Orchestra performs for the first time in its new summer home, Tanglewood, in Lenox, Massachusetts.

COMPOSER PROFILE:

Igor Stravinsky

Stravinsky was one of the most influential and enigmatically charming composers of the 20th century. His composing life is often divided into distinct periods, in much the same way as that of the artist Picasso. For Picasso's blue, cubist and surrealist periods, substitute for Stravinsky, Russian, neoclassical and serial. Stravinsky's three great ballets, *Firebird*, *Petrushka* and *The Rite of Spring*, all belong to his Russian period, with their use of folksong or folk-like motifs. The masterpieces of his neoclassical period, during which he rediscovered classic forms, are the *Symphony of Psalms*, *Symphony in C* and the *Symphony in Three Movements*. In the 1950s and 1960s, he adopted Schoenberg's 12-tone techniques to produce works such as the ballet *Agon* and the choral and orchestral piece *Canticum Sacrum*. Across his long life, he furnished quotation books with many a quip, of which you will find a liberal sprinkling throughout this book.

HALL OF FAME HIT
Claudio Monteverdi: *Vespers*

Recommended Recording
Monteverdi Choir and Orchestra conducted by John Eliot Gardiner; Decca 443 4822

> 'Opera: an exotic and irrational entertainment.'
> SAMUEL JOHNSON IN HIS *DICTIONARY OF THE ENGLISH LANGUAGE* OF 1775

BIRTHS & DEATHS

1637 English dramatist and librettist Ben Jonson dies in London.

1858 German composer Albert Fuchs is born in Basle.

2001 American harmonica player Larry Adler dies in London.

FIRST PERFORMED

1859 Two duets from Hector Berlioz's opera *Les Troyens* are performed for the first time, in Baden.

TODAY'S THE DAY

1803 Ludwig van Beethoven buys a new piano from the Paris-based instrument maker Sebastien Erard.

1826 Ludwig van Beethoven's nephew Karl attempts to shoot himself, but survives. The composer is greatly upset by the incident, as he was awarded custody of Karl as a child.

1859 Richard Wagner finishes work on *Tristan and Isolde* in Lucerne.

1876 King Ludwig arrives in Bayreuth, ready to watch the dress rehearsals for Wagner's *Ring Cycle* over the next four nights.

1921 85-year-old Camille Saint-Saëns performs on the piano for the very last time, in Dieppe.

INSTRUMENT FOCUS:

Pianola

Pianolas, or 'player pianos', were invented in the 1890s, the Aeolian Company of New York being among the most significant manufacturers of the instrument. Indeed, it is its trade name, Pianola, that has stuck as the word for all player pianos, in much the same way as Hoover became synonymous with vacuum cleaners. Player pianos reproduce both the notes and the expression of a given performance by means of piano rolls. The piano roll is first 'cut' (generally not during an actual performance but by a technician). It can subsequently be 'played' by means of suction pedals, which control not just the speed at which the piece is played but the dynamics as well, making playing a pianola fairly tricky. They were intended originally for homes where no one could play the piano, and they have produced a wonderful by-product: rolls 'cut' by famous pianists and even some composers.

 HALL OF FAME HIT

Richard Wagner: *Die Meistersinger von Nürnberg*

Recommended Recording

Various soloists; Bayreuth Festival Orchestra and Choir conducted by Daniel Barenboim; Teldec 2564 678999

AUGUST

'Who hears music, feels his solitude peopled at once.'

ROBERT BROWNING, POET AND PLAYWRIGHT

BIRTHS & DEATHS

1818 French composer Henry Litolff is born in London.

1825 Italian violin maker Gaetano Antoniazzi is born in Cremona.

1868 English composer Granville Bantock is born in London.

FIRST PERFORMED

1912 Sergei Prokofiev's *Piano Concerto No. 1* receives its first performance, in Moscow.

TODAY'S THE DAY

1782 In a letter written today, Wolfgang Amadeus Mozart describes the opening of his 'Haffner' *Symphony No. 35* as needing to be played 'with real fire'.

1814 Carl Maria von Weber is very nearly seriously injured under the wheels of an oncoming train; he is pulled away from the track just in time.

1829 Gioachino Rossini is awarded the Légion d'Honneur.

1829 Felix Mendelssohn reaches Oban on his tour of Scotland. He looks out to sea and is inspired to come up with the theme for his *Hebrides Overture*.

1834 Samuel Wesley gives his last public performance, in London's Exeter Hall.

COMPOSER PROFILE:

John Rutter

Known chiefly for his choral music, composer and conductor John Rutter studied at Clare College, Cambridge, in the 1960s, returning there in 1975 as Director of Music. He left four years later and went on to form his own Cambridge Singers, a group dedicated to performing and recording, among other works, his own extensive body of compositions. Rutter is probably the most widely performed English composer of his generation. He is particularly noted for his Christmas carols, though he has also composed various anthems and, on a grander sale, a notable *Gloria*, a *Magnificat* and a *Requiem*. There is a strong following for his music in the USA. Favourite Rutter works include *A Gaelic Blessing*, which was commissioned by a choir in Nebraska, and *For the Beauty of the Earth*, a resetting of the old hymn.

HALL OF FAME HIT

Ludovico Einaudi: *I Giorni*

Recommended Recording

Ludovico Einaudi (piano); Decca 476 4490

> 'Of all the noises known to man, opera is the most expensive.'
>
> MOLIÈRE, PLAYWRIGHT

08
AUGUST

 BIRTHS & DEATHS

1916 Founder of Japanese musical-instrument manufacturer that bears his name, Torakusu Yamaha, dies in Hamamatsu.

 FIRST PERFORMED

1808 Sixteen-year-old Gioachino Rossini has his first work – a cantata – performed in public in Bologna.

 TODAY'S THE DAY

1526 Spanish composer Cristóbal de Morales is appointed music director of Avila Cathedral.

1704 Georg Philipp Telemann gets a new job as organist and music director of the Neukirche in Leipzig.

1774 Wolfgang Amadeus Mozart finishes work on his *Missa Brevis*, in Salzburg.

1829 Felix Mendelssohn travels by boat to the Scottish island of Staffa, where he sees Fingal's Cave.

1848 Bedřich Smetana opens the doors of a music institute in Prague.

1867 Anton Bruckner leaves the sanatorium in Bad Kreuzen following three months of treatment for a nervous breakdown.

1922 There is a fight – and the police have to be called to restore order – at a performance of Anton Webern's *Five Movements for String Quartet* in Salzburg.

1927 Gustav Holst meets Thomas Hardy in Dorchester. The composer has dedicated his orchestral tone poem *Egdon Heath* to the novelist.

1941 Sergei Prokofiev is evacuated by train from Moscow to Nalchik in the Caucasus.

ENSEMBLE FOCUS:

Academy of Ancient Music

When the conductor Christopher Hogwood founded the Academy of Ancient Music back in 1973, he wanted to perform music from the Baroque and Classical periods in exactly the way that the composers had originally intended it to be heard. That meant that the instruments themselves needed to be authentic, so out went steel strings and in came strings made of animal gut; valves on trumpets and chin rests on violins and violas were jettisoned; and the cellists had to forgo spikes to rest their instruments on the floor, squeezing them between their legs instead. The sound was very different from that of a modern orchestra, and excited audiences and critics alike. The *Independent* described the Academy of Ancient Music as 'the ultimate raspberry to anyone who says Baroque music is predictable'. In 2006, Richard Egarr took over as music director and the orchestra continues to flourish – it now has more than 300 recordings to its name.

 HALL OF FAME HIT

Johann Sebastian Bach: *Cantata No. 208*

Recommended Recording

Bach Collegium Japan conducted by Masaki Suzuki; BIS 1971

09

AUGUST

> 'Music is a higher revelation than all wisdom and philosophy.'
>
> LUDWIG VAN BEETHOVEN, COMPOSER

BIRTHS & DEATHS

1875 English composer Albert Ketelbey is born in Birmingham.
1919 Italian composer Ruggero Leoncavallo dies in Montecatini.
1975 Russian composer Dmitri Shostakovich dies in Moscow, on the anniversary of the first performance of his *Symphony No. 7*.

FIRST PERFORMED

1902 Edward Elgar's hymn 'O Mightiest of the Mighty' and Hubert Parry's anthem 'I Was Glad' are first performed at the Coronation of King Edward VII in Westminster Abbey.
1942 Dmitri Shostakovich's *Symphony No. 7 ('Leningrad')* is premiered in the besieged city after which it is named. Musicians are drafted in from all over the city to take part, and, in an act of defiance, the Russian forces set up loudspeakers so that their German assailants can hear the music as it is played.

TODAY'S THE DAY

1703 Johann Sebastian Bach begins work as the organist at Neuekirche in Arnstadt.
1869 Giuseppe Verdi turns down a request to compose a new work for the opening of the Cairo Opera House and the Suez Canal.
1906 A new design for a phonograph, with the horn inside the cabinet (effectively a modern loudspeaker), is revealed by the Victor Talking Machine Company.
1928 Percy Grainger gets married at the Hollywood Bowl in front of an audience of 22,000 people. He didn't let his marriage get in the way of conducting the LA Philharmonic after the ceremony.

COMPOSER PROFILE:

Ruggero Leoncavallo

Born in the same year as Edward Elgar into a well-off family (his father was a police magistrate), Leoncavallo studied at the Naples Conservatoire. There was little interest in his early output as either a composer or a librettist and he ended up working as a café pianist in places as far apart as Paris, London and Egypt. Leoncavallo was hugely influenced by the operas of Wagner and set out to try to emulate his success. In 1890, though, he heard Mascagni's *Cavalleria Rusticana*, which is as unlike Wagner as anything can be imagined. It fell into the genre of what was christened *verismo* (realistic) opera – that is, operas that took real life as the basis for their stories. Leoncavallo's *Pagliacci* was the result. Today, it is often performed in tandem with *Cavalleria Rusticana* as a double bill (known as 'Cav & Pag' in the trade).

HALL OF FAME HIT

Johannes Brahms: *Piano Concerto No. 1*

Recommended Recording

Nicholas Angelich (piano); Frankfurt Radio Symphony Orchestra conducted by Paavo Järvi; Virgin Classics 50999 5189982

'Without music, life would be a mistake.'

FRIEDRICH NIETZSCHE, PHILOSOPHER AND COMPOSER

10

AUGUST

 BIRTHS & DEATHS

1748 German music publisher Bernhard Schott is born in Eltville.

1806 Austrian composer Michael Haydn dies in Salzburg.

1865 Russian composer Alexander Glazunov is born in St Petersburg.

1909 American electric-guitar maker Leo Fender is born in Anaheim, California.

1929 English choral conductor John Alldis is born in London.

1947 Russian pianist Dmitri Alexeev is born in Moscow.

TODAY'S THE DAY

1787 Wolfgang Amadeus Mozart finishes work on his *Serenade for Strings No. 13 in G ('Eine Kleine Nachtmusik')*.

1788 Wolfgang Amadeus Mozart finishes work on his *Symphony No. 41 ('Jupiter')*.

1850 Samuel Sebastian Wesley is appointed professor of organ at the Royal Academy of Music.

1895 Henry Wood's first Promenade Concert is held at Queen's Hall in London.

ENSEMBLE FOCUS:

London Sinfonietta

Co-founded by impresario Nicholas Snowman and conductor David Atherton in 1968, this chamber orchestra has focused on modern classical music throughout its life, with many of its concerts including world premieres of key works by living composers.

The orchestra has never been afraid to push the boundaries of how a classical music concert should look and sound, on occasions blending in electronic music and working with folk and jazz musicians. Other collaborations have included pieces involving choreographed dance and specially shot film.

In 1969, the orchestra gave the premiere performance of John Tavener's *The Whale*, recording the work for The Beatles' Apple Records label the following year. Today, the London Sinfonietta is resident at London's Southbank Centre and is based at King's Place, the relatively newly built concert hall in the King's Cross area of London. It has enjoyed a particularly close relationship with the composer and conductor Oliver Knussen.

 HALL OF FAME HIT

Gustav Mahler: *Symphony No. 8 ('Symphony of a Thousand')*

Recommended Recording

Various soloists and choruses; City of Birmingham Symphony Orchestra conducted by Simon Rattle; EMI 623 0762

11

AUGUST

'The modern composer builds upon the foundation of truth.'

CLAUDIO MONTEVERDI, COMPOSER

 BIRTHS & DEATHS

1919 American philanthropist Andrew Carnegie, after whom New York's Carnegie Hall is named, dies in Lenox, Massachusetts.

1927 English conductor Raymond Leppard is born in London.

1929 Welsh composer Alun Hoddinott is born in Bargoed.

1996 Czech pianist, composer and conductor Rafael Kubelík dies in Lucerne.

2011 Spanish violinist and conductor José-Luis García dies in London.

 FIRST PERFORMED

1943 Richard Strauss's *Horn Concerto No. 2* is performed for the first time, in Salzburg.

TODAY'S THE DAY

1829 Frédéric Chopin performs his first concert in Vienna, to great popular acclaim.

1832 Giacomo Meyerbeer is appointed court conductor by King Friedrich Wilhelm III of Prussia.

1840 Robert Schumann and Clara Wieck are finally able to marry, after her father ends his legal battle to prevent the union.

1845 Three days of celebrations begin in Bonn to mark the unveiling of a new statue of Ludwig van Beethoven. Queen Victoria and Prince Albert are among the many dignitaries taking part.

1846 Felix Mendelssohn finishes work on the orchestral score for his oratorio *Elijah*.

1922 The International Society for Contemporary Music is founded.

1939 Sergei Rachmaninov performs in Europe for the final time, at the Lucerne Festival.

COMPOSER PROFILE:

Joaquín Rodrigo

The most Spanish of composers, Rodrigo was born not far from Valencia. After contracting diphtheria, he lost most of his eyesight at the age of three, but this did not put a stop to his musical progress. He studied first in Valencia, then with Paul Dukas in Paris, writing all his compositions in Braille. He returned to Spain in 1939, the same year in which he wrote his *Concierto de Aranjuez*. Inspired by the beautiful palace at Aranjuez, the guitar concerto is probably his best-known work, though, curiously enough, Rodrigo himself never mastered the playing of the instrument. In his forties, Rodrigo became director of music at the University of Madrid. There he put himself at the head of the *casticismo* (authenticity) movement, which aimed to revive Spanish music by going back to its folk traditions and rediscovering lost Baroque customs. He was widely travelled, giving lectures and piano recitals, and being honoured by virtually every European country. He was Spain's most enduring musical celebrity in the latter half of the 20th century.

 HALL OF FAME HIT

Patrick Hawes: *Quanta Qualia*

Recommended Recording

Janet Coxwell (soprano); Conventus; English Chamber Orchestra conducted by Patrick Hawes; Black Box BBM 1081

'A good composer does not imitate; he steals.'

IGOR STRAVINSKY, COMPOSER

12
AUGUST

 BIRTHS & DEATHS

1612 Italian composer Giovanni Gabrieli dies in Venice.

1633 Italian composer Jacopo Peri dies in Florence.

1928 Czech composer Leoš Janáček dies in Moravska Ostrava.

1992 American composer John Cage dies in New York.

 FIRST PERFORMED

1858 Johann Strauss Junior's *Champagne Polka* is performed for the first time, in Pavlovsk.

☀ **TODAY'S THE DAY**

1845 A monument commemorating Ludwig van Beethoven is unveiled in Bonn, following a performance of his *Missa Solemnis* conducted by Louis Spohr.

1846 After initially being against the idea, Felix Mendelssohn agrees that his sister Fanny should have her music published under her own name.

1859 Anton Bruckner (by now well into his thirties) passes a correspondence course in counterpoint.

1864 Hector Berlioz is appointed an officer of the Légion d'Honneur by Emperor Napoleon.

1877 Thomas Edison formally receives his patent on a device for recording and playing back sound called the gramophone.

1881 The Prague National Theatre, which opened only two months earlier, is completely destroyed by fire.

ORCHESTRA FOCUS:

Bournemouth Symphony Orchestra

Classic FM's Orchestra in the South of England is not actually based in Bournemouth. Its home in fact is just down the road in Poole. It started life in the 1890s, when Dan Godfrey was appointed to form a new municipal orchestra, drawing players from the Italian military band that for many years had given concerts in the town. Because of this, the orchestra still played in military uniform for the first few years of its life. It was called the Bournemouth Municipal Orchestra until 1954, when it was given its current name. The BSO has a long pedigree of championing English music: when it celebrated its 25th anniversary, the likes of Edward Elgar sent letters of congratulation to mark its achievements in this area. Today, the BSO performs more than 140 concerts a year in venues including Poole, Bournemouth, Exeter, Portsmouth, Winchester, Weymouth, Southampton, Bristol and Basingstoke. It was notable in being the first British orchestra to appoint a female principal conductor – Marin Alsop, who directed the orchestra from 2002 to 2008. The dynamic young Ukrainian Kirill Karabits took over the baton at the beginning of the 2009 season.

 HALL OF FAME HIT
Modest Mussorgsky: *A Night on the Bare Mountain*

Recommended Recording
Los Angeles Philharmonic Orchestra conducted by Esa-Pekka Salonen; Deutsche Grammophon 477 6198

13

AUGUST

'I think a life in music is a life beautifully spent, and this is what I have devoted my life to.'

LUCIANO PAVAROTTI, TENOR

 BIRTHS & DEATHS

1820 English music writer George Grove is born in Clapham. He goes on to edit *Grove's Dictionary of Music and Musicians* – the world's foremost classical music reference work.

1879 English composer John Ireland is born in Cheshire.

1912 French composer Jules Massenet dies in Paris.

1948 American soprano Kathleen Battle is born in Ohio.

1959 English conductor Martyn Brabbins is born in Leicester.

 TODAY'S THE DAY

1742 George Frideric Handel sets off from Dublin to London for the start of the oratorio season at Covent Garden.

1828 Niccolò Paganini leaves Vienna after 14 concerts in which he wowed the crowds. He now sets off to do the same on a tour of no fewer than 30 different European cities.

1876 Richard Wagner's Festspielhaus opens in Bayreuth. There is no denying Wagner's box-office attraction. Among the famous names in the audience: Franz Liszt, Anton Bruckner, Camille Saint-Saëns, Pyotr Ilyich Tchaikovsky and Edvard Grieg. The first complete *Ring Cycle* begins with *Das Rheingold*.

COMPOSER PROFILE:

Jules Massenet

Among the leading opera composers in France in the latter part of the 19th century, Massenet was a child prodigy taught first by his mother and then at the Paris Conservatoire. He made his recital debut at the age of 16 and from then on paid his way by giving music lessons and by performing in cafés, bars and orchestras. When he was 21, he won the Prix de Rome, the major French composition prize. He served alongside Georges Bizet in the army during the Franco–Prussian War, before going on to make a name for himself with his operas. His major successes came in the 1880s, first with *Manon* and later with *Le Cid*. There followed a relatively unsuccessful period, even though it saw the premiere of *Werther*, now considered one of Massenet's greatest successes. Everything changed with *Thaïs*, which proved to be an enduring hit.

 HALL OF FAME HIT

Richard Wagner: *Götterdämmerung*

Recommended Recording

Various soloists; Bayreuth Festival Orchestra and Choir conducted by Daniel Barenboim; Teldec 2564 677140

'All that counts in life is intention.'

ANDREA BOCELLI, TENOR

BIRTHS & DEATHS

1810 English organist Samuel Sebastian Wesley is born in London. He is the first of the seven illegitimate children of composer Samuel Wesley.
1953 American composer James Horner is born in Los Angeles.

FIRST PERFORMED

1876 The first complete run of the *Ring Cycle* at Bayreuth continues with *Die Walküre*.

TODAY'S THE DAY

1703 Johann Sebastian Bach starts a new job as organist at Bonifatiuskirche in Arnstadt.
1763 Michael Haydn starts work as Konzertmeister and court composer to the Archbishop of Salzburg.
1844 Jacques Offenbach gets married.
1949 Aaron Copland has a car crash near Tanglewood in Massachusetts, killing a cow. Copland is arrested and fined $35 for the cow's death.
1975 Dmitri Shostakovich is buried in Moscow; his body has been lying in state at the Moscow Conservatoire.

COMPOSER PROFILE:

Aaron Copland

Born in the USA to a Russian émigré family, Copland went to Paris at the age of 21 to study with the highly influential music teacher Nadia Boulanger. Many of his early works are tough listening because he was a fan of dissonance in his twenties.

He experimented with jazz and also with Mexican infusions to his music, but, as time went by, he started to become more concerned with composing works that were more easily understood by the general public. Accordingly, he created barnstorming American hits, such as *El Salón México, Billy the Kid, Rodeo* and *Fanfare for the Common Man*. Later on in life, composing became less important to him than conducting, and he took every opportunity to spread the word about contemporary American classical music wherever he travelled in the world.

I left my heart in . . . Warsaw

When Chopin died, he was buried in France. But before his body was placed in its coffin, his heart was removed and pickled in alcohol. In accordance with his final wishes, it was then taken to Poland. Except for a short period during the Second World War, when it was removed for safe-keeping, it has remained in a church there ever since.

 HALL OF FAME HIT

Ludwig van Beethoven: *Choral Fantasy*

Recommended Recording

Emanuel Ax (piano); New York Philharmonic Orchestra and New York Choral Artists conducted by Zubin Mehta; RCA Classical Masters 8869 7757492

15

AUGUST

'When [Johann] Strauss was writing his music, it was dance music. Now it's classical music. So how can you tell that in 50 years' time film music will not turn out to be classical music?'

ZBIGNIEW PREISNER, COMPOSER

BIRTHS & DEATHS

1875 English composer Samuel Coleridge-Taylor is born in London.

1890 French composer Jacques Ibert is born in Paris.

1896 Russian inventor Leon Theremin is born in St Petersburg. He gave his name to the 'other-worldly'-sounding electronic musical instrument that he invented.

1907 Hungarian violinist Joseph Joachim dies in Berlin.

1951 Austrian pianist Artur Schnabel dies in Morschach, Switzerland.

FIRST PERFORMED

1808 Giovanni Paisiello's *Mass in D* is performed for the first time, in Paris. He chose this date a year later for the premiere of his *Mass in G*; then, in 1811, he premiered a different *Mass in G*, before also premiering his *Mass in C* in the same city on the same date one year after that.

TODAY'S THE DAY

1690 Johann Pachelbel is formally released from his job as organist, composer and teacher in Erfurt, after he asks to be allowed to move on.

1795 Joseph Haydn leaves England for the final time, having composed his oratorio *The Creation*.

1835 Samuel Sebastian Wesley is appointed organist at Exeter Cathedral.

1868 Camille Saint-Saëns is admitted into the Légion d'Honneur.

1887 Johann Strauss Junior is married for the third time. He turns his back on Catholicism and his fiancée renounces Judaism to allow the marriage to go ahead.

1928 Leoš Janáček's funeral is held in Brno.

1949 Richard Strauss suffers a heart attack, leaving him gravely ill.

COMPOSER PROFILE:

Johann Pachelbel

As well as being a significant composer, Nuremberg-born Pachelbel was also a virtuoso organist, his talents winning him the top job at St Stephen's, Vienna's great cathedral, as well as in Eisenach and Stuttgart. In Eisenach, he grew close to the Bach family and was eventually godfather to one of Johann Sebastian's children. The composer of countless pieces of music in varied forms, his life was scarred by tragedy: his wife and child both died of the plague. He is remembered now for only one work, albeit a beautiful one: his *Canon in D*.

HALL OF FAME HIT

Edward Elgar: *Serenade for Strings*

Recommended Recording

London Philharmonic Orchestra conducted by Paul Daniel; Sony 8869 7642942

'Playing lifts you out of yourself into a delirious place.'

JACQUELINE DU PRÉ, CELLIST

16

AUGUST

🕐 BIRTHS & DEATHS

1960 Austrian conductor Franz Welser-Möst is born in Linz.

🏛 FIRST PERFORMED

1876 Richard Wagner's *Siegfried* is premiered on the third night of the first complete *Ring Cycle*, in Bayreuth.

☀ TODAY'S THE DAY

1613 Claudio Monteverdi becomes the Master of Music for the Republic of Venice.
1783 Giovanni Paisiello is appointed Inspector of Opera by the Committee for the Direction of Imperial Theatres in St Petersburg.
1814 Ludwig van Beethoven finishes work on his *Piano Sonata No. 27*.
1846 Gioachino Rossini gets married in Bologna, ten months after the death of his first wife.
1866 Anton Bruckner writes a letter to a butcher's daughter half his age, asking her to marry him; she turns him down.
1870 Gabriel Fauré enlists in the First Light Infantry Regiment of the Imperial Guard.
1932 The New York Philharmonic Orchestra plays its first concert consisting of music entirely written by a living composer, with a performance of works by George Gershwin; it is also the first full-length classical concert solely of Gershwin's music anywhere.
1941 Dmitri Shostakovich refuses to be evacuated from the besieged city of Leningrad.
1943 La Scala opera house in Milan is damaged in an Allied bombing raid.

INSTRUMENT FOCUS:

Cello

With its name an abbreviation of the word 'violincello', this member of the string family is bigger than a viola and violin, but smaller than a double-bass. It is played between a performer's knees, which has spawned a whole host of double-entendres down the years from conductors ('Madam, you have between your legs an instrument capable of giving pleasure to thousands – and all you can do is scratch it', from Thomas Beecham, comes to mind in particular). The composers Boccherini and Offenbach were both masterly cellists. and the 20th century produced such greats as England's Jacqueline du Pré, Spain's Pablo Casals, France's Paul Tortelier and Russia's Mstislav Rostropovich. We are lucky to have a number of modern-day masters and mistresses including Julian Lloyd Webber, Yo-Yo Ma, Steven Isserlis, Natalie Clein and Alisa Weilerstein all performing today.

🎵 HALL OF FAME HIT

Frédéric Chopin: *Nocturne in E flat major Op. 9 No. 2*

Recommended Recording

Yundi Li (piano); Deutsche Grammophon 479 1302

17

'Every great work of art has two faces, one toward its own time and one toward the future, toward eternity.'

DANIEL BARENBOIM, PIANIST AND CONDUCTOR

AUGUST

 BIRTHS & DEATHS

1887 German composer Franz Commer dies in Berlin.

1968 Portuguese pianist Artur Pizarro is born in Lisbon.

1973 English violinist Daniel Hope is born in Durban, South Africa.

1983 American lyricist Ira Gershwin dies in Beverly Hills, California.

FIRST PERFORMED

1876 The final night of the first complete production of Richard Wagner's *Ring Cycle* sees *Götterdämmerung* performed at Bayreuth.

TODAY'S THE DAY

1752 The English newspaper *General Advertiser* carries a report of George Frideric Handel's blindness.

1768 Michael Haydn gets married in Salzburg.

1807 Carl Maria von Weber is hired as music teacher to the children of Duke Ludwig Friedrich Alexander in Württemburg.

1895 Antonín Dvořák resigns as director of the National Conservatory of New York.

1912 Jules Massenet's funeral is held in Egreville. He had stipulated that no music was to be played at the service.

Mozart, Haydn and the piano

One way of placing the invention of the piano within the history of classical music is to look at the works of Haydn (born 1732) and Mozart (born 1756). That 20-odd-year difference meant that Haydn wrote a dozen keyboard concertos while Mozart penned 27 piano concertos. The latter was one of the first composers to realise the potential of the new pianoforte, writing a stunning body of work that exploited all of its possibilities. Alongside the concertos – Mozart's calling-card showpieces, which he frequently used to gain work in a new town or to show to a new patron what he could do – are the 18 piano sonatas, which demonstrate virtually every facet of the instrument. Mozart's favourite instruments were a Stein piano made in Augsburg, and one built by Walter of Vienna, which is on display at the composer's birthplace museum in Salzburg. If you ever see it, you will notice that Mozart had to work with 22 fewer notes than he would have done with a modern piano. Pianos now have 88 notes, whereas Mozart's Walter had just 66. Pedals were not always pedals, either. The job done by today's 'soft' pedal was often achieved by means of a knob, positioned on the front of the case, which the player would pull with his hand.

HALL OF FAME HIT

Sergei Rachmaninov: *Piano Concerto No. 1 in F# minor*

Recommended Recording

Simon Trpčeski (piano); Royal Liverpool Philharmonic Orchestra conducted by Vasily Petrenko; Avie AV 2191

> 'Subtlety is not a virtue on a Bond movie.'
>
> JOHN BARRY, COMPOSER

BIRTHS & DEATHS

1750 Italian composer Antonio Salieri is born in Legnano.

1916 English pianist Moura Lympany is born in Saltash.

1957 American composer Tan Dun is born in Simao, Hunan Province.

1987 Norwegian trumpeter Tine Thing Helseth is born in Oslo.

2004 American composer Elmer Bernstein dies in California.

FIRST PERFORMED

1938 Benjamin Britten's *Piano Concerto* is premiered in London, with the composer as soloist.

TODAY'S THE DAY

1763 The ever-touring Mozart children give their first public concert in Frankfurt. 15-year-old Johann Wolfgang von Goethe is in the audience.

1829 Because of public demand, 19-year-old Frédéric Chopin performs in concert in Vienna for a second time.

1843 The Berlin Opera House is destroyed by fire.

1857 Conductor Hans von Bülow and Cosima, daughter of Franz Liszt, get married in Berlin.

1861 Edvard Grieg makes his concert debut, in Karlskrona, Sweden.

1931 A performance of Richard Wagner's *Tristan and Isolde* at Bayreuth is the first worldwide television opera broadcast.

1942 A judge overturns a previous court decision that Benjamin Britten should undertake non-combatant war work.

INSTRUMENT FOCUS:

Trumpet

To call the trumpet a lip-vibrated cylindrical bore aerophone, while being technically accurate, would not begin to convey the impressive range of colours that it can produce. This is an instrument that can range from attention-grabbing authority to haunting, elegiac beauty. The modern trumpet, most commonly in B flat (which means all the music is written one whole tone above where it sounds) is the undisputed leader of the brass section, a full 8 feet of coiled tubing, whose every note is produced via just three valves and the ever-changing lipwork (called embouchure) of the player's mouth. Many bridegrooms have had the hairs on the back of their necks raised in a mixture of apprehension and relief at the start of a rousing trumpet voluntary. Despite originally being organ pieces (which made a feature out of using the trumpet stop), they are very often used at weddings, arranged for trumpet or not, to signal the bride's arrival and hopefully elegant procession down the aisle. Great trumpet concertos include those written by Haydn, Hummel and Arutunian.

HALL OF FAME HIT

Ralph Vaughan Williams: *The Wasps*

Recommended Recording

London Symphony Orchestra conducted by André Previn; RCA 8869 7472502

19

'The word "listen" contains the same letters as the word "silent".'

ALFRED BRENDEL, PIANIST

AUGUST

BIRTHS & DEATHS

1881 Romanian composer George Enescu is born in Liveni-Virnaz.

1929 Russian ballet impresario Sergei Diaghilev dies in Vienna.

1944 English conductor Henry Wood dies in Hitchin.

1947 American conductor and trumpeter Gerard Schwarz is born in Weehawkin, New Jersey.

1963 Welsh soprano Rebecca Evans is born near Neath.

FIRST PERFORMED

1820 Robert Schumann's *Andante and Variations for Two Pianos* is given its first performance, in Leipzig. The soloists are Clara Schumann and Felix Mendelssohn.

1957 Leonard Bernstein's musical *West Side Story* has its regional premiere in the National Theatre, Washington, before transferring to Broadway.

TODAY'S THE DAY

1613 Claudio Monteverdi takes over as director of music at St Mark's, Venice.

1816 Carl Maria von Weber signs up to be Kapellmeister in Dresden.

1830 Hector Berlioz wins the First Grand Prize in the Prix de Rome, but the jury is split.

1847 Hector Berlioz turns down the job of director of singing at the Paris Opéra, opting instead to move to London to be music director at the Theatre Royal, Drury Lane.

1905 Fourteen-year-old Bohuslav Martinů makes his concert debut on the violin in Borova, Bohemia.

1961 President Kennedy sends Aaron Copland a telegram congratulating him on winning the MacDowell Medal.

1990 Leonard Bernstein makes his final concert appearance, conducting a performance by the Boston Symphony Orchestra of Britten's *Four Sea Interludes* and Beethoven's *Symphony No. 7*.

Mozart's England

While Vienna was definitely the city of Mozart's dreams, it is possible to find traces of the genius on these shores:

180 Ebury Street, London: A plaque denotes Mozart 'composed his first symphony here in 1764'. He would have been eight years old.

19 Cecil Court, London: Mozart lodged here with a barber.

21 Frith Street (then 'Thrift Street'), London: There is still a plaque opposite Ronnie Scott's Jazz Club, marking another of Mozart's lodgings.

Bourne Park, near Canterbury, Kent: Mozart stayed in this wonderful Queen Anne House to attend the races at nearby Barham Downs.

HALL OF FAME HIT

Giuseppe Verdi: *Rigoletto*

Recommended Recording

Various soloists; Vienna Philharmonic Orchestra; Vienna State Opera Choir conducted by Riccardo Chailly; Deutsche Grammophon 073 4166

> 'We do not play the piano with our fingers but with our mind.'
>
> GLENN GOULD, PIANIST

20

AUGUST

🕐 BIRTHS & DEATHS

1561 Italian composer Jacopo Peri is born in Rome.

1611 Spanish composer Tomás Luis de Victoria dies in Madrid.

1827 Austrian composer (and brother of Johann Junior) Josef Strauss is born in Vienna.

1941 English soprano Anne Evans is born in London.

1974 Russian violinist Maxim Vengerov is born in Novosibirsk.

🎭 FIRST PERFORMED

1828 Gioachino Rossini's opera *Le Comte Ory* is premiered in Paris.

1871 A setting of Gabriel Fauré's *Ave Maria* is performed for the first time, in Switzerland.

1882 Pyotr Ilyich Tchaikovsky's *1812 Overture* is given its first performance, in Moscow.

☀ TODAY'S THE DAY

1918 Italian tenor Enrico Caruso gets married.

COMPOSER PROFILE:

Ludwig van Beethoven

When Beethoven was 16, he travelled to Vienna to play for Mozart, who was 15 years older. Mozart agreed to take on the teenager as a pupil, creating one of the great 'what if?'s of classical music. Shortly after their meeting, Beethoven was called back home to Bonn to look after his sick mother. As a result, the lessons never took place. Around the time of Beethoven's 20th birthday, he met Haydn, who offered to give him lessons in Vienna. Beethoven took up the opportunity and settled in the city for the rest of his life, quickly gaining a reputation as the best keyboard player in town.

Initially, he found public performance a gruelling experience, composing right up to the last minute and suffering stomach pains in the process. In the next few years, his confidence grew considerably and his rate of composition shot up, with piano sonatas, violin sonatas and other chamber works pouring out of him. By the time he was 29, he had completed his first symphony. A year later, he mentioned his deafness in print for the first time, saying it had gradually been worsening for a while. Nevertheless, he continued to compose. During his thirties, many of his greatest works received their premieres, including the *Symphonies Nos 2 to 6*, his *Mass in C*, his *Piano Concertos Nos 3 and 4*, and his *Violin Concerto*. His only opera, *Fidelio*, had a troubled birth, with no fewer than four separate versions of the overture being penned.

Beethoven continued to produce astounding new works well into his fifties, despite his health issues. The most triumphant of all is quite possibly his *Symphony No. 9*, which includes a setting of Schiller's poem 'Ode to Joy'.

🎵 HALL OF FAME HIT

Jean Sibelius: *Lemminkäinen Suite*

Recommended Recording

Helsinki Radio Symphony Orchestra conducted by Okko Kamu; Australian Eloquence 480 3297

21

AUGUST

'The challenge is not so much to change the sound. The challenge is to connect and to create something special.'

GUSTAVO DUDAMEL, CONDUCTOR

🕐 BIRTHS & DEATHS

1893 French composer Lili Boulanger is born in Paris.

1933 English mezzo-soprano Janet Baker is born in Hatfield, Yorkshire.

1951 English composer and conductor Constant Lambert dies in London.

☀ TODAY'S THE DAY

1750 George Frideric Handel is injured when his coach overturns on a journey between The Hague and Haarlem.

1772 Wolfgang Amadeus Mozart is given the job of Second Konzertmeister in Salzburg, on a salary of 150 florins.

1822 Hector Berlioz decides to turn his back on medicine and become a composer instead after seeing an opera written by Christoph Willibald von Gluck in Paris.

1837 Richard Wagner arrives in Riga ready to start work as musical director.

1849 Samuel Sebastian Wesley is appointed Winchester Cathedral organist.

1883 Gustav Mahler begins a new job as assistant conductor in Kassel.

1943 Michael Tippett is released from Wormwood Scrubs prison after serving two months inside for refusing to perform national service in lieu of military duty.

1980 American pop singer Linda Ronstadt stars in a Broadway production of Gilbert and Sullivan's operetta *The Pirates of Penzance*.

ORCHESTRA FOCUS:

Royal Northern Sinfonia

Founded by Michael Hall in 1958, this chamber orchestra was known originally as the 'Sinfonia Orchestra'. A year later, 'Northern' was added to the front of the name. Later still, 'Orchestra' was dropped from the band's title. It was not until 2013 that the Queen issued a Royal charter, allowing the orchestra to change its name to Royal Northern Sinfonia. The orchestra was resident in Newcastle City Hall until 2004; shortly after moving to Sage Gateshead, on the other side of the River Tyne, it became known as Classic FM's Orchestra in the north-east of England. Designed by Lord Foster, this futuristic building contains two acoustically excellent concert halls, another hall, which is used for rehearsals, and a 25-room music education centre. The orchestra has enjoyed artistically strong relationships with a series of impressive conducting talents, including Tamás Vásáry, Ivan Fischer and the current music director, Thomas Zehetmair.

🎵 HALL OF FAME HIT

Johann Sebastian Bach: *Cantata No. 208*

Recommended Recording

Bach Collegium Japan conducted by Masaki Suzuki; BIS 1971

'Audiences are not important for me now and they never were.'

MARTHA ARGERICH, PIANIST

BIRTHS & DEATHS

1862 French composer Claude Debussy is born in St Germain-en-Laye.

1922 Israeli violinist Ivry Gitlis is born in Haifa.

1928 German composer Karlheinz Stockhausen is born near Cologne.

TODAY'S THE DAY

1741 George Frideric Handel begins working on the score for his oratorio *Messiah*. It is all done and dusted just 24 days later.

1760 Johann Christian Bach becomes Milan Cathedral's organist after passing the audition with flying colours.

1861 Alexander Borodin gets engaged in Baden-Baden.

1894 Jean Sibelius decides that he is musically closer to Liszt than to Wagner, writing, 'I am no longer a Wagnerian.'

1959 The New York Philharmonic Orchestra, conducted by Leonard Bernstein, begins a tour of the Soviet Union.

COMPOSER PROFILE:

Claude Debussy

Rather than having formal music lessons, the young Debussy was taught by a family friend. That did not stop him from making it into the Paris Conservatoire or winning the Prix de Rome composing competition in 1884. Debussy went through a musical turning-point in 1889, when, struck (not literally) by the gamelan that he heard at the Paris Exhibition of that year, he realised that he should move forward independently, developing his own individual style, rather than simply following in Wagner's musical slipstream. In the process, he became a true innovator.

In 1893, Debussy began to compose his opera *Pelléas et Mélisande*. A year later came *Prélude à l'après-midi d'un faune,* a piece that, according to some, changed the course of classical music for ever. He became friendly with the Impressionist painters of the period and is often referred to as an 'Impressionist composer'. He also worked as a music critic, using the pseudonym 'M. Croche', which translates as 'Mr Quaver'. An interesting footnote: when he was a music student, Debussy took a summer job teaching the children of Nadezhda von Meck. She was the patron who funded Tchaikovsky on the strict understanding that they should never actually meet.

HALL OF FAME HIT

Franz Liszt: *Hungarian Rhapsody No. 2*

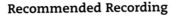

Recommended Recording

Simon Trpčeski; Wigmore Hall Live 0058

23

AUGUST

'The ultimate aim, in all these projects, is of course to move people, to touch their heart with stories, with music, to make them think, or feel something.'

DARIO MARIANELLI, COMPOSER

🎵 BIRTHS & DEATHS

1905 English composer and conductor Constant Lambert is born in London.

1960 American musical librettist Oscar Hammerstein II dies in Pennsylvania.

1961 French composer Alexandre Desplat is born in Paris.

🎵 FIRST PERFORMED

1735 Jean-Philippe Rameau's ballet-opera *Les Indes galantes* is premiered in Paris.

1906 Ralph Vaughan Williams' *Norfolk Rhapsody No. 1* is given its first performance, at the Queen's Hall in London.

1913 Sergei Prokofiev's *Piano Concerto No. 2* receives its first performance, in Pavlovsk.

🎵 TODAY'S THE DAY

1846 Felix Mendelssohn sets off on a specially chartered train from London to Birmingham, along with the orchestra and soloists, for the premiere of his oratorio *Elijah*.

1939 Sergei Rachmaninov sails from Cherbourg for the USA. It is the final time that he sets foot on European soil.

COMPOSER PROFILE:

Jean-Philippe Rameau

Born in Dijon, Rameau was a contemporary of Handel. A celebrated harpsichordist and organist, he travelled pretty much the length and breadth of France. His fame at the time rested as much on his textbooks about music as it did on his composing and playing.

Once he had settled permanently in Paris, from 1722 onwards, he specialised in composing music for the stage. In his fifties, he inherited from Lully the position of being the most respected name in French opera. His pioneering work brought him to the attention of, first, the superbly named financier, Alexandre le Riche de la Poupelinière (for whom he worked), and subsequently for King Louis XV himself. For the last two decades of his life he was the Royal Chamber Music Composer.

🎵 HALL OF FAME HIT
Benjamin Britten: *Peter Grimes*

Recommended Recording
Various soloists; London Symphony Orchestra and Chorus conducted by Colin Davis; LSO Live 0054

> 'I never understand the need for a "live" audience. My music, because of its extreme quietude, would be happiest with a dead one.'
>
> **IGOR STRAVINSKY, COMPOSER**

24
AUGUST

🕐 BIRTHS & DEATHS

1669 Italian composer Alessandro Marcello is born in Venice.

1882 English inventor of the pennywhistle Robert Clarke dies near Manchester.

1948 French composer and synthesizer player Jean-Michel Jarre is born in Lyons.

1952 American organist Carlo Curley is born in North Carolina.

🐘 FIRST PERFORMED

1850 Franz Liszt's overture *Prometheus* is given its first performance, in Weimar, with the composer conducting. The composer later turned it into a symphonic poem.

1878 Arthur Sullivan conducts some of the music to his new operetta *HMS Pinafore* in London's Covent Garden, as a taster for potential ticket buyers.

1907 Edward Elgar's *Pomp and Circumstance March No. 4* is first performed, at the Queen's Hall in London.

☀️ TODAY'S THE DAY

1899 The players of the Vienna Philharmonic hold a vote to choose Gustav Mahler as their conductor, but the decision is nowhere near unanimous and Mahler chooses not to take up the offer.

1918 Sergei Prokofiev is allowed to enter the USA, after being held at the border for three days while immigration officials check out the validity of his credentials.

1925 Wolfgang Amadeus Mozart's *Don Giovanni* is the first performance ever to be broadcast from the Salzburg Festival.

1968 Czech conductor Rafael Kubelík appeals to musicians to boycott the Warsaw Pact nations that invaded Czechoslovakia three days earlier. He is supported by Bernard Haitink, Otto Klemperer, Yehudi Menuhin, Arthur Rubinstein and Igor Stravinsky.

Czech nationalism in music

Czech, Bohemian, Moravian and Slovakian nationalism in classical music all tend to be clubbed together in a group. At the heart of the movement was Smetana, from Bohemia, who scored an early success with his second Czech opera *The Bartered Bride,* into which he incorporated genuine folk melodies and dances. His later work *Má Vlast ('My Fatherland')* is a set of six, separate symphonic poems, each depicting some aspect of his homeland, the most famous being *Vltava,* a musical portrait of the Moldau river. Dvořák championed the cause with his *Slavonic Dances* and *Slavonic Rhapsodies,* while Janáček, a fervent advocate of his native Moravian music, contributed to the cause in the 20th century with works such as his opera, *Jenůfa.*

🎵 HALL OF FAME HIT
Max Bruch: *Kol Nidrei*

Recommended Recording
Alisa Weilerstein (cello); Staatskapelle Berlin conducted by Daniel Barenboim; Decca 478 2735

25

AUGUST

'If I weren't a director, I would want to be a film composer.'

STEVEN SPIELBERG, FILM DIRECTOR

BIRTHS & DEATHS

1909 Welsh composer and conductor Arwel Hughes is born in Rhosllanerchrugog.

1918 American composer and conductor Leonard Bernstein is born in Massachusetts.

TODAY'S THE DAY

1870 Richard Wagner gets married to Cosima Liszt von Bülow near Lucerne.

1939 Olivier Messiaen is called up into the French army.

1943 Leonard Bernstein is offered the role of assistant conductor of the New York Philharmonic on his 25th birthday.

1945 Leonard Bernstein is offered the post of music director of the New York City Symphony Orchestra on his 27th birthday.

COMPOSER PROFILE:

Jeremiah Clarke

Clarke was a composer who also worked as the organist at the Chapel Royal, before moving on to Winchester College and St Paul's Cathedral. He wrote *The Prince of Denmark's March* in about 1700. Today, it is more popularly known as the *Trumpet Voluntary* and for a long time it was wrongly thought to have been composed by Henry Purcell. It remains a popular choice at wedding ceremonies.

10 classical theme tunes

The Apprentice: Prokofiev, *Dance of the Knights* from *Romeo and Juliet*
The X-Factor: Orff, *Carmina Burana*
Horse of the Year Show: Mozart, *A Musical Joke*
The Lone Ranger: Rossini, *William Tell Overture*
Monty Python's Flying Circus: Sousa, *Liberty Bell*
Onedin Line: Khachaturian, *Adagio of Spartacus and Phrygia*
The Sky at Night: Sibelius, *At the Castle Gate* from *Pelléas et Mélisande*
The South Bank Show: Lloyd Webber, *Variations on a Theme of Paganini*
What the Papers Say: Arnold, *English Dance No. 5*
Jonathan Creek: Saint-Saëns, *Danse Macabre*

HALL OF FAME HIT
Edward Elgar: *Salut d'Amour*

Recommended Recording
Tasmin Little (violin); John Lenehan (piano); EMI 085 9002

'When I play a note of Schubert I don't want anybody walking around and talking.'

MITSUKO UCHIDA, PIANIST

🕐 BIRTHS & DEATHS

1819 German musician (and husband of Queen Victoria) Prince Albert is born in Coburg. He was passionate about music and London's Royal Albert Hall is named after him.

1958 English composer Ralph Vaughan Williams dies in London.

1998 Italian musicologist Remo Giazotto dies in Pisa. He was responsible for discovering and piecing together Albinoni's *Adagio*; many people believe he actually wrote it in its entirety.

🎭 FIRST PERFORMED

1846 Felix Mendelssohn's oratorio *Elijah* is first performed, to great critical acclaim, in Birmingham.

1885 Charles Gounod's *Mors et Vita* is given its first performance, in Birmingham, although the composer is not there to see it because of an outstanding debt that would see him arrested as soon as he arrived in England.

☀ TODAY'S THE DAY

1829 Gioachino Rossini meets Vincenzo Bellini for the first time at the latter composer's home in Milan.

1850 A dress rehearsal for Wagner's opera *Lohengrin* is about to begin, but the audience has to be evacuated from the auditorium because of a fire at a nearby prison.

1888 Pyotr Ilyich Tchaikovsky finishes work on his *Symphony No. 5*.

1900 The premiere for Gabriel Fauré's *Prometheus* is delayed for 24 hours after lightning and heavy rain all but destroy the set.

1929 George Gershwin conducts in public for the first time, with a performance of his *An American in Paris* by the New York Philharmonic.

Choirs

We can define a choir as a group of people who get together to sing, with more than one person to a part – so more than one soprano, more than one alto, and so on. In its most common form today, a choir is in four parts: two of them male and two of them female. The females are sopranos (high) and altos (lower), the males are divided into tenors (high) and basses (lower) – often abbreviated to SATB. This is, however, only the most everyday grouping. Choral music can be sung by whatever group the composer specifies: so, SSA (an all-woman set-up), SSAATTBB (two independent parts on each register), SATBSATB (two independent choirs) and the very popular (today at least) SA-Men (sopranos, altos and a mix of tenors and basses). Any setting, more or less, is possible. A good example of the approach is Allegri's *Miserere*, which is written for SSATB/SSAB: two separated choirs, one of double sopranos, altos, tenors and basses, and another of double sopranos, altos and basses.

 HALL OF FAME HIT

Charles Gounod: *St Cecilia Mass*

Recommended Recording

Berlin Radio Symphony Orchestra and Choir conducted by Mariss Jansons; BR Klassik 900 114

'I am not now nor have I ever been a diva . . . I am only Montserrat!'

MONTSERRAT CABALLÉ, SOPRANO

 BIRTHS & DEATHS

1521 French composer Josquin des Prez dies in Condé-sur-l'Escaut.

1886 English composer Eric Coates is born in Hucknall.

1949 Irish mezzo-soprano Ann Murray is born in Dublin.

 FIRST PERFORMED

1900 Gabriel Fauré's *Prometheus,* delayed from yesterday because of a heavy thunderstorm, is first performed at Arènes de Béziers.

1937 Aaron Copland's tone poem *El Salón México* is given its first performance, in Mexico City.

 TODAY'S THE DAY

1849 The original Philharmonic Hall in Liverpool's Hope Street opens with a four-day music festival.

1849 Bedřich Smetana gets married to his childhood sweetheart in Prague.

1862 Johann Strauss Junior gets married for the first of three times in Vienna.

1892 New York's Metropolitan Opera House is virtually destroyed by fire.

1943 Kurt Weill becomes a citizen of the USA.

COMPOSER PROFILE:

Bedřich Smetana

Smetana is generally recognised as being the father of Czech music, with his art and fortunes closely tied to his country's struggle for independence: he manned the barricades during the failed nationalist uprising in 1848.

Having played the piano in public from an early age, he went, via teaching and conducting, into a life as a concert pianist, in order to pay the bills. It was only much later, after doing a job as a music critic in Prague, that he finally gained public acclaim, aged 42. Later, Smetana started to suffer from increasing deafness. He took refuge in the country, where he composed his influential set of musical portraits of his native land, which he titled *Má Vlast* ('My Fatherland'). He eventually fell victim to mental-health problems and died, aged 60, in an asylum.

 HALL OF FAME HIT

Antonio Vivaldi: *Guitar Concerto in D major*

Recommended Recording

Pepe Romero (guitar); Academy of St Martin in the Fields conducted by Neville Marriner; Philips 475 6360

> 'If I miss a day of practice, I know it. If I miss two days, my manager knows it. If I miss three days, my audience knows it.'
>
> **ANDRÉ PREVIN, PIANIST AND CONDUCTOR**

28
AUGUST

🕐 BIRTHS & DEATHS
430 Early-music composer St Augustine, Bishop of Hippo, dies in Algeria.

1949 English pianist Imogen Cooper is born in London..

1959 Czech composer Bohuslav Martinů dies in Liestal, Switzerland.

🕐 FIRST PERFORMED
1850 Richard Wagner's opera *Lohengrin* is premiered in Weimar, directed by Franz Liszt. However, the composer is not there to see it because he would be arrested if he set foot on German soil.

☀ TODAY'S THE DAY
1714 Georg Philipp Telemann gets married in Frankfurt.

1761 Luigi Boccherini asks for a job as a cello player in Lucca. He will have a wait of more than two years to find out the answer.

1777 Leopold and Wolfgang Amadeus Mozart are dismissed from the service of Archbishop Colloredo of Salzburg – much to their relief.

1848 Frédéric Chopin performs at the Gentlemen's Concert Hall in Manchester. He is not at his best and the performance does not go down well with the critics.

1923 Béla Bartók gets married to one of his students from the Budapest Academy of Music, after divorcing his wife.

1924 Arnold Schoenberg gets married to his second wife in the Mödling Lutheran Parish Church.

1949 The Aspen Music Festival is founded in Colorado.

ENSEMBLE FOCUS:

City of London Sinfonia

The City of London Sinfonia was founded by the conductor Richard Hickox in 1971. He remained its music director until his death in 2008. The orchestra is particularly committed to the performance of music of the 20th century and by contemporary British composers; it has made more than 130 recordings of them. Although the orchestra has toured as far afield as Colombia, China, Dubai, Brazil, Australia and Norway, it has specialised in taking world-class live classical-music concerts to small English towns that might not otherwise experience them at all, including Ipswich, King's Lynn, High Wycombe and Chatham. It is not to be confused with either the Sinfonia of London, a studio orchestra founded by the Rank Organisation in 1955, or the London Sinfonietta, a completely separate contemporary-music orchestra.

 HALL OF FAME HIT
Frederick Delius: *Koanga*

Recommended Recording
Hallé Orchestra conducted by John Barbirolli; EMI 084 2102

29

AUGUST

 **BIRTHS & DEATHS**

1661 French composer Louis Couperin dies in Paris.

FIRST PERFORMED

1853 Josef Strauss's '*The First and the Last Waltz*' is given its first performance, in Hernals, Austria. It is Josef's first composition; he was standing in as conductor of the Johann Strauss Orchestra because his older brother, Johann Strauss Junior, was ill.
1952 John Cage's controversial 4'33" (in which no actual instruments are played) receives its first 'performance', in Woodstock, New York.

TODAY'S THE DAY

1780 Wolfgang Amadeus Mozart finishes work on his *Symphony No. 34* in Paris.
1833 Hector Berlioz gives the actress Harriet Smithson a 48-hour ultimatum to respond to his proposal of marriage.
1858 Richard Wagner arrives in Venice for the first time.
1908 Edward Elgar resigns from his job as professor of music at the University of Birmingham.

COMPOSER PROFILE:

Frédéric Chopin

Although he was born in Poland, Chopin lived in France from the age of 21. His father was actually French but had moved to Poland, to work as a private tutor to the sons of a countess. The youngster's musical talent, particularly at the piano, was noticed and nurtured from an early age. After studying at the Warsaw Conservatoire during his teenage years, he went on the road in 1830, giving concerts in cities as far apart as Dresden, Prague, Vienna and Stuttgart. While he was there, he heard that the Russians had marched into Warsaw, so he travelled on to Paris.

French salon society suited Chopin rather well, although he resented having to give so many piano concerts, even though they were wildly popular. He regarded himself as a composer, not a performer. He also disliked having to teach piano to members of Parisian society, even though it helped to pay the bills. By his late twenties, Chopin was enjoying a romantic liaison with the fiery feminist novelist George Sand. They spent a famous Majorcan winter in a monastery, with Chopin desperately ill and yet composing madly. It is said that his '*Raindrop*' *Prelude* came out of the trip as a direct response to the terrible weather. In 1848, Chopin toured around England and Scotland giving concerts. His health worsened considerably and he was packed off back to Paris, where he died from tuberculosis, surrounded by friends in his flat on the Place Vendôme.

 **HALL OF FAME HIT**
Nigel Hess: *Ladies in Lavender*

Recommended Recording
Nicola Benedetti (violin); Bournemouth Symphony Orchestra conducted by Kirill Karabits; Decca 478 3529

> 'When [Spielberg] showed me *Schindler's List*, I was so moved I could barely speak. I remember saying to him, "Steven, you need a better composer than I am to do this film." And he said, "I know, but they're all dead."'
>
> **JOHN WILLIAMS, COMPOSER**

30

BIRTHS & DEATHS

1585 Italian composer Andrea Gabrielli dies in Venice

FIRST PERFORMED

1882 Charles Gounod's 'sacred trilogy', *La Rédemption*, receives its first performance, in Birmingham, with the composer conducting. It is dedicated to Queen Victoria.

1992 Philip Glass's *'Low' Symphony* is given its first performance, in Munich.

TODAY'S THE DAY

1751 Despite suffering from serious problems with his vision, George Frideric Handel completes his final oratorio, *Jeptha*.

1835 Felix Mendelssohn arrives in Leipzig ready for his new job as the director of the Gewandhaus Orchestra.

GENRE FOCUS:

Choral music

Choral music developed enormously during the Early and Renaissance periods, naturally expanding from monophonic singing (a one-line tune) to two lines singing in an antiphonal style (against each other), occasionally with a response element using a soloist. In much the same way as concertos gradually evolved, choral music developed through two parts, then three parts, until it was its own fully fledged genre, of a massed body, singing with more than one person to any number of parts.

The Church, the chief sponsor of music in the Early and Renaissance periods, loved choral music for its ability to set words of praise. Later, the opera house welcomed choruses with open arms. Despite the arrival of opera, composers from Bach to Beethoven and beyond carried on writing religious choral music. It is a tradition that has continued to this day in the works of composers such as John Tavener, John Rutter and Howard Goodall. During the 19th and 20th centuries, the choral sound fattened up, with composers writing for bigger choirs than ever before. Mendelssohn, for example, was not averse to using a choir of 300 to sing in one of his revival performances of J. S. Bach's *St Matthew Passion*. This is around a tenfold increase in the size of the choir from Bach's day. More recently, a predilection for making choral works out of instrumental ones has led to the popularity of Elgar's *Nimrod* (*Lux Aeterna* in its choral setting) and Barber's *Adagio for Strings* (*Agnus Dei* when it is sung).

HALL OF FAME HIT

John Tavener: *Song for Athene*

Recommended Recording

The Choir of King's College, Cambridge conducted by Stephen Cleobury; EMI Classics 50999 22894403

31

'I don't need the money, dear. I work for art.'

MARIA CALLAS, SOPRANO

AUGUST

🔲 BIRTHS & DEATHS

1834 Italian composer Amilcare Ponchielli is born in Paderno Fasolaro (now known as Paderno Ponchielli; the town was renamed after the composer).

1945 Israeli-American violinist and conductor Itzhak Perlman is born in Tel Aviv.

1965 English soprano Susan Gritton is born in Reigate.

1971 Russian violinist Vadim Repin is born in Novosibirsk.

1975 English conductor Daniel Harding is born in Oxford.

🐑 FIRST PERFORMED

1882 Hubert Parry's *Symphony No. 1* is given its first performance, in Birmingham.

1928 Kurt Weill's *Threepenny Opera* is premiered in Berlin.

☀ TODAY'S THE DAY

1792 Jan Ladislav Dussek gets married in St Anne's Church, Westminster.

1835 Felix Mendelssohn meets Robert Schumann for the first time, at a Gewandhaus Orchestra rehearsal.

1851 Robert and Clara Schumann meet Franz Liszt in Düsseldorf. The Schumanns rate Liszt's exuberant piano playing, but can't stand his compositions.

1861 Johann Strauss Junior conducts a performance of orchestral excerpts from Richard Wagner's *Tristan and Isolde,* in Vienna.

1876 Pyotr Ilyich Tchaikovsky writes to his brother to tell him that he is getting married.

1916 Undeterred by the personal risk, Arturo Toscanini conducts a military band in the front line on top of Monte Santo during an assault.

INSTRUMENT FOCUS:

Percussion

Percussion instruments are struck by a stick, a hand or a pedal. They are generally thought to be the second oldest instruments on the planet, beaten only by the voice. The percussion family can be divided into two parts: those instruments with a set pitch and those without. Examples of the former include timpani, xylophones and glockenspiels, while triangles, tambourines and castanets fall into the second category. There are a whole host of other weird and wonderful objects that composers have dreamed up for the percussion section to play, including car horns and assorted pieces of metal in different shapes and sizes. For a long time, percussion instruments tended to be used in Western classical music more for colour, rhythm and other specific musical effects than for anything else. However, over recent years they have emerged as instruments in their own right. Artists such as Evelyn Glennie and Colin Currie have done an enormous amount to raise percussionists' standing and also to grow the repertoire through the commissioning of new, often spectacular works.

HALL OF FAME HIT

Gioachino Rossini: *The Barber of Seville*

Recommended Recording

Maria Callas and Tito Gobbi (soloists); Philharmonia Orchestra and Chorus conducted by Alceo Galliera; EMI Classics 456 4442

Septe

mber

01

'If I weren't reasonably placid, I don't think I could cope with this sort of life. To be a diva, you've got to be absolutely like a horse.'

JOAN SUTHERLAND, SOPRANO

SEPTEMBER

BIRTHS & DEATHS

1715 Enthusiastic musical patron and ruler of France King Louis XIV dies in Versailles.

1854 German composer Engelbert Humperdinck is born in Siegburg.

1912 English composer Samuel Coleridge-Taylor dies in Croydon.

1935 Japanese conductor Seiji Ozawa is born in China.

1944 American conductor Leonard Slatkin is born in Los Angeles.

1957 English horn player Dennis Brain dies in a car crash in London.

FIRST PERFORMED

1910 Ralph Vaughan Williams' *Fantasia on English Folk Songs* is heard for the first time, at the Queen's Hall in London.

TODAY'S THE DAY

1551 Giovanni Pierluigi da Palestrina is appointed choir master at the Cappella Giulia in Rome.

1653 Johann Pachelbel is baptised in Nuremberg.

1761 Five-year-old Wolfgang Amadeus Mozart makes his first public appearance in Salzburg – as a dancer.

1785 Wolfgang Amadeus Mozart dedicates six of his string quartets to Joseph Haydn.

1850 Clara and Robert Schumann leave Dresden to travel to Düsseldorf, where Robert has a new job.

1880 The Saint Louis Symphony Orchestra is founded.

1948 Dmitri Shostakovich is sacked from his roles at the Leningrad and Moscow Conservatoires. It is an attempt by the government to remove 'formalism' from Soviet music.

1953 Francis Poulenc is appointed an officer of the Légion d'Honneur.

ORCHESTRA FOCUS:

Saint Louis Symphony Orchestra

The Saint Louis Symphony is the second-oldest American orchestra (the oldest is the New York Philharmonic). It was founded today in 1880 by Dutch-born choir conductor Joseph Otten with just 31 musicians. It is currently based in the (allegedly haunted) Powell Symphony Hall, with principal conductor American-born David Robertson, who has taken the orchestra to critical heights. Other noted conductors to have stood on the podium include Itzhak Perlman and Leonard Slatkin (who also celebrates his birthday today). It was Slatkin's long musical directorship, from 1979 to 1996, that saw a real growth in the Saint Louis Symphony's musical prestige. There were problems, though. In 2001, the orchestra nearly went bankrupt, while in 2005, the musicians staged a two-month strike.

HALL OF FAME HIT

Wolfgang Amadeus Mozart: *Sinfonia Concertante for Violin and Viola*

Recommended Recording

Rachel Podger (violin); Pavlo Beznosiuk (viola); Orchestra of the Age of Enlightenment; Channel Classics 29309

> 'If your voice is very soft and you don't make it clear that this is the way things should go, they probably won't go.'
>
> **VALERY GERGIEV, CONDUCTOR**

02
SEPTEMBER

🕐 BIRTHS & DEATHS

1956 English oboist and conductor Paul Goodwin is born in Warwick.

🎵 FIRST PERFORMED

1960 William Walton's *Symphony No. 2* is performed for the first time, at the Edinburgh Festival.

☀ TODAY'S THE DAY

1850 Robert and Clara Schumann are given a warm welcome on their arrival in Düsseldorf, at the start of Robert's new role in the city.

1872 Richard and Cosima Wagner visit her father, Franz Liszt, in Weimar. The two men have previously fallen out over her marital problems with her ex-husband, the conductor Hans von Bülow, as a result of her affair with Wagner.

1908 Frank Bridge gets married to a fellow former student of the Royal College of Music at St Mary's Church in Fulham.

1932 Aaron Copland begins a four-month trip to Mexico, during which many of his works will be performed.

INSTRUMENT FOCUS:

French horn

Uncoil the French horn and you would have eleven feet of brass piping on your hands. Originating from the world of hunting, the horn started to make an appearance in the world of orchestral music in France around the time of Jean-Baptiste Lully, in the 17th century. Valves were added in 1827, and composers such as Robert Schumann and Richard Wagner were big fans of this more modern instrument. The effect of the valves was to make it an easier instrument to play, as the performers no longer had to create the different notes by modulating the tension of their lips.

Modern French horns are made in five parts: the main body, the mouthpiece, the 'bell' (the round part the player sticks his or her hand up), the mouth pipe and the valves. French horns make a wonderful sound: when they are played softly, they can sound pastoral and placid; when they are loud, they can be menacing and regal.

🏆 HALL OF FAME HIT

Edward Elgar: *Sea Pictures*

Recommended Recording

Janet Baker (mezzo-soprano); London Symphony Orchestra conducted by John Barbirolli (EMI 623 0752)

03

'Listening to the Fifth Symphony of Ralph Vaughan Williams is like staring at a cow for 45 minutes.'

AARON COPLAND, COMPOSER

SEPTEMBER

BIRTHS & DEATHS
1695 Italian composer Pietro Antonio Locatelli is born in Bergamo.

FIRST PERFORMED
1936 William Walton's music to the film *As You Like It*, starring Laurence Olivier, is heard for the first time at the Carlton Theatre in London.

TODAY'S THE DAY
1850 Ten-year-old Pyotr Ilyich Tchaikovsky sees a performance of Glinka's *A Life for the Tsar* in St Petersburg. It has a massive effect on the young boy.
1890 W. S. Gilbert and Arthur Sullivan finally settle their legal dispute over a carpet, which has resulted in the total disintegration of their personal and artistic relationship.
1939 Michael Tippett starts work on *A Child of Our Time*, as the Second World War begins.

COMPOSER PROFILE:

Howard Goodall

Goodall is among the most successful film and television theme-tune writers of all time: his credits include *Blackadder*, *Mr Bean*, *Red Dwarf*, *The Catherine Tate Show*, *QI* and *The Vicar of Dibley*. He is well known for his choral music and, as Classic FM's Composer in Residence, he wrote *Enchanted Voices*, an album based on the Beatitudes, which stormed to the top of the Specialist Classical Charts on its release and stayed there for months, winning a Gramophone Award in the process. He was named Composer of the Year at the Classical Brit Awards in 2009, following the release of *Eternal Light: A Requiem*, which was incorporated into a ballet by the Ballet Rambert.

As well as presenting a weekly programme on Classic FM, he has become a regular face on television, presenting award-winning series such as *Howard Goodall's Big Bangs* for Channel 4, the BBC and Sky Arts. Goodall is also a passionate advocate of the benefits of music education and was England's first National Singing Ambassador.

HALL OF FAME HIT
César Franck: *Panis Angelicus*

Recommended Recording
Choir of St John's College, Cambridge conducted by Andrew Nethsingha; Chandos CHSA 5085

'Never compose anything unless not composing it becomes a positive nuisance to you.'
GUSTAV HOLST, COMPOSER

04
SEPTEMBER

🕐 BIRTHS & DEATHS
1824 Austrian composer Anton Bruckner is born near Linz.
1892 French composer Darius Milhaud is born in Marseille.
1899 English composer Frederic Curzon is born in London.
1907 Norwegian composer Edvard Grieg dies in Bergen.
1910 Musicologist Remo Giazotto is born in Rome. He is the man who 'discovered' a fragment of Albinoni's *Adagio* (his biggest hit), but might have in fact composed the whole thing himself.
1980 German violinist David Garrett is born in Aachen.

🎭 FIRST PERFORMED
1945 Dmitri Shostakovich and Sviatoslav Richter give the first performance of Shostakovich's *Symphony No. 9*, in a version for two pianos, in Moscow's Philharmonic Hall.
1989 John Tavener's *The Protecting Veil* for cello and strings receives its first performance, at the Royal Albert Hall in London.

☀ TODAY'S THE DAY
1776 Wolfgang Amadeus Mozart writes a letter about his boss in Salzburg, Archbishop Colloredo, who has imposed new rules on church music, requiring an entire Mass to be no longer than 45 minutes.
1830 Gioachino Rossini sets off from Bologna for Paris, leaving his wife at home because the trip is due to last for only a month. As it turns out, they don't see each other for 4 years.
1854 Amilcare Ponchielli takes his music diploma, ahead of becoming a music teacher in Cremona.
1859 Giuseppe Verdi is elected to the town council in Parma.

MUSICAL TERM:

Intermezzo

Literally translated as 'in the middle', an intermezzo was originally a short opera, often featuring comic characters, that was performed between the acts of a more serious opera. By the 19th century, however, the meaning of intermezzo had changed to being a piece of orchestral music that denoted the passage of time. Two good examples are the intermezzi from Mascagni's opera *Cavalleria Rusticana* and *The Walk to the Paradise Garden* from Delius's opera *A Village Romeo and Juliet*.

🎵 HALL OF FAME HIT
John Barry: *Dances with Wolves*

Recommended Recording
Royal Liverpool Philharmonic Orchestra conducted by Carl Davis; Naxos 857 0505

05

SEPTEMBER

'I look forward to hearing his longer works.'

IGOR STRAVINSKY, COMPOSER, ON HEARING JOHN CAGE'S 4'33", WHICH COMPRISES NO MUSIC, JUST FOUR AND A HALF MINUTES OF SILENCE

BIRTHS & DEATHS

1735 German composer Johann Christian Bach is born in Leipzig.
1791 German composer Giacomo Meyerbeer is born near Berlin.
1867 American composer Amy Beach is born in New Hampshire.
1912 American composer John Cage is born in Los Angeles.
1961 Canadian pianist Marc-André Hamelin is born in Montreal.
1997 British conductor Georg Solti dies in Antibes.

FIRST PERFORMED

1913 Sergei Prokofiev's *Piano Concerto No. 2* is given its first performance, in Pavlovsk, with the composer at the piano.

TODAY'S THE DAY

1782 Irish composer John Field is baptised in Dublin.
1844 Johann Strauss Junior gets a licence to perform with an orchestra in restaurants in Vienna.
1901 Lili Boulanger makes her concert debut as a violinist, in Normandy.

ARTIST PROFILE:

Georg Solti

Born György Stern in Budapest, Georg Solti was taught by the best: Bartók and Dohnányi were his piano teachers and Kodály his composition tutor. In the end, he chose conducting, having heard, at the age of 14, Carlos Kleiber's father, Erich, conduct Beethoven's *Symphony No. 5*.

Solti's conducting debut in Budapest on 11 March 1938 was followed the next day by the *Anschluss*, the Nazi annexation of Austria (his father had changed the family name to avoid anti-Semitism), and Solti left Hungary for Switzerland. Post-war jobs with the Munich State Opera and in Frankfurt were followed by a golden period at the Royal Opera House, Covent Garden, in the 1960s, and then by an immensely successful music directorship of the Chicago Symphony Orchestra. His exuberant, demonstrative style on the podium has been preserved in more than 250 recordings. He died on this day in September 1997, by which time he was Sir Georg Solti, a British citizen.

HALL OF FAME HIT

Giovanni Pergolesi: *Stabat Mater*

Recommended Recording

Anna Prohaska (soprano); Bernarda Fink (mezzo-soprano); Academy for Ancient Music, Berlin conducted by Bernhard Forck; Harmonia Mundi HMC 902072

'You have to remain flexible, and you must be your own critic at all times.'

HANS ZIMMER, COMPOSER

BIRTHS & DEATHS

1928 Russian conductor Yevgeny Svetlanov is born in Moscow.

1979 English composer Ronald Binge dies in Ringwood.

2007 Italian tenor Luciano Pavarotti dies in Modena.

FIRST PERFORMED

1791 Wolfgang Amadeus Mozart's *La clemenza di Tito* is premiered at the Prague National Theatre. It forms part of the celebrations of the Coronation of Emperor Leopold II.

1910 Ralph Vaughan Williams' *Fantasia on a Theme of Thomas Tallis* receives its first performance, in Gloucester, with the composer conducting.

TODAY'S THE DAY

1922 In Russia, Alexander Glazunov is named 'People's Artist of the Republic'.

ORCHESTRA FOCUS:

Royal Scottish National Orchestra

Known originally simply as 'The Scottish Orchestra', the Royal Scottish National Orchestra was founded in 1891. Over the years, it has been conducted by an impressive list of great musicians, not least John Barbirolli and George Szell, but, aptly enough, it was thanks to the leadership of Scottish-born Alexander Gibson that the orchestra really flowered to win international renown. From 1959, Gibson conducted the orchestra for 25 years, becoming the longest-serving music director in the orchestra's history. Under him, the orchestra became famous for its performances of Scandinavian music, notably that of Sibelius and Nielsen. Gibson also took the orchestra into the pit when he founded Scottish Opera.

In 1991, the orchestra was granted permission to add the 'Royal' to its title (it had been renamed the Scottish National Orchestra in 1950). Today, under its music director Peter Oundjian, the home of Classic FM's orchestra in Scotland is still Glasgow, though it also performs regularly in Edinburgh, Aberdeen, Perth, Dundee and Inverness, with occasional – but extremely well-received – forays into the more remote parts of Scotland. The orchestra's recording reputation is particularly impressive, with eight Grammy nominations between 2002 and 2009 alone.

HALL OF FAME HIT

Wolfgang Amadeus Mozart: *Exsultate Jubilate*

Recommended Recording

Julia Lezhneva (soprano); Il Giardino Armonico conducted by Giovanni Antonini; Decca 478 5242

07

'Pay no attention to what the critics say. No statue has ever been put up to a critic.'

JEAN SIBELIUS, COMPOSER

 BIRTHS & DEATHS

1961 French pianist Jean-Yves Thibaudet is born in Lyon.

1965 Romanian soprano Angela Gheorghiu is born in Adjud.

 TODAY'S THE DAY

1834 Mikhail Glinka meets his future wife for the first time, in St Petersburg.

1874 Bedřich Smetana writes to the board of the Czech National Theatre, resigning from his role as music director, because of his loss of hearing.

1992 The UK's first national commercial radio station, Classic FM, begins broadcasting at 6 a.m. The first piece of music on air is Handel's *Zadok the Priest*.

ORCHESTRA FOCUS:

Philharmonia Orchestra

The Philharmonia Orchestra's fine reputation is all the more impressive given its relative youth. It was the brainchild of impresario and record company executive Walter Legge, who came up with the plan to establish a new virtuoso orchestra towards the end of the Second World War. It made its debut on 27 October 1945, in London's Kingsway Hall, with Thomas Beecham conducting.

The connection between Beecham and the orchestra did not last for long – he disagreed with Legge over how it should be run and decided to form his own Royal Philharmonic – but other leading figures flocked to conduct it. Within a few years, the orchestra, which Legge had formed primarily to record for EMI, was being conducted by no less a personage than Richard Strauss. It went on to give the world premiere of his *Four Last Songs* for soprano and orchestra in 1950. During that decade, the orchestra blossomed further, taking part in the historic opening concert of London's Royal Festival Hall in 1951 and touring Europe and the USA with Herbert von Karajan in 1952 and 1954 respectively.

In 1964, Legge decided to disband the orchestra. It refused to die, instead re-emerging as the self-governing New Philharmonia Orchestra. The legendary conductor Otto Klemperer, whom Legge had appointed principal conductor of the Philharmonia in 1959, decided to stick by the players. The name stuck until 1977, when it was changed back to the Philharmonia Orchestra. In the years since, the big-name talent has continued to step on to the orchestra's podium: Simon Rattle, Lorin Maazel, Vladimir Ashkenazy, Ricardo Muti and Bernard Haitink were among them. The current principal conductor and artistic advisor is the Finnish conductor and composer Esa-Pekka Salonen.

 HALL OF FAME HIT

Gustav Mahler: *Symphony No. 4*

Recommended Recording

Luba Orgonasova (soprano); Tonhalle Orchestra Zurich conducted by David Zinman; RCA 8869 7690472

08

SEPTEMBER

'To a free man, matrimony is a terrifying thought these days; he exchanges it either for melancholy or for crude sensuality.'

FRANZ SCHUBERT IN A DIARY ENTRY, WRITTEN TODAY IN 1816

BIRTHS & DEATHS

1841 Czech composer Antonín Dvořák is born near Prague.

1929 German conductor Christoph von Dohnányi is born in Berlin.

1934 English composer Peter Maxwell Davies is born in Salford.

1949 German composer and conductor Richard Strauss dies in Garmisch-Partenkirchen.

1970 German pianist Lars Vogt is born in Düren.

FIRST PERFORMED

1761 William Boyce's anthem 'The King Shall Rejoice' and Johann Christian Bach's 'Thanks be to God Who Rules the Deep' are sung for the first time at the wedding of King George III in the Chapel Royal, St James's Palace.

1910 Edward Elgar's *Violin Concerto* has a private performance in Gloucester. It will be a couple more months before its first public outing.

1994 Michael Torke's *Javelin* is given its first performance, to mark the Olympic Games in Atlanta.

TODAY'S THE DAY

1677 Henry Purcell is appointed 'composer to the 24 Violins' – a violin band playing French-style dance music for the English royal court.

1862 Johannes Brahms sets off from his home city of Hamburg to Vienna.

1862 The Russian Music Society opens; eventually it will become the St Petersburg Conservatoire.

1875 Clara Schumann hears a performance of Wagner's *Tristan and Isolde* in Munich, but is unimpressed by the work.

1889 Richard Strauss starts a new job as a conductor in Weimar.

COMPOSER PROFILE:

Peter Maxwell Davies

Known in the classical music world simply as 'Max', this Salford-born composer studied at the Royal Manchester (now Royal Northern) College of Music at the same time as Harrison Birtwistle, Alexander Goehr and the pianist John Ogdon, who together made up the celebrated 'Manchester Group' of musicians. After further study in Rome, he worked as music director at Cirencester Grammar School. He took great delight in composing specifically for youngsters and has been a staunch champion of the value of music education ever since. Then came more study and composition at Princeton and Adelaide Universities, after which he moved to Orkney in 1971. The wild and beautiful island life suited him well and has inspired many of the works he has since composed. He founded the St Magnus Festival there in 1977. Knighted in 1987, he was appointed Master of the Queen's Music in 2004.

HALL OF FAME HIT

Karl Jenkins: *Requiem*

Recommended Recording

Various soloists; Serendipity; Côr Caerdydd; West Kazakhstan Philharmonic Orchestra conducted by Karl Jenkins

09
SEPTEMBER

'I'll get hold of a film and look at it 20 times. I'll spend one week just looking at the time – once in the morning, once in the afternoon – until the film tells me what to do.'

ELMER BERNSTEIN, COMPOSER

BIRTHS & DEATHS
1957 French pianist Pierre-Laurent Aimard is born in Lyon.
1960 Swedish tenor Jussi Björling dies in Slaro, Sweden.

FIRST PERFORMED
1825 Ludwig van Beethoven's *String Quintet No. 15* is performed for the first time, privately in Vienna.
1890 Edward Elgar's *Froissart Overture* receives its first performance, in Worcester, with the composer conducting.
1963 Erik Satie's *Vexations* receives its first performance, in New York. It takes ten pianists working in shifts to play this remarkable piece in full, as it repeats the same few bars over and over and over again – in total, 840 times.

TODAY'S THE DAY
1830 Luigi Cherubini and Jean-François Le Sueur are the last ever superintendents of the French Royal Chapel, as the role is abolished.
1836 Felix Mendelssohn gets engaged.

1836 Frédéric Chopin asks 17-year-old Maria Wodzinski to marry him, but, despite encouraging noises from her mother, she turns him down (although she makes him wait a year for her answer).
1846 Richard Wagner starts work on the music for his opera *Lohengrin*.
1907 40,000 people take part in the funeral held for Edvard Grieg in Bergen.
1971 Antal Doráti conducts the National Symphony Orchestra in the inaugural concert at the Kennedy Center in Washington.

COMPOSER PROFILE:
Ermanno Wolf-Ferrari

Born Ermanno Wolf in Venice, Wolf-Ferrari divided his time between music and art as a boy, choosing to follow in the footsteps of his artist father and study painting at Rome's Accademia di Belle Arti. He switched to music, having moved to Munich when he was 17 years old, studying for a time with the composer Boito. Seemingly, Wolf-Ferrari was more appreciated in Germany than in Italy, certainly during his lifetime. He spent the First World War years in Switzerland, composing little – a silence he broke only when he was in his forties. When he was 63, he was made professor of composition at the prestigious Mozarteum in Salzburg. He died in his native Venice, aged 72.

Royal Opera

Granted its royal title in 1968 (before then, it had been the Covent Garden Opera Company), the Royal Opera performs works in their original language with guest artists singing most major roles (in contrast to English National Opera, which sings in English with a company of contracted singers). The Orchestra of the Royal Opera House is the resident band, playing for both opera and ballet.

HALL OF FAME HIT
Karl Jenkins: *Palladio*

Recommended Recording
London Philharmonic Strings conducted by Karl Jenkins; Sony SK 62276

> '[Musicians] talk of nothing but money and jobs. Give me businessmen every time. They really are interested in music and art.'
>
> JEAN SIBELIUS, COMPOSER

10

SEPTEMBER

🏛 BIRTHS & DEATHS

1659 English composer Henry Purcell's birthday is celebrated today, although historians are unable to confirm the date.

1941 English conductor and harpsichordist Christopher Hogwood is born in Nottingham.

1944 English baritone Thomas Allen is born in Seaham.

2008 English conductor Vernon Handley dies in Skenfrith.

🎶 FIRST PERFORMED

1963 Nearly 19 hours after the performance began yesterday evening, Erik Satie's *Vexations* concludes in New York. The same few bars have been played 840 times by a relay of ten different pianists.

☀ TODAY'S THE DAY

1588 English composer Nicholas Lanier is baptised in London.

1855 Robert Schumann's condition in hospital worsens, as delirium takes hold. His doctors say that he will not recover.

1875 Fifteen-year-old Gustav Mahler begins his studies in music at the Conservatoire in Vienna.

1894 Richard Strauss gets married to an opera singer near Salzburg.

1925 After Erik Satie's death, officials discover his flat has no gas, electricity or water, but does have two pianos – one of which is filled with unopened mail.

COMPOSER PROFILE:

Gregorio Allegri

At the age of nine, Allegri was a boy chorister at Rome's San Luigi dei Francesi. In his early twenties he was ordained as a priest, working as a composer and singer in the cathedrals of Fermo and Tivoli. In 1629, he joined the papal choir, and was elected Maestro di Cappella 21 years later. His most celebrated work is his setting of the *Miserere*. The Vatican refused to allow it to be published, but, in 1770, the 14-year-old Mozart wrote it down from memory after he heard a performance of it in the Sistine Chapel and so it became known to the world. Many musicologists also believe his *Sonata a quattro* was the first piece written specifically for string quartet.

🏆 HALL OF FAME HIT

Aram Khachaturian: *Masquerade Suite*

Recommended Recording

Armenian Philharmonic Orchestra conducted by Loris Tjeknavorian; Alto ALC 1019

11

> 'It is music's lofty mission to shed light on the depths of the human heart.'
>
> **ROBERT SCHUMANN, COMPOSER**

SEPTEMBER

BIRTHS & DEATHS

1733 French composer François Couperin dies in Paris.

1935 Estonian composer Arvo Pärt is born in Paide.

1952 English soprano Catherine Bott is born in Leamington Spa.

1985 English composer Willam Alwyn dies in Southwold.

TODAY'S THE DAY

1711 English composer William Boyce is baptised in London.

1824 Carl Maria von Weber is forced to relinquish artistic control of the German and Italian opera companies in Dresden because of his worsening tuberculosis.

1827 Hector Berlioz falls wildly and passionately in love with the actress Harriet Smithson after seeing her playing Ophelia in *Hamlet* in Paris. His romantic pursuit of her is to last for some time; eventually she weakens and marries him, only for him to turn his amorous attentions elsewhere.

1827 Seven-year-old Clara Wieck (later Schumann) performs a piano concerto in public for the first time.

1850 The international superstar soprano Jenny Lind performs in the USA for the first time at a New York venue managed by the impresario Phineas T. Barnum. She earns $1,000 per concert – an eye-wateringly large amount of money at the time.

1875 The Carl Rosa Opera Company opens its first season in the Princess's Theatre in London with Mozart's *The Marriage of Figaro*.

1884 Edward Elgar is one of the violinists in a performance of Dvořák's *Symphony No. 6* at the Three Choirs Festival in Worcester, with the composer conducting.

1996 The Bridgewater Hall opens in Manchester with a concert by the Hallé Orchestra conducted by Kent Nagano.

COMPOSER PROFILE:

Béla Bartók

Bartók is eclipsed only by Liszt in the pantheon of all-time Hungarian greats. Alongside Zoltán Kodály, his fellow countryman, he made it his life's work to collect and preserve his country's folk music. Without their efforts, a whole body of Hungarian music might well have vanished beyond recall. Although Bartók is now thought of chiefly as a composer, he was better known as a teacher and pianist during his lifetime. His major works include the *Concerto for Orchestra,* a one-act opera *Duke Bluebeard's Castle* and the ballet *The Miraculous Mandarin.*

HALL OF FAME HIT

Zbigniew Preisner: *Requiem for My Friend*

Recommended Recording

Sumi Jo (soprano); Cologne Philharmonic Orchestra conducted by James Conlon; Erato 8573 857722

'God tells me how the music should sound, but you stand in the way!'

ARTURO TOSCANINI, CONDUCTOR, TO AN ORCHESTRAL PLAYER

BIRTHS & DEATHS
1764 French composer Jean-Philippe Rameau dies in Paris.
1957 German composer Hans Zimmer is born in Frankfurt.

FIRST PERFORMED
1910 Gustav Mahler's *Symphony No. 8* ('*Symphony of a Thousand*') is performed for the first time, in Munich, conducted by the composer. It features a massive choir and orchestra, hence its nickname.

TODAY'S THE DAY
1765 Maria Anna Mozart misses out on performing for the Dutch royal family in The Hague because of illness.
1836 Frédéric Chopin, Robert Schumann and Clara Wieck spend the day playing the piano together in Leipzig.
1840 Robert Schumann and Clara Wieck finally get married near Leipzig, after a year-long legal battle with her father.
1875 Charles Villiers Stanford is among those at a concert held in honour of Franz Liszt in Leipzig.

MUSICAL TERM:

Tone poem

Also known as the symphonic poem, 'tone poem' was first coined by the composer Liszt to denote a symphonic work, very often in just one movement, that seeks to portray a descriptive subject. Liszt's tone poems generally took various literary or mythological figures as their subject – Mazeppa, Hamlet and Orpheus were three typical examples.

While later composers followed the same path, they also ventured into new, less definite fields. Delius's *On Hearing the First Cuckoo in Spring* is a tone poem, but one depicting an almost Impressionistic mood, rather than a specific narrative picture. Richard Strauss made something of a speciality of tone poems, with works such as *Don Juan, Till Eulenspiegel, Ein Heldenleben* and *Also Sprach Zarathustra*; the sunrise section of the latter work was used as the opening theme for the cult science-fiction movie *2001: A Space Odyssey*.

HALL OF FAME HIT
Franz Schubert: *Ave Maria*

Recommended Recording
Luciano Pavarotti (tenor); National Philharmonic Orchestra conducted by Kurt Herbert Adler; Cascade Medien 06010

13

SEPTEMBER

> 'I like your opera – I think I will set it to music.'
>
> LUDWIG VAN BEETHOVEN, AFTER HEARING AN OPERA BY ANOTHER COMPOSER

🕐 BIRTHS & DEATHS

1819 German composer and pianist Clara Wieck (later Schumann) is born in Leipzig.

1874 Austrian composer Arnold Schoenberg is born in Vienna.

1894 French composer Emmanuel Chabrier dies in Paris.

1924 French composer Maurice Jarre is born in Lyon.

1977 British conductor Leopold Stokowski dies in Hampshire.

🎵 FIRST PERFORMED

1807 Ludwig van Beethoven's *Mass in C* is given its first performance, in Eisenstadt, with the composer conducting.

☀ TODAY'S THE DAY

1835 Felix Mendelssohn is the guest of honour at Clara Wieck's 16th birthday party.

1866 The Moscow Conservatoire officially opens its doors; Pyotr Ilyich Tchaikovsky, who is on the teaching staff, is among those performing at the opening dinner.

COMPOSER PROFILE:

Pyotr Ilyich Tchaikovsky

Tchaikovsky was born some 600 miles east of Moscow in Votkinsk, an industrial town in the Ural Mountains, where his father was the manager of the local ironworks. Like many composers before him (particularly Russian ones), he eschewed music at first, studying Law and then entering the civil service as a clerk in the Ministry of Justice, before finally turning to music when the composer Anton Rubinstein founded the St Petersburg Conservatoire in 1863.

By the time Tchaikovsky was in his thirties, he was well known enough to come to the attention of one Nadezhda von Meck, a canny businesswoman who had been the driving force behind her husband's railway engineering company. For 13 years, she funded Tchaikovsky – on the strict stipulation that they never met. During this time, Tchaikovsky rose to fame in Russia and beyond, writing masterpieces such as the opera *Eugene Onegin* and the ballet *The Sleeping Beauty*. He also had completed five of his symphonies. He toured the USA in the early 1890s, where he was the star conductor at the opening of the new Carnegie Hall in 1891. He visited England to receive an honorary degree from Cambridge University in 1893, producing the ever popular *Nutcracker* between the two trips.

Despite his successes, life was not easy for Tchaikovsky. He suffered badly from acute depression, not least because of the need to conceal the fact that he was homosexual. His sudden death, four days after the first performance of his *Symphony No. 6* in November 1893, has given rise to various conspiracy theories, although, officially at least, cholera was to blame.

🎵 HALL OF FAME HIT

John Stanley: *Trumpet Voluntary*

Recommended Recording

Maurice André (trumpet); Jane Parker-Smith (organ); EMI 636 5602

> 'Debussy is like a painter who looks at his canvas to see what more he can take out. [Richard] Strauss is like a painter who has covered every inch and then takes the paint he has left and throws it at the canvas.'
>
> **ERNEST BLOCH, COMPOSER**

14
SEPTEMBER

 BIRTHS & DEATHS

1760 Italian composer Luigi Cherubini is born in Florence.

FIRST PERFORMED

1945 William Walton's *Henry V Suite*, arranged by Malcolm Sargent, is given its first performance, at the Royal Albert Hall in London.

1954 Benjamin Britten's opera *The Turn of the Screw* is premiered in Venice, conducted by the composer.

TODAY'S THE DAY

1731 Johann Sebastian Bach begins a series of organ recitals in Dresden.

1737 Austrian composer Michael Haydn (younger brother of Joseph) is baptised in Rohrau.

1741 George Frideric Handel finishes his *Messiah* after just over three weeks of constant work on the oratorio.

1836 The soprano Maria Malibran sings for the final time in public at one of the Gentlemen's Concerts in Manchester. She is taken ill and dies in the Mosley Arms Hotel nine days later.

1850 Richard Wagner first outlines his idea for a new theatre in which to perform his operas, designed and built to his exact specifications.

Ultimately, his wish will come true in Bayreuth.

1860 Franz Liszt writes his first will.

1909 Sergei Prokofiev graduates from the St Petersburg Conservatoire.

1969 Igor Stravinsky settles in New York, after moving from Los Angeles.

COMPOSER PROFILE:

Thomas Tallis

The details of Thomas Tallis's childhood are lost in the mists of time, but we do know that, by his forties, he was first a Gentleman and then organist of the Chapel Royal. In partnership with William Byrd – with whom he shared the position of organist – he was granted the exclusive licence by Elizabeth I to print music. Despite the apparent value of the licence, they failed to make much money out of the venture and were forced to go cap in hand to the Queen to rescue them financially. Known for his church music in general, such as his *Mass for Four Voices* and his *Lamentations*, the staggeringly beautiful *'Spem in Alium'* is possibly Tallis's most breathtaking work, an amazingly skilful combination of 40 separate vocal lines.

 HALL OF FAME HIT

Johann Sebastian Bach: *Cantata No. 140*

Recommended Recording

English Baroque Soloists and Monteverdi Choir conducted by John Eliot Gardiner; Soli Deo Gloria 171

15

SEPTEMBER

'I know I have a reputation for bad tempers, but I am always having good tempers.'

MARIA CALLAS, OPERA SINGER

BIRTHS & DEATHS

1945 American soprano Jessye Norman is born in Augusta.

1945 Austrian composer Anton Webern is mistakenly shot and killed by an American soldier near Salzburg.

FIRST PERFORMED

1969 William Walton's score for the film *The Battle of Britain* is heard for the first time in London's Dominion Cinema.

TODAY'S THE DAY

1750 Christoph Willibald von Gluck gets married in Vienna.

1768 Giovanni Paisiello gets married in Naples. As his wife-to-be is pregnant, he faces prison unless he does the honourable thing.

1866 Bedřich Smetana is appointed principal conductor of the Royal Provincial Czech Theatre.

1876 40 years after Vincenzo Bellini's death, his remains are removed from his tomb in Paris to be taken to his birthplace in Italy.

1892 Antonín Dvořák, his wife, son and daughter leave their home in Prague and set off for America, where he has a new job at the National Conservatory.

1906 Edvard Grieg finishes three of the *Four Psalms* – his final composition.

1922 Gustav Holst conducts a recording of his own music for the first time – with the London Symphony Orchestra playing '*Jupiter*' from *The Planets* for the Columbia Gramophone Company.

1924 Léon Theremin successfully applies for a patent for his new electronic instrument.

1929 Olivier Messiaen gives his first public organ recital, near Grenoble.

1938 Musical instrument inventor Léon Theremin flees the USA for Russia on forged documents; he is being pursued by the US Internal Revenue Service.

1946 The Royal Philharmonic Orchestra gives its first performance, with Thomas Beecham conducting.

VENUE FOCUS:

Barbican Centre

The London Symphony Orchestra performs pretty much all of its UK concerts here – but the Barbican has much more to offer classical-music lovers, with international residencies from the New York Philharmonic, the Los Angeles Philharmonic, the Leipzig Gewandhaus and the Royal Concertgebouw Orchestras. Described by the *Guardian* as 'a building where there is always something rich and strange going on', the Barbican Centre also hosts visual art, dance and wider cultural events. There's a cinema, a theatre, a library, a conference centre, an art gallery, exhibition halls and even a rooftop tropical conservatory alongside the 1,949-seat concert hall – all of which makes a visit to the Barbican Centre whenever you're in London a very good idea indeed.

HALL OF FAME HIT

Hubert Parry: '*I Was Glad*'

Recommended Recording

London Symphony Orchestra and Chorus conducted by Richard Hickox; Chandos CHAN 241-46

'What a name! It suggests fierce whiskers stained with vodka!'

THE MUSICAL COURIER, ABOUT THE COMPOSER NIKOLAI RIMSKY-KORSAKOV

 BIRTHS & DEATHS

1685 English librettist John Gay is baptised in Barnstaple.
1887 French conductor and composition teacher Nadia Boulanger is born in Paris.
1977 Greek soprano Maria Callas dies in Paris.
2003 English clarinettist Jack Brymer dies in Redhill.

 TODAY'S THE DAY

1858 Jules Massenet makes his first public appearance at the piano, in Tournai, Belgium.
1899 Gustav Mahler agrees to become the conductor of the Vienna Philharmonic, after a second vote among the musicians ends up overwhelmingly in his favour (unlike the first).
1904 Sergei Rachmaninov makes his conducting debut at the Bolshoi Ballet.
1920 Enrico Caruso makes his final recording for Victor Records in Camden, New Jersey.
1966 The Metropolitan Opera House opens at New York's Lincoln Center.

MUSICAL TERM:

Variations

The musical form of 'theme and variations' is one in which a theme (original or borrowed from another composer) is subjected to a series of self-contained new interpretations or 'variations'. There are no hard and fast rules about the number of variations or the exact form they take, with the decision on this resting with the composer of the new work.

Possibly the most famous set of theme and variations are Elgar's so-called *Enigma Variations* (more properly known as *Variations on an Original Theme*). This is due to the mystery left behind about the nature of the original tune itself and also because of the puzzle surrounding the people alluded to in each of the variations' titles. The latter has long been solved, but the former continues to exercise musical brains. Another favourite is Rachmaninov's *Rhapsody on a Theme of Paganini*. Part piano concerto, part variations, yet called a rhapsody, this set of 24 reworkings of a tune borrowed from Paganini reaches its high point in Variation 18, when the composer turns both the world and the original tune upside-down to produce three minutes of musical heaven.

 HALL OF FAME HIT
Johann Strauss Junior: *Die Fledermaus*

Recommended Recording
Various soloists; Vienna Philharmonic Orchestra conducted by Herbert von Karajan; Alto ALC 2018

17

'To play the organ properly, one should have a vision of eternity.'

CHARLES-MARIE WIDOR, COMPOSER AND ORGANIST

SEPTEMBER

 BIRTHS & DEATHS

1179 German composer Hildegard of Bingen dies in Rupertsburg.

1803 Austrian composer Franz Xaver Süssmayr, who completed Mozart's *Requiem*, dies in Vienna.

1966 German tenor Fritz Wunderlich dies in Heidelberg.

2011 German conductor Kurt Sanderling dies in Berlin.

FIRST PERFORMED

1931 Frederick Delius's *A Song of Summer* is performed for the first time, in London.

TODAY'S THE DAY

1721 Georg Philipp Telemann becomes music director of the city of Hamburg.

1829 Felix Mendelssohn is injured when the carriage in which he is travelling in London overturns.

1839 Richard Wagner arrives in Paris for the first time.

1859 Giuseppe Verdi is made an honorary citizen of the city of Turin.

1893 Antonín Dvořák heads for New York, after spending three months in Iowa.

1893 Engelbert Humperdinck finishes work on his opera *Hansel and Gretel*.

1945 After being removed for safe-keeping during the Second World War, Frédéric Chopin's heart is returned to its normal resting place in Warsaw Cathedral.

INSTRUMENT FOCUS:

Flute

Flutes go back to ancient Egyptian times and beyond. Variants of the instrument are also present in areas of world music, but here we are concentrating on flutes used in the Western classical music tradition. Despite being part of the woodwind family, the flute is now rarely made of wood, instead being manufactured from metal. The instrument was originally known as the 'transverse flute' or the 'German flute'. It was given the first name because it was designed to be played sideways, unlike, say, a recorder (which was sometimes known as the 'English flute'). The 'German' epithet came about because the instrument seems to have hailed from that country in the distant past. Flutes are distinct from other woodwind instruments because they have no reed. The player blows across an aperture in the side of the instrument; the breath hits the edge of the opening and air is directed into the metal tube. The pitch of the notes is produced by covering the finger holes along the length of the instrument. The flute's range runs three octaves up from middle C – that's a range of 24 notes, hitting the high notes with ease. Famous flautists (the correct name for a flute player) include James Galway, who was a massive hit in the 1970s and 1980s as 'the man with the golden flute', and Emmanuel Pahud, the principal flautist of the Berlin Philharmonic Orchestra.

 HALL OF FAME HIT

John Rutter: *A Gaelic Blessing*

Recommended Recording

Polyphony; Bournemouth Symphony Orchestra conducted by Stephen Layton; Hyperion CDA 30017

> 'Does no one care sufficiently for Saint-Saëns to tell him he has written music enough?'
>
> **CLAUDE DEBUSSY ON HIS FELLOW COMPOSER, CAMILLE SAINT-SAËNS**

18

SEPTEMBER

 BIRTHS & DEATHS

1893 Australian composer Arthur Benjamin is born in Sydney.

1971 Russian soprano Anna Netrebko is born in Krasnodar.

1979 Macedonian pianist Simon Trpčeski is born in Skopje.

 FIRST PERFORMED

1930 Edward Elgar's *Pomp and Circumstance March No. 5* is heard for the first time, at a recording session for HMV in London's Kingsway Hall.

TODAY'S THE DAY

1693 Fifteen-year-old Antonio Vivaldi joins the clergy in Venice.

1700 Antonio Vivaldi is promoted to deacon of a Venice church.

1804 Muzio Clementi gets married in Berlin.

1809 The second Covent Garden Theatre opens in London (the first burned down a year earlier).

1818 The courts rule that Ludwig van Beethoven should remain the guardian of his nephew, Karl, despite legal moves by the boy's mother.

1840 Felix Mendelssohn begins a two-week trip to England – a week in London and a week in Birmingham.

1857 Richard Wagner finishes writing the words to *Tristan and Isolde*.

1858 Gioachino Rossini buys some land in the Bois de Boulogne, on which he plans to build a new home.

1917 Sergei Rachmaninov performs for the final time in Russia, playing Liszt's *Piano Concerto No. 1*.

1918 Gustav Holst changes his name from Gustavus von Holst. With the outbreak of the First World War, he fears that his name sounds too German, although he was born and bred in Cheltenham.

1945 The Stuttgart Chamber Orchestra gives its first concert.

MUSICAL TERM:

Rubato

Music from the Romantic era has a particularly special aural quality: it seems to ebb and flow beautifully, to tug on the heart strings, almost to breathe and sigh. The reason? More often than not, it's because of the use of rubato – an Italian term that literally means 'stolen time'. Rather than rigidly following a very strict beat, the music is pulled and pushed, stretched and squashed, into something that sounds less mechanical and, many would say, more human. Sometimes, composers specify its use; at other times, the performer takes a healthy helping of artistic licence. But either way, when it works, the effect is mesmerising.

 HALL OF FAME HIT

Hubert Parry: *'Jerusalem'*

Recommended Recording

London Chamber Orchestra and the Choir of Westminster Abbey conducted by Christopher Warren-Green; Decca 277 0662

19
SEPTEMBER

'I suddenly realised that I could be as expressive as I wanted. Each film was completely different. To me it was no different than Haydn being kept as a court composer.'

JAMES HORNER, COMPOSER

BIRTHS & DEATHS

1912 German conductor Kurt Sanderling is born in Arys (now Orzysz).

1924 English composer Ernest Tomlinson is born in Rawtenstall.

FIRST PERFORMED

1908 Gustav Mahler's *Symphony No. 7* is given its first performance, in Prague, with the composer conducting.

TODAY'S THE DAY

1958 The ashes of Ralph Vaughan Williams are interred in Westminster Abbey.

Royal Opera House

The original Theatre Royal, Covent Garden (the name comes from its historical convent garden site), was built by actor-manager John Rich out of the fortune he made, aptly enough, from his staging of *The Beggar's Opera*. Many of Handel's great operas were premiered there, but, today in 1808, the theatre was gutted by fire, with 23 firemen losing their lives as the building collapsed in the blaze. The replacement theatre opened a year later; in 1847, it became the Royal Italian Opera. Then, disaster struck again. In 1856, the theatre was destroyed by fire for the second time. The third and present theatre opened two years later. In 1892, it was renamed the Royal Opera House. Up until 1914, it staged spectacular summer opera seasons, but, during the First World War, it served as a furniture store. Opera returned in 1934, but, in 1939, it became a dance hall. Extensively redeveloped in the 1990s, it has been the home of both the Royal Opera and the Royal Ballet since 1946.

Royal Ballet

In 1926 Ninette de Valois founded the Academy of Choreographic Art, out of which grew the Vic-Wells Ballet and, in 1939, Sadler's Wells Ballet, which moved into Covent Garden in 1946 as the resident ballet company, gaining its royal status – as the Royal Ballet – in 1956.

HALL OF FAME HIT

George Gershwin: *Piano Concerto*

Recommended Recording

Denis Matsuev; New York Philharmonic Orchestra conducted by Alan Gilbert; RCA 8876 5492602

> 'He has written nothing that will live, nothing that will make the world better. His name as well as his music will be forgotten.'

OBITUARY IN *THE CHICAGO TRIBUNE* OF JACQUES OFFENBACH, THE MAN WHO COMPOSED THE INFERNAL GALOP – THE QUINTESSENTIAL MUSIC FOR THE CAN-CAN

20

SEPTEMBER

🕐 BIRTHS & DEATHS

1852 Austrian trumpeter Anton Weidinger (for whom both Haydn and Hummel wrote their trumpet concertos) dies in Vienna.

1908 Spanish violinist and composer Pablo de Sarasate dies in Biarritz.

1957 Finnish composer Jean Sibelius dies in Järvenpää.

1958 English saxophonist John Harle, also composer of the theme to the long-running television drama *Silent Witness*, is born in Newcastle upon Tyne.

🎵 FIRST PERFORMED

1818 Carl Maria von Weber's *Jubilee Overture* receives its first performance, in Dresden.

☀ TODAY'S THE DAY

1862 St Petersburg Conservatoire opens, with Pyotr Ilyich Tchaikovsky, still working as a civil servant, as one of its part-time students.

1880 The International Mozart Foundation is set up in Salzburg.

1890 Max Reger begins studying piano and theory at Wiesbaden Conservatoire, although he teaches piano to other students to pay the bills.

VENUE FOCUS:

Bridgewater Hall

The Hallé Orchestra is one of the country's finest ensembles, and its residency at Bridgewater Hall is one of a number of reasons for paying this remarkable venue a visit. It's a truly international concert hall: as well as its three resident UK orchestras, the Bridgewater Hall regularly hosts some of the finest musicians from around the world, and has a performance list that easily rivals the very best of the London concert halls.

The first bricks of this striking structure were laid on 22 March 1993, on a site that formerly housed a bus station and a rather unglamorous car park. The most remarkable aspect of the building can be found right at the bottom. Somewhat bizarrely, the whole structure appears to float off the ground on almost 300 earthquake-proof giant springs, meaning that there is no actual link between the 22,500-tonne building and its foundations. Try not to think about that next time you are sitting there during a concert.

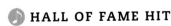

🎵 HALL OF FAME HIT
Max Bruch: *Violin Concerto No. 2*

Recommended Recording
Chloë Hanslip (violin); London Symphony Orchestra conducted by Martyn Brabbins; Warner Classics 9274 56642

21

SEPTEMBER

'I conclude that musical notes or rhythms were first acquired by the male or female progenitors of mankind for the sake of charming the opposite sex.'

CHARLES DARWIN, SCIENTIST AND WRITER

🕐 BIRTHS & DEATHS

1874 English composer Gustav Holst is born in Cheltenham.

1953 English composer Roger Quilter dies in London.

1955 Russian pianist Andrei Gavrilov is born in Moscow.

☀ TODAY'S THE DAY

1819 Seven-year-old Franz Liszt plays for his father's boss, Prince Nikolaus Esterházy. The Prince is so impressed that he agrees to fund the young boy's music education in Vienna.

1848 Fifteen-year-old Johannes Brahms makes his concert debut at the piano, in Hamburg.

1856 Fourteen-year-old Arthur Sullivan begins studying at the Royal Academy of Music.

1962 Igor Stravinsky arrives back in Moscow for his first visit to Russia for 48 years.

1971 Pierre Boulez conducts the New York Philharmonic for the first time.

COMPOSER PROFILE:

Edvard Grieg

Norway's finest composer was born in the same year that the first Christmas card was sent. Although Grieg is always considered Norwegian, his great-grandfather was Scottish. As a youngster, Grieg showed great flair for the piano, and he was sent to Leipzig to study music. Despite not particularly enjoying himself there, Grieg honed his musical genius in the city. He started to build himself up quite a celebrity fan club, with Liszt, Delius and Grainger all fully paid-up members. He was also good friends with the playwright Henrik Ibsen, who asked him to write the incidental music to his play

Peer Gynt. Grieg became a huge star in Norway and something of a national treasure. In his later life, he was famous as a travelling concert pianist, performing his *Piano Concerto* in cities across Europe. Grieg is buried halfway up the side of a rock face, near Troldhaugen. Apparently, the composer was out walking one evening and noticed how the sun hit a spot, halfway up the mountainside. He told a friend who was with him, 'There . . . I would like to rest for ever!'

🎵 HALL OF FAME HIT

Sergei Rachmaninov: *Vespers (All-Night Vigil)*

Recommended Recording

Estonian Philharmonic Chamber Choir conducted by Paul Hillier; Harmonia Mundi HMU 807504

'A gentleman is a man who can play the accordion but doesn't.'

ANONYMOUS

22

SEPTEMBER

 BIRTHS & DEATHS

1946 English bass John Tomlinson is born in Oswaldtwistle.

1958 Italian tenor Andrea Bocelli is born in Lajatico.

1961 American composer Michael Torke is born in Milwaukee.

1989 American composer Irving Berlin dies in New York.

2001 Polish-born American violinist Isaac Stern dies in New York.

 FIRST PERFORMED

1761 Eight new anthems composed by William Boyce are sung at the Coronation of King George III at Westminster Abbey.

TODAY'S THE DAY

1837 Fourteen-year-old César Franck is made a French citizen so that he can study at the Paris Conservatoire.

1888 Edward Elgar becomes engaged to Alice Roberts. Her family most certainly do not approve.

1904 Thirteen-year-old Sergei Prokofiev passes the entrance examination for the Moscow Conservatoire. Nikolai Rimsky-Korsakov and Alexander Glazunov are among his examiners.

1930 Sixteen-year-old Benjamin Britten begins studying at the Royal College of Music in London.

MUSICAL TERM:

Concerto

Originally a term for any music played in a concert, the Italian word *concerto* has now been absorbed into the English language. In modern usage, it is a musical work where a solo instrument is mixed and contrasted with the sound created by the rest of the orchestra. Historians trace the introduction of the concerto back to the turn of the 17th century with the advent of *concerti ecclesiastici* (church concertos). Later came the *concerto grosso* (literally a big concerto), which pitted a group of players against the rest of the orchestra. The Italian composer Corelli was a major force in developing this type of composition. But it was Johann Sebastian Bach who was among the first composers to create the concerto as we know it today – in his case, making the harpsichord the solo star of the show. Mozart took the idea and ran with it, writing concertos for dozens of different instrumental groupings. As with many of the rules surrounding classical music, very few of them are rigid. Although concertos occur most often for solo instruments, some composers have written for larger groupings (for example, Mozart's *Flute and Harp Concerto*). It is usual for concertos to be written in three movements, but this is not always the case (for instance, Brahms' *Piano Concerto No. 2* has four).

 HALL OF FAME HIT

Maurice Ravel: *Piano Concerto*

Recommended Recording

Benjamin Grosvenor (piano); Royal Liverpool Philharmonic Orchestra conducted by James Judd; Decca 478 3527

23

SEPTEMBER

> 'I compose every morning and, when one piece is done, I compose another.'
>
> FRANZ SCHUBERT, COMPOSER

 BIRTHS & DEATHS

1835 Italian composer Vincenzo Bellini dies in Paris.
2006 English composer Malcolm Arnold dies in Norwich.

 TODAY'S THE DAY

1756 Announcements are placed in both the *Whitehall Evening Post* and the *London Evening Post* advertising a proposal to publish a 'Correct and Complete Body of Church Music' by William Boyce.

1777 Wolfgang Amadeus Mozart and his mother head for Paris, leaving Leopold and Maria Anna behind at home in Salzburg.
1872 Pianist Anton Rubinstein performs the first of a 15-concert run in New York, which cements his place as one of the world's greats.
1878 The impresario Richard D'Oyly Carte shows W. S. Gilbert and Arthur Sullivan the site on London's Strand where he plans to build a theatre to house their operettas.
1898 Hans Richter stands down from the Vienna Philharmonic; within hours Gustav Mahler is offered his role of music director.
1929 The RCA Theremin is sold to the public for $175 per instrument; it is put on show in New York's Madison Square Garden.

VENUE FOCUS:

Southbank Centre

Located next to Waterloo station on the south bank of the River Thames, this 21-acre site houses some of the UK's best orchestras, and is also regularly packed to bursting with visiting musicians. The Centre, which includes the Royal Festival Hall and the Queen Elizabeth Hall, has an illustrious history stretching back to the 1951 Festival of Britain. As well as the two concert halls, it also houses the Purcell Room, the Hayward Gallery, the Saison Poetry Library and the Arts Council Collection. Resident ensembles include the Philharmonia Orchestra (Classic FM's Orchestra on Tour), the London Philharmonic Orchestra and the Orchestra of the Age of Enlightenment.

 HALL OF FAME HIT

Jacques Offenbach: *The Tales of Hoffmann*

Recommended Recording

Various soloists; Orchestra and Choir of the Suisse Romande conducted by Richard Bonynge; Decca 417 3632

'I abhor imitation and I abhor the familiar.'

SERGEI PROKOFIEV, COMPOSER

24
SEPTEMBER

 BIRTHS & DEATHS

1813 French composer André Grétry dies in Montmorency.

1914 Polish composer Andrzej Panufnik is born in Warsaw.

1945 English composer and conductor John Rutter is born in London.

 TODAY'S THE DAY

1830 Robert Schumann gives up studying the law and takes up music instead.

1881 Gustav Mahler has his first professional conducting engagement, in Ljubljana.

1898 Gustav Mahler is formally announced as the Vienna Philharmonic's new music director.

1904 Jean Sibelius moves house, to a villa near Tuomala.

1956 Dmitri Shostakovich is awarded the Lenin Prize.

1995 As a tribute to Sergei Rachmaninov, the main manor house on the Ivanokva estate where he lived in Russia is opened to the public. In fact, it's not the actual building where he lived and worked, which was razed to the ground during the Russian Revolution in 1917. Instead, the house and many other surrounding buildings making up the estate have been painstakingly rebuilt from plans, photographic records and the memories of those who were alive at the time.

MUSICAL TERM:
Flats and sharps

If you're new to classical music, the use of the terms 'flat' and 'sharp' can be quite baffling. You'll often come across phrases such as 'in D flat major' or 'in F sharp minor' as part of the title of a work. The good news is that the meaning of 'flat' and 'sharp' is pretty simple: a D flat is slightly lower than a D (on a piano keyboard, it's the black note to the left), whereas a D sharp is slightly higher (the black note to the right). If you hear someone describe a singer as being 'a bit sharp' or 'a bit flat', the chances are they're singing out of tune, a little above or below the right note, and could have done with warming up with some vocal exercises first before opening their mouth. If something is described as being 'in D flat major', then the central note of the piece of music – the note that feels like 'home' – is D flat.

COMPOSER PROFILE:
Alexander Glazunov

Born in St Petersburg, Glazunov had lessons from Rimsky-Korsakov, who said that he progressed 'not by the day, but literally by the hour'. He was lucky enough to find a rich sponsor in Mitrofan Belyayev early on, so a lot of his music was published and paid for without any of the struggles that other composers had to endure. Belyayev introduced him to Liszt, who became an influence on the young composer. Glazunov's music is on the conservative side, and often beautiful – his *Saxophone Concerto* of 1931 is particularly stunning. As an instrumentalist, he was something of a polymath, learning to play the piano, violin, cello, trumpet, French horn, clarinet and a range of percussion instruments.

 HALL OF FAME HIT
Giulio Caccini: *Ave Maria*

Recommended Recording
Inessa Galante (soprano); Latvian National Symphony Orchestra conducted by Alexander Vilumanis; Campion Cameo RRCD 1335

25

'I like to think of composing as a physical business. I compose at the piano and like to feel involved in my work with my hands.'

MICHAEL TIPPETT, COMPOSER

SEPTEMBER

🕐 BIRTHS & DEATHS

1683 French composer Jean-Philippe Rameau is baptised in Dijon.

1849 Austrian composer Johann Strauss Senior dies in Vienna.

1906 Dmitri Shostakovich is born in St Petersburg.

1927 English conductor Colin Davis is born in Weybridge.

1932 Canadian pianist Glenn Gould is born in Toronto.

1997 French composer and pianist Jean Françaix dies in Paris.

🎵 FIRST PERFORMED

1870 Bedřich Smetana's opera *The Bartered Bride* is premiered in Pavlovsk, in what is regarded as its definitive form.

☀️ TODAY'S THE DAY

1717 The Earl of Carnarvon commissions two anthems from George Frideric Handel.

1802 On the orders of Emperor Napoleon, Giovanni Paisiello is given responsibility for the music during the church service in the First Consul's chapel every Sunday.

1833 Felix Mendelssohn arrives in Düsseldorf, having recently accepted the job of music director.

1845 Anton Bruckner is appointed an assistant schoolteacher in the Austrian town of St Florian.

1903 Frederick Delius gets married in Grez-sur-Loing, France.

1929 The first radio broadcast of the Theremin, a newly invented electronic instrument, is transmitted from Madison Square Garden in New York.

1939 With the Second World War in its first weeks, Igor Stravinsky leaves Europe on board a ship from Bordeaux to New York.

1966 On his 60th birthday, Dmitri Shostakovich is weighed down with honours, including a second Order of Lenin, a Gold Medal of the Hammer and Sickle and the title 'Hero of Socialist Labour'. Benjamin Britten sends him a brand new Steinway grand piano as a birthday present.

MUSICAL TERM:

Key signature

This is another musical term associated with flats and sharps (see 24 September). Basically, the whole sound world of pretty much every piece of Western classical music centres on one major or minor chord. The central note – the one that most phrases or passages return to in the end – is the same note as the key signature. The key signature could be anything from C major to B flat minor. To hear a good musical example, try listening to Johann Sebastian Bach's *Well-Tempered Clavier*, a set of 48 preludes and fugues on the piano or harpsichord in every single key signature. And what about 'major' and 'minor'? Well, at its most basic level, music in a major key sounds happy; music in a minor key sounds sad. Every single note on the piano keyboard has a major and minor key signature – so we get E major and E minor, F major and F minor, and so on.

🎵 HALL OF FAME HIT

Edvard Grieg: *Lyric Pieces*

Recommended Recording

Leif Ove Andsnes (piano); Virgin Red Line 232 2862

'It's cruel, you know, that music should be so beautiful.
It has the beauty of loneliness and of pain . . . The
beauty of disappointment and never-satisfied love.'

BENJAMIN BRITTEN, COMPOSER

🕐 BIRTHS & DEATHS

1898 American composer
George Gershwin is born in
New York.

1930 German tenor Fritz
Wunderlich is born in Kusel.

1945 Hungarian composer Béla
Bartók dies in New York.

🎵 FIRST PERFORMED

1835 Gaetano Donizetti's *Lucia
di Lammermoor* is premiered in
Naples.

1892 In Plainfield, New Jersey,
the new Sousa Band, with John
Philip Sousa at its head, performs
its inaugural concert, featuring
his *Liberty Bell March*.

1957 Leonard Bernstein's
musical *West Side Story*, with
words by Stephen Sondheim, is
premiered in New York.

☀ TODAY'S THE DAY

1714 George Frideric Handel's
Te Deum is performed for the
new English king, George I, at
St James's Palace in London.

1777 Previously sacked for
spending too much time away
from court, Leopold and
Wolfgang Amadeus Mozart are
reinstated by Archbishop
Colloredo of Salzburg.

1791 Gioachino Rossini marries
Anna Guidarini in Pesaro.

1804 Jan Ladislav Dussek is
appointed Kapellmeister to
Prince Louis Ferdinand of Prussia.

1854 Richard Wagner finishes
work on *Das Rheingold* in Zurich.

1876 Vincenzo Bellini's remains
are reburied in his birthplace, in
the Duomo of Catania, Sicily; it is
more than 41 years since his
death.

1892 Antonín Dvořák arrives
in New York, after sailing from
Bremen nine days earlier.

1962 Eighty-year-old Igor
Stravinsky performs in concert in
Russia for the first time since the
Revolution. Dmitri Shostakovich
and Aram Khachaturian are in
the audience at the Moscow
Conservatoire.

1971 Otto Klemperer conducts
the final concert of his life, with
the New Philharmonia Orchestra,
at the Royal Festival Hall in
London.

VENUE FOCUS:

Birmingham
concert venues

Birmingham is lucky enough to have not one, but
two world-class venues, just around the corner from
each other. The design of Birmingham's Town Hall is
based on the Roman temple of Castor and Pollux. It
isn't just a concert venue, but also hosts civic events.
It's a great space for small-scale concerts, while
Symphony Hall's stunning acoustics make it the
perfect location for orchestral wizardry. The City of
Birmingham Symphony Orchestra (Simon Rattle's
old stomping ground) is resident there, and the
venue regularly hosts prestigious orchestras and
ensembles from abroad. Classic FM's Orchestra on
Tour, the Philharmonia, is also a frequent visitor.

🎵 HALL OF FAME HIT

Hector Berlioz: *The Childhood of
Christ*

Recommended Recording

La Chapelle Royale; Collegium Vocale Gent; Orchestra of the Champs-
Élysées conducted by Philippe Herreweghe; Harmonia Mundi HMGold
HMG501632/33

27

SEPTEMBER

> 'Hell is full of musical amateurs.'
>
> **GEORGE BERNARD SHAW, WRITER AND MUSIC CRITIC**

BIRTHS & DEATHS

1601 Music patron and composer King Louis XIII of France is born in Paris.

1919 Spanish-born soprano Adelina Patti dies in Brecon.

1921 German composer Engelbert Humperdinck dies in Neustrelitz.

1954 Russian violinist and conductor Dmitry Sitkovetsky is born in Baku.

1956 English composer Gerald Finzi dies in Oxford.

1957 American theatre and opera director Peter Sellars is born in Pittsburgh.

FIRST PERFORMED

1797 Joseph Haydn's *String Quartet Op. 76 No. 3* ('Emperor') is given its first performance, at Eisenstadt.

1907 Ralph Vaughan Williams' *Norfolk Rhapsodies Nos 2 and 3* receive their first performances, in Cardiff, with the composer conducting.

1934 Ralph Vaughan Williams' *Fantasia on Greensleeves* is given its first performance, in the Queen's Hall, London, with the composer conducting.

TODAY'S THE DAY

1738 George Frideric Handel finishes working on his oratorio *Saul* and begins working on *Israel in Egypt*.

10 favourite Baroque works

Pachelbel:	*Canon in D*
Allegri:	*Miserere*
Handel:	*Messiah*
Vivaldi:	*Four Seasons*
Handel:	*Zadok the Priest*
J. S. Bach:	*Double Violin Concerto*
J. S. Bach:	*Toccata and Fugue in D minor*
J. S. Bach:	*Brandenburg Concertos*
Handel:	*Solomon*
Vivaldi:	*Gloria*

1764 A memorial service for Jean-Philippe Rameau is held at the church of the Pères de l'Oratoire in Paris.

1827 Franz Schubert finishes writing his song-cycle *Winterreise*.

1834 Robert Schumann meets Frédéric Chopin in Leipzig.

1835 Frédéric Chopin arrives in Leipzig and visits Felix Mendelssohn.

1849 As many as 100,000 people turn out for the funeral of Johann Strauss Senior in Vienna.

1866 Bedřich Smetana begins work as conductor of Prague's Provisional Theatre.

1881 The new Budapest Opera House opens, with Emperor Franz Joseph and Empress Elisabeth in the audience.

1890 Ferruccio Busoni gets married in Moscow.

1982 Pianist Glenn Gould suffers a massive stroke, just months after branching out into a new career as a conductor.

1999 Spanish tenor Plácido Domingo opens for the 18th time as the headline in an operatic performance at the Metropolitan Opera in New York – beating the record set by Enrico Caruso.

HALL OF FAME HIT

Aaron Copland: *Rodeo*

Recommended Recording

Detroit Symphony Orchestra conducted by Leonard Slatkin; Naxos 8559758

‘Music can name the unnameable and communicate the unknowable.’

LEONARD BERNSTEIN, COMPOSER AND CONDUCTOR

28

SEPTEMBER

 BIRTHS & DEATHS

1790 Joseph Haydn's patron Prince Nikolaus Esterházy dies in Vienna.

1959 English humorist and musician Gerard Hoffnung dies in London.

1987 English violinist Chloe Hanslip is born in Guildford.

 FIRST PERFORMED

1745 The British national anthem, '*God Save the King*', is heard for the first time, at London's Drury Lane Theatre.

2000 Tan Dun's *Crouching Tiger Concerto* is performed for the first time, by the London Sinfonietta, at the Barbican Centre in London.

 TODAY'S THE DAY

1791 Wolfgang Amadeus Mozart finishes work on the overture and *The March of the Priests* for his opera *The Magic Flute* just two days before it is due to receive its premiere in Vienna.

1863 Johannes Brahms conducts a rehearsal of the Vienna Singakademie for the first time.

1866 Bedřich Smetana conducts Carl Maria von Weber's *Der Freischütz* for his opening performance as conductor of Prague's Provisional Theatre.

1889 Fifteen-year-old Gustav Holst comes sixth in a music competition run by *Boy's Own Paper*.

1945 Béla Bartók's funeral is held in New York.

2003 The Three Tenors perform in concert in Columbus. It is the 31st time they have sung together under the Three Tenors brand – and it is to be their final concert.

ENSEMBLE FOCUS:

Aurora Orchestra

Despite being only a decade old, the Aurora Orchestra has cut an impressive swath through the classical-music world, quickly establishing itself as a chamber orchestra to be reckoned with. Its artistic director Nicholas Collon is also making something of a name for himself, with a burgeoning career conducting many other major orchestras. It's no mean feat to establish a brand new orchestra in London – and to get the classical-music establishment and audiences to take notice of what you are doing in the concert hall. Aurora has managed to do this in style, making its home at the recently built King's Place Concert Hall just around the corner from King's Cross station and also at LSO St Luke's, near the Barbican Centre in the City of London. As well as being comfortable performing seasons of Bach and Mozart, the orchestra has built a reputation for developing cutting-edge creative partnerships with other art forms, including dance, film and theatre. Definitely one to listen out for in the future.

 HALL OF FAME HIT
Johannes Brahms: *Symphony No. 2*

Recommended Recording
Orchestre Révolutionnaire et Romantique conducted by John Eliot Gardiner; SDG 703

29

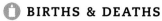

'I often think in music. I live my daydreams in music.'

ALBERT EINSTEIN

SEPTEMBER

🎵 BIRTHS & DEATHS

1930 Australian conductor Richard Bonynge is born in Sydney.

1973 English tenor Alfie Boe is born in Fleetwood.

🎵 FIRST PERFORMED

1918 Gustav Holst's *The Planets* receives its first performance, in the Queen's Hall, London.

☀ TODAY'S THE DAY

1674 Nicholas Staggins is appointed Master of the King's Musick.

1739 George Frideric Handel finishes work on his *Concerto grosso in G, Op. 6 No. 1*.

1789 Wolfgang Amadeus Mozart finishes work on his *Clarinet Quintet*.

1890 Jean Sibelius gets engaged.

1923 Sergei Prokofiev gets married in Ettal, Germany.

1960 Cellist Pablo Casals makes his final public appearance in Britain, conducting a concert at the Royal Festival Hall in London.

COMPOSER PROFILE:

Maurice Ravel

French composer Maurice Ravel studied composition with Fauré. He tried three times to win the Prix de Rome, the most prestigious prize offered by the Paris Conservatoire. His lack of success became something of a scandal; his music was considered too radical by the conservatives who judged the competition. At around the same time as he was battling with the Conservatoire authorities, Ravel joined an avant-garde group of writers, artists and musicians known as the 'Apaches'. He became something of a dandy, with a penchant for showy ties and frilly shirts. Musically, it was a productive period for him. He produced a succession of great works, such as the opera *L'heure espagnole*; *Valse nobles et sentimentales*, which he composed for the piano but later rescored for orchestra; and the ballet *Daphnis and Chloe*, which he wrote for Serge

Diaghilev's Ballets Russes. It was through this commission that Ravel met Stravinsky, who became a firm friend. His relationship with Debussy, however, deteriorated over time. Maybe the older composer took offence at Ravel's reported remark that, if he had the time, he 'would re-orchestrate *La Mer*'. When the First World War broke out, Ravel tried to get into the army, but was turned down because of his ill health. Later, he volunteered to serve as an ambulance driver on the front near Verdun, but was discharged in 1917, suffering from fever, exhaustion and insomnia. After the war, he composed less, though he still produced exceptional works, such as *La Valse* and *Boléro*. Though it became his best-known composition, he came to dislike the latter work, describing it as 'a piece for orchestra without music'.

🎵 HALL OF FAME HIT

Ralph Vaughan Williams: *Symphony No. 1 ('A Sea Symphony')*

Recommended Recording

Various soloists; Royal Liverpool Philharmonic Orchestra and Choir conducted by Vernon Handley; EMI 575 3082

> 'To sing is to pray twice.'
> **ST AUGUSTINE**

30

SEPTEMBER

 BIRTHS & DEATHS

1840 Norwegian composer Johan Svendsen is born in Christiania (now Oslo).
1852 Irish composer Charles Villiers Stanford is born in Dublin.
1908 Ukrainian violinist David Oistrakh is born in Odessa.

 FIRST PERFORMED

1791 Wolfgang Amadeus Mozart's opera *The Magic Flute* is premiered in Vienna.
1863 Georges Bizet's opera *The Pearl Fishers* receives its first performance, in Paris.

1935 George Gershwin's opera *Porgy and Bess* is given its first performance, in Boston.

☀ TODAY'S THE DAY

1808 Eleven-year-old Franz Schubert is auditioned by Antonio Salieri to become a chorister in the Imperial Chapel Royal; he passes.
1816 Carl Maria von Weber conducts his final opera performance in Prague.
1819 Louis Spohr resigns as Kapellmeister of the orchestra at the Theater an der Wien in Vienna. He had fallen out with the management.

1832 Thirteen-year-old Clara Wieck makes her debut at the Leipzig Gewandhaus.
1853 Robert Schumann and Johannes Brahms meet for the first time. The former is immediately wowed by the younger man's musicality.
1939 Igor Stravinsky arrives in New York, having left Europe because of the Second World War.
1957 A funeral for Jean Sibelius is held in Järvenpää.

ENSEMBLE FOCUS:

Britten Sinfonia

Launched in 1992, the Britten Sinfonia might not be the oldest orchestra in this book – but it has certainly made an indelible mark for the better on the country's chamber-music life. Unusually, it does not have a permanent principal conductor or music director. Instead, this role is taken by a series of different guest artists with whom the orchestra collaborates, often performing without anyone taking the traditional conducting role at all. The Britten Sinfonia's work is centred in the East of England, where it has residencies in Cambridge and Norwich, but its performances are by no means limited by these geographical boundaries, with regular concerts in Brighton, at the Barbican Centre in London and also across the European mainland. The orchestra has diversified to include the choral group Britten Sinfonia Voices and the Britten Sinfonia Academy, which trains school-age musicians at weekends.

 HALL OF FAME HIT
Antonín Dvořák: *Slavonic Dances*

Recommended Recording
Berlin Philharmonic Orchestra conducted by Lorin Maazel; EMI 232 2902

Octob

01

> 'Rhythm and harmony find their way into the inward places of the soul.'
>
> PLATO, GREEK PHILOSOPHER

OCTOBER

BIRTHS & DEATHS

1708 English composer John Blow dies in London.

1865 French composer Paul Dukas is born in Paris.

1903 American pianist Vladimir Horowitz is born in Kiev.

FIRST PERFORMED

1872 Georges Bizet's incidental music to Daudet's play *L'Arlesienne* is performed for the first time, in Paris.

1912 Edward Elgar's *The Music Makers* is premiered in Birmingham, conducted by the composer.

1913 Elgar's *Falstaff* is given its first performance, in Leeds, conducted by the composer.

1932 John Ireland's *A Downland Suite* has its first performance, in London's Crystal Palace.

TODAY'S THE DAY

1555 Giovanni Pierluigi da Palestrina becomes maestro di cappella of St Giovanni Laterano in Rome.

1762 Six-year-old Wolfgang Amadeus Mozart performs for the first time in public, at Trinity Inn in Linz.

1820 Brother and sister Fanny and Felix Mendelssohn start singing at the Berlin Singakademie; both are altos.

1833 Felix Mendelssohn begins work as the music director in Düsseldorf.

1853 Robert Schumann hails Johannes Brahms as a 'genius' after Brahms visits him and his wife Clara in their home in Düsseldorf.

1868 Anton Bruckner starts his job as theory and organ teacher at the Konservatorium der Gesellshaft der Musikfreunde in Vienna.

1870 Charles Villiers Stanford begins his studies at Queens' College, Cambridge.

1877 Gustav Mahler becomes a student at the University of Vienna, where Anton Bruckner is among his teachers.

1878 Jules Massenet is given a new job as professor of counterpoint, fugue and composition at the Paris Conservatoire.

1880 John Philip Sousa enlists in the United States Marine Corps for the third time, so that he can become leader of the Marine Band.

1885 Richard Strauss becomes the assistant conductor to Hans von Bülow at Meiningen.

1886 Richard Strauss makes his debut as opera conductor, in Munich.

1892 Antonín Dvořák officially starts work as director of the National Conservatory in New York.

1894 Richard Strauss is made assistant conductor of the Munich Opera.

1896 Continuing his rapid climb up the city's musical hierarchy, Richard Strauss is appointed Munich's Hofkapellmeister.

1905 Gabriel Fauré becomes director of the Paris Conservatoire.

1920 As his deafness worsens, Gabriel Fauré resigns as director of the Paris Conservatoire.

1921 Engelbert Humperdinck is buried near Berlin.

1924 Fourteen-year-old Samuel Barber is among the first cohort of students at the brand new Curtis Institute of Music, Philadelphia.

1934 Arnold Schoenberg moves to Hollywood.

1941 Dmitri Shostakovich and his family are flown out of the besieged city of Leningrad to the relative safety of Moscow.

HALL OF FAME HIT
Felix Mendelssohn: *Elijah*

Recommended Recording
Various soloists; Orchestra of the Age of Enlightenment; Edinburgh Festival Chorus conducted by Paul Daniel; Decca 455 6882

'What passion cannot music raise and quell!'

JOHN DRYDEN, POET

🕐 BIRTHS & DEATHS

1920 German composer Max Bruch dies near Berlin.

1933 French conductor Michel Plasson is born in Paris.

1944 Dutch conductor and organist Ton Koopman is born in Zwolle.

🎵 FIRST PERFORMED

1913 George Butterworth's *A Shropshire Lad* is performed for the first time, at Leeds Festival.

☀️ TODAY'S THE DAY

1826 Hector Berlioz signs up for a counterpoint course at the Paris Conservatoire.

1834 Felix Mendelssohn is impressed after hearing 14-year-old Clara Schumann performing her own music in Leipzig.

1835 Vincenzo Bellini is buried in Paris. Cherubini and Rossini are among the mourners.

1849 Johann Strauss Junior takes over from his father Johann Strauss Senior as conductor of the Vienna Strauss Orchestra.

1860 The Mariinsky Theatre opens in St Petersburg, as the headquarters of the Russian Opera. Its previous home had burned to the ground in 1859.

1869 Richard Wagner begins work on the first complete draft of his opera *Götterdämmerung*. It will take more than six months to complete.

1879 Leoš Janáček passes the entrance exam to the Leipzig Conservatoire, where he will study piano, organ and composition.

1879 Ernest Chausson starts his studies at the Paris Conservatoire; his teachers there include Jules Massenet and César Franck.

1888 Gustav Mahler is appointed the director of the Royal Opera in Budapest.

1897 The Carl Rosa Opera Company opens its first season at London's Covent Garden with Puccini's *La bohème*.

1939 Manuel de Falla leaves Spain on board a ship heading for Buenos Aires.

1948 Leonard Bernstein is appointed music director of the Israel Philharmonic Orchestra.

1956 Igor Stravinsky suffers a cerebral thrombosis in the middle of conducting a concert, struggling on to the end. Although he is seriously unwell afterwards, he eventually makes a full recovery.

1958 Leonard Bernstein conducts the New York Philharmonic for the first time as the orchestra's sole music director.

Classic BRIT Awards: 2 October 2013

Outstanding Contribution to Music – Hans Zimmer
Lifetime Achievement Award – Luciano Pavarotti (posthumous)
International Artist of the Year – Lang Lang
Female Artist of the Year – Nicola Benedetti
Male Artist of the Year – Daniel Barenboim
Breakthrough Artist of the Year – Amy Dickson
Composer of the Year – Hans Zimmer
Critics' Award – Jonas Kaufman
Album of the Year – André Rieu: *Magic of the Movies*

🎵 HALL OF FAME HIT

Wolfgang Amadeus Mozart: *Mass in C minor ('Great')*

Recommended Recording

Various soloists; Gabrieli Consort and Players conducted by Paul McCreesh; Deutsche Grammophon 478 5409

03

OCTOBER

'Where words fail, music speaks.'

HANS CHRISTIAN ANDERSEN, WRITER

 BIRTHS & DEATHS

1882 Polish composer Karol Szymanowski is born near Kiev.

1931 Danish composer Carl Nielsen dies in Copenhagen.

1936 American composer Steve Reich is born in New York.

1953 English composer Arnold Bax dies in Cork.

1967 English conductor Malcolm Sargent dies in London.

FIRST PERFORMED

1836 Felix Mendelssohn's oratorio *St Paul* is premiered in Liverpool.

1888 W. S. Gilbert and Arthur Sullivan's operetta *The Yeomen of the Guard* is premiered at the Savoy Theatre in London.

1900 Edward Elgar's oratorio *The Dream of Gerontius* is given its first performance, at Birmingham Town Hall.

1906 Edward Elgar's oratorio *The Kingdom* receives its first performance, in Birmingham.

1929 William Walton's *Viola Concerto* is performed for the first time, in the Queen's Hall, London.

1943 *Suite No. 1* from Aram Khachaturian's ballet *Gayaneh* receives its first performance, in Moscow.

TODAY'S THE DAY

1773 Wolfgang Amadeus Mozart finishes work on his *Symphony No. 24*, in Salzburg.

1798 Ludwig van Beethoven's *Piano Trio Op. 11* is published.

1829 Fanny Mendelssohn gets married in Berlin. She composes her own music for the ceremony.

1833 Hector Berlioz gets married to the actress Harriet Smithson in Paris. Franz Liszt is one of the guests.

1881 Gustav Mahler makes his debut as an opera conductor, with a performance of Verdi's *Il trovatore* in Ljubljana.

1907 A trio of composers – Paul Dukas, Manuel de Falla and Isaac Albéniz – meet in Paris.

1943 Munich's National Theatre – the home of the State Opera – is destroyed in an Allied bombing raid.

COMPOSER PROFILE:

Peter Warlock

Born in London, Philip Heseltine moved to Wales with his mother at an early age. He went to Eton, but further study at Oxford and then University College London lasted just a year and a term respectively. Both during and after a stay in Ireland when he was 23, he began composing, under the name Peter Warlock (he still used his real name for other work, such as his job as music critic of the *Daily Mail*). He lived a riotous life for a time in Eynsford, Kent, with the composer E. J. Moeran, before moving back to London in 1928. After a creatively fruitless period, including bouts of unemployment and depression, he was found dead from gas poisoning in his flat. His most enduring work, the *Capriol Suite*, comes from his apparently drunken, but productive, three years in Eynsford.

 HALL OF FAME HIT

William Walton: *Spitfire Prelude and Fugue*

Recommended Recording

Royal Northern Sinfonia conducted by Paul Daniel; Naxos 855 3869

> 'Music is the shorthand of emotion.'
> LEO TOLSTOY, WRITER

04

BIRTHS & DEATHS

1940 French conductor Alain Lombard is born in Paris.
1962 French conductor Marc Minkowski is born in Paris.
1982 Canadian pianist Glenn Gould dies in Toronto.

FIRST PERFORMED

1916 A revised version of Richard Strauss's *Ariadne auf Naxos* is premiered in Vienna.
1945 Aaron Copland's orchestral suite *Appalachian Spring* is performed for the first time, in New York.
1982 Philip Glass's film score *Koyaanisqatsi* receives its first performance, at Radio City Music Hall in New York.

TODAY'S THE DAY

1600 Jacopo Peri dedicates his opera *Euridice*, regarded by many music historians as the oldest surviving example of the genre, to Marie de' Medici, the new Queen of France. It is to receive its premiere in two days' time.
1763 The Mozart family arrives in Brussels as their European tour continues.
1820 Carl Maria von Weber performs for the King and Queen of Denmark, in Fredriksborg.
1830 Six-year-old Bedřich Smetana makes his concert debut in Litomysl, Bohemia.
1835 Felix Mendelssohn makes his debut as the director of Leipzig's Gewandhaus Orchestra.

1837 Fourteen-year-old César Franck signs up to study at the Paris Conservatoire.
1848 Frédéric Chopin performs a solo piano recital in Edinburgh.
1848 Richard Wagner writes the prose version of what would become his epic *Ring Cycle*.
1885 Pyotr Ilyich Tchaikovsky finishes work on his *'Manfred' Symphony*.
1890 Pyotr Ilyich Tchaikovsky's patron Madame von Meck writes to him to tell him that she has run out of money and will no longer be able to bankroll him.
1935 Sergei Prokofiev performs a piano score of his ballet *Romeo and Juliet* at Moscow's Bolshoi Theatre.
1951 A film version of George Gershwin's *An American in Paris* is released.

COMPOSER PROFILE:

Gaetano Donizetti

Composers don't tend to be terribly warlike as a breed, but Donizetti was one of relatively few among their number who started off life as a soldier. It was the usual story of parental disapproval of life as a composer that propelled him to arms. He continued to write music in his spare time and was eventually discharged from the army because of the success of his opera *Zoraide di Granata*. He then made up for lost time by composing almost 30 operas in the following eight years – quite some achievement by anyone's

standards. For a while, there was a school of thought that said that speed made his operas somewhat slapdash, but his work has been through something of a reassessment over the past 50 years. His greatest triumph of all is undoubtedly the tragic opera *Lucia di Lammermoor*, which received its premiere on 26 September 1835. He wrote more light-hearted masterpieces as well, notably *L'elisir d'amore*, *La fille du régiment* and *Don Pasquale*.

HALL OF FAME HIT

Ralph Vaughan Williams: *Symphony No. 5*

Recommended Recording

Hallé Orchestra conducted by Mark Elder; Hallé CDHLL 7533

05

'Heard melodies are sweet, but those unheard are sweeter, therefore, ye soft pipes, play on.'

JOHN KEATS, POET

OCTOBER

🕐 BIRTHS & DEATHS

1880 French composer Jacques Offenbach dies in Paris.

🎵 FIRST PERFORMED

1762 Christoph Willibald von Gluck's *Orpheus and Euridice* is premiered in Vienna.

1898 Edward Elgar's oratorio *Caractacus* receives its first performance, in Leeds. Hubert Parry, Gabriel Fauré and Charles Villiers Stanford are among those listening.

1899 Edward Elgar's *Sea Pictures* is given its first performance, in Norwich, with the composer conducting.

1938 Ralph Vaughan Williams' *Serenade to Music* is heard for the first time, at the Royal Albert Hall in London, celebrating Henry Wood's fifty years as a conductor.

☀ TODAY'S THE DAY

1773 Wolfgang Amadeus Mozart finishes work on his *Symphony No. 25*, in Salzburg.

1823 Carl Maria von Weber visits Ludwig van Beethoven in Baden.

1849 Samuel Sebastian Wesley starts work as Winchester Cathedral organist.

1892 Johannes Brahms and Joseph Joachim perform together at the new Bechstein Hall in Berlin.

GENRE FOCUS:

Beginnings of ballet

Ballet is the dance form most closely connected to classical music. It primarily developed in the Renaissance courts of Italy and then in France during the reign of Louis XIV. It was around Louis XIV's time that the dance master Pierre Beauchamp, the choreographer who worked with the composer Jean-Baptiste Lully, codified the five principal positions of the feet, which dancers still use today, centuries later. From its early beginnings as a ballo, simply meaning dance, ballet developed to become part of an operatic spectacle, usually occurring as an interlude during the opera, with especially composed music. From this integrated form, ballet gained a following and, subsequently, its independence. The Paris Opéra, in particular, became a pioneering stage for stand-alone ballet. From the 1700s onwards, ballet had its own stories, characters and, of course, music. By 1800, people were watching the sort of ballets that we still appreciate today. As well as Lully, composers such as Gluck were important in its development. Gluck applied his pioneering style, which had done much to revolutionise opera, to ballet. Much later, in the 1870s, Delibes, a former Paris Opéra rehearsal pianist, had big hits with *Sylvia* and *Coppélia*. Others worthy of mention include Ferdinand Hérold (his *La fille mal gardée*, with its popular Clog Dance, endures perhaps better than does its composer), as well as Adolphe Adam, who wrote, among other ballets, *Giselle* and *Le corsaire*.

🎵 HALL OF FAME HIT

Morten Lauridsen: *O Magnum Mysterium*

Recommended Recording

Polyphony conducted by Stephen Layton; Hyperion CDA 67449

'Why do so many of us try to explain the beauty of music, thus depriving it of its mystery?
LEONARD BERNSTEIN, CONDUCTOR AND COMPOSER

06

OCTOBER

 BIRTHS & DEATHS

1732 Scottish piano maker John Broadwood is born in Cockburnspath.

1820 Swedish soprano Jenny Lind is born in Stockholm.

1930 English composer Stanley Myers is born in Edgbaston.

1935 English conductor, composer and pianist Frederick Cowen dies in London.

 FIRST PERFORMED

1600 Jacopo Peri's opera *Euridice* is premiered in Florence. It is regarded by many musicologists as the oldest surviving opera.

1938 Aaron Copland's ballet *Billy the Kid* is premiered in Chicago.

TODAY'S THE DAY

1802 Ludwig van Beethoven's 'Heiligenstadt Testament' – his will – is filed, ready for opening in the event of his death.

1802 In a letter to his brother, Ludwig van Beethoven describes the onset of his deafness and the debilitating effect it is having on his life.

1820 Six-year-old Charles-Valentin Alkan begins his studies at the Paris Conservatoire.

1858 Edvard Grieg signs up to studying at the Leipzig Conservatoire.

1886 Edward Elgar begins teaching piano to Alice Roberts; she will become his wife.

1927 Recorded film music is presented in the cinema successfully for the first time, in New York City. An audio recording is synchronised with the projection of the Al Jolson movie *The Jazz Singer*.

COMPOSER PROFILE:

Patrick Hawes

Patrick Hawes is one of a long line of English composers who have drawn their inspiration from their native countryside. His music sits comfortably within the English Romantic tradition of Delius and Vaughan Williams. Classic FM's second composer in residence, between 2006 and 2007, he is also a highly proficient organist. Hawes first came to widespread notice with his haunting vocal work 'Quanta Qualia',

taken from his album *Blue in Blue*. It entered our annual listeners' poll, the Classic FM Hall of Fame, shortly after its release on CD, making it the fastest ever new entry for a new composer in the chart. His other major works include the *Highgrove Suite*, written to mark the 60th birthday of HRH The Prince of Wales.

 HALL OF FAME HIT

Jon Lord: *Durham Concerto*

Recommended Recording

Various soloists; Royal Liverpool Philharmonic Orchestra conducted by Mischa Damev; Avie AV 2145

> 'I hardly ever think of ought else but sex, race, athletics, speech and art.'
>
> PERCY GRAINGER, COMPOSER, IN A LETTER TO HIS MOTHER WRITTEN ON THIS DAY IN 1911

BIRTHS & DEATHS

1918 English composer Hubert Parry dies in Rustington.

1936 Swiss conductor Charles Dutoit is born in Lausanne.

1955 American cellist Yo-Yo Ma is born in Paris.

1959 American tenor Mario Lanza dies in Rome.

1978 English trumpeter Alison Balsom is born in Royston.

1982 Chinese pianist Yundi Li is born in Chongqing.

TODAY'S THE DAY

1787 Librettist Lorenzo da Ponte is spreading himself too thin. An angry Antonio Salieri writes to him, demanding that he come back to Vienna from Prague, where he has been working on the opening of Mozart's opera *Don Giovanni*. Salieri wants da Ponte to finish writing the words to his opera *Axur, re d'Omus*.

1797 Ludwig van Beethoven's *Piano Sonata No. 4* is published.

1835 Samuel Sebastian Wesley starts work as the organist at Exeter Cathedral.

1849 Johann Strauss Junior conducts his father's orchestra for the first time, in a concert in Vienna. He will eventually take over the family business full time.

1864 King Ludwig II of Bavaria gives Richard Wagner the finances to allow him to continue composing the *Ring Cycle*.

1877 Pyotr Ilyich Tchaikovsky collapses in St Petersburg. His doctor blames the stress of his relationship with his wife, telling him not to see her again.

1880 Jacques Offenbach's funeral is held in Paris. Johann Strauss Junior and Jules Massenet are among the mourners.

1901 Arnold Schoenberg gets married in Bratislava.

1912 Igor Stravinsky leaves St Petersburg by train; he won't return home for almost five decades.

1932 Thomas Beecham's London Philharmonic Orchestra performs in concert for the first time at the Queen's Hall in London.

1937 The Society of Recorder Players opens for business in London.

1945 Munich's first orchestral concert since the ending of the Second World War is held in the Prince Regent Theatre; virtually all the other major venues have been destroyed by Allied bombs.

HALL OF FAME HIT

Frederick Delius: *On Hearing the First Cuckoo in Spring*

Recommended Recording

Camerata Wales conducted by Owain Arwel Hughes; BIS CD 1589

> 'The end of all good music is to affect the soul.'
> CLAUDIO MONTEVERDI, COMPOSER

08

OCTOBER

BIRTHS & DEATHS
1551 Italian composer Giulio Caccini is born in Rome.
1930 Japanese composer Toru Takemitsu is born in Tokyo.
1944 Brazilian pianist Nelson Freire is born in Boa Esperança.
1953 English contralto Kathleen Ferrier dies in London.

FIRST PERFORMED
1931 William Walton's oratorio *Belshazzar's Feast* is premiered in Leeds Town Hall.

TODAY'S THE DAY
1844 Johann Strauss Junior signs a one-year contract with 24 musicians to create his own orchestra, in competition with the one run by his father.
1848 The family of eight-year-old Pyotr Ilyich Tchaikovsky leaves the countryside behind to move to the bright lights of Moscow.
1866 Jules Massenet gets married near Fontainebleau. Franz Liszt is the piano teacher of Massenet's new wife Louise.

1897 Gustav Mahler is named as the new director of the Vienna Hofoper.
1940 Béla Bartók gives a farewell performance at the Budapest Academy of Music, just before leaving Hungary.
1945 Leonard Bernstein starts work as conductor of the New York City Symphony Orchestra.
1981 The new Leipzig Gewandhaus opens, with Kurt Masur conducting the inaugural concert.

ORCHESTRA FOCUS:

Royal Philharmonic Orchestra

Founded in 1946 by the flamboyant conductor Thomas Beecham, the Royal Philharmonic Orchestra is based in London at Chelsea's Cadogan Hall, though it gives regular performances at the Royal Albert Hall and the Royal Festival Hall. The orchestra's debut performance was at the Davis Theatre in Croydon, and it has continued to perform in the town ever since. The RPO also visits Northampton, Crawley, Lowestoft and Reading on a regular basis. Beecham made the orchestra one of the world's great bands. After his death in 1961, it turned to other notable conductors, including Rudolf Kempe, André Previn, Antal Dorati, Walter Weller and Daniele Gatti. The current artistic director is Charles Dutoit. The RPO has enjoyed a long partnership with the concert promoter Raymond Gubbay, often featuring in his 'Classical Spectacular' concerts. It has recorded extensively and streams its entire Cadogan Hall concert series over the internet.

 HALL OF FAME HIT
John Barry: *The Beyondness of Things*

Recommended Recording
English Chamber Orchestra conducted by John Barry; Decca 460 0092

09

OCTOBER

'I have heard him boast of composing a concerto faster than a copyist could write it down!'

CHARLES DE BROSSES ABOUT ANTONIO VIVALDI

BIRTHS & DEATHS

1835 French composer Camille Saint-Saëns is born in Paris.
1928 Finnish composer Einojuhani Rautavaara is born in Helsinki.
1953 British mezzo-soprano Sally Burgess is born in Durban.

FIRST PERFORMED

1986 Andrew Lloyd-Webber's musical *Phantom of the Opera* is premiered at Her Majesty's Theatre in London.

TODAY'S THE DAY

1770 Fourteen-year-old Wolfgang Amadeus Mozart passes the entrance exam for the Accademia Filarmonica in Bologna.
1848 Nine-year-old Georges Bizet passes the entrance exam to the Paris Conservatoire.
1851 Nine-year-old Jules Massenet fails the entrance exam to the Paris Conservatoire.
1867 Franz Liszt arrives in Tribschen to discuss the relationship between Richard Wagner and Liszt's daughter Cosima von Bülow.
1897 Ralph Vaughan Williams gets married in Hove. The vicar who carries out the service is the Revd Spooner, who gave his name to the term 'Spoonerism'.
1931 A state funeral is held for Carl Nielsen in Copenhagen, with the Danish king and queen in attendance.
1932 Maurice Ravel is injured in a car crash in Paris.
1973 Leonard Bernstein gives the first of his lectures as a Harvard professor. Notably, his professorship is not in music, but in poetry.

COMPOSER PROFILE:

Domenico Scarlatti

The son of composer Alessandro, Domenico Scarlatti was born in Naples in 1865, the same year as Handel and Bach. As well as being a composer himself, he was an outstanding harpsichordist who, according to legend, 'fought' Handel in a keyboard duel (adjudged to be a draw). Early on he worked mainly in Rome before spending nine years in Lisbon, composing for Princess Maria Barbara. Eventually, he followed her to Madrid (she married into the Spanish royal family and ultimately became Queen of Spain), where he remained until he died. While in Spain, he composed an amazing 555 keyboard sonatas, which paved the way for the later sonatas of Mozart and Beethoven.

HALL OF FAME HIT

Sergei Prokofiev: *Lieutenant Kijé*

Recommended Recording

Royal Scottish National Orchestra conducted by Neeme Järvi; Chandos CHAN 10481X

> 'Handel understands effect better than any of us;
> when he chooses, he strikes like a thunderbolt.'
>
> WOLFGANG AMADEUS MOZART, COMPOSER

10
OCTOBER

 BIRTHS & DEATHS

1813 Italian composer Giuseppe Verdi is born near Parma.

1946 Jamaican bass Willard White is born in St Catherine.

1971 Russian pianist Evgeny Kissin is born in Moscow.

2010 Australian soprano Joan Sutherland dies in Montreux.

FIRST PERFORMED

1759 Thomas Arne's *The Beggar's Opera* is premiered in London's Covent Garden.

1935 The official premiere of George Gershwin's opera *Porgy and Bess* takes place in New York.

TODAY'S THE DAY

1774 Antonio Salieri gets married.

1802 Ludwig van Beethoven finishes a second part of his 'Heiligenstadt Testament', a long and detailed account of his despair, which was particularly acute because of the loss of his hearing.

1828 Niccolò Paganini has an operation on his teeth in Prague.

1853 While he is in Paris, Franz Liszt sees his three children for the first time in nine years.

1881 The new Savoy Theatre in London opens with a production of *Patience* by W. S. Gilbert and Arthur Sullivan.

1882 Pietro Mascagni passes the entrance exam to the Milan Conservatoire.

1928 Eric Fenby begins working as the amanuensis to the seriously ill Frederick Delius.

1939 The first of 1,698 classical concerts is given at lunchtime in the National Gallery in London during the Second World War.

COMPOSER PROFILE:

Alexander Scriabin

Born in Moscow, Scriabin was the son of a lawyer and a pianist. Unsurprisingly, he excelled in piano from a young age and, despite being enrolled at military cadet school in early boyhood, managed to keep up his playing. When he was 16, he switched to studying music at the Moscow Conservatoire, tackling composition with the composer Arensky as well as continuing his piano studies. A publishing deal he made while still at college allowed him to tour his own works when he was just 24. Scriabin became piano professor at his old conservatoire aged 26, but gave it up to settle in Switzerland in 1903. He was increasingly attracted to theosophy and other mystical philosophies, composing his works from this time onwards as heralds, so he said, of a forthcoming disaster. He may also have had synesthesia – that is, he 'saw' musical pitches in colour.

 HALL OF FAME HIT
Paul McCartney: *Standing Stone*

Recommended Recording
London Symphony Orchestra and Chorus conducted by Lawrence Foster; EMI Classics 556 4842

11

'The aim and final end of all music should be none other than the glory of God and the refreshment of the soul.'

JOHANN SEBASTIAN BACH, COMPOSER

OCTOBER

BIRTHS & DEATHS

1778 English violinist George Bridgetower is born in Biała, Poland.

1837 English organist and composer Samuel Wesley dies in London.

1896 Austrian composer Anton Bruckner dies in Vienna.

FIRST PERFORMED

1727 George Frideric Handel's *Coronation Anthems* are performed for the first time at Westminster Abbey during the Coronation of King George II. These include *Zadok the Priest*, which is then performed at all future Coronations.

1947 Sergei Prokofiev's *Symphony No. 6* is given its first performance, in Leningrad.

1952 Sergei Prokofiev's *Symphony No. 7* receives its first performance, in Moscow. The composer makes his final public appearance at the concert.

TODAY'S THE DAY

1759 François-Joseph Gossec gets married in Paris.

1830 Although he is only 20 years old, Frédéric Chopin gives his last performance in Warsaw, with the premiere of his *Piano Concerto No. 1*.

1853 Hector Berlioz, Franz Liszt and Richard Wagner have breakfast together at Berlioz's house in Paris.

1912 Leopold Stokowski conducts the Philadelphia Orchestra for the first time.

1962 80-year-old Igor Stravinsky visits President Khrushchev at the Kremlin, shortly before the end of his first trip to Russia for almost 50 years.

MUSICAL TERM:

Sonata

The word 'sonata' means 'sounded' or 'played' and is the opposite of 'cantata', meaning 'sung'. It is a piece for a solo instrumentalist (very often a pianist), a soloist with piano accompaniment or occasionally a small ensemble. Today's interpretation of the sonata is largely that which was prevalent during the Classical and Romantic periods. Sonata form – the rules by which a sonata is written – can also be applied to other genres, though: many symphonies have a movement that, while not being a sonata, is written in sonata form. A standard Classical or Romantic sonata has three movements, usually – but not always – one quick, then one slow and then another quick. The rules of sonata form dictate three sections within each movement: an exposition, containing the big tunes, a development, in which the tunes from the exposition are built on and varied, and finally a recapitulation, where themes from the exposition return.

HALL OF FAME HIT

Ralph Vaughan Williams: *Symphony No. 2 ('A London Symphony')*

Recommended Recording

Hallé Orchestra conducted by Mark Elder; Hallé CDHLL 7529

> 'My Prince was always satisfied . . . and I was in a position to improve, alter and be as bold as I pleased.'
>
> JOSEPH HAYDN, ABOUT HIS EMPLOYER PRINCE NIKOLAUS ESTERHÁZY

12
OCTOBER

🏛 BIRTHS & DEATHS

1692 Italian composer Giovanni Vitali dies in Modena.

1872 English composer Ralph Vaughan Williams is born in Down Ampney.

1935 Italian tenor Luciano Pavarotti is born in Modena.

1944 Dutch harpsichordist and conductor Ton Koopman is born in Zwolle.

🔔 FIRST PERFORMED

1910 Ralph Vaughan Williams' *Symphony No. 1: 'A Sea Symphony'* is given its first performance, in Leeds. The composer conducts.

☀ TODAY'S THE DAY

1742 George Frideric Handel finishes work on his oratorio *Samson*.

1849 Frédéric Chopin partakes of the last sacrament; he lives for only five more days.

1894 Giuseppe Verdi is presented with the Grand Cross of the Légion d'Honneur at the French premiere of his *Otello*.

1895 Pietro Mascagni is offered – and accepts – the job as director of the Liceo Rossini in Pesaro.

1903 Pietro Mascagni accepts a new role as director of the National Music School in Rome.

1922 Gustav Holst is one of a group of friends who surprise Ralph Vaughan Williams by singing to him in his back garden in London, on his 50th birthday.

COMPOSER PROFILE:

Vincenzo Bellini

Born into a close-knit Sicilian family, Bellini was said to have been singing operatic arias by the time he was 18 months old. The success of two of his early operas, *Il Pirata* and *La Straniera*, propelled him centre stage in the Italian operatic world. He cited Rossini as a great influence on his work and, at the height of his success, was matching him in terms of financial earnings. Bellini was one of those composers who relied on a deadline to get his creative juices flowing. He had many lovers in his life, including the famous soprano Giuditta Pasta, who created the role of Norma in Bellini's opera of the same name. Sadly, Bellini died very young. Rossini was one of the pall-bearers at his funeral in Paris.

🎵 HALL OF FAME HIT
James Horner: *Titanic*

Recommended Recording
Original soundtrack; Sony COLS 2K60797

13

OCTOBER

'Hosts of imitators have sprung up since Strauss, but to him will remain the glory of originality, fancy, feeling and invention.'

OBITUARY FOR JOHANN STRAUSS SENIOR, PUBLISHED IN THE *ILLUSTRATED LONDON NEWS*, TODAY IN 1849

🕐 BIRTHS & DEATHS

1937 Armenian composer and conductor Loris Tjeknavorian is born in Borujerd, Iran.

1956 English pianist Melvyn Tan is born in Singapore.

☀ TODAY'S THE DAY

1726 Antonio Vivaldi becomes the director of the Teatro Sant'Angelo in Venice.

1735 Charles Avison is given the job of organist at St John's Church in Newcastle.

1762 Six-year-old Wolfgang Amadeus Mozart and his sister Maria Anna play for Empress Maria Theresa at the Schönbrunn Palace. Their father, Leopold, realises just how talented both children – especially Wolfgang – really are.

1813 The invention of the chronometer by Johann Nepomuk Maelzel is reported in a Viennese newspaper. Ludwig van Beethoven is one of the advocates of the device, which is a forerunner to the metronome.

1833 Felix Mendelssohn conducts for the first time as Düsseldorf's new music director.

1841 Felix Mendelssohn gets a new job as the Royal Kapellmeister for King Friedrich Wilhelm IV of Prussia.

1863 The bodies of Franz Schubert and Ludwig van Beethoven are exhumed for medical examination more than three decades after their deaths.

1870 Ten-year-old Gustav Mahler makes his concert debut at the piano in Jihlava.

1878 Modest Mussorgsky is given a new job in the Office of Government Control, having just been about to be fired from his role in the Forestry Department because of his problems with alcohol.

1879 Engelbert Humperdinck wins the Berlin Mendelssohn Prize, enabling him to study for a year in Italy.

1887 Nellie Melba makes her operatic debut in Brussels, as Gilda in Verdi's opera *Rigoletto*.

1966 The Teatro Real in Madrid reopens as a concert hall, having been closed for more than 40 years.

🎵 HALL OF FAME HIT

Pyotr Ilyich Tchaikovsky: *Piano Concerto No. 2*

Recommended Recording

Stephen Hough (piano); Minnesota Orchestra conducted by Osmo Vänskä; Hyperion CDA 67711/2

'We cannot despair about mankind knowing that Mozart was a man.'

ALBERT EINSTEIN

14
OCTOBER

🕐 BIRTHS & DEATHS

1977 English pianist Freddy Kempf is born in Croydon.
1990 American composer and conductor Leonard Bernstein dies in New York.

🎵 FIRST PERFORMED

1843 Felix Mendelssohn's incidental music to *A Midsummer Night's Dream* is performed for the first time, in Potsdam. The composer wrote the *Overture* to the same play back in 1826.
1883 Antonín Dvořák's *Violin Concerto* is given its first performance, in Prague.
1903 Edward Elgar's oratorio *The Apostles* is premiered in Birmingham, with the composer conducting.

☀️ TODAY'S THE DAY

1826 Gioachino Rossini is made a Chevalier of the Légion d'Honneur. However, he declines the award on the grounds that there are more worthy recipients who should be honoured ahead of him.

1847 Otto Nicolai takes over from Felix Mendelssohn as Kapellmeister at the Royal Opera House in Berlin.
1896 Anton Bruckner's funeral is held in Vienna.
1935 George Gershwin oversees the first commercial recording of his opera *Porgy and Bess* in New York.
1972 36 years after his death, Alexander Glazunov's remains are taken from Paris for burial in St Petersburg.

ORCHESTRA FOCUS:

City of Birmingham Symphony Orchestra

The Birmingham Symphony Orchestra was founded in 1920 and renamed the City of Birmingham Symphony Orchestra 28 years later. There is a long tradition of classical music in the city, with a regular music festival dating back as far as 1768. The current music director is the Latvian Andris Nelsons, but it was the then 25-year-old Simon Rattle who made his name with the orchestra when he took up the baton in 1980. Under his leadership, the CBSO developed a strong reputation both at home and abroad and recorded extensively. In 1991, the city benefited from the opening of a brand new purpose-built concert venue in the heart of Birmingham. Symphony Hall remains one of the finest places anywhere to listen to classical music, with world-class acoustics.

 HALL OF FAME HIT
Léo Delibes: *Coppélia*

Recommended Recording
Orchestra of the Royal Opera House, Covent Garden conducted by Mark Ermler; RCA 8869 1936602

15

OCTOBER

'The audience . . . expected the ocean, something big, something colossal, but they were served instead with some agitated water in a saucer.'

LOUIS SCHNEIDER, COMPOSER, ABOUT CLAUDE DEBUSSY'S LA MER

BIRTHS & DEATHS

1905 Swedish composer Dag Wirén is born in Striberg.

1926 German conductor Karl Richter is born in Plauen.

1953 English choral director and founder of the Tallis Scholars, Peter Phillips, is born in Southampton.

1964 American composer and lyricist Cole Porter dies in Santa Monica.

FIRST PERFORMED

1769 Wolfgang Amadeus Mozart's *Mass in C 'Dominicus'* is given its first performance, in Salzburg.

1880 Camille Saint-Saëns' *Violin Concerto No. 3* receives its first performance, in Hamburg.

1905 Claude Debussy's *La mer* is premiered in Paris.

1933 Dmitri Shostakovich's *Piano Concerto No. 1* is given its first performance, in Lengingrad, with the composer playing the solo.

1946 Benjamin Britten's *Young Person's Guide to the Orchestra* receives its first performance, in Liverpool's Philharmonic Hall.

TODAY'S THE DAY

1825 Felix Mendelssohn finishes composing his earliest notable work, his *Octet*.

1844 Eighteen-year-old Johann Strauss Junior makes his first appearance as a conductor, in competition with his father.

1872 Franz Liszt visits his daughter Cosima and her husband Richard Wagner for the first time in Bayreuth.

1881 A performance at the Paris Opéra basks in electric light for the very first time.

1883 Dallas Opera House opens with a performance of Gilbert and Sullivan's *Iolanthe*.

1884 Johann Strauss Junior is granted the freedom of the city of Vienna to mark the 40th anniversary of the beginning of his career.

1893 Charles Gounod collapses into a coma at his Paris home.

1900 The Boston Symphony Orchestra moves into its permanent home: Symphony Hall, Boston.

1907 Gustav Mahler chooses Beethoven's opera *Fidelio* as his final production as music director of the Vienna Opera.

1955 The Burgtheater in Vienna reopens after considerable Second World War damage is repaired.

1956 Leonard Bernstein becomes the first home-grown conductor of a major American symphony orchestra, when he takes over as joint principal conductor of the New York Philharmonic.

1960 Igor Stravinsky is evacuated from a hotel in Venice, after it floods.

1963 Herbert von Karajan conducts the inaugural concert at Berlin's new Philharmonie; he had been heavily involved in the design of the hall.

HALL OF FAME HIT
Franz Lehár: *The Merry Widow*

Recommended Recording
Various soloists; Monteverdi Choir; Vienna Philharmonic Orchestra conducted by John Eliot Gardiner; Deutsche Grammophon 439 9112

'A Romantic who felt at ease within the mould of Classicism.'

CELLIST AND CONDUCTOR PABLO CASALS, ABOUT COMPOSER FELIX MENDELSSOHN

16

OCTOBER

 BIRTHS & DEATHS

1946 English composer and conductor Granville Bantock dies in London.

1956 American conductor Marin Alsop is born in New York.

1962 Russian baritone Dmitri Hvorostovsky is born in Krasnoyarsk, Siberia.

 FIRST PERFORMED

1791 Wolfgang Amadeus Mozart's *Clarinet Concerto* is premiered in Prague.

1926 Zoltan Kodaly's *Hary Janos* is performed for the first time, at the Hungarian Royal Opera House in Budapest.

1938 A two piano version of Aaron Copland's ballet *Billy the Kid* receives its first performance, in Chicago.

1942 Aaron Copland's ballet *Rodeo* is premiered at the Metropolitan Opera House in New York.

 TODAY'S THE DAY

1842 Felix Mendelssohn tries to leave his job with King Friedrich Wilhelm in Berlin, but the king won't let him go.

1849 Now seriously ill, Frédéric Chopin leaves instructions that all of his unfinished manuscripts should be destroyed and that he wants Mozart's *Requiem* to be sung at his funeral.

1865 Richard Wagner successfully negotiates a lump-sum pension, with further annual payments from his patron, King Ludwig.

1868 Richard Wagner's *Lohengrin* is performed for the first time in Russia, at the Mariinsky Theatre in St Petersburg. Modest Mussorgsky, Nikolai Rimsky-Korsakov and César Cui are among those in the audience. They are less than complimentary about the work.

1887 Johannes Brahms and Clara Schumann return 35 years' worth of correspondence to each other.

1888 Carl Nielsen makes his conducting debut at the Odense Music Society.

1891 The Chicago Symphony Orchestra gives its first performance.

1896 Gabriel Fauré takes over from Jules Massenet as professor of composition at the Paris Conservatoire.

1918 Hubert Parry's funeral is held at St Paul's Cathedral in London. Edward Elgar and Charles Villiers Stanford are among the mourners.

1930 John Ireland gives 16-year-old Benjamin Britten his first composition lesson at the Royal College of Music.

1990 Leonard Bernstein's funeral is held in New York.

Mixed-up kid

The composer John Ireland doesn't actually hail from Ireland. He was in fact from England, having been born in 1879 in Altrincham in Greater Manchester. Just to add to the all-round general confusion, his family originally came from Scotland.

 HALL OF FAME HIT
Franz Schubert: *Impromptus Op. 90*

Recommended Recording
Maria João Pires (piano): Deutsche Grammophon 457 5502

17

OCTOBER

'Had I learned to fiddle, I should have done nothing else.'

SAMUEL JOHNSON, WRITER

BIRTHS & DEATHS

1688 Italian composer Domenico Zipoli is born in Prato.

1837 German composer Johann Nepomuk Hummel dies in Weimar.

1849 Polish composer Frédéric Chopin dies in Paris.

1892 English composer Herbert Howells is born in Lydney.

1940 American pianist Stephen Kovacevich is born in San Pedro, California.

1944 Czech composer Pavel Haas dies in Auschwitz.

FIRST PERFORMED

1831 Felix Mendelssohn's *Piano Concerto No. 1* is performed for the first time, in Munich.

TODAY'S THE DAY

1707 Johann Sebastian Bach gets married to his cousin Maria Barbara.

1823 Eleven-year-old Franz Liszt performs the first of three concerts in Munich. The audience is ecstatic.

1826 Gioachino Rossini is given the rather grand title of First Composer of the King and Inspector General of Singing in France by King Charles X.

1837 Samuel Wesley's funeral is held in London.

1850 On the first anniversary of the composer's death, a monument is unveiled at Frédéric Chopin's grave.

1876 Isaac Albéniz joins the Royal Conservatoire of Music in Brussels.

1894 Mily Balakirev performs on the piano in public for the final time at a concert to mark the 45th anniversary of Chopin's death.

MUSICAL TERM:

Lieder

The German word for 'songs' (in the singular it is 'lied'). It is not just any song though: usually (although not always) the term refers to the songs written by German Romantic composers around the late 18th and early 19th centuries. They often set the words of great poets, such as Goethe or Schiller, to music, and usually (again, not always) the musical accompaniment is provided by a solo piano. Those composers who were particularly adept at writing lieder include Schumann, Brahms, Mahler and Richard Strauss. Probably the greatest of them all was Franz Schubert, who, despite his short life, churned out more than 600 separate songs. In 1815 alone he wrote 140, and even managed eight in just one day. Among those who have made their names as singers of lieder are the Welsh bass-baritone Bryn Terfel, who won the Lieder Prize at the Cardiff Singer of the World competition, and the English tenor Ian Bostridge, whose recordings of Schubert and Schumann lieder have been acclaimed around the world.

HALL OF FAME HIT

Jean-Philippe Rameau: *Les Indes galantes*

Recommended Recording
Collegium Aureum; Deutsche Harmonia Mundi 8869 7959542

'The darling of our nation.'

DESCRIPTION OF JOSEPH HAYDN IN THE AUSTRIAN NEWSPAPER WIENER BIARIUM, ON THIS DAY IN 1766

18
OCTOBER

 BIRTHS & DEATHS

1545 English composer and organist John Taverner dies in Boston.

1893 French composer Charles Gounod dies in Paris.

1931 American inventor of the phonograph, Thomas Edison, dies in West Orange.

1946 Canadian composer Howard Shore is born in Toronto.

1961 American trumpeter Wynton Marsalis is born in New Orleans.

 FIRST PERFORMED

1887 Johannes Brahms' *Double Concerto* is performed for the first time, in Cologne, with the composer conducting.

1904 Gustav Mahler's *Symphony No. 5* is given its first performance, in Cologne, with the composer conducting.

1923 Sergei Prokofiev's *Violin Concerto No. 1* receives its first performance, in Paris.

TODAY'S THE DAY

1754 Christoph Willibald von Gluck is appointed Imperial and Royal Chamber Composer by Empress Maria Theresa.

1774 Empress Maria Theresa promotes Christoph Willibald von Gluck to Imperial Court Composer.

1777 Wolfgang Amadeus Mozart writes to his father Leopold, telling him that the organ is 'in my eyes and ears . . . the king of instruments'.

1841 Samuel Sebastian Wesley accepts a job as organist in Leeds.

1870 Anton Bruckner gets a new job teaching theory, piano and organ at the St Anna Teacher Training Institute for Men and Women in Vienna.

1878 Pyotr Ilyich Tchaikovsky ends his career as a teacher at Moscow Conservatoire.

1885 Richard Strauss makes his debut as a solo pianist in Meiningen. Johannes Brahms is in the audience.

1889 Giuseppe Verdi buys the land on which he will build a retirement home for musicians.

1898 Richard Strauss chooses Beethoven's *Fidelio* as his final production as chief conductor of the Munich Opera, before moving to Berlin.

1961 The film version of Leonard Bernstein's *West Side Story* is premiered in New York.

Master of the Queen's (King's) Music(k)

The role dates back to the reign of Charles I, when Nicholas Lanier, a composer and lute player, became the first to hold the job from 1626 until the post was abolished by Oliver Cromwell. He returned to it in 1660 when Charles II was restored to the throne. The position involved accompanying the monarch on his travels, as well as leading his private band of musicians, which, during Charles II's reign, numbered 24 string players. The present incumbent is the Salford-born composer, Peter Maxwell Davies, who has been a popular and well-respected holder of the post.

HALL OF FAME HIT
Johann Hummel: *Trumpet Concerto*

Recommended Recording
Alison Balsom (trumpet); German Philharmonic Chamber Orchestra of Bremen; EMI 216 2130

19

OCTOBER

'I am affected by everything that goes on in the world . . . and then I long to express my feelings in music.'

ROBERT SCHUMANN, COMPOSER

🕐 BIRTHS & DEATHS

1659 Italian composer Domenico Gabrielli is born in Bologna.

1943 English composer Robin Holloway is born in Leamington Spa.

1950 English composer George Fenton is born in Bromley.

1987 English cellist Jacqueline du Pré dies in London.

🎵 FIRST PERFORMED

1814 'The Star-Spangled Banner' is performed for the first time, in Baltimore.

1845 Richard Wagner's *Tannhäuser* is premiered in Dresden, with the composer conducting.

1901 Edward Elgar's *Pomp and Circumstance Marches Nos 1 and 2* are heard for the first time, in Liverpool.

1922 Modest Mussorgsky's *Pictures at an Exhibition*, orchestrated by Maurice Ravel, is given its first performance, in Paris.

☀ TODAY'S THE DAY

1814 Seventeen-year-old Franz Schubert composes his first significant piece of music, '*Gretchen at the Spinning Wheel*'.

1854 Hector Berlioz gets married in Paris.

1854 Gioachino Rossini's wife writes to a newspaper to deny rumours that her husband has gone insane.

1878 Having turned his back on teaching at the Moscow Conservatoire, Pyotr Ilyich Tchaikovsky sets off for St Petersburg.

1899 Claude Debussy gets married in Paris. Erik Satie is among the witnesses.

1933 Otto Klemperer conducts the Los Angeles Philharmonic for the first time.

1977 The Society for Music Theory is founded at Northwestern University in the USA.

Celluloid success

The London Symphony Orchestra won three Grammy Awards for its performance of the soundtrack to the original *Star Wars* movie. The orchestra has played on every *Star Wars* film since. The LSO is not above a little screen stardom of its own either, having appeared in cartoon form on both *The Simpsons* and *Family Guy*.

🎵 HALL OF FAME HIT

Leonard Bernstein: *Candide* (*Overture*)

Recommended Recording

New York Philharmonic Orchestra conducted by Leonard Bernstein; Sony Classical Masters 8869 7880862

> 'My mind and fingers have worked like two damned ones. Unless I go mad, you will find an artist in me.'
>
> FRANZ LISZT, PIANIST AND COMPOSER

20

OCTOBER

🕐 BIRTHS & DEATHS

1874 The American composer Charles Ives is born in Danbury.

1958 Croatian pianist Ivo Pogorelich is born in Belgrade.

1977 American violinist Leila Josefowicz is born in Toronto.

🎵 FIRST PERFORMED

1877 Franz Schubert's *Symphony No. 2* is given its first performance, in Berlin.

1883 Max Bruch's *Kol Nidre* is heard for the first time, in Liverpool.

1921 Arnold Bax's *Tintagel* is premiered at the Winter Gardens in Bournemouth.

☀️ TODAY'S THE DAY

1828 Nine-year-old Clara Wieck plays the piano in concert at the Leipzig Gewandhaus for the first time.

1837 Johann Nepomuk Hummel's funeral takes place in Weimar.

1865 Cosima von Bülow collects a 40,000-florin payment from King Ludwig II of Bavaria to Richard Wagner. Treasury officials have no paper money, so they hand it over in coins. It takes two cabs to transport the money.

1874 Bedřich Smetana becomes deaf in his left ear.

1878 Clara Schumann is given a rapturous welcome by both staff and students, as she becomes a teacher at the Frankfurt Conservatoire.

1940 Béla Bartók and his wife head off to the USA on a ship from Lisbon.

1973 The Sydney Opera House is officially opened by Queen Elizabeth II.

COMPOSER FOCUS:

Henry Litolff

Litolff was one of those people always destined to have an event-filled life. His mother was Scottish and his father was a dance-master prisoner-of-war from the Alsace region of France. After studying music, Litolff eloped to Gretna Green to get married at the age of 17. He separated from his wife and ended up in prison, before escaping with the assistance of the jailer's daughter. He was finally divorced and then married again, before getting divorced for a second time and married for a third time. His third wife died and – at the age of 55 – he married once again, this time to a 17-year-old. He is chiefly noted for the Scherzo from his *Concerto Sinfonique No. 4*.

🎵 HALL OF FAME HIT

Pyotr Ilyich Tchaikovsky: *Serenade for Strings*

Recommended Recording

Camerata Lausanne conducted by Pierre Amoyal; Warner Classics 2564 652182

21

‘I had another dream the other day about music critics.
They were small and rodent-like with padlocked ears,
as if they had stepped out of a painting by Goya.’

IGOR STRAVINSKY, COMPOSER

OCTOBER

BIRTHS & DEATHS

1879 French composer Joseph Canteloube is born in Annonay.

1912 Hungarian (later British) conductor Georg Solti is born in Budapest.

1921 English composer Malcolm Arnold is born in Northampton.

FIRST PERFORMED

1858 Jacques Offenbach's opera *Orpheus in the Underworld* is premiered in Paris.

2001 Philip Glass's *Cello Concerto* is given its first performance, in Beijing.

TODAY'S THE DAY

1722 Georg Philipp Telemann asks his employers, Hamburg Council, for a big pay rise to prevent him from decamping to Leipzig; they agree.

1762 Six-year-old Wolfgang Amadeus Mozart falls ill in Vienna with scarlet fever.

1765 Maria Anna Mozart is so ill with typhus that she receives the last rites in The Hague. However, she gradually recovers.

1838 Gaetano Donizetti arrives in Paris and ends up living in the same building as fellow composer Adolphe Adam.

1848 Eight-year-old Pyotr Ilyich Tchaikovsky arrives in Moscow with his family, to discover that the job his father has been expecting to take is no longer available. The family head on to St Petersburg instead.

1861 Franz Liszt and Princess Carolyne Sayn-Wittgenstein are all set to get married tomorrow. However, late tonight a messenger arrives with news that her marriage to Liszt would be illegal. It never happens.

1892 Antonín Dvořák conducts his first concert on American soil – at Carnegie Hall in New York.

1926 A monument to Jules Massenet is unveiled in Paris, 14 years after the composer's death,

INSTRUMENT FOCUS:

Prepared piano

This does not refer to a piano that has been tuned and given the once-over with furniture polish and a vigorous rubbing with a duster. The term 'prepared piano' was coined by the 20th-century composer John Cage. In this instance the piano is prepared by having items placed inside the case on the strings. These could range from spoons, to bells, to nuts and bolts. The object is to trigger not only the notes of the piano but a series of extraneous random sounds, too. Cage's sonatas and interludes are still considered the benchmark in this area.

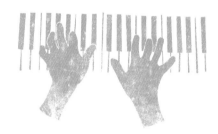

HALL OF FAME HIT

Gaetano Donizetti: *Lucia di Lammermoor*

Recommended Recording

Various soloists; Coro e Orchestra del Maggio Musicale Fiorentino, Tullio Serafin; EMI 735 9482

> 'Schubert's life was one of inner, spiritual thought, and was seldom expressed in words but almost entirely in music.'
>
> FRANZ ECKEL ABOUT HIS CHILDHOOD FRIEND, COMPOSER FRANZ SCHUBERT

22
OCTOBER

🕐 BIRTHS & DEATHS

1725 Italian composer Alessandro Scarlatti dies in Naples.

1764 French composer Jean-Marie Leclair dies in Paris.

1811 Hungarian composer and pianist Franz Liszt is born in Raiding.

1859 German composer Louis Spohr dies in Kassel.

1973 Spanish cellist and conductor Pablo Casals dies in San Juan, Puerto Rico.

1979 French pianist, teacher and conductor Nadia Boulanger dies in Paris.

🎭 FIRST PERFORMED

1987 John Adams' opera *Nixon in China* is premiered at Houston Grand Opera.

☀ TODAY'S THE DAY

1872 Ten-year-old Claude Debussy begins his studies on the piano at the Paris Conservatoire.

1880 Edvard Grieg conducts Harmonien, the Bergen Symphony Orchestra, for the first time.

1881 The Boston Symphony Orchestra gives its inaugural concert in the city's Music Hall.

1883 The USA's first permanent opera company opens at the Metropolitan Opera House in New York with a production of Charles Gounod's *Faust*.

1888 Alexander Glazunov takes to the stage as a conductor for the first time, in St Petersburg.

1904 Giacomo Puccini writes the first of an astonishing 700 letters to Sybil Seligman, the wife of a banker.

1917 Leopold Stokowski conducts the Philadelphia Orchestra in its first recording session for Victor Records in Camden, New Jersey.

1959 Dmitri Shostakovich begins a tour of American cities, as part of a cultural-exchange programme.

1983 Joan Sutherland, Plácido Domingo and Luciano Pavarotti are among the opera stars taking part in a special concert to mark the 100th anniversary of New York's Metropolitan Opera.

VENUE FOCUS:

Wigmore Hall

Based in London, this is one of the UK's busiest concert venues, hosting in excess of 400 events every year, and it's a particularly great place to go if you like the idea of more intimate chamber-music concerts and recitals, rather than the full-blown orchestral and operatic affairs available elsewhere. Completely restored in 2004, the Wigmore Hall was built at the turn of the 20th century and was commissioned by the German piano-making firm Bechstein, which had a showroom in Wigmore Street and whose directors wanted a venue in which to showcase their wares. Wigmore Hall was designed by the same architect who created the rooms on a number of P&O cruise liners: one Thomas Colcott. It's a simply beautiful place. Concerts are held there nearly every lunchtime throughout the year, so if you happen to find yourself in Mayfair in the middle of the day and you have an hour to spare, this is most definitely the place to head.

🎵 HALL OF FAME HIT

Antonio Vivaldi: *Double Concerto for 2 Mandolins RV 532*

Recommended Recording
Il Giardino Armonico; Warner Classics 2564 698542

23

OCTOBER

'Bruckner! He is my man!'

RICHARD WAGNER, COMPOSER

🎵 BIRTHS & DEATHS

1941 American conductor Lawrence Foster is born in Los Angeles.

2004 American baritone Robert Merrill dies in New York.

🎵 FIRST PERFORMED

1890 Alexander Borodin's opera *Prince Igor* is premiered in St Petersburg. Alexander Glazunov and Nikolai Rimsky-Korsakov have helped to complete the work.

1913 Frederick Delius's *On Hearing the First Cuckoo in Spring* and *Summer Night on the River* are given their first performances, in the Leipzig Gewandhaus.

☀ TODAY'S THE DAY

1828 The newspaper *Le Corsaire* publishes an obituary for 17-year-old Franz Liszt. He turns out to be very much alive.

1859 Richard Wagner and Hector Berlioz bump into each other by chance in the street in Paris. Wagner comments on Berlioz's poor health.

1910 The Orquesta Sinfónica of Barcelona performs for the first time in public.

1961 Seventeen-year-old John Tavener passes the entrance exam for the Royal Academy of Music in London.

COMPOSER PROFILE:

Charles Villiers Stanford

Though he is not among the most remembered composers now, it is a mark of the esteem in which Charles Villiers Stanford was held in his day that he was buried in Westminster Abbey, next to Henry Purcell. He was born in Dublin in 1852 and was educated there and at Queens' College, Cambridge, where, at his father's insistence, he read Classics rather than Music. Nevertheless, it was his time in Cambridge – he conducted the Music Society orchestra and became organist at Trinity College while still an undergraduate – that put him firmly on the musical map. After further study in Germany, Stanford began composing in earnest. His prodigious musical output includes 7 symphonies, 10 operas, 15 concertos, chamber, piano and organ pieces, songs, and more than 30 large-scale choral works. However, it was his role as composition professor at the then new Royal College of Music that enabled him to leave a real mark on musical posterity.

🎵 HALL OF FAME HIT

John Barry: *Out of Africa* (original soundtrack)

Recommended Recording

MCA Records; MCA 6158

'Without craftsmanship, inspiration is a mere reed shaken in the wind.'

JOHANNES BRAHMS, COMPOSER

24

OCTOBER

 BIRTHS & DEATHS

1799 Austrian composer and violinist Karl Ditters von Dittersdorf dies in Neuhaus.

1913 Italian baritone Tito Gobbi is born in Bassano del Grappa.

1925 Italian composer Luciano Berio is born in Oneglia.

1948 Hungarian composer Franz Lehár dies in Bad Ischl.

 FIRST PERFORMED

1919 George Gershwin's song 'Swanee' is sung for the first time, at the opening of the Capitol Theatre in New York. It becomes a huge hit and sets him on the pathway to becoming one of classical music's richest composers of all time.

1945 Revised for a second time, Igor Stravinsky's suite from his ballet *The Firebird* is given its first performance, in New York.

1948 Francis Poulenc's *Sinfonietta* is heard for the first time, in London as part of a radio broadcast.

 TODAY'S THE DAY

1725 Alessandro Scarlatti's funeral is held in Naples.

1818 Nine-year-old Felix Mendelssohn performs in his first public concert, in Berlin.

1836 Gioachino Rossini moves from Paris to Italy, where he will live for the next 19 years.

1836 At Franz Liszt's home in Paris, Frédéric Chopin meets George Sand, the writer who will become the love of his life.

The attraction is not instant for him though – he might well have been slightly confused by the fact that she is dressed in men's clothes.

1850 Robert Schumann conducts his first concert in Düsseldorf, with his wife Clara the star piano soloist.

1867 Richard Wagner finishes work on *Die Meistersinger von Nürnberg*.

1878 The city of Leipzig celebrates Clara Schumann and the 50th anniversary of her first public performance at the Leipzig Gewandhaus.

1919 The Los Angeles Philharmonic Orchestra gives its inaugural concert, in Trinity Auditorium.

COMPOSER PROFILE:

John Stanley

John Stanley was an English composer, born in London in 1712, who was blind from the age of two, following a fall. He was taught the organ by Maurice Greene, organist at St Paul's Cathedral, and soon was playing in his own church, aged just 11. When he was 17, he became the youngest-ever music graduate from Oxford University. Aged 22, he was made organist at the Temple Church, a job he held for the rest of his life, becoming a composing and performing phenomenon – his organ voluntaries were famous. On Handel's death, when Stanley was 48, it was he who continued the oratorio tradition at Covent Garden.

 HALL OF FAME HIT

Joaquín Rodrigo: *Fantasia para un gentilhombre*

Recommended Recording

Andrés Segovia (guitar); Symphony of the Air conducted by Enrique Jorda; Naxos Classical Archives 980916

25

OCTOBER

> 'I am Russian in the completest possible sense of that word.'
>
> PYOTR ILYICH TCHAIKOVSKY, COMPOSER

BIRTHS & DEATHS

1825 Austrian composer and conductor Johann Strauss Junior is born in Vienna.

1838 French composer Georges Bizet is born in Paris.

1895 British pianist and conductor Charles Hallé dies in Manchester.

1971 Japanese violinist Midori is born in Osaka.

FIRST PERFORMED

1821 The *Kyrie* and *Gloria* from Ludwig van Beethoven's *Missa Solemnis* are performed for the first time, in Vienna.

1873 Johann Strauss Junior plays his *Csárdás für Gesang* for the first time in Vienna. It goes down a storm with the crowds, and this spurs him on to complete the work from which it comes – his operetta *Die Fledermaus (The Bat)*.

1875 Pyotr Ilyich Tchaikovsky's *Piano Concerto No. 1* is given its first performance, in Boston.

1885 Johannes Brahms' *Symphony No. 4* receives its first performance, in Meiningen, with the composer conducting.

1912 Richard Strauss's opera *Ariadne auf Naxos* is premiered in Stuttgart.

TODAY'S THE DAY

1681 Johann Pachelbel gets married in Erfurt.

1859 Louis Spohr's funeral is held in Kassel.

1925 Steinway Hall in New York opens.

1945 The Philharmonia Orchestra gives its first concert in Kingsway Hall, London, conducted by Thomas Beecham.

The Strauss family: part I

The Strauss family is dominated by one man – Johann Strauss Junior – whose reputation overshadowed that of his father, and of his younger brothers. In the fiercely fought battleground for musical supremacy as master of the Viennese waltz, father and son ran rival orchestras. When his brother Eduard Strauss set up his own orchestra, there were three. Johann Strauss Senior was a proficient violinist and viola player, who became the founding father of the Strauss dynasty. He formed his own band when he was just 22 years old, after playing in those of the composer Joseph Lanner. Strauss was eventually booked at the Sperl Ballroom in Vienna, where he became famous. He also played for the court balls. Despite composing a couple of hundred waltzes, he would eventually be eclipsed by his son, and remembered, pretty much, for one work: the '*Radetzky March*'.

HALL OF FAME HIT

Joseph Haydn: *Cello Concerto No. 1*

Recommended Recording

Jacqueline du Pré (cello); English Chamber Orchestra conducted by Daniel Barenboim; EMI 586 5972

'The symphony must be like the world. It must embrace everything.'

GUSTAV MAHLER, COMPOSER

26
OCTOBER

 BIRTHS & DEATHS

1685 Italian composer and keyboard player Domenico Scarlatti is born in Naples.

1797 Italian soprano Giuditta Pasta is born near Milan.

1934 French pianist Jacques Loussier is born in Angers.

1955 American soprano Christine Brewer is born in Grand Tower.

1965 Finnish conductor Sakari Oramo is born in Helsinki.

 FIRST PERFORMED

1783 Wolfgang Amadeus Mozart's *Mass in C minor* is performed for the first time, in Salzburg, with the composer conducting and his wife Constanze singing a solo soprano part.

 TODAY'S THE DAY

1767 Eleven-year-old Wolfgang Amadeus Mozart begins to show signs of suffering from the smallpox epidemic that has been sweeping through Vienna.

1842 Felix Mendelssohn tries to get out of his job working for King Friedrich of Prussia for a second time. The king compromises and Mendelssohn's workload is scaled down, allowing him to travel more widely.

1921 In Paris, Nadia Boulanger agrees to take on Aaron Copland as a piano student.

1933 The German government takes over the directorship of the Berlin Philharmonic. This means that the players become civil servants, enabling the government to force Jewish players out of the orchestra, as Jewish people are barred from working for the civil service.

1969 Leonard Bernstein presides over a concert in New York to mark the official opening of the Juilliard School and the completion of building work on the Lincoln Center.

1979 Nadia Boulanger's funeral is held in Paris.

The Strauss family: part II

Despite being a composer and conductor himself, Johann Strauss Senior forbade his son from following in his footsteps. As a result, Johann Strauss Junior became a bank clerk, learning music in secret. Eventually, he set up his own orchestra (aged just 19) in opposition to his father. On his father's death, he merged both bands and became famous for his waltzes (nearly 400 of them). Spotting the potential of the stage, he switched to operetta when he was 56; his greatest example, *Die Fledermaus (The Bat)*, is a staple of the operatic repertory. He could count Brahms, Wagner and Schoenberg among his fans.

 HALL OF FAME HIT
Antonio Vivaldi: *La forza del destino*

Recommended Recording
Various soloists; Vienna State Opera Orchestra and Chorus conducted by Dimitri Mitropoulos; Andromeda ANDRCD 9110

27

OCTOBER

'There is no such thing as abstract music; there is good music and bad music. If it is good, it means something.'

RICHARD STRAUSS, COMPOSER

 BIRTHS & DEATHS

1782 Italian composer and violinist Niccolò Paganini is born in Genoa.

1961 Swedish trumpeter Håkan Hardenberger is born in Malmö.

1978 British violinist Vanessa Mae is born in Singapore.

1991 Polish conductor and composer Andrzej Panufnik dies in Twickenham.

 FIRST PERFORMED

1919 Edward Elgar's *Cello Concerto* receives its first performance, in Queen's Hall in London, with the composer conducting.

 TODAY'S THE DAY

1781 Newly rebuilt, the Paris Opéra reopens.

1824 Five-year-old Clara Wieck begins taking piano lessons from her father in Leipzig.

1886 Modest Mussorgsky's *A Night on the Bare Mountain*, reorchestrated by Rimsky-Korsakov, is given its first performance, in St Petersburg.

1893 Charles Gounod's funeral is held in Paris, with Gabriel Fauré playing the organ for the service.

1897 Sergei Rachmaninov conducts Camille Saint-Saëns' *Samson and Delilah* in Moscow. It's the first time he has conducted an opera, and also the first time he has conducted music that he himself has not written.

1917 Sixteen-year-old violinist Jascha Heifetz makes his American debut at New York's Carnegie Hall.

The Strauss family: part III

Josef and Eduard Strauss, the brothers of Johann Strauss Junior, were by no means the leading lights of the Strauss family, but they did perform an important role in keeping the tradition going. Josef deputised as conductor of the band and had a hand in the composition of the 'Pizzicato Polka', with his elder brother Johann. Eduard took over the band in 1872, and brought it to the UK. A polka specialist rather than a waltz king, he is also responsible for burning all the original manuscripts of the entire Strauss clan, which is why we have some works to this day available only in piano versions.

 HALL OF FAME HIT

Gerald Finzi: *Clarinet Concerto*

Recommended Recording

Andrew Marriner (clarinet); Academy of St Martin in the Fields conducted by Neville Marriner; Decca 476 2163

> 'There is music in the air. All you have to do is take as much as you require.'
>
> EDWARD ELGAR, COMPOSER

28

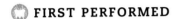

BIRTHS & DEATHS

1936 American (now British) composer and conductor Carl Davis is born in New York.

1938 English composer Howard Blake is born in London.

1943 Northern Irish conductor Kenneth Montgomery is born in Belfast.

FIRST PERFORMED

1893 Pyotr Ilyich Tchaikovsky's *Symphony No. 6* ('*Pathétique*') is given its first performance, in St Petersburg, with the composer conducting.

1915 Richard Strauss's *Alpine Symphony* is heard for the first time, in Berlin, with the composer conducting.

TODAY'S THE DAY

1544 Giovanni Pierluigi da Palestrina gets a new job as organist and choirmaster at St Agapito Cathedral in Palestrina.

1612 John Dowland is appointed 'Musician For the Lutes' by King James I.

1818 Nine-year-old Felix Mendelssohn makes his debut public performance in Berlin.

1838 Giuseppe Verdi hands in his notice as director of music in Busseto.

1847 Felix Mendelssohn suffers a mild stroke while having lunch with his wife, temporarily losing the ability to speak.

1856 Following the death of her husband Robert, Clara Schumann needs to work to support her seven children. Tonight, she gives her first concert after his death.

1873 Fire destroys the Paris Opéra.

1892 Illness forces Anton Bruckner to resign from his role as director of music at the Vienna Hofkapelle.

1926 A charter is granted to the Juilliard School of Music in New York.

1952 Soprano Joan Sutherland makes her debut at the Royal Opera House, as the First Lady in Mozart's *The Magic Flute*.

The Bach family

In a letter written today in 1730, Johann Sebastian Bach talked about his children as 'born musici'. In truth, they were born into one of the most remarkable musical clans of all time. There were 53 different members of the Bach family who held positions as organists or as church or town musicians. Johann Sebastian's principal composer offspring were: Carl Philipp Emanuel Bach, Johann Christian Bach, Johann Christoph Friedrich Bach and Wilhelm Friedmann Bach. As with their father, they tend to be known by their initials. By the way, in German the word 'Bach' means 'stream' or 'brook', which prompted Beethoven to say: 'His name should not be brook, it should be ocean!'

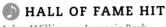

HALL OF FAME HIT
John Williams: *Jurassic Park*

Recommended Recording
Royal Liverpool Philharmonic Orchestra conducted by Carl Davis; Naxos 857 0505

29

OCTOBER

'What we want in England is real music, even if it be only music-hall song.'

RALPH VAUGHAN WILLIAMS, COMPOSER

 BIRTHS & DEATHS

1888 English composer, organist and conductor Harold Darke is born in London.

1982 English composer William Lloyd Webber dies in London.

 FIRST PERFORMED

1787 Wolfgang Amadeus Mozart's opera *Don Giovanni* is premiered in Prague. Staging it is a close-run thing though, with the composer finishing work on the overture only the previous night – forcing the orchestra to perform it without any rehearsal.

1955 Dmitri Shostakovich's *Violin Concerto No. 1* is heard for the first time, in Leningrad.

1956 Leonard Bernstein's musical *Candide* is premiered at the Colonial Theatre in Boston, ahead of its official opening in New York.

 TODAY'S THE DAY

1741 George Frideric Handel finishes work on the first draft of his oratorio *Samson*.

1787 Giovanni Paisiello is given the job of *maestro della real camera* in the Neapolitan court.

1813 Niccolò Paganini performs at La Scala, Milan, for the first time.

1873 As fire continues to rage through the Paris Opéra building, the roof collapses in the early hours of the morning. The flames are finally brought under control shortly after.

1918 Sergei Prokofiev performs his first concert in the USA at the Brooklyn Museum.

1926 John Ireland gives up his job as organist and choirmaster at St Luke's Church in Chelsea.

1940 Béla Bartók and his wife arrive in New York, after travelling from Lisbon.

1956 Soprano Maria Callas makes her debut at New York's Metropolitan Opera, in Bellini's *Norma*.

ORCHESTRA FOCUS:

Berlin Philharmonic Orchestra

Founded in 1882, the same year as Tottenham Hotspur Football Club, the Berliner Philharmoniker (to give it its correct name) is one of the world's greatest orchestras. Its list of principal conductors reads like a *Who's Who* of the greats, including Hans von Bülow, Richard Strauss, Wilhelm Furtwängler and Herbert von Karajan. The last is credited with improving the orchestra's already formidable reputation by transforming the sound and raising playing standards. Claudio Abbado succeeded von Karajan in 1989 and, 13 years later, the Liverpudlian conductor Simon Rattle was appointed to the top job, having previously made his name at the City of Birmingham Symphony Orchestra. Critics and audiences the world over continue to regard both orchestra and conductor as still being at the top of their game.

 HALL OF FAME HIT

Franz Schubert: *Die Forelle (The Trout)*

Recommended Recording

Matthias Goerne (baritone); Andreas Haefliger (piano); Harmonia Mundi HMC902141

> 'All I heard was something akin to a meteor, and then was unable to account for it.'
>
> **JOHANN WOLFGANG GOETHE DISCUSSING A PERFORMANCE BY NICCOLÒ PAGANINI IN WEIMAR, 1829**

30
OCTOBER

BIRTHS & DEATHS

1894 English composer Peter Warlock is born in London. (His real name was Philip Heseltine.)

1946 Belgian countertenor and conductor René Jacobs is born in Ghent.

1949 English conductor James Judd is born in Hertfordshire.

FIRST PERFORMED

1876 Johannes Brahms' *String Quartet No. 3* is given its first performance, in Berlin.

1881 Pyotr Ilyich Tchaikovsky's *Serenade for Strings* is heard for the first time, in Moscow.

1908 Sergei Rachmaninov's *Piano Sonata No. 1* receives its first performance, in Moscow.

1957 Dmitri Shostakovich's *Symphony No. 11* ('*The Year 1905*') is premiered in Moscow.

☀ TODAY'S THE DAY

1822 Franz Schubert completes two of the movements of his *Symphony No. 8* ('*Unfinished*').

1849 Frédéric Chopin's funeral is held in Paris. As he requested, Mozart's *Requiem* is sung. His body is buried in a Parisian cemetery, while his heart is removed and sent to the Church of the Holy Cross in Warsaw.

1859 Franz Liszt is rewarded with a place in the Australian nobility. He is to be known as Franz Ritter von Liszt.

1861 Richard Wagner shares his idea for a 'grand comic opera' called *Die Meistersinger von Nürnberg* with the publisher Schott.

1894 Richard Strauss is made conductor of the Musical Academy concerts in Munich.

1924 Ten-year-old Benjamin Britten hears an orchestra performing in concert for the very first time, in Norwich.

COMPOSER PROFILE:

Max Reger

Among the very few composers with a palindrome for a name, Reger was born in Bavaria. As well as being a composer, he was a virtuoso organist, whose performances did much to rekindle popularity for the instrument. He also had a passion for the music of Bach and Beethoven. Having settled in Munich at the age of 28, Reger won fame as a solo performer and as an accompanist, before moving to take up the post of director of music at the University of Leipzig. A heavy drinker, he died from a heart attack, aged only 43.

HALL OF FAME HIT
Klaus Badelt: *Pirates of the Caribbean*

Recommended Recording
Royal Liverpool Philharmonic Orchestra conducted by Carl Davis; Naxos 857 0505

31

OCTOBER

'My music is not modern, it is merely badly played.'

ARNOLD SCHOENBERG, COMPOSER

BIRTHS & DEATHS

1179 German composer Hildegard of Bingen dies in Rupertsberg, near Bingen.

1947 English composer Howard Skempton is born in Chester.

FIRST PERFORMED

1841 A revised version of part of Gioachino Rossini's *Stabat Mater* is heard for the first time, in Paris.

1866 Jacques Offenbach's opera *La vie parisienne* is premiered in Paris.

1875 Camille Saint-Saëns' *Piano Concerto No. 5* receives its first performance, in Paris, with the composer as soloist.

1887 Nikolai Rimsky-Korsakov's *Capriccio espagnol* is given its first performance, in St Petersburg.

1918 Frederick Delius's *Cello Sonata* receives its first performance, at the Wigmore Hall in London.

TODAY'S THE DAY

1768 Carl Philipp Emanuel Bach gives the first of 20 subscription concerts he has announced for that winter, in Hamburg.

1828 Franz Schubert falls ill after eating some fish at a restaurant. It is the beginning of a rapid decline in his health.

1867 Mily Balakirev makes his concert debut as director of the Russian Music Society, in St Petersburg.

1874 Anton Bruckner's application to become a teacher of music theory at the University of Vienna is turned down.

1877 Edward MacDowell wins a scholarship to the Paris Conservatoire.

1905 A ceremony to open the Juilliard School (then known as the Institute of Musical Art) takes place in New York.

1933 Arnold Schoenberg arrives in New York, having left Germany for the very last time.

Scandinavian nationalism

In Norway and Finland, Grieg and Sibelius were both musical firebrands in the countries' respective nationalist movements. Under the influence of the Norwegian violinist and folk historian Ole Bull, Grieg composed a huge body of music, particularly for the piano, in the national style. He is best remembered for works such as *Peer Gynt*, written as incidental music for Henrik Ibsen's fairytale play. Sibelius's music is all totally original, yet Finnish-sounding. He became a hero of Finland's struggle for full independence from Tsarist Russia with tone poems such as *Finlandia*, which occupies the same place in Finnish hearts as 'Land of Hope and Glory' does in England or 'Men of Harlech' in Wales.

HALL OF FAME HIT

Ludwig van Beethoven: *Missa Solemnis*

Recommended Recording

Various soloists; London Philharmonic Orchestra and Choir conducted by Christoph Eschenbach; LPO Live 0061

Novel

nber

01

NOVEMBER

'Verdi has bursts of marvellous passion. His passion is brutal, it is true, but it is better to be impassioned in this way than not at all.'

GEORGES BIZET ON FELLOW COMPOSER GIUSEPPE VERDI

BIRTHS & DEATHS

1877 English composer Roger Quilter is born in Hove.

1923 Spanish soprano Victoria de los Ángeles is born in Barcelona.

1934 Welsh composer William Mathias is born in Whitland.

FIRST PERFORMED

1862 The *Prelude* to Richard Wagner's *Die Meistersinger von Nürnberg* is heard for the first time, in the Leipzig Gewandhaus, with the composer conducting.

1868 Books 1 and 2 of Johannes Brahms' *Hungarian Dances* (as a duet for two pianos) are performed for the first time, in Oldenburg, with Clara Schumann joining the composer at the keyboards.

TODAY'S THE DAY

1738 George Frideric Handel finishes work on his oratorio *Israel in Egypt*.

1769 Karl Ditters (at this point without the 'von Dittersdorf' appended) starts work for the Prince-Bishop of Breslau.

1791 Antonio Salieri is sacked as the music director of the Burgtheater, although Emperor Leopold II allows him to stay on as Hofkapellmeister.

1837 Fellow composers Luigi Cherubini, Giacomo Meyerbeer, Adolphe Adam and Hector Berlioz are in the crowd to see Johann Strauss Senior and his orchestra perform Viennese waltzes at a concert in Paris.

1853 Richard Wagner begins work on his operatic triumph *Das Rheingold*.

1869 The Cairo Opera House opens with Verdi's *Rigoletto* as its first production.

1871 Richard Wagner writes to the authorities in Bayreuth to tell them about his plan for a new opera house; he receives a favourable response.

1885 At only 21 years old, and still rather wet behind the ears, Richard Strauss takes over from Hans von Bülow as court conductor in Meiningen.

1895 Antonín Dvořák starts teaching composition at the Prague Conservatoire once again,

after returning from New York.

1898 Richard Strauss begins a new job as conductor of the Berlin Opera.

1902 The Philadelphia Orchestra Association is registered as a legal entity.

1918 Sergei Rachmaninov leaves Oslo on board a ship heading for the USA.

1945 Created by the British at the end of the Second World War, in an attempt to reintroduce normal life to Germany, the Northwest German Radio Symphony Orchestra makes its debut performance in Hamburg.

1954 Maria Callas makes her debut in America in a performance of Bellini's opera *Norma*, in Chicago.

1986 Aaron Copland is awarded the Congressional Gold Medal, the US Congress's highest civilian honour.

1989 Russian pianist Vladimir Horowitz makes his final recording, just four days before his death.

HALL OF FAME HIT

Antonín Dvořák: *Serenade for Strings*

Recommended Recording

Amsterdam Sinfonietta; Channel 24409

'If one has not heard Wagner at Bayreuth, one has heard nothing!'

GABRIEL FAURÉ ON FELLOW COMPOSER RICHARD WAGNER

BIRTHS & DEATHS

1739 Austrian composer Karl Ditters von Dittersdorf is born in Vienna.

1880 English composer John Foulds is born in Manchester.

1887 Swedish soprano Jenny Lind (known as 'The Swedish Nightingale') dies at Malvern.

1946 Italian conductor Giuseppe Sinopoli is born in Venice.

FIRST PERFORMED

1979 Peter Shaffer's play with music, *Amadeus*, about the life of Wolfgang Amadeus Mozart, opens at the National Theatre in London.

TODAY'S THE DAY

1792 Ludwig van Beethoven leaves Bonn to travel to Vienna, to become a pupil of Joseph Haydn.

1830 Frédéric Chopin heads to Vienna from his home city of Warsaw; he will never return.

1834 Felix Mendelssohn resigns as opera conductor in Düsseldorf.

1842 Franz Liszt is promoted to the rather grand new title of 'Kapellmeister Extraordinary' by Grand Duke Carl Friedrich of Weimar.

1862 Nikolai Rimsky-Korsakov sets off on his first voyage as a Russian naval officer. It is to last for two and a half years.

1893 Pyotr Ilyich Tchaikovsky falls seriously ill in St Petersburg.

1907 Jean Sibelius visits Gustav Mahler while the latter is staying at a hotel in Helsinki. The two men don't fall out – but they don't exactly hit it off either.

1966 Leonard Bernstein announces that he will leave his role at the New York Philharmonic at the end of his contract in three years' time.

GENRE FOCUS:

Baroque Opera

The elder Scarlatti, Lully and Rameau all quickly got to grips with the new-style opera that had been pioneered by Monteverdi, with his *La favola d'Orfeo*. Scarlatti alone wrote well over 100 different operas. He is considered the father of the Neapolitan opera school. Purcell's *Dido and Aeneas,* from 1689, is a landmark in English opera. For some people, no composer has ever bettered the hauntingly beautiful aria '*When I am Laid in Earth*'. Handel, having learned his operatic trade in Italy, wrote 40 or so operas for Britain in his thirties. Many of them were premiered at London's Covent Garden.

HALL OF FAME HIT

Georges Bizet: *Symphony in C*

Recommended Recording
Les Siècles conducted by François Xavier Roth; Mirare MIR036

03

NOVEMBER

'If I belong to a tradition, it is a tradition that makes the masterpiece tell the performer what to do, and not the performer telling the piece what it should be like, or the composer what he ought to have composed.'

ALFRED BRENDEL, PIANIST

BIRTHS & DEATHS

1801 Italian composer Vincenzo Bellini is born in Sicily.

1933 English composer John Barry is born in York.

1993 Electronic musical-instrument inventor Leon Theremin dies in Moscow.

FIRST PERFORMED

1888 Nikolai Rimsky-Korsakov's *Scheherazade* is premiered in St Petersburg.

1945 Dmitri Shostakovich's *Symphony No. 9* in its full orchestral version is heard for the first time, in Leningrad. It had previously been performed in a piano-duet version.

TODAY'S THE DAY

1587 German organist and composer Samuel Scheidt is baptised in Halle.

1752 George Frideric Handel undergoes an operation on his eyes, to correct his failing sight. Although things initially look promising, the outcome is not positive.

1783 Wolfgang Amadeus Mozart finishes work on his *Symphony No. 36*, the day before it's due to be premiered in Linz.

1916 Fourteen-year-old William Walton wins the Composition Prize at the choir school at Oxford.

Mozart operas

To Mozart, opera was the finest medium in which a composer could operate. It is not surprising then that he contributed works that are still thought of as being the creation of a genius. He wrote three works with the librettist Lorenzo da Ponte (*The Marriage of Figaro*, *Don Giovanni* and *Così fan tutte*). Many musical historians believe that these operas have never been bettered for the synthesis of singers and orchestra, not to mention melodic beauty and level of invention.

HALL OF FAME HIT

Craig Armstrong: *Romeo and Juliet*

Recommended Recording

Royal Philharmonic Orchestra conducted by Paul Bateman; Classic FM CFMD1 10

'I have more skill, but he is greater.'

RICHARD STRAUSS ON FELLOW COMPOSER JEAN SIBELIUS

04
NOVEMBER

🎵 BIRTHS & DEATHS

1847 German composer Felix Mendelssohn dies in Leipzig.

1924 French composer Gabriel Fauré dies in Paris.

1935 English conductor and trumpet player Elgar Howarth is born in Cannock.

1957 Uzbekistani (now Australian) composer Elena Kats-Chernin is born in Tashkent.

1957 French composer Joseph Canteloube dies in Paris.

1961 English trumpeter and Principal of the Royal Academy of Music Jonathan Freeman-Attwood is born in Woking.

🎵 FIRST PERFORMED

1783 Wolfgang Amadeus Mozart's *Symphony No. 36* is first performed, in Linz.

1863 The second part of Hector Berlioz's opera *Les Troyens* is premiered in Paris.

1876 Johannes Brahms' *Symphony No. 1* is performed for the first time, in Karlsruhe.

1883 Emanuel Chabrier's *España* receives its first performance, in Paris.

1883 Johann Strauss Junior's *Lagoon Waltz, Op. 411*, is heard for the first time, in the Musikverein, Vienna.

1890 Alexander Borodin's opera *Prince Igor* (with help from Nikolai Rimsky-Korsakov and Alexander Glazunov) is premiered at the Mariinsky Theatre in St Petersburg.

1899 Jean Sibelius's *Finlandia* receives its first performance, in Helsinki.

1943 Dmitri Shostakovich's *Symphony No. 8* is given its first performance, in Moscow.

☀️ TODAY'S THE DAY

1737 The San Carlo Opera House opens in Naples.

1817 Carl Maria von Weber gets married to the soprano Caroline Brandt in Prague.

1818 Legal authorities reject Ludwig van Beethoven's appeal of the decision to allow his nephew Karl to remain living with the boy's mother.

1821 Felix Mendelssohn meets the poet Johann Wolfgang von Goethe for the first time, in Weimar. The two get on famously.

1828 All of Niccolò Paganini's lower teeth are removed in a dental operation.

1847 Hector Berlioz arrives in London ready to start work as music director of the opera company at the Drury Lane Theatre.

1879 Thirteen-year-old Erik Satie takes the entrance exam for the Paris Conservatoire. His teachers there will find his performance unremarkable.

1889 Fourteen-year-old Maurice Ravel is offered a place at the Paris Conservatoire, after passing an audition at which he played the music of Chopin.

1893 Crowds begin to gather outside the flat of Pyotr Ilyich Tchaikovsky's brother. The composer is seriously ill inside.

1909 Sergei Rachmaninov makes his debut as a solo pianist and also on American soil at Smith College, Northampton, Massachusetts.

1937 Nadia Boulanger becomes the first woman to conduct an entire Royal Philharmonic Society orchestral concert in London.

HALL OF FAME HIT
Stuart Mitchell: *Seven Wonders Suite*

Recommended Recording
Prague Symphony Orchestra; Kuhn Mixed Choir conducted by Mario Klemens; Stuart Mitchell Music DNAVAR1433

05

NOVEMBER

> 'I have commissioned 170 pieces: that's still not enough, there are still lots and lots of composers I would like to approach. When I see a composer and I see a performer, I think to combine those forces.'
>
> EVELYN GLENNIE, PERCUSSIONIST

BIRTHS & DEATHS

1940 English tenor Anthony Rolfe-Johnson is born in Tackley.

1971 English classical composer (and member of the rock band Radiohead) Jonny Greenwood is born in Oxford.

1989 Ukrainian-born American pianist Vladimir Horowitz dies in New York.

2012 American composer Elliott Carter dies in New York.

FIRST PERFORMED

1846 Robert Schumann's *Symphony No. 2* receives its first performance, in Leipzig, with Felix Mendelssohn conducting.

1882 Bedřich Smetana's *Má Vlast* is performed in full for the first time, in Prague.

1886 Alexander Glazunov's *Symphony No. 2* is given its first performance, in St Petersburg.

1910 Igor Stravinsky's *Firebird Suite* is premiered in St Petersburg.

1938 Samuel Barber's *Adagio for Strings* is heard for the first time, in New York, with Arturo Toscanini conducting a radio broadcast by the NBC Symphony Orchestra.

TODAY'S THE DAY

1832 Felix Mendelssohn is commissioned by the Philharmonic Society of London to write a symphony, an overture and a vocal composition.

1847 As soon as he learns that Felix Mendelssohn is dead, Robert Schumann hurries from Dresden to Leipzig.

1879 W. S. Gilbert and Arthur Sullivan are given an extremely warm response as they arrive in New York, ahead of productions of *HMS Pinafore* and *The Pirates of Penzance*.

1886 W. S. Gilbert reads the complete libretto of *Ruddigore* to Arthur Sullivan, ahead of the composer setting the words to music.

1894 Anton Bruckner lectures for the final time at the University of Vienna.

1898 Wagner's *Tristan and Isolde* is Richard Strauss's work of choice for his debut performance as conductor at the Berlin Court Opera.

1903 The Minneapolis Symphony Orchestra gives its first concert as a permanent body.

1936 John Barbirolli conducts the New York Philharmonic Society Orchestra for the first time.

1955 The recently rebuilt Vienna State Opera reopens after being damaged in Allied bombing.

GENRE FOCUS:

Bel canto opera

Bel canto opera is generally considered to be opera in the Italian style, written in the early 19th century, a time when singers became superstars. It seems as if audiences of the time could not get enough of these showy, coloratura classics, where sopranos were given the chance to impress with their fast, agile singing. Donizetti's *Lucia di Lammermoor* and Bellini's *Norma* are both masterpieces of this type of opera.

HALL OF FAME HIT

Camille Saint-Saëns: *Piano Concerto No. 2*

Recommended Recording

Benjamin Grosvenor (piano); Royal Liverpool Philharmonic Orchestra conducted by James Judd; Decca 478 3527

'Music is given to us with the sole purpose of establishing an order in things, including, and particularly, the coordination between man and time.'

IGOR STRAVINSKY, COMPOSER

BIRTHS & DEATHS

1814 Belgian instrument maker Adolphe Sax is born in Dinant.

1854 American composer and bandmaster John Philip Sousa is born in Washington DC.

1893 Russian composer Pyotr Ilyich Tchaikovsky dies in St Petersburg.

1941 English countertenor James Bowman is born in Oxford.

1961 Italian conductor Daniele Gatti is born in Milan.

1965 French composer Edgard Varèse dies in New York.

GENRE FOCUS:

Opera styles

The three towering figures in late-Romantic opera all specialised in their chosen discipline and rarely wrote anything else. Verdi's work is in a direct line from that of Donizetti, with an emphasis on increased drama and a huge wealth of tunes. Puccini's brand of *verismo* opera (telling real-life stories) was often considered near scandalous; as late as the 1950s, his *Tosca* was described by one critic as 'a shabby little shocker'. Wagner is a stand-alone giant in the opera world, taking the form to its absolute limit. He did away with the idea of having recitative (a form of speech-like singing) and then an aria, instead blending the whole opera into one continuous, overflowing bath of musical delight.

FIRST PERFORMED

1825 Ludwig van Beethoven's *String Quartet No. 15, Op. 132,* is performed for the first time, in Vienna.

1924 Leoš Janáček's opera *The Cunning Little Vixen* is premiered in Brno.

1935 William Walton's *Symphony No. 1* is heard in full for the first time, at the Queen's Hall in London.

1936 Sergei Rachmaninov's *Symphony No. 3* is given its first performance, in Philadelphia.

1954 Dmitri Shostakovich's *Festive Overture* receives its first performance, in Moscow.

TODAY'S THE DAY

1717 Johann Sebastian Bach is sent to prison for three weeks because he had taken a new job without permission, thereby breaking the terms of his existing employment contract.

1767 Carl Philipp Emanuel Bach is appointed music director of the five main churches in Hamburg.

1868 Alexander Borodin writes to his wife admitting that he has been having an affair with a younger woman.

1887 An incredibly generous philanthropist towards the end of his life, Giuseppe Verdi sees the hospital he has funded and project managed open its doors at Villanova near Sant'Agata.

1898 Gustav Mahler conducts the Vienna Philharmonic for the first time, performing the music of Mozart and Beethoven.

1923 Jean Sibelius is given a major cash scholarship in Helsinki, to recognise his promotion of Finnish music.

1956 The Boston Symphony Orchestra is the first American orchestra to perform in Russia, with a concert at the Leningrad Conservatoire.

HALL OF FAME HIT

Wolfgang Amadeus Mozart: *Horn Concerto No. 2*

Recommended Recording

Alessio Allegrini (horn); Orchestra Mozart conducted by Claudio Abbado; Deutsche Grammophon 477 8083

07

NOVEMBER

> 'When you hear strong, masculine music like this, stand up and use your ears like a man!'
>
> CHARLES IVES TO A CONCERTGOER WHO WAS CRITICAL OF A NEW WORK BY FELLOW COMPOSER CHARLES RUGGLES

🕐 BIRTHS & DEATHS

1866 German composer Paul Lincke is born in Berlin.

1905 English composer William Alwyn is born in Northampton.

1926 Australian soprano Joan Sutherland is born in Sydney.

1936 Welsh soprano Gwyneth Jones is born in Pontnewynydd.

1983 French composer and the only female member of 'Les Six', Germaine Tailleferre, dies in Paris.

🎭 FIRST PERFORMED

1857 Franz Liszt's *Dante Symphony* is premiered in Dresden.

1934 Sergei Rachmaninov's *Rhapsody on a Theme of Paganini* is heard for the first time, in Baltimore, with the composer at the keyboard.

☀ TODAY'S THE DAY

1847 Felix Mendelssohn's funeral takes place in Leipzig. Thousands of people watch as his coffin is loaded onto a train to be taken to Berlin.

1871 Richard Wagner is given planning permission for his new opera house in Bayreuth.

2003 Chinese pianist Lang Lang makes his recital debut at New York's Carnegie Hall.

COMPOSER PROFILE:

Johann Sebastian Bach

Among the greatest composers of all time, Johann Sebastian Bach strode like a colossus across the Baroque period of classical music. His life fell into three main sections, divided up neatly by where he was working: Weimar for nine years from the age of 23, Cöthen for six years from when he was 32 and Leipzig for 27 years from when he was 38 until his death. His huge musical output is testament to the fact that Bach was undoubtedly a hard-working man. But he was also somewhat feisty, always seeming to be arguing with someone important – more often than not the person who was paying his wages. He even ended up in prison for a month when he first started working in Cöthen: he had annoyed his previous employers at Weimar so much that they ordered him to be locked up for disloyalty. Writing church music was how Bach earned his living day to day, with a deluge of cantatas coming from his pen, as well as the *St Matthew Passion*, the *St John Passion* and the great Mass in B minor. Alongside this, there was a constant stream of secular instrumental music, such as the *Brandenburg Concertos*. These were written speculatively in the hope of gaining patronage and further commissions.

🎵 HALL OF FAME HIT

Ludwig van Beethoven: *Piano Sonata No. 23 ('Appassionata')*

Recommended Recording

Alfred Brendel (piano); Alto ALC 1016

'I do not compose, I assemble materials.'

AARON COPLAND, COMPOSER

08
NOVEMBER

 BIRTHS & DEATHS

1883 English composer Arnold Bax is born in Streatham.

1890 French composer César Franck dies in Paris.

1941 English violinist Simon Standage is born in High Wycombe.

1947 Japanese (later British) conductor Tadaaki Otaka is born in Kamakura.

FIRST PERFORMED

1879 Johannes Brahms' *Violin Sonata in G* is given its first performance, in Vienna, with the composer at the piano.

TODAY'S THE DAY

1692 Johann Pachelbel is appointed the town organist in Gotha.

1768 Giovanni Battista Sammartini is appointed *maestro di cappella* of the Regia Ducal Corte, in Milan.

1770 In Spain, Luigi Boccherini is given the job of 'violincellist of his Chamber and composer of music with the authorisation of H. M. Charles III'.

1793 The Institut National de Musique is set up in France, with François-Joseph Gossec as its first director.

1830 Eleven-year-old pianist Clara Wieck makes her official debut at the Leipzig Gewandhaus.

1838 Frédéric Chopin arrives in Mallorca for a working break, along with George Sand and her two children.

1847 Felix Mendelssohn's funeral train arrives in Berlin, where his body is buried close to the grave of his sister Fanny, who has been dead for less than a year.

1873 Budapest throws a three-day festival to celebrate Franz Liszt's half-century as a composer and performer.

1909 The Boston Opera Company gives its debut performance at the new Boston Opera House.

1924 Gabriel Fauré is honoured with a state funeral in Paris, at which his own *Requiem* is performed.

1949 Maria Callas makes her first commercial recording in Turin.

1952 Maria Callas makes her debut at London's Covent Garden.

10 favourite ballets

Tchaikovsky:	*Swan Lake*
Tchaikovsky:	*The Sleeping Beauty*
Tchaikovsky:	*Nutcracker*
Adam:	*Giselle*
Prokofiev:	*Romeo and Juliet*
Massenet:	*Manon*
Hérold:	*La fille mal gardée*
Prokofiev:	*Cinderella*
Stravinsky:	*The Rite of Spring*
Delibes:	*Coppélia*

 HALL OF FAME HIT

Camille Saint-Saëns: *Introduction and Rondo Capriccioso*

Recommended Recording

Kyung-Wha Chung (violin); Royal Philharmonic Orchestra conducted by Charles Dutoit; Decca 444 5522

09
NOVEMBER

> 'I don't think there has been such an inspired melodist on this earth since Tchaikovsky.'
>
> **LEONARD BERNSTEIN ON FELLOW COMPOSER GEORGE GERSHWIN**

 BIRTHS & DEATHS

1965 Welsh baritone Bryn Terfel is born in Pant Glas.

1993 English composer Stanley Myers, whose *Cavatina* was featured in the film *The Deer Hunter*, dies in London.

 FIRST PERFORMED

1881 Johannes Brahms' *Piano Concerto No. 2* is given its first performance, in Budapest, with the composer as soloist.

1896 The second movement of Gustav Mahler's *Symphony No. 3* is heard for the first time, in Berlin.

1901 Sergei Rachmaninov's *Piano Concerto No. 2* is performed in full for the first time, in Moscow, with the composer as soloist.

1940 Joaquín Rodrigo's *Concierto de Aranjuez* is given its first performance, in Barcelona.

1940 A suite from Aaron Copland's ballet *Billy the Kid* receives its first performance, in New York.

 TODAY'S THE DAY

1734 George Frideric Handel begins his first season at London's Covent Garden with his opera *Il pastor fido*.

1766 Leopold, Wolfgang and Maria Anna Mozart end their European tour in Munich, before heading home to Salzburg.

1823 Gioachino Rossini visits Paris for the first time, en route to England.

1835 Sixteen-year-old Clara Wieck performs her own *Piano Concerto* at the Leipzig Gewandhaus with Felix Mendelssohn conducting.

1884 Pyotr Ilyich Tchaikovsky visits Mily Balakirev at his home in St Petersburg. While he is there, he meets Nikolai Rimsky-Korsakov and Alexander Glazunov.

1893 Three requiems are sung for Pyotr Ilyich Tchaikovsky, as his body is taken from his brother's flat to a St Petersburg cemetery. He is buried not far from Alexander Borodin, Modest Mussorgsky and Mikhail Glinka.

VENUE FOCUS:

Concertgebouw

Concertgebouw is Dutch for 'concert building' and the Royal Concertgebouw Orchestra has the Concertgebouw in Amsterdam as its home. The orchestra came to international prominence under its second conductor, Willem Mengelberg. He was forbidden to conduct after the Second World War because of his collaboration with the Nazi occupiers of the Netherlands. More recent conductors have included Bernard Haitink and Riccardo Chailly. Mariss Jansons, regarded by some as the greatest living conductor, took over the baton in 2004. In 1988, the orchestra was granted 'Royal' status by Queen Beatrix of the Netherlands and, in 2008, *Gramophone* magazine named the Concertgebouw as the top orchestra in the world.

 HALL OF FAME HIT

Ludwig van Beethoven: *Fidelio*

Recommended Recording

Various soloists; Metropolitan Opera Orchestra and Chorus conducted by Karl Böhm; Sony 8869 7853092

> 'With my whole heart I consign Mussorgsky's music to the devil; it is the most vulgar and foul parody of music.'
>
> CLAUDE LÉVI-STRAUSS, ANTHROPOLOGIST

10
NOVEMBER

 BIRTHS & DEATHS

1483 German hymn composer and religious reformer Martin Luther is born in Eisleben.

1668 French composer and organist François Couperin is born in Paris.

1928 Italian composer Ennio Morricone is born in Rome.

1944 English lyricist Tim Rice is born in Amersham.

1955 English organist and choirmaster David Flood is born in Guildford.

1967 German counter-tenor Andreas Scholl is born in Eltville.

 **FIRST PERFORMED**

1862 Giuseppe Verdi's opera *La forza del destino* is premiered in St Petersburg.

1872 The first suite from Georges Bizet's incidental music to *L'arlésienne* is performed for the first time, in Paris.

1910 Edward Elgar's *Violin Concerto* is given its first performance, in Queen's Hall, London, with the composer conducting and Fritz Kreisler as soloist.

 TODAY'S THE DAY

1872 Johannes Brahms conducts the Vienna Gesellschaftskonzerte for the first time, launching a campaign to promote the music of Johann Sebastian Bach and George Frideric Handel, both of whom have been dead for more than 100 years.

1888 Thirteen-year-old violinist Fritz Kreisler makes his American debut at the old Steinway Hall in New York.

1890 César Franck is buried at Montrouge. Emanuel Chabrier, Léo Delibes, Gabriel Fauré, Charles-Marie Widor and Edouard Lalo are all among the mourners.

COMPOSER PROFILE:

Léo Delibes

A graduate of the Paris Conservatoire, Delibes was an organist as well as a composer. After leaving his student years behind him, he took up playing the piano at the Théâtre Lyrique. From this point, he never looked back, specialising particularly in writing operettas and ballets. His big hits include the ballets *Coppélia* and *Sylvia* and his opera *Lakmé*. Delibes is buried in Montmartre Cemetery in Paris, alongside Degas, Dumas and other famous Ds.

 HALL OF FAME HIT

Claude Debussy: *La mer*

Recommended Recording

Seoul Philharmonic Orchestra conducted by Myung-Whun Chung; Deutsche Grammophon 476 4498

11

NOVEMBER

'I have always kept one end in view, namely, with all good will to conduct a well-regulated church music to the honour of God.'

JOHANN SEBASTIAN BACH, COMPOSER

🛈 BIRTHS & DEATHS
1858 Italian castrato Alessandro Moreschi is born near Rome.
1930 English conductor Vernon Handley is born in London.

🐾 FIRST PERFORMED
1760 William Boyce's anthem '*The Souls of the Righteous*' is performed for the first time, during the funeral of King George II.
1889 Richard Strauss's symphonic poem *Don Juan* is given its first performance, in Weimar, with the composer conducting.
1889 Edward Elgar's *Salut d'amour* is heard for the first time, in London's Crystal Palace.

1898 English composer Samuel Coleridge-Taylor's *Hiawatha* is premiered in London.

☀ TODAY'S THE DAY
1821 Twelve-year-old Felix Mendelssohn is compared to the child prodigy Wolfgang Amadeus Mozart after his *Piano Quartet in D* is performed in Weimar.
1830 The family of 17-year-old Giuseppe Verdi is forced to move into a pub after failing to pay the rent.
1846 Frédéric Chopin arrives in Paris without the love of his life, George Sand. Their relationship has hit the rocks.
1891 Gustav Holst makes his public concert debut, performing

Brahms' *Hungarian Dances* with his father at the Montpelier Rotunda in Cheltenham.
1918 Richard Strauss becomes the interim artistic adviser for the Berlin Opera.
1923 In a diary entry today, the Finnish composer Jean Sibelius writes of his battle with alcoholism, which has begun to affect his work: 'Alcohol, which I gave up, is now my most faithful companion. And the most understanding! Everything and everyone else have largely failed me.'

ENSEMBLE FOCUS:
Southbank Sinfonia

Southbank Sinfonia bridges the gap for professional musicians between the time when they finish their training at a music conservatoire and being offered their first job as part of a professional orchestra. Every year, a group of mostly twenty-something musicians from around the world comes together in the Waterloo area of London, on the south bank of the River Thames, for a nine-month programme of performance and professional development, led by Music Director Simon Over, as well as other distinguished conductors. The Southbank Sinfonia can often be heard on Classic FM accompanying performances by the Parliament Choir, which is made up of members of both the House of Commons and the House of Lords.

🎵 HALL OF FAME HIT
Maurice Ravel: *Piano Concerto for the Left Hand*

Recommended Recording
Philippe Entremont (piano); New York Philharmonic Orchestra conducted by Pierre Boulez; Sony 8287 6873742

> 'Prince, what you are, you are by the accident of your birth; what I am, I am of myself.'
>
> **LUDWIG VAN BEETHOVEN, IN A LETTER TO PRINCE LICHNOWSKY**

12
NOVEMBER

🏛 BIRTHS & DEATHS

1883 Alexander Borodin is born in St Petersburg.

2010 Polish composer Henryk Górecki dies in Katowice.

2013 English composer John Tavener dies in Dorset.

🎭 FIRST PERFORMED

1881 Pyotr Ilyich Tchaikovsky's *Piano Concerto No. 2* is given its first performance, in New York.

1887 Nikolai Rimsky-Korsakov's *Capriccio Espagnol* is heard for the first time, in St Petersburg. Tchaikovsky is in the audience.

☀ TODAY'S THE DAY

1806 Music publisher Muzio Clementi arrives in Vienna. While he's in the city he will buy the rights to some of Ludwig van Beethoven's recent compositions.

1837 Franz Liszt writes glowing reviews for a set of piano works by Robert Schumann in the Paris *Gazette musicale*.

1848 Franz Liszt conducts the overture to Richard Wagner's *Tannhäuser* in the Court Theatre in Weimar. It's the first time he has conducted Wagner's music.

1902 The first million-selling record is recorded – Enrico Caruso singing '*Vesti la giubba*' from Leoncavallo's opera *Pagliacci*.

1913 Heitor Villa-Lobos gets married to pianist Lucília Guimarães in Rio de Janeiro.

1931 The first recording is made in the now legendary Abbey Road studios in London's St John's Wood. Edward Elgar conducts a recording of his *Falstaff*.

1962 In Gorky, Dmitri Shostakovich conducts his own music in a public concert performance for the only time in his career.

Fantasia

Today, in 1940, Walt Disney released his classical music cartoon *Fantasia*, which sees Mickey Mouse joining Leopold Stokowski conducting the Philadelphia Orchestra. It followed a long tradition of using classical music in Disney animations, with the *Silly Symphonies* series dating back to 1928. But this took it to a new level, embracing revolutionary sound-recording techniques. The Philadelphia Orchestra was booked by Disney for 42 days of recording to get the soundtrack just right. The classical music featured in the film includes:

Johann Sebastian Bach:	*Toccata and Fugue in D*
Pyotr Ilyich Tchaikovsky:	*Nutcracker Suite*
Paul Dukas:	*The Sorcerer's Apprentice*
Igor Stravinsky:	*The Rite of Spring*
Ludwig van Beethoven:	*The Pastoral Symphony*
Amilcare Ponchielli:	*The Dance of the Hours*
Modest Mussorgsky:	*A Night on the Bare Mountain*

HALL OF FAME HIT

Frédéric Chopin: *Fantaisie-Impromptu in C sharp minor*

Recommended Recording

Yundi Li (piano); Deutsche Grammophon 479 1302

13

'An opera must draw tears, cause horror, bring death, by means of a song.'

VINCENZO BELLINI, COMPOSER

NOVEMBER

🎵 BIRTHS & DEATHS

1817 French organist and composer Louis Lefébure-Wely is born in Paris.

1868 Italian composer Gioachino Rossini dies in Paris.

1988 Hungarian conductor Antal Dorati dies in Gerzensee.

🌅 TODAY'S THE DAY

1756 Leopold Mozart gets a new job as violin teacher at the Kapellhaus in Salzburg.

1762 Johann Christian Bach makes his professional concert debut in London.

1767 Carl Philipp Emanuel Bach agrees to become music director of a group of five churches in Hamburg.

1840 Hector Berlioz is sent to prison for 24 hours as punishment for not turning up for National Guard duty.

1842 King Friedrich II offers Felix Mendelssohn the role of Kapellmeister. The composer declines, saying that he would prefer it if the king funded a new conservatoire in Leipzig.

1855 Anton Bruckner half-heartedly takes part in a competition in Linz to find the new cathedral organist there. He is clearly the outstanding candidate and a surprised Bruckner is offered the job.

1915 In a mark of the growing respect for his musical output, the first mainstream concert of

Heitor Villa-Lobos's work is held in Brazil.

1951 Aaron Copland gives the first of his six lectures as a professor at Harvard University.

1972 Alexander Glazunov is buried in Leningrad, after his body is repatriated from Paris.

COMPOSER PROFILE:

Christoph Willibald von Gluck

This German cellist was lucky enough to spend his formative years fairly loaded down with princely patrons, who paid his way. He studied in Milan and developed a penchant for opera, becoming much in demand as a composer. By the 1750s, he started to develop the idea of enhancing the drama in operas, as well as singing. The reform did not always go down well with the divas on stage, but it was a huge step forward in the history of opera and set a new benchmark for the composers who followed him. He made plenty of cash along the way and was to be found living in quite some style in Vienna at the end of his life. He died after quaffing an after-dinner liqueur – against his doctor's orders.

🎵 HALL OF FAME HIT

Dmitri Shostakovich: *Symphony No. 7 ('Leningrad')*

Recommended Recording

Royal Liverpool Philharmonic Orchestra conducted by Vasily Petrenko; Naxos 8573057

> 'Such sweet compulsion doth in music lie.'
> JOHN MILTON, AUTHOR

14
NOVEMBER

🎵 BIRTHS & DEATHS

1719 German-Austrian composer Leopold Mozart, father of Wolfgang Amadeus, is born in Augsburg.

1778 German composer and pianist Johann Nepomuk Hummel is born in Pressburg.

1805 German composer Fanny Mendelssohn is born in Hamburg.

1900 American composer Aaron Copland is born in Brooklyn.

1927 Spanish guitarist Narciso Yepes is born in Marchena.

1930 British pianist Peter Katin is born in London.

1946 Spanish composer Manuel de Falla dies in Alta Gracia, Argentina. His full name was Manuel Maria de los Dolores Clemente Ramon del Sagrado Corazon de Jesus de Falla y Matheu.

1946 American composer Jay Ungar is born in New York.

1977 English composer Richard Addinsell dies in London.

🎵 FIRST PERFORMED

1906 The overture to Leoš Janáček's opera *Jenůfa* is premiered in Paris.

☀ TODAY'S THE DAY

1769 Thirteen-year-old Wolfgang Amadeus Mozart is given the job of Third Konzertmeister to the Salzburg court, although the role doesn't come with any remuneration.

1787 Christoph Willibald von Gluck suffers a stroke for a fourth time.

1815 Ludwig van Beethoven's brother, who is seriously ill, draws up a will making his wife and brother co-guardians of his young son. The composer is outraged.

1816 Niccolò Paganini is ordered to pay damages to the father of a woman who has become pregnant by him. The composer and violin virtuoso refuses to pay.

1875 The National Hungarian Royal Academy of Music opens with Franz Liszt as its president.

1915 Enrique Granados performs in public for the final time, at his home in Barcelona.

1937 Leonard Bernstein and Aaron Copland meet for the first time, at the latter's birthday party in New York.

1943 Leonard Bernstein steps in as conductor of the New York Philharmonic when the conductor Bruno Walter suddenly falls ill. The concert is broadcast live and Bernstein proves to be an instant sensation.

COMPOSER PROFILE:

Orlando Gibbons

Gibbons moved in exalted 17th-century circles: born in Oxford, he sang in the choir of King's College, Cambridge, and studied music at the university. The organist at both the Chapel Royal and Westminster Abbey, he also worked as one of the king's chamber musicians. He died in Canterbury after suffering an apoplectic fit and was buried in the Cathedral there. During his relatively short life, he wrote some notable church anthems, including 'This is the Record of John'.

HALL OF FAME HIT
Pyotr Ilyich Tchaikovsky: *Eugene Onegin*

Recommended Recording
Various soloists; St Petersburg Chamber Choir; Orchestre de Paris conducted by Semyon Bychkov; Philips 475 7017

15

NOVEMBER

> 'The metronome has no value . . . for I myself have never believed that my blood and a mechanical instrument go well together.'
>
> **JOHANNES BRAHMS, COMPOSER**

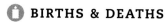 BIRTHS & DEATHS

1738 German astronomer and composer William Herschel is born in Hanover.

1787 German composer Christoph Willibald von Gluck dies in Vienna.

1905 English conductor and violinist Annunzio Paolo Mantovani is born in Venice.

1942 Israeli conductor and pianist Daniel Barenboim is born in Buenos Aires.

FIRST PERFORMED

1807 Ludwig van Beethoven's *Symphony No. 4* receives its first performance, in Vienna.

1891 Edvard Grieg's *Peer Gynt Suite No. 2* is heard for the first time, in Oslo.

1920 Gustav Holst's *The Planets* is given its first complete performance at the Queen's Hall in London, with the composer conducting.

1928 George Gershwin's *An American in Paris* is premiered in New York.

TODAY'S THE DAY

1810 Twelve-year-old Gaetano Donizetti wins a place at art school – a pathway he chose because he was worried that he wasn't good enough to be allowed to study music.

1815 Ludwig van Beethoven's brother dies of tuberculosis in Vienna. A protracted battle begins between the composer and his sister-in-law over custody of the dead man's son.

1863 Johannes Brahms conducts the first concert performance by the Vienna Singakademie.

1874 Giuseppe Verdi is appointed to the Italian Senate, but he isn't sworn in to his new role as he is desperate not to become involved in a production of his opera *Aida* taking place in Rome, so he avoids going to the capital.

1875 Verdi finally goes to Rome to be sworn into the Italian Senate – a year later than he should have done.

1893 Nikolai Rimsky-Korsakov resigns his position as assistant superintendent of the Imperial Court Chapel – mainly because he can't stand the man who is superintendent, fellow composer Mily Balakirev.

COMPOSER PROFILE:

Gerald Finzi

One of the most underrated English composers, Finzi deserves to be mentioned in the same breath as Elgar and Vaughan Williams. His settings of the poems of Thomas Hardy are particularly beautiful. He did a lot to revive the music of earlier and lesser-known English composers, such as William Boyce and John Stanley, with performances of their works being given by his group, the Newbury String Players. Two interesting footnotes: between 1941 and 1945, he worked in the Ministry of War Transport; he also became an expert cultivator of rare apples.

HALL OF FAME HIT

Jon Lord: *Boom of the Tingling Strings*

Recommended Recording

Nelson Goerner (piano); Odense Symphony Orchestra conducted by Paul Mann; EMI Classics 390 5282

> 'I want to attain the unknown. What I already know is boundless. But I want to go even further. The final word still eludes me.'
>
> **FERRUCCIO BUSONI, COMPOSER**

16

NOVEMBER

 BIRTHS & DEATHS

1895 German-born American composer and viola player Paul Hindemith is born in Hanau.

1946 English organist and choral director Edward Higginbottom is born in Kendal.

1954 Scottish conductor Donald Runnicles is born in Edinburgh.

FIRST PERFORMED

1908 Widely acknowledged as the first proper film score, *L'assassinat du Duc de Guise* by Camille Saint-Saëns is heard for the first time, in Paris.

TODAY'S THE DAY

1821 Seventeen-year-old Hector Berlioz begins his studies for a medical degree in Paris.

1848 Frédéric Chopin makes his final public performance, at a fundraising concert in aid of Polish refugees at London's Guildhall.

1851 Georges Bizet wins the second prize for piano at the Paris Conservatoire.

1862 Johannes Brahms performs in concert in Vienna for the first time, to great critical acclaim.

1868 Cosima von Bülow walks out on her husband, the conductor Hans von Bülow, to move in with the father of her two daughters, Richard Wagner.

1875 Arthur Sullivan performs with the Glasgow Choral Union for the first time as its conductor.

1900 The Philadelphia Orchestra gives its first concert at the Academy of Music in Philadelphia.

1909 Béla Bartók marries one of his students in Budapest.

COMPOSER PROFILE:

Arvo Pärt

Pärt studied in Talinn, the capital city of his native Estonia, doubling up as a recording engineer for Estonian Radio and writing film music in his free time. Early on, he was considered one of the firebrands of modern Estonian music, before entering two periods of self-imposed silence. The first came about as the result of the banning of his *Credo* by the Soviet regime and the second resulted from his decision to transform his musical style. As a result, his music became minimalist and ethereal, reflecting Pärt's passion for plainchant. Soon, he became well known for what he called his 'tintinnabuli' pieces, hypnotic works in which there are very few notes and the music is saturated with bell-like motifs. Indeed, Pärt's word for them comes from the Latin for 'little bells'.

 HALL OF FAME HIT
Johannes Brahms: *Academic Festival Overture*

Recommended Recording
Berlin Philharmonic Orchestra conducted by Claudio Abbado; Deutsche Grammophon 2542 120

17

NOVEMBER

> 'There are two kinds: one takes the music too fast, and the other too slow. There is no third.'
>
> **COMPOSER CAMILLE SAINT-SAËNS ON CONDUCTORS**

🎵 BIRTHS & DEATHS

1925 Australian conductor Charles Mackerras is born in Schenectady.

1959 Brazilian composer Heiter Villa-Lobos dies in Rio de Janeiro.

1984 Czech composer Jan Novák dies in Neu-Ulm, Germany.

🎵 FIRST PERFORMED

1828 Ferdinand Hérold's ballet *La fille mal gardée* is premiered in Paris.

1876 Pyotr Ilyich Tchaikovsky's *Marche slave* receives a rapturous reception at its first performance, in Moscow.

1877 W. S. Gilbert and Arthur Sullivan's *The Sorcerer* – their first major collaboration – opens in London.

1878 Antonín Dvořák's *Slavonic Rhapsodies Nos 1 and 2* are heard for the first time, in Prague.

1888 Pyotr Ilyich Tchaikovsky's *Symphony No. 5* is given its first performance, in St Petersburg, with the composer conducting.

🎵 TODAY'S THE DAY

1774 Wolfgang Amadeus Mozart finishes work on his *Symphony No. 28* in Salzburg.

1787 Chistoph Willibald von Gluck's funeral takes place in Vienna.

1873 Antonín Dvořák gets married to one of his students.

1898 W. S. Gilbert and Arthur Sullivan take a bow on stage at London's Savoy Theatre to mark the 21st anniversary of their first full-length joint work. By now, though, their relationship has collapsed and the two will never set eyes on each other again.

1940 A German bombing raid on London destroys scenery and costumes being stored by the D'Oyly Carte Opera Company productions of Gilbert and Sullivan's operettas *The Sorcerer*, *HMS Pinafore*, *Princess Ida* and *Ruddigore*.

COMPOSER PROFILE:

Zoltán Kodály

Kodály was the son of a music-loving employee of the state railway company. His first orchestral piece was played by his school orchestra while he was still a pupil. After studying at Budapest University, he began his lifelong love affair with the folk music of Hungary and was an avid collector of tunes that had previously only been handed down by word of mouth from generation to generation. He became a good friend of fellow Hungarian composer Béla Bartók and together they indulged their passion for folk music, as well as setting up an organisation that promoted the performance of contemporary music. Kodály became an important figure in the Hungarian music scene, occupying some of the most prestigious academic music jobs in the country. Towards the end of his life, he was still travelling extensively around Europe and the USA conducting his own works.

🎵 HALL OF FAME HIT
Jeremiah Clarke: *The Prince of Denmark's March*

Recommended Recording
Maurice André (trumpet); Jane Parker-Smith (organ); EMI 476 9542

'After silence, that which comes nearest to expressing the inexpressible is music.'

ALDOUS HUXLEY, WRITER

18
NOVEMBER

🕐 BIRTHS & DEATHS

1836 English playwright and lyricist William Schwenck Gilbert is born in London.

1860 Composer, pianist and first premier of Poland Ignacy Jan Paderewski is born in Vinnytsia Oblast.

1899 Hungarian conductor Eugene Ormandy is born in Budapest.

1978 Latvian conductor Andris Nelsons is born in Riga.

2003 American film composer Michael Kamen dies in London.

2012 English organist and choral conductor Philip Ledger dies in the Cotswolds.

🎹 FIRST PERFORMED

1821 Franz Schubert's song 'Der Wanderer' is given its first performance, in Vienna.

1866 Johann Strauss Junior's *Express-Polka Schnell*, the waltz *Feen-Marchen* and the polka française *Wildfeuer* are performed for the first time, in Vienna.

1875 Johannes Brahms' *Piano Quartet No. 3* receives its first performance, with the composer at the piano.

☀ TODAY'S THE DAY

1741 George Frideric Handel arrives in Dublin ready for a series of six sell-out concerts in the city.

1763 Leopold, Wolfgang and Maria Anna Mozart arrive in Paris on the latest leg of their European tour.

1779 A fire in the Esterházy palace destroys some of Joseph Haydn's musical manuscripts.

1791 Wolfgang Amadeus Mozart is seen in public for the final time, at a masonic meeting in Vienna.

1839 Mikhail Glinka writes to his wife to tell her that he is leaving her on account of her unfaithfulness – although he himself has previously strayed from the marital bed.

1875 Anton Bruckner gets a new job as teacher of harmony and counterpoint at the University of Vienna – although it doesn't come with a salary.

1883 The Czech National Opera House opens in Prague.

1892 The New York Philharmonic gives its first concert in New York's Carnegie Hall.

1893 Eleven-year-old Igor Stravinsky hears a performance of Tchaikovsky's *Symphony No. 6*, just days after the older composer's death.

1951 Joaquín Rodrigo is made a member of the Academy of Fine Arts of San Fernando, in Madrid.

🎵 HALL OF FAME HIT

Frédéric Chopin: *Prelude Op. 28 No. 15 ('Raindrop')*

Recommended Recording

Martha Argerich (piano); Deutsche Grammophon 463 6632

19

NOVEMBER

'I've not heard a greater artist!'

COMPOSER LEOŠ JANÁČEK ON HEARING A PERFORMANCE IN LEIPZIG IN 1879 BY PIANIST ANTON RUBINSTEIN

BIRTHS & DEATHS

1786 German composer Carl Maria von Weber is born in Eutin.

1828 German composer Franz Schubert dies in Vienna.

1859 Russian composer Mikhail Ippolitov-Ivanov is born in Gatchina.

1934 English conductor David Lloyd-Jones is born in London.

FIRST PERFORMED

1810 Carl Maria von Weber's *Piano Concerto No. 1* is given its first performance, in Mannheim.

1826 Felix Mendelssohn's overture to *A Midsummer Night's Dream* is heard for the first time, in Berlin.

1849 Franz Schubert's *Symphony No. 4* receives its first performance, in Leipzig, 21 years after the composer's death.

1875 Pyotr Ilyich Tchaikovsky's *Symphony No. 3* is performed for the first time, in Moscow.

TODAY'S THE DAY

1736 Johann Sebastian Bach is appointed court composer by King Augustus III of Poland.

1816 Carl Maria von Weber gets engaged to the soprano Caroline Brandt in Berlin.

1839 Franz Liszt wows Viennese audiences with the first of six recitals in the city.

1871 Giuseppe Verdi hears Richard Wagner's opera *Lohengrin* in Bologna. His verdict is not altogether positive, though, with him branding the opera 'mediocre'.

1888 Edward MacDowell makes his debut as a pianist in Boston.

1936 In a technological first, the London Philharmonic Orchestra and their conductor Thomas Beecham record a performance on magnetic tape at BASF's concert hall in Germany.

1957 Leonard Bernstein is appointed music director of the New York Philharmonic.

ORCHESTRA FOCUS:

Los Angeles Philharmonic

One of the greatest American orchestras, the Los Angeles Philharmonic is based at the Walt Disney Concert Hall in the winter and at the Hollywood Bowl in the summer. It was unsurprising when the Los Angeles Philharmonic came calling for Gustavo Dudamel, known to many as 'The Dude', and appointed him its music director. There can be few individuals who are both a credible classical music performer and who have a big enough personality to stand out in Tinseltown. It's testament to Dudamel's magnetic charm that he has appeared in a television advertisement for California alongside Governor Arnie Schwarzenegger. Aside from its work in the concert hall, the LA Phil is also making a name for itself in the area of music education, with a community music programme for young people in neighbourhoods right across the city built around the Youth Orchestra Los Angeles (YOLA) project. The orchestra records on the Deutsche Grammophon label, as well as making its concerts available across the world online, including the first full-length classical music video released on iTunes.

HALL OF FAME HIT

Erik Satie: *6 Gnossiennes*

Recommended Recording

Alexandre Tharaud (piano); Harmonia Mundi HMX 2908450/51

> 'A great name has disappeared from the world. His was the most extensive, the most popular reputation of our time. And it was an Italian glory.'
>
> **GIUSEPPE VERDI ON FELLOW COMPOSER GIOACHINO ROSSINI**

20

NOVEMBER

 BIRTHS & DEATHS

1894 Russian pianist, composer and conductor Anton Rubinstein dies in Petrodvorets.

1948 American soprano Barbara Hendricks is born in Stephens, Arkansas.

 FIRST PERFORMED

1805 Ludwig van Beethoven's opera *Leonore* is premiered in Vienna. It doesn't go down well with the audience or the critics and he never writes an opera again, although he continues polishing this work, with it eventually being premiered all over again as *Fidelio* some nine years later. At that point, it is a two-act work, rather than the three acts of today's original performance. Luigi Cherubini is in the audience for tonight's premiere.

1889 Gustav Mahler's *Symphony No. 1* is heard for the first time, in Budapest, with the composer conducting.

1911 Gustav Mahler's *Das Lied von der Erde* is premiered in Munich.

1919 Claude Debussy's *Fantaisie* for piano and orchestra receives its first performance, in London.

☀ **TODAY'S THE DAY**

1663 Johann Christoph Bach is given the job of organist of the Arnstadt castle chapel.

1847 Fourteen-year-old Johannes Brahms gives his first public concert, in Birgfeld.

1868 Gioachino Rossini's body is moved to L'Eglise de la Trinité in Paris in readiness for his funeral.

1882 Ten-year-old Alexander Scriabin performs on the piano for the first time in public at a concert given by the Cadet Corps in Moscow.

1895 To mark the 200th anniversary of Henry Purcell's death, the first performance of *Dido and Aeneas* for two centuries is staged by the Royal College of Music. Ralph Vaughan Williams and Gustav Holst – both of whom are students at the College – are among the performers.

1918 Sergei Prokofiev appears for the first time in the USA, in a concert in New York. Sergei Rachmaninov is among those in the audience.

OPERETTA FOCUS:

The Mikado

Today in 1884, W. S. Gilbert handed over the libretto of *The Mikado* to composer Arthur Sullivan. This comeback operetta, following the less successful *Princess Ida*, gave the Gilbert and Sullivan partnership its longest ever run of 672 performances. It ran in London and New York and eventually transferred to Vienna and Berlin, before the show moved on to France, Holland, Hungary, Spain, Belgium, Germany and Russia. This helps to give some sense of the scale of the Gilbert and Sullivan phenomenon.

 HALL OF FAME HIT

Leonard Bernstein: *West Side Story Suite*

Recommended Recording

New York Philharmonic Orchestra conducted by Leonard Bernstein; Sony 8869 7700432

21
NOVEMBER

'Music expresses that which cannot be said and on which it is impossible to be silent.'

VICTOR HUGO, WRITER

BIRTHS & DEATHS

1694 French philosopher, author and librettist Voltaire is born in Paris.

1695 English composer Henry Purcell dies in Westminster.

1852 Spanish composer and guitarist Francisco Tárrega is born in Villareal.

1931 Australian composer Malcolm Williamson is born in Sydney.

1938 American pianist and composer Leopold Godowsky dies in New York.

FIRST PERFORMED

1937 Dmitri Shostakovich's *Symphony No. 5* receives its first performance, in Leningrad.

1939 Dmitri Shostakovich's *Symphony No. 6* is heard for the first time, in Leningrad.

1976 Philip Glass's *Einstein on the Beach* is premiered at the Metropolitan Opera in New York.

TODAY'S THE DAY

1747 Leopold Mozart and Anna Maria Pertl get married. Their son Wolfgang Amadeus, born nine years later, is to become arguably the greatest composer of them all.

1822 Hector Berlioz stops his formal studies of medicine after his college is closed down because of political unrest.

1828 Franz Schubert's funeral is held in Vienna. His body is buried not far from that of Ludwig van Beethoven.

1861 Anton Bruckner faces an exam in harmony and counterpoint in Vienna in his quest to become a professor. He was so good that the adjudicators told him that he should have been examining them.

1868 Gioachino Rossini's funeral is held in Paris before a congregation of 4,000 people. Later in the day, his music is performed in many of the major Paris theatres.

1874 Richard Wagner finally finishes his epic *Ring Cycle*, writing the final note of *Götterdämmerung*.

1895 Hubert Parry and Charles Villiers Stanford are among the big names in English music to lay wreaths at Westminster Abbey to commemorate the 200th anniversary of the death of Henry Purcell.

1930 The Mayor of Philadelphia declares today 'John Philip Sousa day'. Sousa responds with a performance of his march *'Harmonica Wizard'* by the Philadelphia Harmonica Band, which has no fewer than 52 harmonica players in its ranks.

1941 Béla Bartók performs as a solo recitalist for the final time, in Chicago.

1967 William Walton is honoured with the Order of Merit.

1985 Trumpeter Wynton Marsalis makes his debut with the New York Philharmonic in a performance of Haydn's *Trumpet Concerto*.

HALL OF FAME HIT
Leoš Janáček: *Sinfonietta*

Recommended Recording
Vienna Philharmonic Orchestra conducted by Charles Mackerras; Decca 478 5670

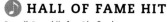

> 'Music produces a kind of pleasure which human nature cannot do without.'
>
> **CONFUCIUS, PHILOSOPHER**

22
NOVEMBER

🎵 BIRTHS & DEATHS

1710 German composer Wilhelm Friedemann Bach is born in Weimar.

1859 English folk music and dance expert Cecil Sharp is born in London.

1900 English composer Arthur Sullivan dies in London.

1901 Spanish composer Joaquín Rodrigo is born in Sagunto.

1913 English composer Benjamin Britten is born in Lowestoft.

1930 English opera, film and theatre director Peter Hall is born in Bury St Edmunds.

1951 American conductor Kent Nagano is born in Morro Bay.

1961 English pianist Stephen Hough is born in Heswell.

1962 Korean soprano Sumi Jo is born in Seoul.

1974 English conductor Edward Gardner is born in Gloucester.

FIRST PERFORMED

1795 Ludwig van Beethoven's *Twelve Minuets* and *Twelve German Dances* are heard for the first time, at a masked ball in Vienna. Joseph Haydn is in the crowd.

1928 Maurice Ravel's ballet *Boléro* is premiered in Paris.

1931 Ferde Grofe's *Grand Canyon Suite* receives its first performance, in Chicago.

1944 The film *Henry V*, with a score by William Walton, is screened for the first time, in London.

☀ TODAY'S THE DAY

1815 Ludwig van Beethoven and his sister-in-law Johanna are appointed joint guardians of Ludwig's nephew Karl.

1826 Prince Nicholas Galitzin receives the three of Ludwig van Beethoven's late string quartets that he had commissioned, in Vienna.

1827 Hector Berlioz makes his public conducting debut in Paris.

1828 After complaints by concertgoers about the smell, the Covent Garden Theatre announces that it is doing away with the gas lights that were introduced 11 years earlier, reverting to candles instead.

1833 Felix Mendelssohn conducts Handel's *Alexander's Feast* for his first performance as music director in Düsseldorf.

1842 King Friedrich Wilhelm of Prussia formally confirms Felix Mendelssohn as general music director for church music.

1845 Robert Schumann changes his mind about Richard Wagner's opera *Tannhäuser*, after seeing it again. He writes to Mendelssohn to say that his view is now far more positive.

1874 Gabriel Fauré is appointed Secretary of the Société Nationale de Musique.

1900 Edward Elgar receives an honorary doctorate in Music from Cambridge University.

St Cecilia's Day

Today is the feast day for St Cecilia, the patron saint of music. To be honest, it isn't entirely clear exactly what she did to earn this honour. However, that hasn't stopped many composers penning tributes to her over the years.

 HALL OF FAME HIT
Michael Nyman: *The Piano*

Recommended Recording
Ksenia Bashmet (piano); Quartz QTZ 069

23

NOVEMBER

'[*Also Sprach*] *Zarathustra* is glorious – by far the most important of all my pieces, the most perfect in form, the richest in content and the most individual in character.'

RICHARD STRAUSS, COMPOSER

🕐 BIRTHS & DEATHS

1585 English composer Thomas Tallis dies in Greenwich.

1750 Italian composer Giuseppe Sammartini dies in London.

1876 Spanish composer Manuel de Falla is born in Cadiz.

1933 Polish composer Krzysztof Penderecki is born in Dębica.

1955 Italian composer and pianist Ludovico Einaudi is born in Turin.

1961 Austrian violinist and conductor Thomas Zehetmair is born in Salzburg.

2008 English conductor Richard Hickox dies in Cardiff.

🎭 FIRST PERFORMED

1834 Hector Berlioz's symphony for viola and orchestra *Harold in Italy* is given its first performance, in Paris.

1916 Gabriel Fauré's *Barcarolle No. 12* and *Nocturne No. 12* are performed for the first time, in Paris.

1916 Camille Saint-Saëns' *Elégie* for violin and piano receives its first performance.

☀ TODAY'S THE DAY

1903 Tenor Enrico Caruso makes his American debut at New York's Metropolitan Opera.

1906 Enrico Caruso is found guilty of inappropriately touching a woman in the monkey house at New York's Central Park Zoo. He is fined the maximum penalty of ten dollars.

2002 David Daniels is the first counter-tenor to give a solo performance at New York's Carnegie Hall.

2004 The British Academy of Composers and Songwriters presents the Fellowship of the Academy to the American composer John Adams at London's Barbican Centre.

COMPOSER PROFILE:

Ludovico Einaudi

Born in Turin in 1955, Einaudi studied piano and composition first at the Milan Conservatoire and then with the highly regarded contemporary Italian composer Luciano Berio. He came to prominence in Britain in the mid-1990s with his solo piano album *Le Onde*. Although he has written for film and for full orchestra, his other solo piano albums *I Giorni* and *Una Mattina* have become more enduringly popular. His compositions embrace the sparse, repetitive style of many of the minimalist composers and his music has great ambient and contemplative qualities.

🎵 HALL OF FAME HIT

Ludwig van Beethoven: *Piano Trio No. 7 ('Archduke')*

Recommended Recording

Chung Trio; EMI 381 7512

'In the olden days, everybody sang. You were expected to sing as well as talk. It was a mark of the cultured man to sing.'

LEONARD BERNSTEIN, CONDUCTOR AND COMPOSER

24
NOVEMBER

BIRTHS & DEATHS
1934 Russian composer Alfred Schnittke is born in Engels.
1966 English singer Russell Watson is born in Salford.

FIRST PERFORMED
1839 Hector Berlioz's *Romeo and Juliet* is premiered in Paris.
1852 Johann Strauss Junior's *Zehner-Polka* is performed for the first time, in Vienna.
1919 The final version of Jean Sibelius's *Symphony No. 5* is given its first performance, in Helsinki.

TODAY'S THE DAY
1833 A fundraising concert is held in Paris to help pay off debts run up by Hector Berlioz and Harriet Smithson. Although they manage to raise the necessary cash, the concert is a disorganised disaster.
1836 Richard Wagner gets married to Minna Planer, in Tragheim.
1859 Sixteen-year-old soprano Adelina Patti makes her debut at New York's Metropolitan Opera, in Donizetti's *Lucia di Lammermoor*.
1873 Seven-year-old pianist Ferruccio Busoni makes his concert debut in Trieste.
1888 Erik Satie advertises the publication of the third of his *Trois Gymnopédies*, although the second won't be published for another seven years.
1891 Jean Sibelius makes his debut as a conductor, in Helsinki.

1907 Gustav Mahler, who is moving on from his job in Vienna, conducts his *Resurrection Symphony* for his goodbye performance. He sheds a tear after taking no fewer than 30 bows on stage at the end.
1924 Surgeons operate on Giacomo Puccini's throat cancer after he has undergone ten days of radiotherapy.
1936 Nadia Boulanger conducts the Royal Philharmonic Orchestra in London's Queen's Hall. She is the first woman to do so.
1938 Tenor Jussi Björling makes his debut at New York's Metropolitan Opera in *La bohème*.
1950 Benjamin Britten and Peter Pears drop in on Igor Stravinsky's Hollywood home during their tour of the USA.

COMPOSER PROFILE:

Jay Ungar

Jay Ungar was born in New York to Hungarian immigrant parents, and his Greenwich Village upbringing may seem a million miles from the Catskill strains of his famous hit tune, *The Ashokan Farewell*. In actual fact, the moving melody, originally a country waltz, was written for fondly felt final nights at his annual Fiddle and Dance Camp, run out of the Ashokan Campus of New York State University. It came to prominence after being used in Ken Burn's television film *The Civil War*, and its arrangement by Captain J. R. Perkins, then of the Band of Her Majesty's Royal Marines, propelled it to the higher echelons of the Classic FM Hall of Fame.

HALL OF FAME HIT
Maurice Ravel: *Daphnis and Chloe*

Recommended Recording
Boston Symphony Orchestra conducted by Seiji Ozawa; Australian Eloquence 476 8429

25

'My job is to make sure, at every turn of the film, it's something the audience can feel with their heart.'

JAMES HORNER, FILM COMPOSER

NOVEMBER

BIRTHS & DEATHS

1835 Scottish businessman Andrew Carnegie, who endowed New York's Carnegie Hall, is born in Dunfermline.

1895 German pianist Wilhelm Kempff is born in Jüterbog.

1937 Lilian Baylis, founder of the Sadler's Wells Opera and Ballet companies, dies in London.

1950 Australian soprano Yvonne Kenny is born in Sydney.

1965 English pianist Myra Hess dies in London.

FIRST PERFORMED

1731 Johann Sebastian Bach's cantata 'Wachet auf' is performed for the first time, in Leipzig.

1811 Carl Maria von Weber's *Clarinet Concerto No. 2* is given its first performance, in Munich.

1869 Camille Saint-Saëns' *Piano Concerto* receives its first performance, in Leipzig.

1879 Three scenes from Alexander Borodin's opera *Prince Igor* are performed for the first time, in St Petersburg.

1882 W. S. Gilbert and Arthur Sullivan's operetta *Iolanthe* is premiered at the Savoy Theatre in London.

1901 Gustav Mahler's *Symphony No. 4* is given its first performance, in Munich, with the composer conducting.

1928 Dmitri Shostakovich's *The Nose Suite*, *Tahiti Trot* and *Tea for Two* are all performed for the first time, at the Moscow Conservatoire.

TODAY'S THE DAY

1720 George Frideric Handel's first collection of keyboard suites is published in London.

1781 The first concert is staged at the Leipzig Gewandhaus.

1824 Gioachino Rossini signs up as directeur de la musique et de la scène at the Théâtre-Italien in Paris.

1841 Franz Liszt bumps into Robert and Clara Schumann while he is on a visit to Weimar.

1869 Louis Moreau Gottschalk collapses on stage in Rio de Janeiro, suffering from malaria.

1896 Jean Sibelius shares his passion for folk music in a lecture at the University of Helsinki entitled 'Some Perspectives on Folk Music and its influence on the Art of Music'.

1918 Wanting to go to Vienna, Richard Strauss tells the Berlin Opera that he is giving up his role as interim artistic adviser.

1927 Eleven-year-old Yehudi Menuhin makes his debut as a solo violinist, performing the Beethoven *Violin Concerto* with the New York Symphony Society Orchestra.

HALL OF FAME HIT
Sergei Rachmaninov: *Vocalise*

Recommended Recording
Renée Fleming (soprano); English Chamber Orchestra conducted by Jeffrey Tate; Decca 458 8582

> 'Music is the poetry of the air.'
> JEAN PAUL RICHTER, WRITER

26

NOVEMBER

🎵 BIRTHS & DEATHS

1959 British composer Albert Ketèlbey dies on the Isle of Wight.

🎵 FIRST PERFORMED

1865 Pyotr Ilyich Tchaikovsky's *Overture in F* is given its first performance, at St Petersburg Conservatoire, with the composer appearing for the first time as a conductor.
1907 Jean Sibelius's *Symphony No. 3* receives its first performance, in Helsinki, with the composer conducting.
1937 Robert Schumann's *Violin Concerto* is performed for the first time in Berlin, 81 years after the composer's death. The manuscript's owner, the celebrated violinist Joseph Joachim, had in fact stipulated in his will that the world should wait a full 100 years after Schumann's death before the work should be heard.
1938 Sergei Prokofiev's *Cello Concerto* is premiered in Moscow.

☀️ TODAY'S THE DAY

1755 William Boyce learns that the existing Master of the Royal Musicians, Maurice Greene, is gravely ill. He takes the opportunity to write to the prime minister to offer his services as a replacement. He is ultimately successful in his quest.
1760 Joseph Haydn gets married in St Stephen's Cathedral in Vienna, to the daughter of a wig maker.
1820 Nine-year-old Franz Liszt makes his second public concert appearance to great acclaim. This time, it's in Bratislava.
1869 Louis Moreau Gottschalk attempts to conduct a concert in Rio de Janeiro but, for a second consecutive night, he collapses on stage.
1887 Pyotr Ilyich Tchaikovsky conducts the first concert in Moscow programmed entirely from music he has himself written.
1940 Sviatoslav Richter makes his concert debut at the piano at the Moscow Conservatoire with a concert of pieces written by Russian composers.

ERA FOCUS:

Modern music: part I

With the dawn of the 20th century, the Romantic period was drawing to a close. Many composers now seemed to be at a loss as to what to do next with music. There was almost a feeling that everything had been done in terms of musical development, and that, with the death of Wagner, an era had come to an end. Many composers decided that a young Austrian, called Arnold Schoenberg, was right to start everything all over again. He developed entirely new rules for how composers might use harmony, melody and rhythm: a system he called '12-tone music' or 'serialism'. Serialism won an immediate following at the time, starting with Schoenberg's pupils. They became known as the Second Viennese School, its main proponents being Anton Webern and Alban Berg. The style gained momentum as the century progressed, not least due to Schoenberg's teaching when he took up residence in the USA.

🎵 HALL OF FAME HIT

Léo Delibes: *Sylvia*

Recommended Recording

New Philharmonia Orchestra conducted by Richard Bonynge; Decca 478 3628

27

NOVEMBER

> 'Music is the art which is most nigh to tears and memory.'
>
> OSCAR WILDE, WRITER

BIRTHS & DEATHS

1474 Belgian composer Guillaume Dufay dies in Cambrai.

1759 Czech composer Franz Krommer is born in Kamenice u Jihlavy.

1804 British conductor and composer Julius Benedict is born in Stuttgart.

1955 French composer Arthur Honegger dies in Paris.

1959 Russian violinist Viktoria Mullova is born in Moscow.

1961 Swedish trumpeter Håkan Hardenberger is born in Malmö.

1979 American violinist Hilary Hahn is born in Lexington.

FIRST PERFORMED

1896 Richard Strauss's tone poem *Also Sprach Zarathustra* is performed for the first time, in Frankfurt.

1939 Heitor Villa-Lobos's *Bachianas Brasileiras No. 4* is given its first performance, in Rio de Janeiro.

TODAY'S THE DAY

1872 After being petitioned by Charles Villiers Stanford, Cambridge University Music Society allows women to join its choir.

1900 Arthur Sullivan's funeral takes place in London. Even though it wasn't what he wanted, he is buried in St Paul's Cathedral.

1900 Antonín Dvořák finishes work on his opera *Rusalka*.

1911 The New Hungarian Music Society gives its first concert performance in Budapest. Béla Bartók and Zoltán Kodály are among its founders.

1953 There is a distinct change of political direction in Moscow with an article in the official Communist Party newspaper *Pravda* underlining 'the importance of encouraging new departures in art, of studying the artist's individual style'. It goes on to encourage the need to recognise 'the artist's right to be independent, to strike out boldly on new paths'. This is a sharp about-turn from the official view during Stalin's lifetime and there is no coincidence that it comes nine months after his death.

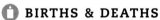

ERA FOCUS:

Modern music: part II

Schoenberg's advocacy of serialism was by no means universally accepted. Stravinsky, for one, adopted as many or as few of Schoenberg's methods as he needed, sometimes incorporating 12-tone, sometimes not. Richard Strauss, while also being starkly modernist, was not interested in serialism at all, preferring instead to push his own brand of tonality to its limits. Many other composers, who had been around from the middle half of the 19th century, preferred to continue in the traditional manner, seeing nothing wrong with keys and tonality. Puccini, Elgar and Rachmaninov were just a few of the composers who continued to plough the Romantic furrow in a Modernist field.

♪ HALL OF FAME HIT
Christian Forshaw: *Mortal Flesh*

Recommended Recording
Christian Forshaw (saxophone); Sanctuary Voices; Integra Records ING 1001

> 'If I don't become Brahms or Tchaikovsky or Stravinsky when I'm conducting their works then it won't be a great performance.'
>
> **LEONARD BERNSTEIN, CONDUCTOR AND COMPOSER**

28

NOVEMBER

 BIRTHS & DEATHS

1829 Russian pianist, conductor and composer Anton Rubinstein is born in the Ukraine.

1976 English composer and organist Harold Darke dies in Cambridge.

 FIRST PERFORMED

1811 Ludwig van Beethoven's *Piano Concerto No. 5 'The Emperor'* is premiered, in Leipzig.

1858 Charles Gounod's *St Cecilia Mass* is heard for the first time, in Paris.

1896 Nikolai Rimsky-Korsakov's orchestration of Modest Mussorgsky's opera *Boris Godunov* is premiered in St Petersburg.

1909 Sergei Rachmaninov's *Piano Concerto No. 3* receives its first performance, in New York, with the composer as soloist.

TODAY'S THE DAY

1835 Robert Schumann and Clara Wieck (later Schumann) share their first kiss after he visits her at home in Leipzig before she goes off on a concert tour.

1853 Johannes Brahms and Hector Berlioz meet for the first time, in Hanover. They are introduced by the violinist Joseph Joachim.

1863 In Berlin, Richard Wagner and Cosima von Bülow begin a serious relationship, despite the fact that she is married to the renowned conductor Hans von Bülow.

1880 Anton Bruckner begins to receive a regular annual salary from the Austrian government.

1894 Anton Rubinstein is buried in St Petersburg, on what would have been his 65th birthday.

1935 The Italian government bans performances of music written by composers from countries such as Great Britain, France, Spain and the United States, who all voted to impose sanctions against Italy, after her invasion of Ethiopia.

1938 Dmitri Shostakovich's *Jazz Suite No. 2* is among the works performed at the debut concert of the State Jazz Orchestra of the USSR.

2013 A Greek Orthodox funeral is held for the composer John Tavener in Winchester Cathedral.

ERA FOCUS:

Modern music: part III

Good old-fashioned tunes and harmonies did survive intact throughout the 20th century, thanks to composers such as Vaughan Williams, Holst and Britten in Britain, Rodrigo in Spain, the composers who called themselves 'Les Six' in France, and, to some extent, the likes of Copland in the USA. Come the 21st century and tonality is still alive and well. Minimalism is still thriving, as is a rediscovered neo-classicism, which sees composers using an audience-friendly musical language that would not be out of place in a film score.

 HALL OF FAME HIT

Frédéric Chopin: *Nocturne in C sharp minor Op. post.*

Recommended Recording

Lise de la Salle (piano); Naïve V5310

29

'When words leave off, music begins.'

HEINRICH HEINE, POET

BIRTHS & DEATHS

1632 Italian-French composer Jean-Baptiste Lully is born in Florence.

1643 Italian composer Claudio Monteverdi dies in Venice.

1797 Italian composer Gaetano Donizetti is born in Bergamo.

1924 Italian composer Giacomo Puccini dies in Brussels.

1957 American composer Erich Korngold dies in Los Angeles.

FIRST PERFORMED

1925 A suite from Sergei Prokofiev's opera *The Love for Three Oranges* is given its first performance, in Paris.

TODAY'S THE DAY

1766 After more than three years on the road touring around Europe, the Mozart family returns home to Salzburg.

1779 Domenico Cimarosa is given the job of organist at the Royal Chapel in Naples, although he isn't paid for doing it.

1825 An Italian opera is staged in Italian in the USA for the first time. Gioachino Rossini's *The Barber of Seville* takes the honour.

1829 Felix Mendelssohn heads to Berlin, after spending two months in England recovering from illness.

1841 Franz Liszt makes his first public performance in Weimar, which will in time become the centre of his music-making.

1877 Inventor Thomas Edison gives a demonstration of his new hand-cranked phonograph.

1926 Giacomo Puccini's body is removed from its resting place in Milan to be reinterred at his villa at Torre del Lago. It is the second anniversary of his death.

ERA FOCUS:

Modern music: part IV

Many 20th- and 21st-century composers, such as Ludovico Einaudi, Howard Goodall, Karl Jenkins, John Rutter and John Tavener, feature in their own entries in this book. Other critically acclaimed modern composers include:

Gavin Bryars (born 1943): the most famous (and quite possibly the only famous) composer from Goole in East Yorkshire. His *Jesus' Blood Never Failed Me Yet* was a big hit in the mid-1990s.

Judith Weir (born 1954): a former pupil of John Tavener; the opera house and theatre are ideal places to experience her fresh, modern sounds.

James MacMillan (born 1959): possibly the best-known Scottish composer of his generation. His *Veni, Veni, Emmanuel*, a concerto for percussion first performed in 1992 by Evelyn Glennie, is considered a modern classic.

George Benjamin (born 1960): studied with Olivier Messiaen before having an early 'modern' hit with *Ringed by the Flat Horizon*.

Mark-Anthony Turnage (born 1960): another man at home writing music for the theatre. His opera derived from Steven Berkoff's play *Greek* is breathtaking.

HALL OF FAME HIT

Wolfgang Amadeus Mozart: *Piano Concerto No. 27*

Recommended Recording

Mitsuko Uchida (piano); Cleveland Orchestra; Decca 478 2596

'I dig Strauss and Wagner, those cats are good.'
JIMI HENDRIX, MUSICIAN

30

NOVEMBER

 BIRTHS & DEATHS

1813 French composer Alkan (Charles-Valentin Morhange) is born in Paris.

1939 Austrian conductor and violinist Walter Weller is born in Vienna.

1952 Russian conductor Semyon Bychkov is born in St Petersburg.

1954 German conductor Wilhelm Furtwängler dies in Ebersteinberg.

 FIRST PERFORMED

1877 Pyotr Ilyich Tchaikovsky's *Variations on a Rococo Theme* for cello and orchestra is performed for the first time, in Moscow.

1885 Jules Massenet's opera *Le Cid* is premiered in Paris.

☀ TODAY'S THE DAY

1625 Charles I appoints Nicholas Lanier as Master of the King's Musick.

1833 Fourteen-year-old Jacques Offenbach signs up to study at the Paris Conservatoire.

1870 Eighteen-year-old Charles Villiers Stanford performs for the first time at Cambridge University.

1892 Antonín Dvořák tells the *Boston Post* that women cannot add to the development of American music because of their intellectual inferiority.

1908 The cornerstone is laid for the new Boston Opera House.

COMPOSER PROFILE:

Philip Glass

This American composer has an unconventional classical-music background, having studied with both the legendary French teacher Nadia Boulanger and the Indian sitar virtuoso Ravi Shankar. In 1967, he formed the Philip Glass Ensemble, and writing for this group of seven musicians formed the core of his output for many years. The style of music that he developed was dubbed 'minimalism'. It is distinctive, catchy and mesmerising and Glass has sustained his popularity ever since, both as a composer of core classical works and of film soundtracks.

ENSEMBLE FOCUS:

Manchester Camerata

A leading chamber orchestra, Manchester Camerata reaches audiences of 70,000 people every year with residencies at the Bridgewater Hall and the Royal Northern College of Music in its home city, as well as regular appearances in towns and cities as varied as Hull, Leeds, Bolton, Blackburn, Chester, Lancaster, Kendal, Bridlington, Sheffield, Hanley, Malvern, Ulverston, Stafford and Colne. Its artistic director is the Hungarian Gábor Takács-Nagy.

♫ HALL OF FAME HIT

Wolfgang Amadeus Mozart: *Piano Concerto No. 3*

Recommended Recording

Gidon Kremer (violin); Kremerata Baltica; Nonesuch 7559 798863

Decer

nber

01

> 'Nature has given us two ears but only one mouth.'
>
> BENJAMIN DISRAELI, POLITICIAN

BIRTHS & DEATHS

1707 English composer Jeremiah Clarke dies in London.

1997 French violinist Stéphane Grappelli dies in Paris.

FIRST PERFORMED

1883 The third version of Pyotr Ilyich Tchaikovsky's *Symphony No. 1* is given its first performance, in Moscow.

1913 Claude Debussy's celebrated solo flute work *Syrinx* is heard for the first time, in Paris.

1935 Sergei Prokofiev's *Violin Concerto No. 2* receives its first performance, in Madrid.

1944 Béla Bartók's *Concerto for Orchestra* is first performed, in Boston.

1951 Benjamin Britten's opera *Billy Budd* is premiered at Covent Garden in London, with the composer conducting.

1956 Leonard Bernstein's comic operetta *Candide* is premiered in New York.

TODAY'S THE DAY

1813 Although many have laid claim to inventing the metronome, the timekeeping device was patented by Johann Nepomuk Maelzel. Reports of his prototype appear today.

1822 Franz Liszt makes his public concert debut in Vienna. He is already studying piano with Carl Czerny and composition with Antonio Salieri.

1861 Richard Wagner reads the plot of *Die Meistersinger von Nürnberg* to the music publisher Schott and is offered 10,000 francs for it on the spot.

1919 Richard Strauss starts work as director of the Austrian State Opera.

1924 Giacomo Puccini's funeral is held in Brussels, before his body is taken by train to Milan.

COMPOSER PROFILE:

Franz Lehár

This Hungarian composer studied at the Prague Conservatoire, but learned much about music from his father, who was a military bandmaster. Despite being told by Dvořák to spend as much time as he possibly could composing, he pursued commitments as an orchestral violin player and performing in his father's band, as well as taking on a variety of different conducting jobs. Lehár got his break as an operetta composer somewhat fortuitously. When the librettists of *The Merry Widow* were casting around to find a composer to set their lyrics to music, his name was suggested, though in fact he was only their second choice. He got the job when the original composer failed to come up with the goods. Lehár auditioned for the role by playing a song over the telephone. The operetta initially received a somewhat mixed reception, nearly closing before it properly opened, but eventually Lehár found that he had a hit on his hands.

HALL OF FAME HIT

Astor Piazzolla: *Libertango*

Recommended Recording

Miloš Karadaglić (guitar); Deutsche Grammophon 479 1421

'Music is the universal language of mankind.'

HENRY WADSWORTH LONGFELLOW, POET

02

🕐 BIRTHS & DEATHS

1899 English conductor John Barbirolli is born in London.

1923 Greek-American soprano Maria Callas is born in New York.

1931 French composer Vincent d'Indy dies in Paris.

1990 American composer Aaron Copland dies in New York.

🎵 FIRST PERFORMED

1877 Camille Saint-Saëns' opera *Samson and Delilah* is premiered in Weimar with Franz Liszt conducting.

1883 Johannes Brahms' *Symphony No. 3* receives its first performance, in Vienna, with Hans Richter conducting.

1949 Olivier Messiaen's *Turangalîla* is given its first performance, in Boston, with Leonard Bernstein conducting.

☀️ TODAY'S THE DAY

1717 Johann Sebastian Bach agrees to become Kapellmeister in Cöthen.

1804 Giovanni Paisiello provides the music for the coronation of Napoleon Bonaparte as Emperor of the French.

1833 Ten-year-old César Franck takes up harmony lessons at the Royal Conservatoire of Liège.

1879 The librettist Arrigo Boito sends the words for the opera *Otello* to Giuseppe Verdi.

1879 Edvard Grieg asks Clara Schumann to help pave his way for a trip to England by providing him with letters of introduction.

1962 Zoltán Kodály is given Hungary's highest honour, the Order of the Hungarian People's Republic.

ORCHESTRA FOCUS:

National Children's Orchestra of Great Britain

A jewel in the UK's music-education crown, the National Children's Orchestra brings together the most promising young musicians aged between seven and thirteen from right across the country to perform together as a symphony orchestra. It was founded in 1978 by Vivienne Price MBE because she wanted to create an ensemble that enabled children who were younger than the normal youth orchestra age group to perform together. It proved so successful that the National Children's Orchestra set up a training orchestra to operate alongside the main ensemble to help provide an even earlier taste of orchestral life for young musicians. The organisation's track record for spotting talent is pretty impressive, with the cellist Guy Johnston, the violinist Nicola Benedetti and the conductors Robin Ticciati and Daniel Harding all former members of the National Children's Orchestra – not to mention a legion of musicians now playing professionally in many of Britain's leading orchestras. Many of the youngsters who play in the National Children's Orchestra graduate on to the National Youth Orchestra once they become old enough.

🎵 HALL OF FAME HIT

Anton Bruckner: *Symphony No. 8*

Recommended Recording

Vienna Philharmonic Orchestra conducted by Herbert von Karajan; Deutsche Grammophon 479 0528

03

'Rachmaninov has some kind of weird dark edge to his music which I don't think I've heard with any other kind of music before.'

MATT BELLAMY, ROCK MUSICIAN

DECEMBER

BIRTHS & DEATHS

1596 Italian cello and violin maker Nicolò Amati is born in Cremona.

1883 Austrian composer Anton Webern is born in Vienna.

1911 Italian composer Nino Rota is born in Milan.

1938 Uruguayan conductor and composer José Serebrier is born in Montevideo.

FIRST PERFORMED

1712 Pyotr Ilyich Tchaikovsky's *Serenade for Strings* is given its first performance, at the Moscow Conservatoire.

1908 Edward Elgar's *Symphony No. 1* is performed for the first time, in Manchester.

1925 George Gershwin's *Concerto in F* receives its first performance, in New York's Carnegie Hall.

1926 *Suite No. 1* from *Façade* by William Walton is premiered in London, with the composer conducting.

1934 The first three movements of William Walton's *Symphony No. 1* are heard for the first time, in London.

1942 Aram Khachaturian's ballet *Gayaneh* is premiered, in Molotov.

1953 The musical *Kismet*, based on the tunes of Alexander Borodin, opens on Broadway.

1954 William Walton's opera *Troilus and Cressida* is premiered at London's Covent Garden.

TODAY'S THE DAY

1721 Johann Sebastian Bach gets married for a second time. His new wife, Anna, is to give birth to thirteen of his children.

1787 Domenico Cimarosa arrives in St Petersburg. He has accepted a new job there as Maestro di Cappella to the court of Catherine the Great.

1810 The London-based music publisher Chappell opens its doors for business.

1818 Ludwig van Beethoven's nephew Karl runs away from his uncle's home back to his mother. Beethoven calls the police and promptly packs the youngster back off to boarding school.

1837 Clara Wieck (later Schumann) performs for the first time at the keyboard in Vienna.

1924 Italian premier Benito Mussolini gives the funeral oration at a service for Giacomo Puccini in Milan Cathedral.

Big-screen controversy

The film director Ken Russell specialised in making movies about the lives of many of the great composers. Often highly controversial and containing scenes that are very definitely of an adult nature, Russell's classical music films for the big and small screens have included: *Elgar* (1962); *The Debussy Film* (1965); *Song of Summer* (1968 – about Delius); *Dance of the Seven Veils* (1970 – about Richard Strauss); *The Music Lovers* (1970 – about Tchaikovsky) *Mahler* (1974); *Lisztomania* (1975); and *The Secret Life of Arnold Bax* (1992).

HALL OF FAME HIT
Kashif Saleem: *Queen Symphony*

Recommended Recording
Nicola Loud (cello); Royal Philharmonic Orchestra conducted by Tolga Kashif; Classic FM CFMCD 41

'It should sound like good music; it should always have a structure to it . . . And it should be able to, away from the picture, conjure up the same sort of feelings and images that it was meant to on screen.'

PATRICK DOYLE, ON COMPOSING FOR FILM

04
DECEMBER

BIRTHS & DEATHS
1879 Northern Irish composer and conductor Herbert Hamilton Harty is born in Hillsborough.
1976 English composer Benjamin Britten dies in Aldeburgh.

FIRST PERFORMED
1816 Gioachino Rossini's opera *Otello* is premiered in Naples.
1845 Robert Schumann's *Piano Concerto* is given its first performance, in Dresden, with Clara Schumann as soloist.
1878 The first complete performance of Antonín Dvořák's *Slavonic Dances Nos 1–4* are given, in Dresden.
1881 Pyotr Ilyich Tchaikovsky's *Violin Concerto* receives its first performance, in Vienna.
1909 Ermanno Wolf-Ferrari's *Susanna's Secret* is premiered in Munich. The secret in question? She smoked.

TODAY'S THE DAY
1830 Franz Liszt and Hector Berlioz meet for the first time in Paris, becoming firm friends.
1845 Students at Leipzig Conservatoire protest after their usual cut-price tickets are withdrawn because a concert by the soprano Jenny Lind under the baton of Felix Mendelssohn is so over-subscribed that there is no room in the concert hall.
1893 Leading soprano Nellie Melba makes her debut at New York's Metropolitan Opera.
1903 Ralph Vaughan Williams starts collecting English folk songs, after hearing a labourer in Essex sing '*Bushes and Briars*'. The composer writes down the notes sung and begins to catalogue music that has been handed down from generation to generation without ever having been formally recorded.

1912 Ballet promoter Sergei Diaghilev introduces Arnold Schoenberg and Igor Stravinsky in Berlin.
1934 Wilhelm Furtwängler resigns as deputy president of the Reichsmusikkammer, director of the Berlin State Opera and conductor of the Berlin Philharmonic.

HALL OF FAME HIT
Howard Goodall: *Eternal Light: A Requiem*

Recommended Recording
Various soloists; London Musici; Christ Church Cathedral Choir, Oxford conducted by Stephen Darlington; EMI 215 0472

'Technique is communication: the two words are synonymous in conductors.'

LEONARD BERNSTEIN, CONDUCTOR AND COMPOSER

 BIRTHS & DEATHS

1791 Austrian composer Wolfgang Amadeus Mozart dies in Vienna.

1940 Czech violinist and composer Jan Kubelík dies in Prague.

1946 Spanish tenor José Carreras is born in Barcelona.

1962 Argentine tenor José Cura is born in Rosario.

 FIRST PERFORMED

1786 Wolfgang Amadeus Mozart's *Piano Concerto No. 25* is heard for the first time, in Vienna.

1822 Thirteen-year-old Felix Mendelssohn's *Concerto for Piano and Strings* is given its first performance, in Berlin.

1830 Hector Berlioz's *Symphonie fantastique* receives its first performance, in Paris.

1837 Hector Berlioz's *Grand messe des morts* is premiered in Paris.

1927 Leoš Janáček's *Glagolitic Mass* is given its first performance, in Brno.

1942 Benjamin Britten's *A Ceremony of Carols* receives its first performance, in Norwich Castle.

☀ **TODAY'S THE DAY**

1839 Charles Gounod heads off to Rome from Paris, after winning the Prix de Rome.

1844 Clara Schumann performs Beethoven's *Piano Concerto No. 5* ('*The Emperor*') in Leipzig, calling it 'the hardest concerto I know'.

1867 The man who wrote the librettos to operas including *Rigoletto* and *La traviata*, Francesco Maria Piave, suffers a stroke in Milan. He will survive, paralysed, for another eight years, during which time Giuseppe Verdi ensures that he and his daughter are able to survive financially.

1882 Eighteen-year-old Richard Strauss performs in public as a pianist for the first time.

British Music Conservatoires

Although it is possible to study for a music degree in many universities across the country, many people believe the best possible training to become a professional musician is offered by the network of smaller specialist institutions known as conservatoires. The Royal Academy of Music, the Royal College of Music, the Guildhall School of Music and Drama and Trinity Laban Conservatoire of Music and Dance make up the London contingent, while Birmingham Conservatoire (part of Birmingham City University), the Royal Northern College of Music in Manchester and Leeds College of Music are the other English conservatoires. The Royal Conservatoire of Scotland is based in Glasgow and the home of the Royal Welsh College of Music and Drama (part of the University of South Wales) is in Cardiff.

 HALL OF FAME HIT
Franz Schubert: *Rosamunde*

Recommended Recording
Swedish Chamber Orchestra conducted by Thomas Dausgaard; BIS 1987

> 'Music is the one incorporeal entrance into the higher world of knowledge which comprehends mankind but which mankind cannot comprehend.'

LUDWIG VAN BEETHOVEN, COMPOSER

06

DECEMBER

BIRTHS & DEATHS

1896 American librettist and lyricist Ira Gershwin is born in New York.

1929 Austrian conductor Nikolaus Harnoncourt is born in Berlin.

1933 Polish composer Henryk Górecki is born in Czernica.

FIRST PERFORMED

1846 Hector Berlioz's *The Damnation of Faust* is premiered in Paris.

1890 More than two decades after his death and more than three decades after it was composed, the first part of Hector Berlioz's *Les Troyens* is performed for the first time, in Karlsruhe.

1906 Gabriel Fauré's *Dolly Suite* is given its first performance, in Monaco.

TODAY'S THE DAY

1786 Wolfgang Amadeus Mozart finishes work on his *Symphony No. 38*, in Vienna.

1847 The Drury Lane Theatre opens for business in London, with Hector Berlioz in charge. Donizetti's *Lucia di Lammermoor* is the first production.

1950 American President Harry Truman is outraged at reading a negative review of a concert given by his daughter Margaret. He leaves the critic in no uncertainty about his views on the subject, writing to him, 'Some day I hope to meet you. When that happens, you'll need a new nose, a lot of beefsteak for black eyes, and perhaps a supporter below.'

COMPOSER PROFILE:

Michael Nyman

A prolific and commercially successful British composer, Michael Nyman studied at the Royal Academy of Music in the 1960s, where his compositions at the time were at the cutting edge of new music. He went on to study at King's College in London, where he turned back the clock, specialising in 17th-century musicology. He put composing on the back-burner for a while, concentrating on musicology and also on music criticism. While he was writing for the *Spectator*, he became the first critic to use the term 'Minimalism' when writing about the music of Steve Reich and Philip Glass. Gradually, he spent more time writing music than writing words, forming a highly successful professional partnership with the film director Peter Greenaway, which saw him composing soundtracks for movies such as *The Draughtsman's Contract* and *The Cook, The Thief, His Wife and Her Lover*. However, he is best known for his beautiful soundtrack to the 1993 Jane Campion film, *The Piano*.

HALL OF FAME HIT
Gustav Holst: *St Paul's Suite*

Recommended Recording
Royal Philharmonic Orchestra conducted by Vernon Handley; Alto ALC 1013

07

DECEMBER

'I call architecture frozen music.'

JOHANN WOLFGANG VON GOETHE, WRITER

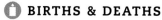 BIRTHS & DEATHS

1863 Italian composer Pietro Mascagni is born in Livorno.

FIRST PERFORMED

1823 Fourteen-year-old Felix Mendelssohn's *Concerto for Two Pianos* is heard for the first time, at his family home in Berlin.

1889 W. S. Gilbert and Arthur Sullivan's operetta *The Gondoliers* is premiered at the Savoy Theatre in London.

1939 William Walton's *Violin Concerto* is given its first performance, in Cleveland.

TODAY'S THE DAY

1732 The Theatre Royal opens in London's Covent Garden. It will eventually become the Royal Opera House.

1787 Wolfgang Amadeus Mozart takes over from the recently deceased Christoph Willibald von Gluck as Imperial and Royal Chamber Composer.

1791 Wolfgang Amadeus Mozart is buried in Vienna.

1814 Luigi Cherubini is appointed a chevalier of the Légion d'Honneur by King Louis XVIII.

1842 The New York Philharmonic Orchestra makes its concert debut.

1857 Camille Saint-Saëns begins work as organist at the Madeleine in Paris.

1881 Leoš Janáček gets a new job as the first director of the Organ School in Brno.

1887 Charles Villiers Stanford becomes Professor of Music at Cambridge University.

1892 Enrique Granados gets married in Barcelona.

1897 Richard Strauss appears as a conductor in England for the first time. Royal College of Music student trombonist Gustav Holst is among the performers in the orchestra's brass section.

1901 Gustav Mahler and Alma Schindler decide to get married in secret.

1902 Max Reger gets married in Württemberg, but as his new wife is a divorcee, the composer is excommunicated from the Roman Catholic Church.

1921 British military bands decide to standardise their instrumentation, removing the tenor horn and introducing the saxophone.

1976 Benjamin Britten's funeral is held in Aldeburgh.

1980 Leonard Bernstein is awarded the Kennedy Center Honour for Lifetime Contributions to American Culture through the Performing Arts.

1982 Aaron Copland appears on stage as a conductor for the final time, with the New Haven Symphony Orchestra.

Musical meaning

The word 'philharmonic' is liberally sprinkled throughout the names of many of the world's greatest orchestras. In the UK, we have the Royal Philharmonic Orchestra, the Royal Liverpool Philharmonic Orchestra, the London Philharmonic Orchestra and even the Philharmonia Orchestra. But what does the word actually mean? It comes from the two Greek words *phileo* and *harmonikos*. When they're welded together 'philharmonic' translates as 'harmony loving'.

HALL OF FAME HIT

Giuseppe Verdi: *Il trovatore*

Recommended Recording

Various soloists; Orchestra and Chorus of La Scala, Milan conducted by Tullio Serafin; Deutsche Grammophon 453 1182

'There is no truer truth obtainable by man than comes of music.'

ROBERT BROWNING, POET AND PLAYWRIGHT

08

DECEMBER

🎵 BIRTHS & DEATHS

1865 Finnish composer Jean Sibelius is born in Hämeenlinna. He is named Johan, changing his name to Jean later in life.

1890 Czech composer Bohuslav Martinů is born in Polička.

1939 Northern Irish flautist James Galway is born in Belfast.

🎵 FIRST PERFORMED

1813 Ludwig van Beethoven's *Symphony No. 7* and *Wellington's Victory* are performed for the first time, in Vienna. The supporting cast is somewhat star-studded: Ignaz Moscheles and Antonio Salieri assist Beethoven in directing *Wellington's Victory*, while the orchestra includes Louis Spohr in the violin section and Giacomo Meyerbeer and Johann Nepomuk Hummel among the percussionists.

1915 Jean Sibelius's *Symphony No. 5* receives its first performance, in Turku, with the composer conducting.

1949 A film version of Leonard Bernstein's *On the Town* is screened for the first time, in New York.

🌅 TODAY'S THE DAY

1790 Johann Peter Salomon and Joseph Haydn sign a contract to produce a series of concerts of Haydn's works – including new commissions – in London.

1881 As many as 650 people are killed when fire breaks out on stage at a performance of *The Tales of Hoffman* in Vienna's Ringtheater.

1911 The San Francisco Symphony Orchestra is founded.

1918 Despite suffering from a nasty bout of flu, Sergei Rachmaninov appears in concert on Rhode Island. It is his first American date since leaving Europe.

1940 Queen's Hall in London is damaged in a German air raid.

COMPOSER PROFILE:

Paul Mealor

The youngest composer featured in this book sprang into the nation's musical consciousness at the biggest event of 2011 – the wedding of the Duke and Duchess of Cambridge at Westminster Abbey. His motet '*Ubi Caritas*' was heard by 2.5 billion people around the world – the largest television audience in broadcasting history. At the end of 2011, he was the darling of the media once again after composing the music to '*Wherever You Are*', a choral work that stormed to the top of the charts after being recorded by the Military Wives. This choir, made up of wives and girlfriends of soldiers serving in Afghanistan, was put together by the inspirational choirmaster Gareth Malone. Mealor studied music at the University of York and combines his work as a choral composer with life as an academic at the University of Aberdeen. The best collection of his music to date comes on the album *A Tender Light*, where it is performed by the choir Tenebrae under the direction of Nigel Short.

🎵 HALL OF FAME HIT

Ludwig van Beethoven: *Symphony No. 8*

Recommended Recording

Leipzig Gewandhaus Orchestra conducted by Riccardo Chailly; Decca 478 3496

09

'Only when I experience do I compose – only when I compose do I experience.'

GUSTAV MAHLER, COMPOSER

🕐 BIRTHS & DEATHS

1837 French composer Charles Emile Waldteufel is born in Strasbourg.

1915 German soprano Elisabeth Schwarzkopf is born in Jarocin.

1967 American violinist Joshua Bell is born in Bloomington.

🎭 FIRST PERFORMED

1836 Mikhail Glinka's opera *A Life for the Tsar* is premiered in St Petersburg.

1842 Mikhail Gilnka's opera *Russlan and Ludmilla* is premiered in St Petersburg.

1882 Gabriel Fauré's *Chanson d'amour* is performed for the first time, in Paris.

1905 Richard Strauss's opera *Salome* is premiered in Dresden.

☀ TODAY'S THE DAY

1820 Franz Schubert's song '*The Trout*' is published in Vienna.

1907 Gustav Mahler and his family set off from Vienna to America. Anton Webern and Arnold Schoenberg are among the guests at their leaving party.

ORCHESTRA FOCUS:

National Youth Orchestra of Great Britain

Founded in 1948, the National Youth Orchestra set out to prove that British teenagers could form a top-quality symphony orchestra that performed core classical repertoire with a proficiency and flair that belied the performers' age. Today, the National Youth Orchestra is the foremost training ground for the musicians who go on to make their careers in professional British orchestras. The statistics speak for themselves: one-fifth of the London Symphony Orchestra's ninety players are NYO graduates; there are thirteen former NYO players in the Philharmonia Orchestra; and the Orchestra of the Royal Opera House and the City of Birmingham Symphony Orchestra have among their ranks twelve and nine NYO alumni respectively. The orchestra draws its players, who are all teenagers, from all corners of the British Isles, for three intensive residential sessions each year. At the end of each period, during which the players receive coaching from top professional musicians, the orchestra performs in concert, often under the baton of Principal Conductor Vasily Petrenko. In 2013, the National Youth Orchestra was awarded the Queen's Medal for Music for its significant contribution to the country's musical life. It remains one of the most important organisations for ensuring that the future of classical music in the UK continues to shine brightly. The *Guardian* has described the orchestra as 'a credit to Britain'.

🎵 HALL OF FAME HIT

Wolfgang Amadeus Mozart: *Symphony No. 39*

Recommended Recording

Scottish Chamber Orchestra conducted by Charles Mackerras; Linn CKD 308

> 'I think and feel in sounds.'
>
> MAURICE RAVEL, COMPOSER

10
DECEMBER

🕭 BIRTHS & DEATHS

1618 Italian composer Giulio Caccini dies in Florence.

1822 Belgian composer César Franck is born in Liège.

1908 French composer and organist Olivier Messiaen is born in Avignon.

1938 Russian conductor Yuri Temirkanov is born in Nalchik.

1958 English pianist Kathryn Stott is born in Nelson.

1980 American violinist Sarah Chang is born in Philadelphia.

1987 Russian-American violinist Jascha Heifetz dies in Los Angeles.

🏛 FIRST PERFORMED

1791 Part of Wolfgang Amadeus Mozart's unfinished *Requiem* is performed for the first time at a memorial service for the composer in St Michael's Church, Vienna.

1818 Ludwig van Beethoven's *String Quintet in C minor, Op. 104*, is given its first performance, in Vienna.

1854 Hector Berlioz's oratorio *L'enfance du Christ* is heard for the first time, in Paris.

1896 Modest Mussorgsky's *Boris Godunov*, in the version orchestrated and completed by Nikolai Rimsky-Korsakov, is premiered at the St Petersburg Conservatoire.

☀ TODAY'S THE DAY

1832 After becoming obsessed with her over a five-year period, Hector Berlioz finally gets to meet the actress Harriet Smithson properly, in Paris.

1895 Giacomo Puccini finishes work on the score for his opera *La bohème*.

1918 Sergei Prokofiev gives his first concert performance in the USA, playing his *Piano Concerto No. 2* with the Russian Symphony Orchestra in New York.

COMPOSER PROFILE:

Giuseppe Verdi

Verdi showed musical promise very early. By the time he was seven, he was already helping the organist at his local church. Though he was turned down for a place at the Milan Conservatoire because of his age, a local grocer paid for him to have lessons with a leading Milanese composer. Verdi was always determined to succeed as an opera composer. Things went well for him from the start – *Oberto*, his first opera, was a success – but then tragedy struck. His two young children perished in quick succession.

Then, his wife died of a brain fever. His first attempt at a comic opera was booed off stage at its premiere. Luckily, the director of La Scala, Milan, sent him the libretto for *Nabucco*. It was a hit, as were the operas that followed, including *Rigoletto* and *Il trovatore*. By contrast, *La traviata* didn't do so well at the start, but *Don Carlos*, *La forza del destino*, *Aida*, *Otello* and *Falstaff* all proved to be sure-fire winners. When he died, some 28,000 people lined the streets of Milan for his funeral.

🎵 HALL OF FAME HIT

Malcolm Arnold: *The Padstow Lifeboat*

Recommended Recording
London Philharmonic Orchestra conducted by David Parry; LPO 0063

11

DECEMBER

'The artist who does not feel satisfied with elegant lines, well-balanced colours and a beautiful succession of harmonies does not understand art.'

CAMILLE SAINT-SAËNS, COMPOSER

🕛 BIRTHS & DEATHS

1803 French composer Hector Berlioz is born in La Côte-Saint-André.

1908 American composer Elliott Carter is born in New York.

1960 English composer Rachel Portman is born in Haslemere.

☀ TODAY'S THE DAY

1784 Wolfgang Amadeus Mozart finishes work on his *Piano Concerto No. 19*, in Vienna. This is also the day he becomes a freemason.

1818 Ludwig van Beethoven admits in court, during the custody battle for his nephew, that he is not of noble birth and that the 'van' in his name is an affectation. It means that the legal hearing needs to take place all over again in a court that is specifically for commoners.

1819 Although they undoubtedly wrote music before today, Felix and Fanny Mendelssohn's earliest datable works are performed in Berlin, as a birthday present for their father.

1920 Tenor Enrico Caruso suffers a throat haemorrhage while singing at the Brooklyn Academy of Music.

1936 Dmitri Shostakovich withdraws his *Symphony No. 4*, which was due to be performed tonight in Leningrad, after a sustained campaign by Communist Party bosses.

COMPOSER PROFILE:

Nikolai Rimsky-Korsakov

A hugely influential Russian composer, orchestrator and teacher, Rimsky-Korsakov started out in life wanting to be a sailor. He took time out for piano lessons along the way and it was his piano teacher who introduced him to the composer Mily Balakirev. He then met Cui, Mussorgsky and Borodin (the group known as 'The Five' or 'The Mighty Handful'). While still serving in the Navy, he was made Professor of Composition and Orchestration at the St Petersburg Conservatoire at the spectacularly early age of 27.

Later, he was able to combine his two passions when he became Inspector of Naval Bands, a post created for him by the Russian Admiralty. In all, he wrote 15 operas. As well as being a fine composer in his own right, he was a keen completer and orchestrator of other people's music, as his work on Mussorgsky's *Boris Godunov* and Borodin's *Prince Igor* testifies. Perhaps his best-known work is his symphonic suite *Scheherazade*, which is based on *One Thousand and One Nights*.

🎵 HALL OF FAME HIT

Franz Schubert: *String Quartet in D minor ('Death and the Maiden')*

Recommended Recording

Alban Berg Quartet; EMI 735 8702

> 'Musical training is a more potent instrument than any other, because rhythm and harmony find their way into the secret places of the soul.'
>
> **PLATO, GREEK PHILOSOPHER**

12

DECEMBER

BIRTHS & DEATHS

1937 English organist and conductor Philip Ledger is born in Bexhill-on-Sea.

FIRST PERFORMED

1920 Maurice Ravel's *La valse* is performed for the first time as an orchestral work, in Paris.

TODAY'S THE DAY

1793 Eleven-year-old pianist John Field makes his concert debut in London.

1823 Franz Liszt's father asks Luigi Cherubini to consider letting his 12-year-old son study at the Paris Conservatoire, but he is rebuffed, as the college is open only to French citizens.

1835 Niccolò Paganini impresses the Grand Duchess Marie-Louise so much at her birthday concert in Parma that he is awarded complete control of all court music.

1836 Teatro La Fenice in Venice is almost completely destroyed by fire.

1852 Georges Bizet is awarded the first prize for piano at the Paris Conservatoire.

1872 The musicians and audience at the Prague Provisional Theatre give Bedřich Smetana a ten-minute standing ovation at the start of a performance. They're showing their support for the conductor after attempts to oust him from his job.

1877 Antonín Dvořák writes to Johannes Brahms to thank him for his support in getting him onto the list of artists who receive state funding.

1893 Nikolai Rimsky-Korsakov conducts a concert of Tchaikovsky's music in St Petersburg as a tribute to the recently deceased composer.

1907 Gustav and Alma Mahler set sail for New York from Cherbourg.

COMPOSER PROFILE:

Sergei Prokofiev

Prokofiev studied with the composers Glière, Rimsky-Korsakov and Liadov. He became enveloped in the Russian Romantic tradition, although he managed to combine this with a natural leaning towards 20th-century modernism. His early works, such as his *Piano Concerto No. 1*, show off his more lyrical side, as does his *Symphony No. 1* (known as the *Classical Symphony*), which was written when he was just 26 years old. An accomplished concert pianist,

Prokofiev left Russia the year after the 1917 Russian Revolution, returning home only in 1936. At first, the authorities approved of his music, but his *Symphony No. 6* got him into the Communist Party's bad books. Aside from his work for the concert hall, Prokofiev became widely respected for his ballets, including *Romeo and Juliet*. He also composed some striking film scores and the mammoth opera *War and Peace*. He died on 5 March 1953 – the very same day as Stalin.

HALL OF FAME HIT

Francis Poulenc: *Gloria*

Recommended Recording

Susan Gritton (soprano); Polyphony; Britten Sinfonia; Choir of Trinity College, Cambridge conducted by Stephen Layton; Hyperion CDA 67623

13

> 'The most difficult things written by one perfectly versed in the difficulties of the keyboard are far easier to play than the easiest things conceived by an amateur.'
> ROBERT SCHUMANN, COMPOSER

DECEMBER

🕐 BIRTHS & DEATHS

1835 American clergyman Phillips Brooks, who wrote the Christmas carol 'Oh, Little Town of Bethlehem', is born in Boston.

🎵 FIRST PERFORMED

1895 Gustav Mahler's *Symphony No. 2* ('*The Resurrection*') is performed for the first time in its complete form, in Berlin.
1928 George Gershwin's *An American in Paris* is given its first performance, in New York's Carnegie Hall.
1944 Leonard Bernstein's musical *On the Town* is premiered in Boston.

☀ TODAY'S THE DAY

1768 Wolfgang Amadeus Mozart finishes work on his *Symphony No. 8*, in Vienna.
1769 Leopold and Wolfgang Amadeus Mozart set off on a tour of Italy, playing concerts along the way.
1836 For the third time, Frédéric Chopin sees the woman who will become the love of his life, George Sand, in Paris. On this occasion, she is dressed in women's (rather than her usual men's) clothes.
1844 The Schumann family moves to Dresden, but Robert's mental and physical state is reaching a low point. His doctor diagnoses acute depression, insomnia and exhaustion and suggests that his work as a composer is not helping matters.
1863 Modest Mussorgsky takes up a job as Collegiate Secretary at Russia's Central Engineering Authority.
1885 Alexander Borodin makes his debut as a conductor in front of the Orchestra of the Medical Academy in St Petersburg.
1907 Ralph Vaughan Williams begins three months of studies with fellow composer Maurice Ravel.
1917 Richard Strauss conducts the 100th performance of his opera *Der Rosenkavalier*, in Dresden.
1948 William Walton marries Susana Valeria Rosa Maria Gil Passo, in Argentina.

GENRE FOCUS:

Verismo opera

The brand of opera championed by the likes of Giacomo Puccini is often labelled as *verismo*, the Italian for realist (from the word *vero*, meaning 'truth'). Such operas concentrate on realistic subject-matter – occasionally considered sordid, and sometimes scandalous, at the time. They also tend to be what is technically termed through-composed, rather than a series of stops and starts for arias and recitatives. As well as Puccini, Mascagni, Leoncavallo, Cilea and Giordano are all considered leading *verismo* composers.

Messiah

Premiered in Dublin in 1742, this is Handel's greatest oratorio, beloved of choral societies the world over. In some ways, it is odd that Handel is most remembered for a religious work, as he spent far more time composing secular operas. The libretto was put together from the Bible by Handel's friend, Charles Jennens, and the music took Handel just three weeks to compose. The *Hallelujah Chorus* is a wonderfully life-affirming highlight of the work. It is worth noting that this work's correct title does not include the definite article.

HALL OF FAME HIT
Simon Dobson: *Penlee*

Recommended Recording
Leyland Band; Faber Music 0571 522165

'This will be our reply to violence: to make music more intensely, more beautifully, more devotedly than ever before.'

LEONARD BERNSTEIN, CONDUCTOR AND COMPOSER, IN RESPONSE TO THE ASSASSINATION OF JOHN F. KENNEDY

14
DECEMBER

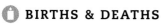 BIRTHS & DEATHS

1788 German composer Carl Philipp Emanuel Bach dies in Hamburg.

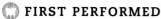 FIRST PERFORMED

1828 Franz Schubert's *Symphony No. 6* is given its first performance, in Vienna.
1916 Claude Debussy's *Etudes* are heard for the first time, in Paris.
1916 Jean Sibelius's *Symphony No. 5* receives its first performance, in Helsinki.
1918 Giacomo Puccini's *Il trittico* – a series of three operas: *Il tabarro*, *Suor Angelica* and *Gianni Schicchi* – is premiered at the Metropolitan Opera in New York.
1924 Ottorino Respighi's *The Pines of Rome* is given its first performance, appropriately enough, in Rome.
1925 Alban Berg's opera *Wozzeck* is premiered in Berlin.
1936 Samuel Barber's *String Quartet, Op. 11*, is performed for the first time, in Rome. The composer rearranged this piece twice – first taking the middle movement and using it to form his very famous *Adagio for Strings* and then giving it a choral setting as his '*Agnus Dei*'. He certainly knew how to make a good tune work hard for his royalty cheques.

☀ TODAY'S THE DAY

1725 Antonio Vivaldi's *The Four Seasons* is published.
1837 Eighteen-year-old Clara Wieck (later Schumann) gives the first of six concerts at the Musikvereinsaal in Vienna. She quickly achieves superstar status across the city.
1885 Jean Sibelius gives his first public performance, at the Helsinki Music Institute. However, his timing is poor, as all the city's classical music critics are round the corner in a different concert hall listening to the local premiere of Tchaikovsky's *Piano Concerto No. 1*.
1901 Béla Bartók earns cash for playing music for the first time – after performing in a casino.
1921 Ralph Vaughan Williams conducts his first concert in charge of the Bach Choir, in Westminster Central Hall.

COMPOSER PROFILE:

Joby Talbot

Joby Talbot was Classic FM's first ever Composer in Residence. The album *Once Around the Sun* was the culmination of that year-long project. A graduate of the Guildhall School of Music and Drama in London, Talbot was a member of the pop band The Divine Comedy before turning to composing classical music, and film and television scores. Talbot's film work includes scores for Alfred Hitchcock's *The Lodger* and for *The Hitchhiker's Guide to the Galaxy*, with his television work including the scores to *Robbie the Reindeer* and *The League of Gentlemen*.

♪ HALL OF FAME HIT
Tomaso Vitali: *Chaconne*

Recommended Recording
Sarah Chang (violin); EMI 56791

15

'Why do rhythms and melodies, which are mere sounds, resemble dispositions, while tastes do not, nor yet colours or smells?'

ARISTOTLE, PHILOSOPHER

DECEMBER

🕊 BIRTHS & DEATHS

1909 Spanish composer Francisco Tárrega dies in Barcelona.

🎼 FIRST PERFORMED

1883 Gabriel Fauré's *Elégie* for cello and piano receives its first performance, in Paris.
1900 Sergei Rachmaninov performs the second and third movements of his *Piano Concerto No. 2* for the first time, in Moscow. The positive reaction encourages him to finish work on the first movement.
1901 Sergei Rachmaninov's *Cello Sonata* is given its first performance, in Moscow, with the composer playing the piano.
1920 Ralph Vaughan Williams' *The Lark Ascending* is heard for the first time, in an arrangement for violin and piano, in Shirehampton Public Hall.

1927 Zoltán Kodály's *Háry János* orchestral suite is given its first performance, in New York.
2000 John Adams' oratorio *El Niño* is premiered, in Paris.

☀ TODAY'S THE DAY

1763 Johann Christian Bach is granted a royal privilege by King George III, enabling him to publish and copyright his works in Britain.
1790 Joseph Haydn travels from Vienna to London for the first time.
1791 A memorial service for Wolfgang Amadeus Mozart is held in the Nicolai Church in Prague.
1815 Gioachino Rossini agrees a deal with Duke Francesco Sforza Cesarini to write an opera to be staged at the Nobile Teatro della Torre Argentina. The opera in question is *The Barber of Seville*.

1826 The biggest of the Schubertiad parties celebrating the music of Franz Schubert is held in Vienna.
1838 The owner of the house in which they are staying in Parma tells Frédéric Chopin and George Sand, along with her two children, to leave after his discovery that the composer's constant coughing is caused by tuberculosis.
1852 Richard Wagner finishes work on the text of the entire *Ring Cycle*.
1888 The foundation stone for the Royal English Opera House is laid in London's Shaftesbury Avenue.

Mrs Haydn

Luigi Boccherini's musical style was, on occasions, somewhat reminiscent of that of the great Haydn. So, if you ever hear Boccherini referred to as 'the wife of Haydn', this is a nickname he was given during his lifetime, because of the stylistic similarities of their music.

♪ HALL OF FAME HIT

Felix Mendelssohn: *Octet*

Recommended Recording
Members of the Australian Chamber Orchestra; BIS 1984

'People who make music together cannot be enemies, at least not while the music lasts.'

PAUL HINDEMITH, COMPOSER

16

DECEMBER

 BIRTHS & DEATHS

1770 Today is believed to be the day German composer Ludwig van Beethoven is born in Bonn.

1882 Hungarian composer Zoltán Kodály is born in Kecskemét.

1899 English composer and lyricist Noël Coward is born in Teddington.

1921 French composer Camille Saint-Saëns dies in Algiers.

1946 English harpsichordist and conductor Trevor Pinnock is born in Canterbury.

ORCHESTRA FOCUS:

Simón Bolívar Symphony Orchestra

 FIRST PERFORMED

1893 Antonín Dvořák's *Symphony No. 9, 'From the New World'*, is given its first performance, in New York.

1921 Sergei Prokofiev's *Piano Concerto No. 3* receives its first performance, in Chicago, with the composer as soloist.

1938 Francis Poulenc's *Organ Concerto* is heard for the first time, at a private performance in Paris, with Maurice Duruflé at the organ and Nadia Boulanger conducting.

 TODAY'S THE DAY

1785 Wolfgang Amadeus Mozart finishes work on his *Piano Concerto No. 22* in Vienna.

1838 Niccolò Paganini hears Hector Berlioz's *Harold in Italy*, which was composed for the great violinist and viola player, for the first time. Paganini is seriously ill with throat cancer, but is greatly moved by the performance.

1854 Richard Wagner writes to Franz Liszt, telling him about his idea for the opera *Tristan and Isolde*.

1890 Johannes Brahms meets Gustav Mahler at a performance of the opera *Don Giovanni* in Budapest, which the latter is conducting.

2002 The Three Tenors perform their 30th concert together in Saint Paul.

The genesis for this orchestra came back in 1975, when a Venezuelan economist called José Antonio Abreu founded a music-education programme in his native land, with the aim of creating a national network of orchestras for young people across the country. It became known as 'El Sistema' and four decades later it has grown to a web of 125 separate, but affiliated, orchestras. More than 300,000 children take part in the programme, with the vast majority coming from economically deprived backgrounds. The Simón Bolívar Symphony Orchestra is the most famous of these Venezuelan orchestras. It first came to prominence in the UK and the USA in 2007, with its engaging young conductor Gustavo Dudamel playing a significant part in the orchestra's success. Originally made up solely of young players, these musicians are now in some cases well into their thirties, so the orchestra no longer presents itself with the word 'Youth' in its title. Despite the advancing of the years, their sound remains big and bold and their performances crackle with vibrant energy – unsurprising really, when you consider that the orchestra is twice the size of a standard symphony outfit.

 HALL OF FAME HIT

Hans Zimmer: *Pirates of the Caribbean*

Recommended Recording

Original soundtrack; Walt Disney Records 0946 39570324

17

DECEMBER

'My music is best understood by children and animals.'

IGOR STRAVINSKY, COMPOSER

 BIRTHS & DEATHS

1749 Italian composer Domenico Cimarosa is born in Aversa.

1889 Ukrainian ballet dancer Vaslav Nijinsky is born in Kiev.

1894 American violinist and conductor Arthur Fiedler is born in Boston.

1930 English composer Philip Heseltine, who wrote music under the name Peter Warlock, dies in London.

 FIRST PERFORMED

1853 Johannes Brahms' *Piano Sonata No. 1* is performed for the first time, in Leipzig.

1865 Franz Schubert's *Symphony No. 8* ('*Unfinished*') is given its first performance, in Vienna, some 43 years after it was composed.

1953 Dmitri Shostakovich's *Symphony No. 10* receives its first performance, in Leningrad.

 TODAY'S THE DAY

1770 Ludwig van Beethoven is baptised in Bonn.

1779 The librettist to many of Wolfgang Amadeus Mozart's most successful operas, Lorenzo Da Ponte, is exiled from Venice because of his rather liberal view of the world – both in terms of his politics and also when it comes to relationships with married women. As an ordained priest, he was expected to toe the line on both counts.

1825 Boston piano manufacturer Alpheus Babcock is issued with a patent to put a one-piece metal frame inside a wooden piano to help prevent the casing expanding or contracting depending on the ambient temperature.

1858 Franz Liszt conducts a performance of Beethoven's music for his final concert as Kapellmeister in Weimar.

1926 John Ireland gets married to a student 30 years his junior at Chelsea Registry Office. The marriage lasts for only two years.

2000 The Three Tenors perform their 26th concert together in Chicago.

Slowly decomposing

After they died, it took a while for many of the greatest composers to be allowed to rest in peace. Bach, Mozart, Haydn, Beethoven and Schubert were all exhumed and reburied at various times. Mozart's, Haydn's and Donizetti's skulls were also parted from their bodies when they were buried. There seems to have been a roaring trade in Haydn skulls – with several doing the rounds in the years after his death. Many years later, the Australian composer and pianist Percy Grainger left an instruction in his will that his skeleton should be put on show at the University of Melbourne. The university turned down the generous offer on the grounds of public decency.

 HALL OF FAME HIT

Alexander Glazunov: *The Seasons*

Recommended Recording

Royal Philharmonic Orchestra conducted by Vladimir Ashkenazy; Decca 4783106

> 'It will generally be admitted that Beethoven's Fifth Symphony is the most sublime noise that has ever penetrated the ear of man.'
>
> E. M. FORSTER, WRITER, HOWARD'S END, 1910

18
DECEMBER

🕐 BIRTHS & DEATHS

1707 English clergyman and hymn writer Charles Wesley is born in Epworth.

1737 Italian violin maker Antonio Stradivari dies in Cremona.

1860 American composer Edward MacDowell is born in New York.

1869 American composer and pianist Louis Moreau Gottschalk dies in Tijuca, Brazil.

1944 English trumpeter Crispian Steele-Perkins is born in Exeter.

1948 English conductor William Boughton is born in Birmingham.

🎵 FIRST PERFORMED

1795 Ludwig van Beethoven's *Piano Concerto No. 1* is given its first performance, in Vienna, with the composer at the keyboard.

1853 Eighteen-year-old Camille Saint-Saëns hears his *Symphony No. 1* performed for the first time, in Paris.

1878 Antonín Dvořák's *Slavonic Dance Nos 5–8* are heard for the first time, in Dresden, following on from *Nos 1–4* on 4 December.

1880 Pyotr Ilyich Tchaikovsky's *Capriccio Italien* receives its first performance, in Moscow.

1892 Pyotr Ilyich Tchaikovky's ballet *The Nutcracker* is premiered in St Petersburg.

1908 Claude Debussy's piano suite *Children's Corner* is given its first performance, in Paris.

2002 The film *The Hours*, with a score by Philip Glass, is screened for the first time.

☀ TODAY'S THE DAY

1732 The Theatre Royal, Covent Garden, is founded in London.

1852 Over the next two days, Richard Wagner gives a reading of the complete poem for the *Ring Cycle*, just outside Zurich.

1905 Alexander Glazunov is appointed director of the Moscow Conservatoire.

1905 Hubert Parry is appointed a Knight Commander of the Royal Victorian Order by King Edward VII.

GENRE FOCUS:

Crossover classical music

The boundaries of what is, and what isn't, classical music can sometimes become quite blurred. A singer might have a selection of popular operatic arias in his repertoire, which he sings in an operatic style. These fall comfortably into the definition of classical music and, although he does not perform full operas, we would be happy to agree that this is genuine classical music. But at the same time, a singer might also perform what are essentially pop songs in an operatic style. This definitely doesn't make them opera and they shouldn't really be thought of as classical music in its strictest sense. However, many crossover performers have enjoyed huge success in selling records and at getting audiences along to large-scale live concerts. For many people, they offer a route into listening to classical music, and they should hold no threat to the core classical music world. Crossover classical music comes at the point where pop music and classical music collide. Sometimes it doesn't quite work, but sometimes this fusion can create quite a stir.

HALL OF FAME HIT
Gustav Holst: *A Moorside Suite*

Recommended Recording
London Symphony Orchestra conducted by Richard Hickox; Regis RRC 1200

19

DECEMBER

'Medicine, to produce health, must know disease;
music, to produce harmony, must know discord.'
PLUTARCH, HISTORIAN

BIRTHS & DEATHS

1746 Italian castrato Venanzio Rauzzini is born in Camerino.
1944 American harpsichordist and conductor William Christie is born in Buffalo.
1958 English cellist Steven Isserlis is born in London.

FIRST PERFORMED

1865 Nikolai Rimsky-Korsakov's *Symphony No. 1* is performed for the first time, in St Petersburg.

TODAY'S THE DAY

1788 Carl Philipp Emanuel Bach is buried in Hamburg.
1839 Mikhail Glinka asks Tsar Nicholas I to let him leave his job as Imperial Kapellmeister due to ill health.
1869 Louis Moreau Gottschalk is buried in Rio de Janeiro.
1906 Béla Bartók and Zoltán Kodály publish *Hungarian Folk Songs*.
1922 Dmitri Shostakovich and Alexander Glazunov are in the audience in Petrograd for the first night of a tour by Léon Theremin and his eponymous new electric instrument.
1937 Doctors operate on Maurice Ravel's brain. Shortly afterwards, he falls into a permanent state of coma.

COMPOSER PROFILE:

Sergei Rachmaninov

Rachmaninov was born into an aristocratic family that was frequently strapped for cash. While still a student, he wrote *Aleko*, a prize-winning one-act opera, his *Piano Concerto No. 1* and *Morceaux de fantaisie*, a set of piano pieces that included one that was to make the young Rachmaninov world famous. It was his *Prelude in C sharp minor*. However, his publishers let him down by failing to copyright it outside Russia, so they – and Rachmaninov – could only look on as it was reprinted around the globe without earning any of them a rouble. Disaster struck again when the premiere of his *Symphony No. 1* was a total flop, not least because the conductor Alexander Glazunov was said to be drunk. Rachmaninov fell into a state of acute depression and stopped composing altogether. He recovered only with the help of a psychotherapist, to whom he dedicated his stunning *Piano Concerto No. 2*.

The Russian Revolution of 1917 forced Rachmaninov out of his homeland and he settled in the USA. He became an incredibly popular performer and conductor of his own works across America. Part of the reason for his brilliance at the piano was due to his unusually large hands, with very long fingers and thumbs, which enabled him to stretch further across the keyboard than the majority of other pianists at the time.

HALL OF FAME HIT

Ralph Vaughan Williams: *Toward the Unknown Region*

Recommended Recording

London Symphony Orchestra and Chorus conducted by Malcolm Sargent; EMI 216 1512

> 'Music is only understood when one goes away singing it and only loved when one falls asleep with it in one's head, and finds it still there the next morning.'

ARNOLD SCHOENBERG, COMPOSER

 BIRTHS & DEATHS

1948 British-Japanese pianist Mitsuko Uchida is born near Tokyo.

1982 American pianist Arthur Rubinstein dies in Geneva.

2010 English choral director John Alldis dies in London.

 FIRST PERFORMED

1823 Franz Schubert's opera *Rosamunde* is premiered in Vienna.

1879 Pyotr Ilyich Tchaikovsky's *Orchestral Suite No. 1* is performed for the first time, in Moscow.

1886 Johannes Brahms' *Piano Trio No. 3 in C* is given its first performance, in Budapest.

1905 Alexander Glazunov's *Symphony No. 3* receives its first performance, in New York.

 TODAY'S THE DAY

1775 Wolfgang Amadeus Mozart finishes work on his *Violin Concerto No. 5*, in Salzburg.

1826 Doctors operate on Ludwig van Beethoven in his Vienna home to remove fluid from his body. He will undergo the procedure on three further occasions.

1862 Alexander Borodin is appointed Assistant Professor of Chemistry at the Medical-Surgical Academy in St Petersburg.

1915 Igor Stravinsky makes his conducting debut at a Red Cross fundraising concert organised by the ballet promoter Sergei Diaghilev. The orchestra performs his *Firebird Suite*.

ORCHESTRA FOCUS:

Orchestra of the Age of Enlightenment

One of the more prosaically named ensembles in this book, the OAE is different from nearly all the other orchestras we feature because it tends not to play by the same set of rules as everyone else. Now, don't misunderstand us, because artistically the OAE is absolutely top notch, but it likes to be a little different. So, there's no single principal conductor running things, while the players perform on period instruments without any of the snazzy modern technological advances that would make, say, a 21st-century clarinet unfamiliar to a composer such as Mozart. Conductors Simon Rattle, Mark Elder, Ivan Fischer and Vladimir Jurowski are regular fixtures on the podium each season and the orchestra has carved out a new niche for itself with its 'Night Shift' performances that place classical music in non-traditional late-night settings, with the aim of taking the genre to a group of listeners who would otherwise quite probably never encounter classical music in a live setting at all. By the way, the 'Age of Enlightenment' was an era from around the start of the 18th century, during which 'reason' and 'individualism' were emphasised over 'tradition'. Intellectuals of the period placed great store in using science to question ideas that had previously been seen as unchallengeable – so it's easy to see from where the musicians behind the OAE have drawn their inspiration.

 HALL OF FAME HIT

Carl Maria von Weber: *Clarinet Concerto No. 1*

Recommended Recording

Maximiliano Martin (clarinet); Scottish Chamber Orchestra conducted by Alexander Janiczek; Linn CKD409

21

DECEMBER

'Music creates order out of chaos; for rhythm imposes continuity upon the disjointed, and harmony imposes compatibility upon the incongruous.'

YEHUDI MENUHIN, VIOLINIST AND CONDUCTOR

BIRTHS & DEATHS

1944 American pianist and conductor Michael Tilson Thomas is born in Hollywood.

1953 Hungarian pianist András Schiff is born in Budapest.

1955 Canadian violinist and conductor Peter Oundjian is born in Toronto.

1957 English composer Eric Coates dies in Chichester.

FIRST PERFORMED

1934 Sergei Prokofiev's *Lieutenant Kijé Suite* is heard for the first time, on Moscow Radio.

TODAY'S THE DAY

1907 Gustav and Alma Mahler arrive in New York. They are housed in a suite in the Hotel Majestic, which has been furnished with two grand pianos.

1953 NBC chooses Gian Carlo Menotti's one-act opera *Amahl and the Night Visitors* as its first colour broadcast of a commercial television programme in the USA.

COMPOSER PROFILE:

Joseph Haydn

Haydn was one of the big names of the Classical period of classical music. By the time he was just five years old, he was showing amazing musical talent. Three years later, he became a choirboy at St Stephen's Cathedral in Venice. At the age of 29, his life changed when he was given a job by Prince Paul Esterházy. He remained in the service of the noble family for the next three decades.

Haydn was a prolific composer and his name is particularly associated with the symphony. In total, he wrote 104 catalogued symphonies and, in doing so, changed the direction of the genre completely. Haydn's fame spread when he was in his forties and fifties. He took the opportunity to travel to England, Spain and France and bought a house for himself in Vienna. He took on pupils, such as Ludwig van Beethoven, who was just a teenage boy. Wherever he went, his visits were treated as major musical events, with other composers, members of royal families and academics falling over themselves to pay their respects. His music was both critically acclaimed and highly lucrative. Alongside his symphonies, he is also admired for his oratorios *The Creation* and *The Seasons*. It's true to say that Haydn might not have led the most adventurous or exciting life, but his relatively comfortable circumstances allowed him the time and space to compose many masterpieces.

HALL OF FAME HIT

César Franck: *Symphonic Variations for Piano and Orchestra*

Recommended Recording

Pascal Rogé (piano); Cleveland Orchestra conducted by Lorin Maazel; Australian Eloquence 480 4864

'I cannot conceive of music that expresses absolutely nothing.'

BÉLA BARTÓK, COMPOSER

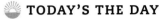 BIRTHS & DEATHS

1858 Italian composer Giacomo Puccini is born in Lucca.
1883 French composer and conductor Edgard Varèse is born in Paris.

FIRST PERFORMED

1789 Wolfgang Amadeus Mozart's *Clarinet Quintet* is given its first performance, in Vienna.
1808 Ludwig van Beethoven's *Symphony No. 5*, *Symphony No. 6*, *Choral Fantasy* and *Piano Concerto No. 4* all receive their first performances in one mammoth concert in Vienna, which lasts for more than four hours in an unheated theatre in the middle of winter. It is the last time that Beethoven performs a piano concerto on stage.
1894 Claude Debussy's *Prelude à l'après-midi d'un faune* is given its first performance, in Paris.
1922 Igor Stravinsky's *Pulcinella Suite* is performed for the first time, in Boston.
1982 John Tavener's choral work *The Lamb* is heard for the first time, in Winchester Cathedral.

TODAY'S THE DAY

1823 Twelve-year-old Franz Liszt's piano playing takes Paris by storm and he will perform 38 concerts in the French capital over the next three months.

COMPOSER PROFILE:

Johannes Brahms

Brahms' background was not at all well to do; he had to go out to work from the age of 13 to earn extra cash to help to support his family. He ended up, so it is said, playing the piano in Hamburg bars that doubled as brothels. Initially, this was the extent of his ambitions, but a meeting with Robert Schumann when Brahms was aged 20 changed all that for the good. Schumann marvelled at the innate talent of Brahms, saying that he had 'sprung like Minerva fully armed from the head of the son of Cronus'. Over the years, Brahms proved himself masterly at all types of classical music, except opera, which he never apparently found tempting. His output of major works, however, was not fast and furious in his early years. He did have a particularly creative period from the age of 35, during which he produced an amazing body of work, including his *Symphonies Nos 1–4*, *Violin Concerto* and *Piano Concerto No. 2*. All of this music was Romantic and lyrical, but at the same time it was musically progressive. Some 50 years later the great modernist Schoenberg wrote an essay about how he took inspiration from Brahms and his music.

HALL OF FAME HIT

Gustav Mahler: *Symphony No. 3*

Recommended Recording

Birgit Remmert (contralto); City of Birmingham Youth Chorus; City of Birmingham Symphony Orchestra and Chorus conducted by Simon Rattle; EMI 556 6572

23

DECEMBER

> 'The art of music above all other arts is the expression of the soul of a nation. The composer must love the tunes of his country and they must become an integral part of him.'
>
> **RALPH VAUGHAN WILLIAMS, COMPOSER**

BIRTHS & DEATHS

1934 Italian conductor Claudio Scimone is born in Padua.
2000 American pianist and comedic musician Victor Borge dies in Greenwich, Connecticut.

FIRST PERFORMED

1785 Wolfgang Amadeus Mozart's *Piano Concerto No. 22* is given its first performance, in Vienna.
1806 Ludwig van Beethoven's *Violin Concerto* receives its first performance, in Vienna. The composer finishes the score only in the nick of time, with the soloist forced to sight-read his part.
1893 Engelbert Humperdinck's opera *Hansel and Gretel* is premiered in Weimar, with Richard Strauss conducting.

TODAY'S THE DAY

1828 A memorial service and concert in honour of Franz Schubert are held in Vienna.
1841 Fanny Mendelssohn completes *The Year*, a set of 12 piano pieces depicting the passage of the year, one per month. Only one will be published before her death.
1891 Antonín Dvořák signs a two-year contract to direct the National Conservatory of Music in New York.
1901 Gustav Mahler and Alma Schindler get engaged in Vienna.
1913 Edward Elgar signs his first recording contract, which guarantees him two-thirds of the net royalties paid from 'mechanical instrument reproduction'.
1934 George Gershwin's three-month series of Sunday-night radio programmes of his music comes to an end.
1989 Leonard Bernstein conducts the first of two concerts of Beethoven's *Symphony No. 9* to celebrate the falling of the Berlin Wall. Tonight's concert is in the Philharmonie in West Berlin.
1997 Peter Maxwell Davies arrives in the Antarctic to spend a month researching the *Antarctic Symphony* he is due to compose following a commission from the Philharmonia Orchestra and the British Antarctic Survey.

Summer snow

Leroy Anderson's *Sleigh Ride* is a perennial Christmas favourite, but if you thought that he composed it in the deep midwinter, then you would be wrong. The musical score comes complete with a horsewhip and was actually written during the height of a summer heatwave.

HALL OF FAME HIT

Louis Léfebure-Wely: *Sortie in E flat major*

Recommended Recording

Katherine Dienes-Williams (organ); Herald HAVP 371

'The flute is not an instrument with a good moral effect. It is too exciting.'

ARISTOTLE, PHILOSOPHER

BIRTHS & DEATHS

1453 English composer John Dunstable dies in London.

1577 Patriarch of the Amati violin-making dynasty, Andrea Amati dies in Cremona.

1906 American conductor and composer Franz Waxman is born in Königshütte.

1935 Austrian composer Alban Berg dies in Vienna.

2012 English composer and pianist Richard Rodney Bennett dies in New York.

FIRST PERFORMED

1818 Organist Franz Gruber performs his composition 'Silent Night, Holy Night' for the first time, at the St Nicholas Church in Oberndorf, near Salzburg. The assistant priest, Joseph Mohr, wrote the words in 1816, but showed them to Gruber only this afternoon, asking him to compose a melody.

1871 Giuseppe Verdi's opera *Aida* is premiered at the Cairo Opera House.

1931 Benjamin Britten's *A Shepherd's Carol* is heard for the first time, during a BBC Home Service broadcast.

1951 Gian Carlo Menotti's opera *Amahl and the Night Visitors* is premiered on the NBC television network.

TODAY'S THE DAY

1781 Wolfgang Amadeus Mozart and Muzio Clementi hold a piano-playing duel in front of members of European royalty. It is felt that Mozart just edges it, by the slimmest of margins.

1835 Gioachino Rossini's finances are settled for the rest of his life, after the French government decides to pay him the annuity promised to him five years earlier. He is also to receive all the money he is owed.

1840 A huge fan of music, Queen Victoria's consort Prince Albert, who is a composer in his own right, turns the Queen's wind band into a full orchestra.

1880 Claude Debussy begins composition lessons at the Paris Conservatoire.

1903 The first performance of Richard Wagner's opera *Parsifal* outside Bayreuth takes place, at the Metropolitan Opera in New York.

1920 Enrico Caruso gives his final performance at New York's Metropolitan Opera.

1921 The funeral of Camille Saint-Saëns is held in Paris.

Favourite carols

Every year, Classic FM listeners vote in their thousands in our annual poll of the nation's favourite carols. Here is the Top 30 from Christmas 2013:

No. 1: *O Holy Night*
No. 2: *Silent Night*
No. 3: *In the Bleak Midwinter* (Gustav Holst version)
No. 4: *Hark! The Herald Angels Sing*

No. 5: *In the Bleak Midwinter* (Harold Darke version)
No. 6: *O Come, All Ye Faithful*
No. 7: *O Little Town of Bethlehem*
No. 8: *Once in Royal David's City*
No. 9: *O Come, O Come Emmanuel*
No. 10: *Carol of the Bells*
No. 11: *Ding Dong! Merrily on High*
(continues on next page)

HALL OF FAME HIT

Giacomo Puccini: *La rondine*

Recommended Recording

Various soloists; London Symphony Orchestra conducted by Antonio Pappano; EMI 640 7482

25

DECEMBER

> 'Listen to music religiously, as if it were the last strain you might hear.'
>
> HENRY DAVID THOREAU, WRITER AND PHILOSOPHER

🕑 BIRTHS & DEATHS

1964 English tenor Ian Bostridge is born in London.

2005 Swedish soprano Birgit Nilsson dies in Vastra Karup.

🎭 FIRST PERFORMED

1723 Johann Sebastian Bach's *Magnificat* is performed for the first time, in Leipzig.

1734 Johann Sebastian Bach's *Christmas Oratorio* is given its first performance, in Leipzig.

1870 Richard Wagner gives his wife Cosima a surprise birthday and Christmas present of his new *Siegfried Idyll*, performed for the first time, by musicians on the stairs outside her bedroom.

1997 Philip Glass's score to the movie *Kundun* is heard for the first time.

☀ TODAY'S THE DAY

1583 English composer Orlando Gibbons is baptised in Oxford.

1777 Wolfgang Amadeus Mozart finishes work on his *Flute Quartet in D*, in Mannheim.

1808 Johann Nepomuk Hummel is sacked by Prince Nikolas Esterházy for spending too much time composing for the theatre in Vienna, instead of working for the Prince. Hummel appeals and is given his job back.

1816 Carl Maria von Weber is sent a letter telling him that he has been given the job of Kapellmeister to the King of Saxony in Dresden.

1834 Franz Liszt and Frédéric Chopin perform in concert together at Stoepel's Music School in Paris.

1835 Niccolò Paganini is given complete control of music in the Duchy of Parma by royal decree.

1875 Samuel Sebastian Wesley plays the Gloucester Cathedral organ for the last time, at Evensong.

1892 Charles Villiers Stanford finishes work as organist at Trinity College Chapel in Cambridge.

1908 Giacomo Puccini's wife Elvira launches a public row with her servant Doria Manfredi over allegations that she has been having an affair with the composer behind her back.

1989 Leonard Bernstein conducts a performance of Beethoven's *Symphony No. 9* in the Schauspielhaus, East Berlin, to celebrate the fall of the Berlin Wall.

Favourite carols

(continued from the previous page)

No. 12: *God Rest Ye Merry, Gentlemen*
No. 13: *Joy to the World*
No. 14: *Away in a Manger*
No. 15: *It Came Upon the Midnight Clear*
No. 16: *Coventry Carol*
No. 17: *The Three Kings*
No. 18: *Sussex Carol*
No. 19: *The Holly and the Ivy*
No. 20: *Gaudete*

No. 21: *In Dulci Jubilo*
No. 22: *Candlelight Carol*
No. 23: *Gabriel's Message*
No. 24: *See Amid the Winter Snow*
No. 25: *Angel's Carol*
No. 26: *The First Nowell*
No. 27: *Jesus Christ the Apple Tree*
No. 28: *Shepherd's Pipe Carol*
No. 29: *What Sweeter Music*
No. 30: *Shepherd's Farewell*

🎵 HALL OF FAME HIT

Carl Maria von Weber: *Clarinet Concerto No. 2*

Recommended Recording

Maximiliano Martin (clarinet); Scottish Chamber Orchestra conducted by Alexander Janiczek; Linn CKD409

'Words seem to me so ambiguous, so vague, so easily misunderstandable in comparison with genuine music, which fills the soul with things a thousand times better than words.'

FELIX MENDELSSOHN, COMPOSER

26

DECEMBER

 BIRTHS & DEATHS

1901 English composer Victor Hely-Hutchinson is born in Cape Town.

1925 English clarinettist Thea King is born in Hitchin.

1953 English choral conductor Harry Christophers is born in Goudhurst.

1976 Ukrainian conductor Kirill Karabits is born in Kiev.

1986 Swedish composer Lars-Erik Larsson dies in Helsingborg.

 FIRST PERFORMED

1767 Christoph Willibald von Gluck's opera *Alceste* is premiered in Vienna.

1831 Vincenzo Bellini's opera *Norma* is premiered, in Milan.

1833 Gaetano Donizetti's opera *Lucrezia Borgia* is premiered, in Milan.

1880 Johannes Brahms' *Tragic Overture* is given its first performance, in Vienna.

1897 Nikolai Rimsky-Korsakov's *Sadko* receives its first performance, in Moscow.

TODAY'S THE DAY

1737 George Frideric Handel begins work on his oratorio *Xerxes*. He will finish it on Valentine's Day next year.

1803 Joseph Haydn makes his final appearance as a conductor, in a performance of his *The Seven Last Words*, in Vienna.

1837 Teatro La Fenice reopens in Venice after burning down just over a year earlier.

1837 Following a performance at the Imperial Court in Vienna, 18-year-old Clara Wieck (later Schumann) is appointed Imperial Court Pianist by Emperor Ferdinand.

1862 Richard Wagner gives a concert performance of some of the music from his as yet unperformed operas *Das Rheingold*, *Die Walküre* and *Die Meistersinger von Nürnberg*, in Vienna.

1898 Arturo Toscanini conducts Wagner's *Die Meistersinger*. It is his first performance in his new role of artistic director of La Scala, Milan.

1900 Tenor Enrico Caruso is ill for his debut at Teatro alla Scala, Milan, and it doesn't go at all well for him.

1921 Arturo Toscanini conducts at the reopening of La Scala, Milan.

1936 The Palestine Symphony Orchestra gives its first concert in Tel Aviv, with Arturo Toscanini conducting.

Christmas music

The tunes of some of the best-loved carols were, in fact, written by classical music greats ('*Hark the Herald*' by Mendelssohn, '*In the Bleak Midwinter*' by Holst). As well as the hymns we sing each year, there's also a festive sack-load of longer pieces, such as the *Carol Symphony* by Victor Hely-Hutchinson, or the *Christmas Overture* by Nigel Hess, both of which are perfect for having on in the background throughout the Christmas festivities.

 HALL OF FAME HIT

Felix Mendelssohn: *Hear My Prayer* (*O for the Wings of a Dove*)

Recommended Recording

Jeremy Budd (treble); St. Paul's Cathedral Choir conducted by John Scott; Helios CDH 55445

27

DECEMBER

BIRTHS & DEATHS
1944 American composer Amy Beach dies in New York.

FIRST PERFORMED
1892 Jules Massenet's opera *Werther* is heard for the first time in French, in Geneva.
1956 Aram Khachaturian's ballet *Spartacus* is premiered, in the Kirov Opera and Ballet Theatre in Leningrad.

TODAY'S THE DAY
1801 Niccolò Paganini is given the job of first violin in the orchestra of the Republic of Lucca.
1824 Tomorrow's performance of Hector Berlioz's *Messe en grande symphonie* is cancelled after today's rehearsal proves to be a disaster because of poorly copied parts for the musicians to play.
1841 Lisztomania officially breaks out in Berlin following a concert by the pianist and composer Franz Liszt. He ends up playing no fewer than 21 concerts there over the next ten weeks.
1854 Richard Wagner finishes work on the first complete draft of his opera *Die Walküre*.
1857 Louis Spohr trips and breaks his arm. The injury prevents him from ever playing the violin professionally again.

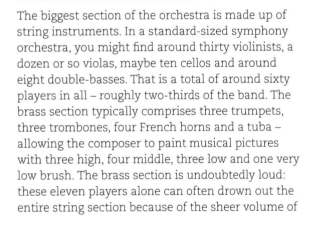

The make-up of the orchestra

The biggest section of the orchestra is made up of string instruments. In a standard-sized symphony orchestra, you might find around thirty violinists, a dozen or so violas, maybe ten cellos and around eight double-basses. That is a total of around sixty players in all – roughly two-thirds of the band. The brass section typically comprises three trumpets, three trombones, four French horns and a tuba – allowing the composer to paint musical pictures with three high, four middle, three low and one very low brush. The brass section is undoubtedly loud: these eleven players alone can often drown out the entire string section because of the sheer volume of sound that their instruments produce. Next up are the woodwind instruments, which are not necessarily made of wood these days. This section is made up of two or three flutes, a piccolo, a couple of oboes, four clarinets and perhaps a bass clarinet, two bassoons and possibly a contra-bassoon. The final part of the orchestra is a percussion section of three or four players, playing various instruments such as timpani, cymbals, side-drums, bass drums, xylophones and triangles. One or sometimes two harpists and a pianist, who might play the celesta when required, more or less complete the complement of a full standard symphony orchestra.

HALL OF FAME HIT
Franz Liszt: *Liebestraum No. 3*

Recommended Recording
Pascal Rogé (piano); Australian Eloquence 480 3150

> 'Nothing is wrong when done to music.'
> JEROME KERN, COMPOSER

28
DECEMBER

 BIRTHS & DEATHS

1916 Austrian composer Eduard Strauss dies in Vienna.

1937 French composer Maurice Ravel dies in Paris.

1956 English violinist Nigel Kennedy is born in Brighton.

1963 German composer Paul Hindemith dies in Frankfurt.

1971 American composer Max Steiner dies in Los Angeles.

FIRST PERFORMED

1878 The first four scenes of Pyotr Ilyich Tchaikovsky's opera *Eugene Onegin* are rehearsed before an audience at the Moscow Conservatoire.

1944 Leonard Bernstein's musical *On the Town* is premiered in New York.

 TODAY'S THE DAY

1832 Duke Carl Friedrich of Saxe-Weimar-Eisenach bestows the Order of the White Falcon on his kapellmeister, Johann Nepomuk Hummel.

1881 London's Savoy Theatre, home of many of Gilbert and Sullivan's greatest hits, is the first theatre to be lit completely by electric light. Promoter Richard D'Oyly Carte is a great fan of the new invention.

1935 Alban Berg is buried in Vienna.

1945 Igor Stravinsky becomes a naturalised American citizen.

2012 Antonio Pappano is awarded a knighthood in the New Year's Honours.

ARTIST PROFILE:

Nigel Kennedy

One of the most recognisable classical music performers alive today, Nigel Kennedy studied piano with his mother, before going to the Yehudi Menuhin School in Surrey at the age of seven. He also studied in New York at the Juilliard School. It emerged recently that Menuhin himself paid the youngster's school fees throughout his childhood. Alongside Menuhin, Kennedy's other great influence was the jazz violinist Stéphane Grappelli. Kennedy made his debut with the Berlin Philharmonic at the age of 24 and immediately became the talk of the music world. His recording of Elgar's *Violin Concerto* was voted record of the year at the 1985 Gramophone Awards, setting him on the road to repeated success in the recording studio, with best-selling concerto recordings of Bach, Beethoven, Berg, Brahms, Bruch, Mendelssohn, Sibelius, Tchaikovsky and Walton, alongside chamber music and recital discs. His version of Vivaldi's *Four Seasons*, recorded with the English Chamber Orchestra in 1989, shot him into the big time, with sales of over 2 million worldwide. Kennedy remains passionate about jazz and is as at home performing at Ronnie Scott's jazz club in London's Soho as he is on the stage of a major European concert hall. He is also a devoted follower of Aston Villa football club, and has often been photographed wearing the team scarf while playing the violin. He is artistic director of the Polish Chamber Orchestra and divides his time between homes in London and Kraków.

 HALL OF FAME HIT
Wolfgang Amadeus Mozart: *Horn Concerto No. 1*

Recommended Recording
Alessio Allegrini (horn); Orchestra Mozart conducted by Claudio Abbado; Deutsche Grammophon 477 8083

29

DECEMBER

'I have never encountered anything more false and foolish than the effort to get truth into opera. In opera everything is based upon the not-true.'

PYOTR ILYICH TCHAIKOVSKY, COMPOSER

 BIRTHS & DEATHS

1876 Spanish cellist, conductor and composer Pablo Casals is born in Catalonia.

1970 Welsh singer and Classic FM presenter Aled Jones is born in Bangor.

 TODAY'S THE DAY

1823 Gioachino Rossini sings two of his arias for King George IV at the Royal Pavilion in Brighton.

1868 Franz Liszt writes to Edvard Grieg congratulating him on his compositions – and his *Violin Sonata No. 1* in particular.

1911 The San Francisco Symphony Orchestra gives its first concert performance.

1999 The Three Tenors perform their 21st concert together in San Jose.

COMPOSER PROFILE:

Giacomo Puccini

Puccini was born into a family that was steeped in music: his father, grandfather and great-grandfather were all musicians. He studied at the Lucca music school and then in Milan at the Conservatoire, where the young Mascagni was a fellow student. The future king of Italian opera started off his career at the age of 14 as a church organist. It was only after attending a performance of Verdi's *Aida* four years later that he was bitten by the opera bug. Inspired by what he had heard, he eventually entered a competition for a new one-act opera. Not only did Puccini's entry *Le Villi* fail to win, it was disqualified because the judges said that Puccini's manuscript was illegible.

Nevertheless, some of the composer's friends decided they could read the spidery score and organised a staging at a local theatre in Milan. Giulio Ricordi, who had been Verdi's publisher, heard the opera and was impressed enough by it to put its composer on a retainer. *Edgar*, the first opera Puccini wrote for Ricordi, was a flop, but *Manon Lescaut*, which followed in 1893, was a smash hit. *La bohème* (1896), *Tosca* (1900) and *Madam Butterfly* (1904) followed. After a period of silence, Puccini returned to the theatre with *La fanciulla del West* (1910) and then *La rondine* (1917) and *Il trittico* (1918), which consists of three one-act operas performed one after another. He did not finish *Turandot*, his final masterpiece.

 HALL OF FAME HIT

Franz Schubert: *String Quartet D103*

Recommended Recording

Endellion String Quartet; 2564 657207

'The English may not like music, but they absolutely love the noise it makes.'

THOMAS BEECHAM, CONDUCTOR

BIRTHS & DEATHS

1904 Russian composer and pianist Dmitri Kabalevsky is born in St Petersburg.

1919 English organist, composer and conductor David Willcocks is born in Newquay.

1959 English conductor and pianist Antonio Pappano is born in Epping.

1962 American conductor Paavo Järvi is born in Talinn.

1979 American composer Richard Rodgers dies in New York.

FIRST PERFORMED

1852 A revised version of Robert Schumann's *Symphony No. 4* is given its first performance, in Düsseldorf.

1877 Johannes Brahms' *Symphony No. 2* is heard for the first time, in Vienna.

1879 W. S. Gilbert and Arthur Sullivan's operetta *The Pirates of Penzance* is premiered at the Royal Bijou Theatre in Paignton, Devon. The purpose of the performance in a rather more off-the-beaten-track venue than normal is to ensure that Gilbert and Sullivan control the British copyright of the production just before its official premiere in New York.

1905 Franz Lehár's operetta *The Merry Widow* is premiered, in Vienna.

1921 Sergei Prokofiev's opera *The Love of Three Oranges* is premiered in Chicago, with the composer conducting.

1938 Sergei Prokofiev's ballet *Romeo and Juliet* is premiered in Brno.

1961 Dmitri Shostakovich's *Symphony No. 4* is heard for the first time, in Moscow some 25 years after it was originally composed. Back then, Shostakovich had fallen foul of the Communist Party leadership and the planned premiere never took place.

TODAY'S THE DAY

1771 Wolfgang Amadeus Mozart finishes work on his *Symphony No. 14*, in Salzburg.

1839 Mikhail Glinka is allowed to leave his job as Imperial Kapellmeister in St Petersburg because he has become depressed over his marriage split.

1876 Nadezhda von Meck, the patron of Pyotr Ilyich Tchaikovsky, writes to the composer for the first time. They have a bizarre relationship: she funds him for many years, but they agree never to speak.

1899 Composer Samuel Coleridge-Taylor marries Jessie Walmisley, a fellow student at the Royal College of Music in London.

1937 Maurice Ravel's body is buried in Levallois cemetery. Igor Stravinsky and Francis Poulenc are among the mourners.

2013 Simon Rattle is appointed a member of the Order of Merit in the New Year Honours.

2013 Peter Maxwell Davies is appointed a Companion of Honour in the New Year Honours.

HALL OF FAME HIT
Murray Gold: *Dr Who*

Recommended Recording
BBC National Orchestra of Wales conducted by Ben Foster; Silva Screen SILCD 1224

31

'I can't live one day without hearing music, playing it, studying it, or thinking about it.'

LEONARD BERNSTEIN, CONDUCTOR AND COMPOSER

DECEMBER

 BIRTHS & DEATHS

1859 German conductor Max Fiedler is born in Zittau.

1869 French organist and composer Louis Lefébure-Wely dies in Paris.

1948 English conductor Stephen Cleobury is born in Bromley.

FIRST PERFORMED

1775 George Frideric Handel's *Messiah* is performed for the first time in German, in Hamburg, with Carl Philipp Emanuel Bach conducting.

TODAY'S THE DAY

1782 Wolfgang Amadeus Mozart finishes work on the first of his 'Haydn' String Quartets.

1895 Jules Massenet is appointed a Commander of the Légion d'Honneur.

1899 A retirement home for ailing musicians in Milan, funded in its entirety by Giuseppe Verdi, is founded by royal decree.

1908 Seventeen-year-old Sergei Prokofiev performs in public for the first time, in St Petersburg.

1963 The South African government is unhappy at the message of racial harmony and equality in the Rodgers and Hammerstein musical *South Pacific*, so bans it from being performed in the country.

1980 A concert is staged for the seriously ill Samuel Barber inside University Hospital, New York. His own *Adagio for Strings* is among the works performed.

1986 Peter Maxwell Davies is given a knighthood in the New Year Honours.

1992 German baritone and conductor Dietrich Fischer-Dieskau gives his final performance before retirement, at the National Theatre in Munich.

1996 The Three Tenors perform their 11th concert together in Vancouver.

Finales

Anton Webern is just one composer who met a rather sad and unfortunate end. He was shot by an American soldier at the end of the Second World War having gone outside to smoke a cigar during a curfew. His contemporary, Alban Berg, met his end after being stung by a bee. Then there was Jean-Baptiste Lully, who hit himself in the toe with a conducting stick, and died from the wound after gangrene set in. And the list of strange composer deaths doesn't end there. The Spaniard Enrique Granados drowned after the passenger cruise ship he was travelling on was torpedoed by a German U-boat during the First World War. The Russian Alexander Borodin dropped dead in full national dress on the dance floor at a grand winter ball in St Petersburg, while the Frenchman Charles-Valentin Alkan was crushed to death by a bookcase, which fell on top of him. Alkan's fellow countryman Ernest Chausson died after riding his bicycle into a brick wall. Compared to all that, Alexander Scriabin's death from a shaving cut seems, well, rather pedestrian.

 HALL OF FAME HIT

Frédéric Chopin: *Etude Op. 10 No. 3* ('Tristesse')

Recommended Recording

Jan Lisiecki (piano); Deutsche Grammophon 479 1039

Where to find out more

If this book has whetted your appetite to find out more, one of the best ways to discover what you like about classical music is to tune in to Classic FM. We broadcast 24 hours a day across the UK on 100–102 FM, on Digital Radio, online at www.classicfm.com, on Sky Channel 0106, on Virgin Media channel 922 and on FreeSat channel 722, or direct to your mobile phone or tablet via our free Android and iOS apps. We play a huge breadth of different classical music each week.

As well as being able to listen online, you will find a host of interactive features about classical music, composers and musicians on our website, classicfm. com. When we first turned on Classic FM's transmitters 22 years ago, we changed the face of classical music radio in the UK for ever. Two decades later, we are doing the same online. So, we've packed our website with up-to-the-minute classical music news, details of the latest recordings and upcoming concerts, big-name interviews and lots of information for anyone who wants to make a personal journey through the world of classical music.

If books are more your thing than websites, then we would very much like to recommend five companion volumes to *The Big Book of Classical Music*, all of which are published by Elliott & Thompson. The first, *Classic Ephemera*, is a musical miscellany, packed with all manner of handy information: telling trivia, curious quotes and fascinating facts. The second, *The Classic FM Hall of Fame*, profiles the three hundred greatest classical works and their composers – as voted by Classic FM listeners. The third, *Everything You Ever Wanted To Know*

About Classical Music … But Were Too Afraid To Ask takes readers on a journey through the history of classical music, while also demystifying the genre's terminology and traditions. *50 Moments That Rocked the Classical Music World* centres on our selection of fifty of the most significant occasions in classical music. Finally, once you have digested all this newfound knowledge about classical music, you can test yourself with our handy *Classic FM Quiz Book*.

If you would like to delve far, far deeper into the subject, the universally acknowledged authority on the subject is *The New Grove Dictionary of Music and Musicians*. The original version was edited by Sir George Grove, with the eminent musicologist Stanley Sadie for this new edition (published in 1995). But be warned – this is a weighty tome, running to 20 hardback volumes with around 29,000 separate articles.

In truth, this massive resource is far more detailed than most music lovers would ever need; a more manageable reference book is *The Concise Oxford Dictionary of Music*, edited by Michael Kennedy (Oxford Reference), or *The Penguin Companion to Classical Music*, edited by Paul Griffiths (Penguin). Paul Griffiths has also written *A Concise History of Western Music* (Cambridge University Press) – a highly readable discussion of the way in which classical music has evolved over time.

The *DK Eyewitness Companions: Classical Music*, edited by John Burrows (Dorling Kindersley), is a very colourful and reliable source of information on the chronology of classical music. Howard Goodall delves into five episodes that changed musical history, including the invention of musical notation and the creation of the recording industry, in his excellent book *Big Bangs* (Vintage) and, more recently, Howard has also written an excellent new book *The Story of Music*. For a slightly quirkier walk through the subject, we recommend Stephen Fry's *Incomplete & Utter History of Classical Music* (Macmillan), based on the award-winning Classic FM radio series of the same name, written by Tim Lihoreau.

Other excellent general guides to classical music include: *The Rough Guide to Classical Music*, edited by Joe Staines (Rough Guides); *The Encyclopedia of Music* by Max Wade-Matthews and Wendy Thompson (Hermes House); *Good Music Guide* by Neville Garden (Columbia Marketing); *The Chronicle of Classical Music* by Alan Kendall (Thames & Hudson); *The Lives & Times of The Great Composers* by Michael Steen (Icon); *The Lives of the Great Composers* by Harold C. Schonberg (Abacus); and *Music for the People: The Pleasures and Pitfalls of Classical Music* by Gareth Malone (Collins), whose television series on singing are fast making him a national treasure.

Three excellent books on the subject of opera are *DK Eyewitness Companions: Opera* (Dorling Kindersley); *The Good Opera Guide* by Denis Forman (Phoenix); and *The Rough Guide to Opera* by Matthew Boyden (Rough Guides).

For younger classical music lovers or discoverers, *The Story of Classical Music* and *Famous Composers* are both published by Naxos Audiobooks. Engagingly read by Classic FM presenter Aled Jones, these titles are aimed at 8- to 14-year-olds and contain musical excerpts and CD-ROM elements.

The very best way of finding out more about which pieces of classical music you like is by going out and hearing a live performance for yourself. There is simply no substitute for seeing the whites of the eyes of a talented soloist as they perform a masterpiece on a stage only a few feet in front of you. If you are a first time attender, then before you leave home, make sure that you read our guide to going to a live classical concert in our book *Everything You Ever Wanted To Know About Classical Music … But Were Too Afraid To Ask.*

Classic FM has a series of partnerships with orchestras across the country: the Royal Scottish National Orchestra, Royal Northern Sinfonia, the Royal Liverpool Philharmonic Orchestra, the Orchestra of Opera North, the Philharmonia Orchestra, the Orchestra of Welsh National Opera, the London Symphony Orchestra and the Bournemouth Symphony Orchestra. To see if they have a concert coming up near you, log on to our website at classicfm.com and click on the 'Concerts and Events' section. It will also include many of the other classical concerts – both professional and amateur – that are taking place near to where you live.

Happy listening!

About the authors

Darren Henley is the managing director of Classic FM. The author of two independent government reviews into music and cultural education, as well as 26 books about classical music, he chairs the government's Cultural Education Board and the Mayor of London's Music Education Advisory Group. He is a member of the governing body of the Associated Board of the Royal Schools of Music; a Vice President of the Canterbury Festival; and a Commissioner for the University of Warwick's Commission on the Future of Cultural Value. Named 'Commercial Radio Programmer of the Year' in 2009, his radio work has been honoured by the Radio Academy Awards, the Arqiva Commercial Radio Awards, the New York International Radio Festival, the Grammy Awards and the United Nations. Darren studied Politics at the University of Hull. He is a Fellow of the Royal Society of Arts, of the Radio Academy and of the London College of Music; an Honorary Fellow of Canterbury Christ Church University and of Trinity Laban Conservatoire of Music and Dance; an Honorary Member of the Royal Northern College of Music and of the Incorporated Society of Musicians; and a Companion of the Chartered Management Institute. He holds honorary doctorates from the University of Hull and from Buckinghamshire New University. The recipient of the Sir Charles Groves Prize for 'his outstanding contribution to British music', he was appointed an OBE in the 2013 New Year Honours for services to music.

Sam Jackson is the managing editor of Classic FM, responsible for all of the station's on-air programming and music output, a role he has held since 2011. Before then, he spent four years as the Executive Producer in charge of Classic FM's music programming. In his ten years at Classic FM, his programmes have been honoured by the Radio Academy Awards, the Arqiva Commercial Radio Awards and the New York International Radio Festival. He was chosen as one of the Radio Academy's '30 Under 30' for two consecutive years and, in 2012, he was the only person working in radio to be included in *Music Week*'s '30 Under 30'. In 2013, the Hospital Club named him as one of 'the 100 most influential, innovative and interesting individuals in the media and creative industries'. A proficient pianist and clarinettist, Sam holds a first-class degree in Music from the University of York. He sits on the governing body of Trinity Laban Conservatoire of Music and Dance and on the University of York Music Department's advisory board, as well as being a trustee of the Radio Academy. Previously, he enjoyed a career in front of the microphone, as a presenter on the children's digital radio station, Fun Kids. The author of two *Sunday Times* bestselling books about classical music, his new book about bringing up young children, *Diary of a Desperate Dad*, is published by Elliott & Thompson and he blogs regularly online about family life at diaryofadesperatedad.com

Tim Lihoreau is the presenter of Classic FM's *More Music Breakfast*, which can be heard every weekday morning between 6 a.m. and 9 a.m. Previously Tim presented the programme at the weekends, before moving to weekdays and taking over the reins of the UK's most listened-to classical music breakfast show in 2012. His career as a presenter, which stretches back more than a decade, has operated in tandem with his role as Classic FM's creative director and has seen him presenting programmes for the station at all hours of the day and night. He has been responsible for writing and producing many of Classic FM's biggest programmes and he has won a string of major accolades on both sides of the Atlantic at the Radio Academy Awards, the New York International Radio Festival and the Arqiva Commercial Radio Awards. He studied Music at the University of Leeds and worked as a professional pianist and in the classical record industry before making the move to Classic FM as a producer in 1993. He is the author of 15 books, including *The Incomplete and Utter History of Classical Music*, which accompanied the award-winning Classic FM series of the same name, presented by Stephen Fry. Tim's *Modern Phobias* book has been translated into eleven different languages, whilst *The Little Black Book of Schadenfreude* is his latest humorous title published by Elliott & Thompson. Alongside his wife, Tim runs three amateur choirs in his home village in Cambridgeshire and regularly plays his local church organ.

ACKNOWLEDGEMENTS

Writing a book like this is something of a mammoth undertaking and it simply wouldn't have happened without lots of help along the way from the people with whom we work every day at Classic FM. So we want to say a very big 'thank you' to Nick Bailey, Jamie Beesley, Catherine Bott, Alex Brooksbank, John Brunning, Stuart Campbell, Lucy Chisholm-Batten, Alistair Cockburn, Lucy Coward, Jamie Crick, Tim Edwards, Howard Goodall CBE, Charlotte Green, Alex James, Aled Jones MBE, Jane Jones, Will Kisby, Myleene Klass, Laurence Llewelyn-Bowen, Kyle Macdonald, James Marshall, David Mellor, Anne-Marie Minhall, Jenny Nelson, Phil Noyce, Bill Overton, Nicholas Owen, Emma Oxborrow, Clare Patterson, Alexandra Philpotts, Sam Pittis, Dan Ross, Mel Spencer, John Suchet, Margherita Taylor, Alan Titchmarsh MBE and Rob Weinberg.

We are also greatly indebted to Global Radio's Founder and Executive President, Ashley Tabor; to Group Chief Executive, Stephen Miron; to Director of Broadcasting, Richard Park; and to Chairman, Lord Allen of Kensington CBE. Thanks also to Global's Will Harding, Mike Gordon, Giles Pearman, Andrea Flamini, Laxmi Hariharan, John Chittenden, Damaris Brown and especially to Caeshia St Paul.

As always, we are incredibly grateful to Lorne Forsyth, Olivia Bays, Jennie Condell, Pippa Crane, Jill Burrows, Charlie Bailey, Alison Menzies, and Thomas Ogilvie at our publishers Elliott & Thompson for all of their help, support and expertise throughout the long journey of turning our idea for this book into the reality you are holding in your hands.

Index